To Bill

From Peter Nockles

29 April 2005.

RELIGIOUS IDENTITIES IN BRITAIN, 1660-1832

Religious Identities in Britain, 1660-1832

Edited by
WILLIAM GIBSON and ROBERT G. INGRAM

ASHGATE

© William Gibson and Robert G. Ingram, 2005

All rights reserved. No part of this publication may be reproduced, stored in a retrieval system, or transmitted in any form or by any means, electronic, mechanical, photocopying, recording or otherwise without the prior permission of the publisher.

William Gibson and Robert G. Ingram have asserted their moral right under the Copyright, Designs and Patents Act, 1988, to be identified as the editors of this work.

Published by
Ashgate Publishing Limited
Gower House
Croft Road
Aldershot
Hants GU11 3HR
England

Ashgate Publishing Company
Suite 420
101 Cherry Street
Burlington
Vermont, 05401–4405
USA

Ashgate website: http://www.ashgate.com

British Library Cataloguing in Publication Data
Religious Identities in Britain, 1660–1832
   1. Great Britain – Church history – 18th century. I. Gibson, William, 1959– .
II. Ingram, Robert G.
274'.07

US Library of Congress Cataloging in Publication Data
Religious Identities in Britain, 1660–1832 / edited by William Gibson and Robert G. Ingram.
     p.   cm.
Includes index.
1. Great Britain – Church history – 18th century. 2. Clergy – Religious life – Great Britain – History – 18th century. I. Gibson, William, 1959– . II. Ingram, Robert G.
BR758.R385 2004
274.1'07–dc22   2004005418

ISBN 0 7546 3209 1

This book is printed on acid free paper.

Printed and bound in Great Britain by MPG Books Ltd, Bodmin, Cornwall

Contents

Contributors   vii

1   Introduction
      William Gibson and Robert G. Ingram   1

2   Roger Morrice and the History of Puritanism
      Mark Goldie   9

3   Charles Leslie and the Political Implications of Theology
      Robert Cornwall   27

4   Altitudinarian Equivocation: George Smalridge's Churchmanship
      William Gibson   43

5   How Heterodox was Benjamin Hoadly?
      Guglielmo Sanna   61

6   The Jacobite Failure to Bridge the Catholic/Protestant Divide, 1717-1730
      Jeffrey S. Chamberlain   81

7   William Warburton, Divine Action, and Enlightened Christianity
      Robert G. Ingram   97

8   James Boswell and the Bi-Confessional State
      James J. Caudle   119

9   'In the Church I will live and die': John Wesley, the Church of England, and Methodism
      Jeremy Gregory   147

10   The Waning of Protestant Unity and Waxing of Anti-Catholicism? Archdeacon Daubeny and the Reconstruction of 'Anglican' Identity in the Later Georgian Church, c.1780-c.1830
      Peter B. Nockles   179

Contents

11 Richard Price on Reason and Revolution
   H.T. Dickinson 231

12 The 'most horrid and unnatural state of man':
   John Henry Williams and the French Wars, 1793-1802
   Colin Haydon 255

13 Sir George Pretyman-Tomline: Ecclesiastical Politician
   and Theological Polemicist
   G.M. Ditchfield 277

14 'Achitophel Firebrand' at St. Asaph:
   Dean Shipley and the Withering of Whiggism
   in the Church of England, 1775-1825
   Nigel Aston 299

Index 321

Contributors

Nigel Aston is Reader in History at the University of Leicester. He is the author of numerous works on the history of religion in Britain and France, c.1660-1790, including *Christianity and Revolutionary Europe, 1750-1830* (2002) and *Religion and Revolution in France, 1780-1804* (2000). He has also edited, with Matthew Cragoe, *Anticlericalism in Britain, 1500-1800* (2001).

James J. Caudle is Associate Editor of the Yale Editions of the Private Papers of James Boswell. He co-edited *The General Correspondence of James Boswell, 1757-1763* (2003-04), and is the author of essays on Richard Francklin and on political sermons in Parliament, 1702-60. He has also contributed a number of articles to *The Oxford Dictionary of National Biography*. His current work is on Georgian dynastic loyalism, sermon culture in Britain, Georgian ecclesiopolitical holidays, and the history of the book.

Jeffrey S. Chamberlain is Professor of History at the University of St. Francis in Joliet, Illinois. He is the author of *Accommodating High Churchmen: the Clergy of Sussex, 1700-1745* (1997) and co-editor (with Jeremy Gregory) of *The National Church in Local Perspective* (2003). He has published several articles on the Church of England in the eighteenth century, and has contributed numerous entries to *The Oxford Dictionary of National Biography*.

Robert Cornwall holds the Ph.D. in historical theology from Fuller Theological Seminary. He is the author of *Visible and Apostolic: The Constitution of the Church in High Church Anglican and Nonjuror Thought* (1993) and the editor of *Gilbert Burnet's Discourse of the Pastoral Care* (1997).

H.T. Dickinson is Richard Lodge Professor of British History at the University of Edinburgh and president of the Historical Association of Great Britain. He is the author and editor of numerous books, including *Bolingbroke* (1970), *Walpole and the Whig Supremacy* (1973), *Liberty and Property: Political Ideology in Eighteenth-Century Britain* (1977), *The Politics of the People in Eighteenth-Century Britain* (1994), and *A Companion to Eighteenth-Century Britain* (2002). He edited the journal *History* from 1993 to 2000.

G.M. Ditchfield is Reader in Eighteenth-Century History at the University of Kent. He is the author of numerous works on eighteenth-century political and religious history, including *George III: An Essay in Monarchy* (2002) and *The Evangelical Revival* (1998).

William Gibson is Academic Director of Lifelong Learning at Oxford Brookes University. He has written widely on the eighteenth- and nineteenth-century Church of England, including, most recently, *The Church of England 1688-1832: Unity and Accord* (2001) and *Enlightenment Prelate: Benjamin Hoadly (1676-1761)* (2004). He was recently awarded a D.Litt. by the University of Wales.

Mark Goldie is a lecturer in History at the University of Cambridge and a Fellow of Churchill College. He has published extensively on British political, intellectual, and religious history, 1660-1750. He is editor of *John Locke: Political Essays* (1997) and *John Locke: Selected Correspondence* (2002).

Jeremy Gregory is Senior Lecturer in the History of Modern Christianity at the University of Manchester. He has published widely on the Church of England in the long eighteenth century, notably *Restoration, Reformation, and Reform, 1660-1828: Archbishops of Canterbury and their diocese* (2000). He has edited the *Speculum of Archbishop Thomas Secker, 1758-68* for the Church of England Record Society (1995), and, with Jeffrey S. Chamberlain, edited *The National Church in Local Perspective: the Church of England and the Regions, 1660-1800* (2003). He is currently researching the Church of England in North America, c.1680-1783.

Colin Haydon is Reader in Early Modern History at University College, Winchester. He edited, with John Walsh and Stephen Taylor, *The Church of England, c.1689-c.1833: From Toleration to Tractarianism* (1993) and is the author of *Anti-Catholicism in Eighteenth-Century England, c.1714-80* (1994). He is currently preparing a book on religion and society in South Warwickshire c.1660-c.1800

Robert G. Ingram is Assistant Professor of History at Ohio University and is preparing a book on Thomas Secker.

Peter B. Nockles is director of the Methodist Church Archives and Research Centre at the John Rylands University Library of Manchester. He has written extensively on eighteenth- and nineteenth-century British religious history. He is the author of *The Oxford Movement in Context: Anglican High Churchmanship in Britain, 1760-1857* (1994) and has contributed chapters to *A History of Canterbury Cathedral* (1995), and to volume 6 of the *History of the University of Oxford* (1997).

Guglielmo Sanna lectures in history at the University of Sassari, Italy. He has published on the British press in the eighteenth century, together with several articles and essays on the religious and political culture of Anglicanism in the age of the Glorious Revolution and the Hanoverian succession. He is now completing a book on Benjamin Hoadly and the Bangorian controversy.

Chapter 1

Introduction

William Gibson and Robert G. Ingram

Historians of sixteenth- and seventeenth-century religion have the luxury of their subject being regarded as integral to the wider history of their eras. From the Protestant Reformations through the Civil Wars and on to the Glorious Revolution, religion served as one of the driving motors of historical change in Britain. Rightly, few would ask Diarmaid MacCulloch, Patrick Collinson, or Peter Lake to justify a study of the Edwardian Reformation, Edmund Grindal, or Puritanism in early Stuart England. Yet scholars of religion in eighteenth-century Britain have often felt compelled to prove their subject's very worth. The reasons for this extra burden of proof are various and have been considered in detail by others, but three stand out as particularly important. In the post-revolutionary calm of the eighteenth century when religious strife did not spark internecine war, religious conviction recedes from the centre stage of historical causation. Likewise, the centrality of religion to the nation's political, cultural, and social life fits uneasily into the prevailing grand narratives of the period, which stubbornly continue to understand the eighteenth century as a jumping-off point for the modern (hence, secular) world.[1] And, finally, the established Church of England—which, until the late eighteenth century, commanded at least the nominal support of nearly 90 per cent of the population—has come in for sustained criticism from many of those who have written its history: anticlericals attacked its privileged legal position, later high churchmen found it too latitudinarian, Tractarians thought it too erastian, evangelicals faulted it for its intolerance of Methodism, and Victorian church reformers thought it corrupt and negligent.[2] Indeed, the

---

[1] See, for instance, Alan Houston and Steve Pincus, 'Introduction: Modernity and later-seventeenth-century England', in idem (eds.), *A Nation Transformed: England after the Restoration* (Cambridge, 2001). pp. 1-19 and Roy Porter, *The Creation of the Modern World: The Untold Story of the British Enlightenment* (New York and London, 2000). For Europe more generally, see Jonathan I. Israel, *Radical Enlightenment: Philosophy and the Making of Modernity, 1650-1750* (Oxford and New York, 2001). B.W. Young, 'Religious History and the Eighteenth-Century Historian', *Historical Journal* 43:3 (September 2000), pp. 849-68 illumines the increasing secularization of the historiography of religion in eighteenth-century Britain.

[2] William Gibson, *The Church of England, 1688-1832: Unity and Accord* (London, 2001), pp. 1-27; idem, *The Achievement of the Anglican Church, 1689-1800: The Confessional State in Eighteenth Century England* (Lewiston, 1996), pp. 5-31; John Walsh and Stephen Taylor, 'Introduction: the Church and Anglicanism in the

religious groups who have garnered the most scholarly attention have tended to be those, like the Rational Dissenters or the Methodists, who sniped at the established church from the periphery or sought significantly to reform it from within.

Historians of eighteenth-century religion have responded to the marginalization of their subject in a number of ways. Some have spotlighted the influence of religion on eighteenth-century intellectual and cultural life. Jonathan Clark and Isabel Rivers, for instance, have argued that theology should not be hived off from the period's wider intellectual history; Clark, in particular, has done much to show theology's formative influence on political allegiances, identities, and ideologies in the century and a half after the Restoration.[3] Brian Young has given flesh to J.G.A. Pocock's suggestive arguments about the clerical, conservative nature of England's Enlightenment,[4] while Ian Green, Jeremy Gregory, and others have demonstrated Christianity's cultural importance during the period.[5]

On a different front, others have illumined the centrality of religion to politics and government. James Bradley, for instance, has carefully elucidated the connections between religious nonconformity and political radicalism in the latter half of the eighteenth century.[6] Regarding the established Church of England's role in politics and government, Norman Sykes's work remains the point of departure. Beginning in the mid-1920s, Sykes inaugurated the modern, archivally-based scholarship of the established church in his enormously influential examinations of church-

---

"long" eighteenth century', in John Walsh, Colin Haydon, and Stephen Taylor (eds.), *The Church of England, c.1689-c.1833: From Toleration to Tractarianism* (Cambridge, 1993), pp. 1-64 succinctly summarize the historiography of the eighteenth-century Church of England.

[3] See, for instance, Isabel Rivers, *Reason, Grace, and Sentiment: a study of the language of religion and ethics in England, 1660-1780*, 2 vols., (Cambridge, 1991, 2000); J.C.D. Clark, 'Religion and Political Identity: Samuel Johnson as a Nonjuror', in idem and Howard Erskine-Hill (eds.), *Samuel Johnson in Historical Context* (London, 2002), pp. 79-145; and idem, *Samuel Johnson: Literature, religion and English cultural politics from the Restoration to Romanticism* (Cambridge, 1994).

[4] B.W. Young, *Religion and Enlightenment in Eighteenth-Century England: Theological Debate from Locke to Burke* (Oxford, 1998); J.G.A. Pocock, 'Post-Puritan England and the Problem of the Enlightenment', in Perez Zagorin (ed.), *Culture and Politics From Puritanism to the Enlightenment* (Berkeley and Los Angeles, 1980), pp. 91-112.

[5] See, for instance, Ian Green, *Print and Protestantism in early modern England* (Oxford, 2000); idem, *The Christian's ABC: catechisms and catechizing in England, c.1530-1740* (Oxford, 1996); Jeremy Gregory, 'Christianity and Culture: Religion, the Arts and the Sciences in England, 1660-1800', in Jeremy Black, *Culture and Society in Britain, 1660-1832* (Manchester and New York, 1997), pp. 102-23.

[6] James E. Bradley, *Religion, Revolution, and English Radicalism: Nonconformity in Eighteenth-Century Politics and Society* (Cambridge, 1990).

state relations.[7] In all his work, Sykes tried to judge the religious actors of the eighteenth century by the standards of their contemporaries, rather than by anachronistic nineteenth-century ones.[8] 'To understand the ethos of the Georgian Church', he argued, '...it is necessary to regard it from the standpoint of the pre-reform age to which, alike in constitution and temper, it belonged'.[9] From this vantage, the close connections between church and state, particularly regarding patronage, appeared less insidious and corrupt than the eighteenth-century church's later critics would suggest. Stephen Taylor, Grayson Ditchfield, and a number of others have pushed even further down trails Sykes originally blazed. Whereas Victorians chastened the eighteenth-century episcopate for its subservience, for instance, Taylor argues that the bishops tried to avoid political controversy because it inhibited their pastoral work and formed an alliance with Newcastle and the Whigs to protect and defend the church.[10] The underlying premise of their research is that 'the relationship between church and state cannot be compartmentalized, separated from the rest of eighteenth-century politics and society, and called ecclesiastical history'.[11] Jonathan Clark has gone even further, arguing that eighteenth-century England was an *ancien regime* confessional state.[12]

Finally, historians of the established church have tried to vindicate their subject in local and regional studies that examine closely the institution's pastoral performance. Critics have long charged the Georgian church with rampant pluralism and non-residence and pilloried its clergy

---

[7] A bibliography of Sykes's work appears in G.V. Bennett and J.D. Walsh (eds.), *Essays in Modern English Church History. In Memory of Norman Sykes* (New York: Oxford University Press, 1966), pp. 217-20. His most lastingly influential work is *Church and State in England in the XVIIIth Century* (Cambridge, 1934).

[8] B.W. Young, '"Knock-Kneed Giants": Victorian Representations of Eighteenth Century Thought', in Jane Garnett and Colin Matthew (eds.), *Revival and Religion since 1700: Essays for John Walsh* (London, 1993), pp. 79-84.

[9] Norman Sykes, 'The Church', in A.S. Turberville (ed.), *Johnson's England: An Account of the Life & Manners of his Age* (Oxford, 1933), p. 15.

[10] See, for instance, Stephen Taylor, 'The Government and the Episcopate in the Mid-Eighteenth Century', in Charles Giry-Deloison and Roger Mettam (eds.), *Patronages et Clientélismes, 1550-1750 (France, Angleterre, Espagne, Italie)* (London, 1995), 191-205; idem, '"The Fac Totum in Ecclesiastic Affairs"? The Duke of Newcastle and the Crown's Ecclesiastical Patronage', *Albion* 24:3 (Fall 1992), pp. 409-33; idem, 'The Bishops at Westminster in the Mid-Eighteenth Century', in Clyve Jones (ed.), *A Pillar of the Constitution: the House of Lords in British politics, 1640-1784* (London, 1989), pp. 137-63; and idem, 'Sir Robert Walpole, the Church of England, and the Quakers Tithe Bill of 1736', *Historical Journal* 28:1 (March 1985), pp. 51-77.

[11] S.J.C. Taylor, 'Church and State in England in the Mid-Eighteenth Century: The Newcastle Years, 1742-1762' (University of Cambridge PhD thesis, 1987), p. 3.

[12] Clark made this argument most succinctly in 'England's Ancien Regime as a Confessional State', *Albion*, 21:3 (Fall 1989), 450-74. See also, idem, *English Society, 1688-1832: Ideology, social structure and political practice during the ancien regime* (Cambridge, 1985), the second edition of which is *English Society, 1660-1832: Religion, ideology and politics during the ancien regime* (Cambridge, 2000).

for being worldly, negligent, and ineffective.[13] Particularly in the last quarter century, scholars have tested these judgments against the actual evidence on the ground from across England and Wales. Jeremy Gregory and Jeffrey Chamberlain's excellent *The National Church in Local Perspective*—a recent collection of essays that brings together the work of scholars who have done the careful archival work that enables us to assess the church's pastoral performance—marks an admirable culmination of the development of local studies.[14] The picture of pastoral performance that emerges from this research, while not entirely roseate, is not gloomy either. The clergy across England and Wales resembled their peers in mid-century York, 'a body of dutiful and conscientious men, trying to do their work according to the standards of the day'.[15] More importantly, conclude Gregory and Chamberlain, the local studies prove the church's importance to eighteenth-century life: 'Whether or not England could be considered a "confessional state", these [studies] confirm that [William] Cobbett was undoubtedly right in stating that the clergy's "aggregate influence" was still "astonishingly great" in the long eighteenth century'.[16]

As a result of these researches, we know a great deal about the practical workings of religious organizations and groups in the eighteenth century. In particular, we have a solid appreciation of the nexus between religion, politics, and government and of the pastoral performance of both the established Church of England and its confessional rivals. What we lack, though, and what inspires this volume of essays, is a sense of what religion meant to the individuals involved. Addressing that neglect requires us to ask questions about personal religious identity, something scholars of sixteenth- and seventeenth-century British religion have done with much profit.[17] We believe that the study of eighteenth-century British religious life might be enriched equally by an exploration of religious identities. What did it mean to hold religious convictions during the eighteenth century? How diverse and variegated, how consistent or heterogeneous were individuals' religious tenets? How did religious belief affect the way people viewed and behaved in the world in which they lived? These are among the questions that concern us here. And while

---

[13] Peter Virgin, *The Church in an Age of Negligence: Ecclesiastical Structure and Problems of Church Reform, 1700-1840* (Cambridge, 1989) is but the most recent work to argue this case. M.F. Snape, *The Church of England in Industrialising Society: The Lancashire Parish of Whalley in the Eighteenth Century* (Woodbridge, 2003) echoes some of these themes.

[14] Jeremy Gregory and Jeffrey S. Chamberlain (eds.), *The National Church in Local Perspective: The Church of England and the Regions, 1660-1800* (Woodbridge, 2002), which also contains a substantial bibliography (pp. 285-295).

[15] Quoted in Sykes, *Church and State in England in the XVIIIth Century*, p. 6.

[16] Jeremy Gregory and Jeffrey S. Chamberlain, 'National and local perspectives on the Church of England in the long eighteenth century', in idem (eds.), *The National Church in Local Perspective*, p. 27.

[17] For a recent example, see Muriel C. McClendon, Joseph P. Ward, Michael Macdonald (eds.), *Protestant Identities: Religion, Society, and Self-fashioning in Post-Reformation England* (Stanford, 1999).

there are a number of ways to examine religious identities,[18] we have done so through studies of individuals. For as much as this volume is an exploration of religious identities in eighteenth-century Britain, it is also an experiment in the historiographical possibilities of biography.

There is a distinguished tradition of biographical studies in eighteenth-century British religious history. Norman Sykes first laid out his revisionist view of the eighteenth-century Church of England in what remains the standard study of Edmund Gibson and capped his career with his *magnum opus* on William Wake.[19] Edward Carpenter, Tindal Hart, G.V. Bennett, and Fred Mather also cast new light on the office and work of the eighteenth-century bishop in a series of biographies.[20] Likewise, biographies have helped shape significantly the historiography of groups outside the Church of England. Almost no significant Methodist, nonconformist, or evangelical religious figures now remains without a biographical treatment, with the Wesleys and Whitefield attracting particular attention.[21]

While the existing biographical studies of eighteenth-century religious figures no doubt enrich our understanding of the period, many suffer by not broadening their view to focus on larger historiographical problems. Of the episcopal biographies written during the last century, only Sykes's study of Wake and Bennett's work on Atterbury truly stepped outside the clerical, theological, and diocesan preoccupations of their subjects to locate them in wider historical perspective. As a result, beyond the comparatively

---

[18] Tony Claydon and Ian McBride (eds.), *Protestantism and National Identity: Britain and Ireland, c.1650- c.1850* (Cambridge, 1998) is an excellent examination of religious identities and large groups. The extensive literature of identity may be accessed through Joseph E. Davis, (ed.), *Identity and Social Change* (New Brunswick, NJ, and London, 2000); James Holstein and Jaber F. Gubrium, *The Self We Live By: Narrative identity in a postmodern world* (Oxford, 2000); Stuart Hall and Paul Du Gay (eds.), *Questions of Cultural Identity* (Thousand Oaks, CA, 1996); and Charles Taylor, *Sources of the Self: The Making of the Modern Identity* (Cambridge, MA, 1989).

[19] Norman Sykes, *Edmund Gibson, Bishop of London, 1669-1748. A study in politics and religion in the eighteenth century* (Oxford, 1926); idem, *William Wake, Archbishop of Canterbury, 1657-1737*, 2 vols. (Cambridge, 1957).

[20] Edward Carpenter, *Thomas Sherlock, 1678-1761* (London, 1936); idem, *Thomas Tenison, Archbishop of Canterbury. His Life and Times* (London, 1948); idem, *The Protestant Bishop: being the life of Henry Compton, 1632-1713, Bishop of London* (London, 1956); A. Tindal Hart, *The Life and Times of John Sharp, Archbishop of York* (London, 1949); idem, *William Lloyd 1627-1717: Bishop, politician, author, and prophet* (London, 1952); G.V. Bennett, *White Kennett, 1660-1728, Bishop of Peterborough: A study in the political and ecclesiastical history of the early eighteenth century* (London, 1957); idem, *The Tory Crisis in Church and State, 1688-1730: the career of Francis Atterbury, Bishop of Rochester* (Oxford, 1975); F.C. Mather, *High Church Prophet: Bishop Samuel Horsley (1733-1806) and the Caroline tradition in the later Georgian church* (Oxford, 1992).

[21] G.M. Ditchfield, *The Evangelical Revival* (London, 1998); and W.R. Ward, *The Protestant Evangelical Awakening* (Cambridge, 1992) are reliable guides to the voluminous scholarship on the subject. See, also, Jeremy Gregory's contribution to this collection.

narrow circle of ecclesiastical historians, most of these biographies achieved little purchase or influence on the broader historiography of the period. Biographers of non-Anglican subjects similarly tend to wear confessional blinkers, for individuals such as the Wesleys, Whitefield, Priestly and others have implicitly endorsed the prevailing traditional historiography that challenged the strength and vitality of the established church. Biographical studies of Howell Harris, Philip Doddridge, and even those clergy who remained evangelicals within the church, were presented as confirmation of the ineffectiveness of the church and tended to underestimate the varieties and complexity of nonconformist religious views.[22]

The contributors to this volume have aimed purposefully to make their subjects speak to wider historical and historiographical problems in eighteenth-century British history. While we do not seek to offer a single meta-interpretation of the period, we do hope that our individual studies together will inspire others in our field to consider the problem of religious identities in greater depth. For it is our conviction that we will only fully appreciate the place of religion in eighteenth-century British life when we appreciate how religion shaped or reflected the identities and attitudes of individual Britons. Only then can we find our way to understand how to integrate the apparently exclusive narratives of an increasingly secular and modern Britain populated by a 'polite and commercial people' with that of a decidedly pre-modern *ancien regime* confessional state.

This book began life in a discussion in a Pasadena, California, coffee shop in October 2000. We thank Professor James Bradley for being an excellent host in Pasadena and all our contributors for their enthusiasm for the project and their good humour in response to nagging editors. The entire editorial team at Ashgate, and particularly Tom Gray, Carolyn Court, and Kirsten Weissenberg have proved supportive, helpful, and patient throughout the oft-delayed production of the final typescript. The Center on Religion and Democracy at the University of Virginia deserves our special thanks for providing generous financial support for copy-editing. James Hunter, Joe Davis, Steven Jones, and Suellen Hill enabled the subvention, while Kristine Harmon had the unenviable task of copy-editing a camera-ready text produced by academics in the humanities. Kevin Uhalde generously agreed to read a draft of this introduction on short notice and offered much helpful advice. Robert Ingram would also like to thank his wife, Jill, for being a 'real trooper' and his father, Dr. Glynn Ingram, for showing a son the value of hard work.

---

[22] See, for instance, Geoffrey F. Nuttall (ed.), *Philip Doddridge, 1702-51: His Contribution To English Religion* (London, 1951); Geraint Tudur, *Howell Harris: From Conversion to Separation* (Cardiff, 2002); George G. Cragg, *Grimshaw of Haworth. A study in eighteenth-century evangelicalism* (London, 1947); Ken Smallbone, *James Potter, Quaker. A record of dissent in the 17th and 18th centuries* (York, 1989); and A.S. Wood, *Thomas Haweis, 1734-1820* (London, 1957), though, as Jeremy Gregory notes, there has been a tradition of both 'Anglican' and 'Methodist' biographies of Wesley.

Finally, we dedicate this book to Canon William Price and Dr. Charles R. Perry, both friends and early supporters of our work.

William Gibson
Robert G. Ingram

20 December 2003

Chapter 2

Roger Morrice and the History of Puritanism[*]

Mark Goldie

Roger Morrice's dearest ambition was to write the history of the Puritans, and he devoted the 1690s to the attempt. He failed. He published nothing, and died obscurely.[1] But at his demise in 1702 he left behind a massive corpus of manuscripts, some written by himself as notes towards his intended 'politico-ecclesiastical' history of England since the Reformation, and some collected by him as an archive of primary sources. It is this body of material which became indispensable to future attempts, from Daniel Neal's *History of the Puritans* (1732-38) to Patrick Collinson's *The Elizabethan Puritan Movement* (1967) and beyond.

As a collector, Morrice's most important find was a folio called *The Seconde Parte of a Register*. He acquired it in 1690 from a descendant of the Elizabeth Puritan MP, Sir John Heigham, and it has remained among his papers ever since. He was captivated by this discovery: if it did not germinate, it certainly spurred his ambition to write a history of Puritanism. One measure of the *Register*'s significance is that it is the source of the phrase 'but halfly reformed'—the rebuke of 1585 so frequently quoted by historians as emblematic of the Puritan perception of the Church of England. Another is that eight of the twenty-seven documents printed in Harry Porter's anthology, *Puritanism in Tudor England* (1971), derive from it. The *Register* was the work of John Field, who was, for Morrice, 'the nonconformist so often mentioned in our story', and, for Harry Porter, 'the great Puritan impresario'.[2] Field was an indefatigable agitator for the

---

[*] This essay is drawn from material that will appear in Volume One of the six-volume edition of Roger Morrice's *Entring Book*, to be published by Boydell and Brewer in association with the Parliamentary History Yearbook Trust. The co-editors are Tim Harris, Mark Knights, Jason McElligott, John Spurr, and Stephen Taylor; the shorthand decoder is Frances Henderson. The Morrice Project is funded by the Arts and Humanities Research Board and Dr. Williams's Library, London. In the notes below 'RM MS' refers to Roger Morrice Manuscripts, Dr. Williams's Library, London.

[1] For Morrice see *Dictionary of National Biography: Missing Persons*, C.S. Nicholls (ed.), (Oxford, 1993), pp. 477-8; A.G. Matthews, *Calamy Revised* (Oxford, 1988), p. 355; Mark Goldie, 'Roger Morrice and his *Entring Book*', *History Today* 51:11 (November 2001), pp. 38-44.

[2] RM MS, H 311(2); H.C. Porter (ed.), *Puritanism in Tudor England* (London, 1970), p. 120. See Patrick Collinson, 'John Field and Elizabethan Puritanism', in

further reformation of the church: for the reconstruction of episcopacy, the creation of a zealous preaching ministry, and the purging of the residues of popery from the Book of Common Prayer. Into his *Register* he gathered campaign petitions, designed to show the weight of clerical and gentry support, and surveys of the condition of the ministry, designed to show the inadequacy of pastoral provision. Field published the first *Parte* in 1593, but Archbishop Bancroft tried to seize the *Seconde Parte* and it was never printed. Today it is chiefly known from the calendar published in 1915 by the Congregationalist historian Albert Peel.[3]

Roger Morrice leads a fugitive double life in the footnotes of two sorts of historians, working a century apart, for he is known not only to students of Tudor Puritanism, but also to those who study the late seventeenth century. His *Entring Book*, nearly one million words long, is a chronicle of his own times, which he compiled between 1677 and 1691 on behalf of a group of Puritan Whig politicians who sought to challenge the threat of 'popery and arbitrary power', which they detected in the policies of Charles II and James II. It, too, was never published. When Morrice ceased composing it, he turned immediately to a programme of relentless historical scholarship. Both the *Entring Book* and the 'politico-ecclesiastical' history belonged to a single master project, for both were attempts to record the trials of the godly party which had leavened the English church for more than a century. Morrice saw himself as John Field *redivivus*, a chronicler of the Puritan cause, his *Entring Book* a latter-day counterpart of Field's *Register*, and his unfinished history a bridge between the two.

That Morrice never completed his history was owed in part to the hazards of scholarship and mortality: he was overwhelmed by the weight of documentation, by his own erudition, by overambition, and by serious illness. Arguably he was also debilitated by the difficulty of achieving a coherent vision of the past of English Puritanism.

Morrice was a Dissenter, one of the Presbyterian clergyman ejected from the Church of England in the great expulsion of 1662. During the next quarter century his colleagues suffered harassment and prosecution, and in the 1680s real fear and persecution. Yet at the heart of Restoration Dissent there lay a paradox. Moderate Puritans like Morrice were separatists who did not believe in separation. They believed in a legally established, uniform, parochially organized, national church, and their earnest hope was for 'Comprehension', a restoration of unity and a healing of schism. Meanwhile, they were forced to come to terms with their marginalized and sectarian status. Not until lingering hopes of Comprehension were destroyed with the passing of the Act of Toleration in 1689 did they accept that their future lay in denominational independence. Toleration was a blessed release from persecution, but, by confirming the Dissenters'

S.T. Bindoff, Joel Hurstfield, and H. Williams (eds.), *Elizabethan Government and Society* (London, 1961), reprinted in Collinson's *Godly People* (London, 1983).

[3] Albert Peel (ed.), *The Seconde Parte of a Register: Being a Calendar of Manuscripts under that title intended for publication by the Puritans about 1593, and now in Dr. Williams's Library*, 2 vols. (Cambridge, 1915).

exclusion from the church, it marked the final failure of the Puritan ideal of reform from within.[4]

About the year 1690 it was hard to know what kind of history of Puritanism to write: of insiders or of outsiders? Should it seek to show that the Elizabethan and Jacobean church was in essence of a moderate Calvinist sort, containing Puritan bishops and university professors within it, who strove for 'further reformation' and the purging of popish corruptions? Such an account would read the Elizabethan settlement as open to revision. Or should it dwell on the righteous sufferers who, from an early stage, stood apart from an incorrigible establishment in the name of a purer religion? Such an account would readily slip into martyrology, a meditation on heroic outcasts. Was the history of Puritanism the story of attempts to capture the soul of the national church, or the story of the origins of a separatism that renounced that church?

For two-and-a-half centuries, from the early 1700s until the mid-twentieth century, the latter was the main historical tendency. The Dissenters, as an independent, organized, and vigorous stream in national life, constructed histories of their traditions. Puritanism came to seem, from the moment of Elizabeth's accession, a discrete, coherent, and continuous movement of opposition. 'Puritan' and 'Anglican' were made to lock horns, and, among much else, it became rather easy to explain the Civil War.[5] By the time that Daniel Neal wrote his *History of the Puritans*, it seemed natural that he should define his aim as being 'to account for the rise and progress of...separation', and that he should dwell on the Puritans' struggle to assert the rights of private conscience against the evil of church establishments.[6] Neal's book, which went through half a dozen editions down to 1863, became a cornerstone of the Dissenting historiographical tradition. In 1910 R.G. Usher pronounced that 'most secondary histories of Puritanism are Neal plus a little of something else'.[7]

By contrast, the whole trend of Puritan historiography in the final third of the twentieth century has reflected the ecumenism—and secularism—of its time: its instinct is to find convergences and affinities between Puritans and their contemporaries. Patrick Collinson has been a signal figure in this

---

[4] For recent surveys see John Spurr, 'From Puritanism to Dissent, 1660-1700', in Christopher Durston and Jacqueline Eales (eds.), *The Culture of English Puritanism, 1560-1700* (Basingstoke, 1998); Nicholas Tyacke, 'The "Rise of Puritanism" and the Legalizing of Dissent, 1571-1719', in Ole Peter Grell, Jonathan I. Israel, and Nicholas Tyacke (eds.), *From Persecution to Toleration: the Glorious Revolution and Religion in England* (Oxford, 1991), reprinted in his *Aspects of English Protestantism, c.1530-1700* (Manchester, 2001).

[5] See, for example, William Haller, *The Rise of Puritanism* (New York, 1938); J.F. New, *Anglican and Puritan: The Basis of their Opposition, 1558-1640* (London, 1964); Michael Walzer, *The Revolution of the Saints* (London, 1966). For the fortunes of the term 'Puritanism' after the seventeenth century see Raphael Samuel, 'The Discovery of Puritanism, 1820-1914', in Jane Garnett and Colin Matthew (eds.), *Revival and Religion since 1700* (London, 1993).

[6] Daniel Neal, *The History of the Puritans* (London, 1822), I, p.v.

[7] R.G. Usher, *The Presbyterian Movement* (London, 1910), II, p. 392.

transformation. Today it is held that, at least before 1640, Puritanism was a tendency, an attitude, *within* the established church, which had little in common with the tiny number of outright separatists. Puritans did not seek to set themselves apart; rather, they sought to be at the heart of the national church. Puritans were churchmen who wished to evangelize, to moralize, not to separate; they sought to inspire and invigorate the church, not to reject it. The Elizabethan and Jacobean church, it is now argued, was not 'Anglican'—the word is a misleading Victorian coinage—but Calvinist, so that the Puritans under Charles I had good reason to claim that *they* were the church, and that the Laudian hierarchy was, in John Pym's notorious words, 'an innovative, papistical, and schismatical sect'. On this view, the Puritans were no revolutionary insurgents against church and state, but a defensive reaction which aimed to reclaim the church from an Arminian, anti-Calvinist takeover. The term 'Anglican' falsely posits a stable centre, a status quo, in contrast to which Puritanism must seem peripheral and aberrant. Similarly, though it is legitimate to speak of 'nonconformists' under Elizabeth and the Stuarts, it needs to be understood that they were mostly parish ministers, who baulked at some rubrics of the Prayer Book, or had a taste for religious meetings which supplemented Prayer Book services: they were not 'Nonconformists' in the sense of making new denominations. Some historians, in this revisionist mood, have gone so far as to propose the abandonment of 'Puritanism' as a viable historical category altogether.[8]

Collinson has helpfully characterised these contrasting approaches to the history of Puritanism as 'vertical' and 'horizontal'.[9] A 'vertical' history traces a tunnel-like denominational tradition from its beginnings down to the present time, offering a history of a people set apart, whereas a 'horizontal' one contextualizes and integrates. Collinson criticizes denominationally committed historians who take an 'excessively vertical, or linear' approach. They operate with assumptions that are genetic and genealogical: they search for the birth and bloodline of a new church, sourced to the fountainhead of the Reformation, and they tend to be hagiographic, martyrological, and defiantly sectarian. He gives the example of Albert Peel, doyen among Congregationalist historians, whose grand aim was to bring to light the lives of 'the fathers of Separatism'. Collinson chides Peel for anachronistically seeking to pin down 'the first

---

[8] Classics of this revisionist account are Patrick Collinson, *The Elizabethan Puritan Movement* (London, 1967); idem, *The Religion of Protestants: The Church in English Society, 1559-1625* (Oxford, 1982); Nicholas Tyacke, 'Puritanism, Arminianism, and Counter-Revolution', in Conrad Russell (ed.), *The Origins of the English Civil War* (London, 1973), reprinted in Tyacke's *Aspects of English Protestantism*; idem, *Anti-Calvinists: The Rise of English Arminianism, 1590-1640* (Oxford, 1987); Peter Lake, *Moderate Puritans and the Elizabethan Church* (Cambridge, 1982).

[9] Patrick Collinson, 'Towards a Broader Understanding of the Early Dissenting Tradition', in Robert C. Cole and Michael E. Moody (eds.), *The Dissenting Tradition: Essays for Leland H. Carson* (Athens, OH, 1975), reprinted in Collinson's *Godly People*.

Congregationalists'.[10] Collinson does, however, note that the vertical approach tends to be self-fulfilling, for the very act of writing such history is a principal instrument in constructing a coherent tradition and identity. Peel's predilections could hardly have been other than they were. He was a child of Gladstonian liberalism, of a period when Nonconformity was a robust social and political force rivaling the established church, a rivalry that involved a whole array of perceived distinctions, between chapel and church, urban and rural, trade and land, reform and reaction, Manchester and Barchester. The consequence was a Puritan historiography that was imbued with a distinctive teleology.

In his own very different historical situation, Roger Morrice stood poised between the two historiographical possibilities. Arguably this produced an intellectual tension he could not resolve. Bred in the 'Comprehensive' tradition, he remained interested in defining the Puritan past as identifiable with, compatible with, the national church. Equally, after a generation of persecution during the Restoration, it was difficult to avoid writing Puritanism as the story of a suffering sect. The result was that Morrice's draft history was a unique hybrid of the 'horizontal' and the 'vertical'. Elegiac martyrology, sectarian self-righteousness, and a (sometimes literal) genealogical tracing of inherited nonconformity among Puritan clerical and gentry dynasties, were interwoven with an emphatically national and integrative vision of England's 'long Reformation'. His was undoubtedly a history of successive generations of victims of persecutory authority. Conscience cost the Puritans 'their worldly interest, ease, and contentment, and [they] have all of them been exposed to the displeasure of the government, the rage of their enemies, and many of them to impoverishment and imprisonment'. Yet it was also a history which aimed to prove that Puritan principles were central to the Elizabethan and Jacobean church, and had firmly repudiated separatism. The Puritans, Morrice insisted, were not to be associated with 'the familists or any heretics or blasphemers', or with anabaptists or sectaries who 'entertained many giddy and fantastical opinions'.[11]

Morrice's collection of manuscripts laid a foundation for the denominational histories of Dissent written in the eighteenth and nineteenth centuries. They are therefore partly responsible for a school of historiography which recent historians, in their wholesale turn towards a 'horizontal' approach, have found unsatisfactory. Yet, by not publishing his history, Morrice obscured from view the 'horizontal' and anti-sectarian aspects of his own approach. His generation, still in touch with pre-Civil War Puritanism, whose nonconformity had subsisted within the national church, was the last, before the late twentieth century, that could write its history 'horizontally'. Accordingly, Morrice's historical argument has striking similarities with what has become the present orthodoxy, most

---

[10] Collinson, *Godly People*, pp. 527-9. Cf. Norman Sykes, 'Dr. Albert Peel and Historical Studies', *Transactions of the Congregational Historical Society* 17 (1952-55), pp. 4-7.
[11] RM MS, G 123, 847.

notably in the work of Collinson, and of Nicholas Tyacke, who has argued strongly for the Calvinist nature of the Elizabethan and Jacobean church.[12]

I

Most of Morrice's notebooks on the history of Puritanism are arranged annalistically, and they often read as an ill-digested *omnium gatherum*. He had a penchant for encyclopedism, for making lists: of Marian martyrs, of clergy suspended and prosecuted by vindictive prelates, of clergy who fled to New England, of MPs who supported the Puritan cause, of bishops who were 'forward tools' of Laudianism, of godly divines who providentially died in the pulpit. These notebooks cast doubt on whether Morrice was capable of constructing a coherent narrative. Yet in one notebook we find 16,000 words of connected prose, the beginnings of a synthesis. It is headed, 'A History of the Plots and Proceedings of the Papists, and their Tools the Hierarchists, against the Reformers, Puritans, and Abbotists for the Destruction of the Reformation and the Restoration of Popery, from Edward VI to the Civil War'.[13]

As this title suggests, Morrice's narrative is driven by an obsessively bipolar vision of the contest between the 'hierarchists' and the Puritans. As a work of historical imagination, it is flawed by his inability to find anything but popish perfidy on the one hand, and patriot piety on the other. He is apt to offer formulaic commendations of those of whom he approves. Thomas Wilson was 'a learned, holy, humble, self-denying, useful, and frequent preacher', Sir Anthony Denny an 'excellent patriot', John Foxe a man of 'exemplary piety'.[14]

Occasionally, however, Morrice is more subtle. His negative judgments upon individuals are sometimes mitigated by admiration for their scholarship. He had an acute sense of the *trahison des clercs*, of the tragedy of refined erudition serving evil causes. Ralph Bane, bishop of Lichfield, 'was an excellent Latinist, Grecian and Hebraecian, and a most virulent persecutor'. The despised Peter Heylyn, Laud's propagandist, is granted to have been a 'master of a sound masculine language'. Such compliments extended even to papists. Nicholas Harpsfield (the biographer of Thomas More) 'most indefatigably and cruelly butchered the poor Reformers; he was a learned man'; the Jesuit Edmund Campion was 'of good parts,

---

[12] See n. 8 above.
[13] RM MS, U. The principal relevant notebooks are MS F-J. For the historiography of the Reformation in Morrice's time see J.A.I. Champion, *Pillars of Priestcraft Shaken: The Church of England and its Enemies, 1660-1720* (Cambridge, 1992); A.G. Dickens and John M. Tonkin, *The Reformation in Historical Thought* (Oxford, 1985); Rosemary O'Day, *The Debate on the English Reformation* (London, 1986).
[14] RM MS, G 911, H 68(2), 83(18), I 373(8), 395(21).

ability and eloquence'.[15]

Morrice was also capable of literary affect. Reflecting on the propensity of the 'hierarchists' to extol the absolute authority of monarchs, when it suited their purposes, Morrice shaped a nicely ironic passage about their blindness to the danger that monarchical authority might rebound upon them:

> If the king might make rules without authority of Parliament against the Puritan conformable clergy, and deprive them thereupon...when the Church of England had the ascendant upon him, he may do the same to the Church of England clergy, if they conform not to such rules as he shall please at any time to prescribe, when the popish clergy hath the like interest in him, this may be easily foretold without the spirit of prophecy. But the hierarchical, prelatical clergy has this excellent gift (though it is verified every century, and in some three or four times over, by experience) not to believe it possible that the same arbitrary power that they gave life to may be executed against themselves, but when they see it, then like wise men, they lift up their hands and say, who would have thought it.[16]

Morrice's subtler arts—and cynicism—are visible too in a passage about the folly of Charles I and Archbishop Laud in cruelly punishing the lawyer William Prynne in 1637, which was, he suggests, more consequential than the punishing of the two clergymen alongside him, Henry Burton and William Bastwick. Morrice judged it politically disastrous for the crown and the church to attack an eminent lay lawyer. The case would have

> given a fainter alarm to the kingdom had they all three been of the short robe [clergymen], for the hierarchists cannot but know very many of the laity are no further concerned in the animosities, hatred and cruelty of the clergy one against another, than to clap them on the back, and laugh at them, &c and to rejoice in the peace and quiet they enjoy, while those are warring one upon another.

But in 1637 Laud and the king unwittingly provoked the sleeping giant of the long robe (the lawyers), 'who have been a greater pillar, not only to liberty and property, but to religion, than any other profession'. To anger lawyers is to 'stir up a wasp's nest'.[17]

---

[15] RM MS, D 25, 56, G 787, H 311(8).
[16] RM MS, U 9. Morrice wrote that Bishop John Fell died wracked with guilt in 1686 when he saw the popery of James II unleashed, having so fervently upheld James's right of inheritance to the throne: RM MS, J 1686(2).
[17] RM MS, U 47.

II

Morrice greatly admired John Foxe, 'that faithful and impartial historian'. The *Acts and Monuments* (the *Book of Martyrs*), he wrote, is so accurate a book that 'it is thought to be more free from errors and mistakes in proportion than any book hitherto written so large'.[18] Morrice might have been drawn to dwell solely on victimhood, on godly men and women who suffered under oppression, a Puritan continuation of Foxe. Certainly he put on record the sufferings of nonconformists. But he was Foxean also in another sense. His was a national history. A constant theme was the struggle for national independence from the thrall of Rome. Rome was idolatrous and anti-Christian, it was a tyranny and usurpation, it aspired to 'universal monarchy'. Morrice's history was, like Foxe's, magisterial and Constantinian. That is to say, it adhered to the Tudor doctrine that reformation was work for godly princes, modeling themselves on the first Christian emperor, Constantine. A godly prince was a lay pastor, a divine instrument for reform. The potency of princes was not necessarily despotic: on the contrary, it could be liberating, for the redeemer-prince was one who freed a people from Rome's crushing impediments to godliness and the gospel. If this was the ideology of the Henrician and Edwardian Reformations, it could still be the idiom of those who celebrated William III in the 1690s.[19] The Foxean theme is given voice in the opening paragraph of Morrice's draft essay:

> When God in his most just displeasure against us for our sins had suffered the pope of Rome who calleth himself the Vicar of Christ, by force and fraud to usurp to himself and to enjoy less, or more, by his predecessors, for some ages past an absolute sovereignty over England and most Christian kings, states, and potentates in the Western Empire. And to introduce idolatry into the church of God, and defile it with such gross corruption and superstition...That God whose will all created being must obey, and who therefore never wants instruments to do his own work, was pleased to raise up King Henry the 8th, a prince of an undaunted courage and resolution as any historians acquaint us with, to encounter this grand usurper the pope, which king in a little time, without any war, deprived him of his pretended supremacy and authority in this realm, and passed an Act of Parliament to that purpose in anno [blank] And gave his own subjects liberty to have the bible in English, and some other godly books whereby they came to understand the will of God revealed in his word and the idolatry, superstition and corruption of the papacy. This king lived and died in the communion of Rome, and continued to persecute the servants of God till his death in Anno 1546. But thus he removed one of the greatest impediments to, and prepared the way for the Reformation

---

[18] RM MS, H 83(22), I 395(19). Morrice helped raise subscriptions for the 1684 edition of the *Book of Martyrs*, the last edition of the book to be published until 1837: RM MS, P 354. See Eirwen Nicholson, 'Eighteenth-Century Foxe: Evidence for the Impact of the *Acts and Monuments* in the "long" Eighteenth Century', in David Loades (ed.), *John Foxe and the English Reformation* (Aldershot, 1997), pp. 143-77.

[19] Tony Claydon, *William III and the Godly Revolution* (Cambridge, 1996).

following.[20]

Henry VIII had repudiated Rome's authority, but not its doctrine. The real transformation began with Edward VI, who was 'zealously addicted to the carrying on of the Reformation'. 'From the beginning of his reign we account the era of the Reformation in this kingdom'. Edward—who died aged sixteen—was the only monarch about whom Morrice is unequivocally enthusiastic. He is likened to the Israelite King Josiah, who pulled down the altars and priesthood of the pagan god Baal.[21]

Queen Mary was of course a disaster: 'Parliaments packed, and members corrupted and bribed...liberty and property invaded, and the Spanish Inquisition and tyranny like to be established'. Naturally Morrice revered the Protestant martyrs whom Mary burnt: Cranmer, Latimer, and Ridley, who suffered hideous deaths 'for the truth of Jesus'. The lesser-known martyr John Bradford is singled out, for Morrice was satisfied that he was 'such a one as men now call a Puritan', for, like 'Nonconformists at this day', he so objected to the 'abuses' in the church that he did not consent to them when ordained a minister, and was allowed to express his dissent by the 'tender' Bishop Ridley.[22]

Elizabeth's reign was the most ambiguous of all. In sanguine moments, Morrice could write of 'the Church of England in the best times she ever saw, that is of Queen Elizabeth'. More sombrely, he argued that though the cause of further reformation did advance under her, ultimately she allowed it to be frustrated, driven in part by reason of state and by her own superstitious inclinations, but chiefly because of a successful coalition between 'papists' and 'prelatists'. It was a coalition that came to the fore in the later years of her reign. After the defeat of the Spanish Armada, the papists turned increasingly to methods of secret insurgency and the subtle undermining from within of court and church. By the time of James I's reign England's ability to hold the balance abroad between France and Spain was emasculated. At home, the papists followed the Machiavellian advice of such Jesuits as Adam Contzen, on how to divide and rule, and how to debauch the common people in order to detach them from their godly pastors.[23] The coalition of popery and prelacy would blight the Stuart century. It was a coalition which successfully marginalized the mainstream of the reform movement and pinned upon it the name of 'Puritan' as a term of reproach.

In the early part of Elizabeth's reign there had been room for reformers to rise. Thomas Cartwright became professor at Cambridge. Laurence Humphrey, who 'sowed...seeds of Calvinism', was professor at Oxford and stocked Magdalen College with Puritans. Miles Coverdale was offered a bishopric. Walter Travers acquired a lectureship at the Inns of Court. Morrice gathered every instance he could find of those 'afterwards called

---

[20] RM MS, G 1; another version at F 1.
[21] RM MS, F 3, 31, G 71, U 1.
[22] RM MS, F 75, D 52.
[23] RM MS, M 2, U 2-3, 7, 11.

Puritans, or Nonconformists' holding public positions in Elizabeth's reign.[24] These men could be shown to have rejected popish ceremonies and prelatical deviations. That, at the birth of the Elizabethan age, the true reformers were at the heart of the national church is the cornerstone of Morrice's account.

Morrice devoted close attention to the turning points of the reign, to the beginnings of the purges of ministers for nonconformity. He documents the Vestiarian Controversy of the 1560s, and the Presbyterian movement and the 'prophesyings' of the 1570s. He shows how the pernicious demand that ministers subscribe to every iota of the Prayer Book steadily drove a wedge between Puritans and 'hierarchists'. Bishops who at first did not enforce the wearing of 'popish' vestments were made to enforce it. Petitions to Parliament against subscription were unavailing, though they did serve to mark out those laymen who were of the godly party. One early turning point was signaled by the coining, in Morrice's estimation in about 1566, of the term 'Puritan', to fix the odium of factiousness upon a party.[25]

During Elizabeth's reign a 'new generation' rose up, who 'set back the Reformation'. Archbishops Whitgift and Bancroft, who embarked upon the systematic crushing of nonconformity, were the calamities of her later years. After 1588, in alliance with Sir Christopher Hatton and William Cecil (Lord Burghley), they 'set themselves to break the Puritan interest'. Morrice lambastes their episcopal allies. Bishop Overall was 'an entire tool to Archbishop Bancroft and that faction'. Samuel Harsnett was an 'agent, spy or informer' for Bancroft at Cambridge: he interfered at Caius College, 'because Puritanism abounded there'.[26]

III

Notwithstanding Morrice's venom against the Bancroftians, he never condemned bishops as a class. On the contrary, there had always been good bishops as well as bad, reformed as well as 'prelatical'. Morrice, a lifelong enemy of 'prelacy', counted bishops among his friends and he remembered three of them in his will.[27] He showed how, from the 1540s onwards, the retardation of reformation was the consequence of prelatists getting the upper hand over reformers in the leadership of the church. The struggle for the principles later dubbed 'Puritan' was thus an intramural contest at the highest level within the establishment. Cranmer and Ridley were true reformers, frustrated by the popish bishop Stephen Gardiner.

On the whole, the first generation of Elizabethan bishops were good

---

[24] RM MS, F 115, G 113, I 431(6).
[25] RM MS, F 193, G 193, H 117(2).
[26] RM MS, I 546(12), 631(6), 667(2), J 1630(2-4).
[27] Edward Fowler, Richard Kidder, John Moore. Public Record Office, Kew, PROB 11/463.

and holy men. Morrice approves of Elizabeth's first archbishop, Matthew Parker. He was 'well inclined to the nonconformists (though the contrary be generally received)'; he administered the sacrament to people standing, not requiring them to kneel; he licensed Puritan preachers; he was favourable to private meetings for spiritual nourishment, the 'prophesyings'.[28] Archbishop Grindal he approved of too, who was suspended for refusing to suppress prophesyings. The verdict on Bishop John Jewel is mixed. He had Puritan friends, and he 'held not the bishops to be a superior order by divine right', but he was unsympathetic to those who made an issue of wearing popish vestments, and he did not favour prophesyings.[29]

The bishop upon whom Morrice dwells at greatest length is John Hooper, a 'blessed martyr' burnt at the stake under Mary, a model for what the English reformed church should have become.[30] Hooper, in the words of a modern historian, was 'the prototype of the Protestant pastor bishop'.[31] Had Edward VI lived longer, Morrice wistfully remarks, Hooper's churchmanship would have triumphed. Hooper encouraged a godly preaching clergy and was himself an itinerant preacher. He instilled discipline and sobriety. He had paupers to his dinner table and examined them in the catechism. He hoped for a reform of episcopacy that would have made bishops superintendents over groups of just ten parishes.[32] Among the documents Morrice acquired was the record of Hooper's visitation of his diocese in 1551, which revealed the pastoral task before him, for it exposed a shocking number of clergy who could not repeat the Ten Commandments.[33] Hooper's significance lay especially in his being persecuted by his Protestant superiors. He at first refused to wear the vestments at his consecration as bishop, though he was finally bullied into submission. Morrice was shocked that Cranmer and Ridley should perpetrate such oppression. It was 'an amazing example indeed to see the flames of persecution kindled among brethren of the same reformed religion'. He half excuses them, putting their actions down not to 'their temper and dispositions' but to the 'common notions' of the time, that 'fire and sword were evangelical and effectual means to suppress heresy and schism'. Hooper had not refused conformity from 'obstinacy, pride, vainglory', but from 'mere conscience'. Futile impositions in matters of 'vestibus et gestibus' ('vestures and gestures') had bedeviled the church

---

[28] RM MS, H 275(6).
[29] RM MS, H 251(6), 275(6).
[30] RM MS, H35(2). In this he followed Foxe. See Tom Betteridge, 'From Prophetic to Apocalyptic: John Foxe and the Writing of History', in Loades (ed.), *John Foxe and the English Reformation*, pp. 210-32.
[31] W.J. Sheils, *The English Reformation, 1530-1570* (London, 1989), pp. 44-5.
[32] RM MS G 51, L 87.
[33] RM MS, L 3. Printed in *Later Writings of Bishop Hooper*, edited by Charles Nevinson (Cambridge, 1852), pp. 117-56; and James Gairdner, 'Bishop Hooper's Visitation of Gloucester', *English Historical Review* 19 (1904), pp. 98-121.

ever since. For Morrice, Hooper was the archetype of the nonconformist *and* he was a bishop, so that he was emblematic of nonconformity's presence at the heart of the church.[34] Ever since, the church had profligately wasted the talent and zeal of godly ministers by groundlessly oppressing or expelling them. Nonconformity was never meant to be a tradition, the stirring of an independent church, rather it was a tragic and unnecessary distraction from the pastoral tasks of the national church.

One of Morrice's preoccupations was the necessity of a preaching ministry, and for improving the quality of the clergy. It was a terrible failure of the Reformation that it had been so neglectful of clerical education, filling the church 'with illiterate, ignorant and scandalous priests that could not preach'.[35] Field's *Register* provided him with plenty of evidence, as did the records of episcopal visitations. One item in Morrice's collection is a report on 'the lamentable state of the ministry in Staffordshire', dating from 1604, showing that many curates were 'very ignorant' or 'of a loose life', and that outlying chapels lacked preachers.[36] Morrice singles out preaching as a cardinal virtue in those he approves. The early reformer Miles Coverdale preached every Sunday and holy day and gave two lectures midweek. Not the least fault of the system of prelacy was its concentration of wealth in the hands of bishops, which could better have been used to ensure provision of a preacher in every town and a schoolmaster in every village. Morrice noted the 'commonweal' tradition among the early reformers, anxious to convert monastic and episcopal revenues to educational uses. In this connection, he cites Simon Fish's *Supplication of the Beggars* (1528) and Aylmer's *Harborowe for Faithfull and Trewe Subjects* (1559).[37]

Morrice turned from the Tudor era to the Stuart. Writing in the immediate aftermath of the providential deliverance of 1688, a sense of the Stuart century as a continuous calamity quickly acquired fixity. Under James I and Charles I Bancroft's 'little faction' was enlarged by William Laud, who 'carried it on vigorously, till a civil war, the most desperate of remedies, put a stop to his measures'. The 'despotic influence' and 'superstitious novelties' of Laud drew Morrice's unmitigated condemnation. His popish innovations (the erecting of altars, the insistence on vestments), his rooting out of the godly (the suppression of Puritan lectureships), his 'profanation of the Lord's day by sports', his instruments of repression (Star Chamber and the Court of High Commission) are tallied.[38] In Laud's wake there came a formidable faction, men like Richard Neile, that 'popish Arminian prelate, a persecutor of all orthodox godly ministers', and Matthew Wren, 'a professed Arminian, a superstitious,

---

[34] RM MS, F 35, G 45, 167, H 35(6), 35(15), 35(28), 36(6), 39(4); cf. F 35-47.
[35] RM MS, F 53.
[36] RM MS, M 5. Printed in Albert Peel, 'A Puritan Survey of the Church in Staffordshire in 1604', *English Historical Review* 26 (1911), pp. 338-52.
[37] RM MS, H 85(2), 221(8), I 631(6).
[38] RM MS, I 417(8), 631(6), J 1644(18), 1644(22), 1644(24). Collinson, *Elizabethan Puritan Movement*, p. 387 quotes Morrice.

popish, dissolute, impious, corrupt clergyman'.[39]

Yet even the early Stuart era produced commendable bishops: James Ussher in particular, who originated the scheme for 'reduced episcopacy' which so captivated moderate Dissenters during the Restoration; John Williams, the thorn in Laud's side, who committed the 'original sin' of lenity to Puritans; George Carleton, that 'excellent philosopher and divine'; and, above all, the Jacobean archbishop, George Abbot, under whom 'Puritanism and religion got much countenance'.[40] Morrice sometimes used the term 'Abbotists' generically, to refer, across two centuries, to godly churchmen, and he does so also in his *Entring Book*.[41] He defined Abbotists thus:

> by whom I mean those formerly called Queen Elizabeth's Protestants, Archbishop Abbot's Protestants, conformable or nonconformable Puritans, according to the then *a la mode* dialect, since then Presbyterians or Independents, of late Nonconformists, Dissenters, Fanatics, who adhere to the articles of the Church of England, and preserve the substance and practice of religion before the paint and shadow of it, and that generally concurred to Archbishop Armagh's [Ussher's] episcopacy in his Reduction.[42]

Morrice makes plain here his commitment to 'primitive episcopacy'. A bishop should be *primus inter pares*, first among equals; he is to preside not dictate. 'The difference lieth in degree, not in order'. He insists that the Puritans were never hostile to episcopacy as such, and his vilification of 'hierarchists' never obliterates this commitment. He contends that the Millenary Petition of 1603 was not against bishops fundamentally; nor was the Covenant of 1643; nor even the Westminster Assembly of the 1640s. The Puritans 'were universally for episcopacy...though not for this hierarchy, much less the *jus divinum* it now claims'. Calvin did not condemn episcopacy as unlawful, only 'such a hierarchy or prelacy as obtained in England'. The evil of prelacy lay partly in the merging of secular with spiritual jurisdiction. Some of what was imagined to be spiritual power in the bishops was, Morrice argued, no more than temporal power licensed to them by the crown. When bishops acted beyond their spiritual function they were but 'king's officers only, or ecclesiastical sheriffs'. The fault in prelacy lay above all in usurped spiritual authority, the monopolization of the ordination of clergy, and of ecclesiastical jurisdiction and censure.[43] The prelatical insistence on episcopal ordination of clergy especially irked Morrice: he himself had not been episcopally ordained and he was violently affronted that the church should deem his ministry a nullity. As to the offensive judicial power of bishops, Morrice

---

[39] RM MS, I 615(5), 667(9), J 1640(2), 1667(2), U 31.
[40] RM MS, G 633, 649, 735, J 1625(8), 1628(2), U 23, 25.
[41] As, for example, George Gifford, deceased rector of St. Dunstans in the East, d.1686, a 'grave sober person' who 'had some tincture of Archbishop Abbot's principles': RM MS, P 591.
[42] RM MS, U 32-3.
[43] RM MS F 23-7, G 7, 27, 545, J 1654(1), U 21.

had in mind the diocesan church courts and the central prerogative courts. Here his animus is not only against bishops but also against the ecclesiastical prerogative usurped by the crown and exercised in the Court of High Commission before 1640—and revived by James II in the Ecclesiastical Commission of 1686-88.

Morrice's approval of moderate episcopacy led him to gloss over the dogmatic Presbyterianism of some of the Elizabethan Puritans. He dwells on vestments, prophesyings, and a preaching ministry; but he avoids John Field's demand for the abolition of bishops in the *Admonition* of 1572, and does not discuss the 'classical' movement of that decade, the organizing of a synodical church independent of episcopacy. He briefly concedes that the Puritans were sometimes too scurrilous and abusive. He had in mind those notoriously savage libels against the bishops, the Marprelate tracts of 1588-9. He remarks that the violence of the differences between prelatists and Puritans was a help to the papists. Breaches were so sinfully kept open 'that God has been to this day punishing us for it'.[44]

If discussion of the 'root and branch' Presbyterianism of the 1570s is a telling absence in Morrice's account, so too is his almost complete neglect of the separatists. He does not discuss the Brownists, except only to stress that the Puritans repudiated them. The Puritan Arthur Hildersham was 'a great opposer of the Brownist separation'. One of Morrice's most profound objections to Archbishop Laud's regime was that it drove people 'into separation and into giddy sects'.[45]

Morrice showed little taste for theology, but he did detect, around the turn of the seventeenth century, a decisive shift in doctrine. The Laudians were a faction which, in capturing the church, manipulated its teaching. Morrice is emphatic that the mainstream of the English church before Laud's time was Calvinist in doctrine, had taught that the pope was antichrist, and had not asserted that episcopacy was by divine right.[46] The places he looked to for evidence were the chairs and divinity theses at Oxford and Cambridge universities. The Oxford professors and heads of colleges—Robert Abbot, Thomas Holland, and Lawrence Humphrey—were 'very learned orthodox and vigilant divines', under whom 'the doctrine of religion was preserved there in its purity, free from Arminianism, Pelagianism, and Socinianism'. It was the young William Laud who deviated: what he taught 'was new doctrine in that university'. A telling development was the advent of the doctrine of *jure divino* episcopacy. In 1604 Laud upheld the thesis 'that there could be no true churches without diocesan bishops', for which he was rebuked by Dr Holland. But by the time of George Downame's sermon of 1608, Laud's

---

[44] RM MS, G 173, 421. Of John Knox's *First Blast of the Trumpet Against the Monstrous Regiment of Women* (1558), Morrice notes that the cruelties of the popish queens of England, Scotland, and France 'transported him beyond all bounds, so that he imputeth that to the sex, which was the fault of the persons': H 85(2).

[45] RM MS, J 1631(8), 1644(38).

[46] RM MS, F 177, G 637, 644-5.

novelty was rapidly gaining ground.[47]

From Morrice's notebooks a coherent thesis emerges. The Tudor church had become doctrinally a fully reformed Calvinist church, albeit backward in its pastoral programme for instilling practical godliness and building a preaching ministry. The coming of the Bancroftians, and signally of the Laudians, marked an ecclesiastical revolution. Laud's was a 'new party', the party of 'Arminianism', a 'faction' which seized the commanding heights of the church from the old 'Calvinistical party (which adhered to the doctrine of the Church of England)'. 'Puritanism and Calvinism prevailing much' until the 1620s, Laud then launched a successful counter-revolution against it.[48] What has ever since been labeled Puritanism was in fact no other than the heart and soul of the Reformation church. That, during the Stuart age, it was thrust to the margins, an oppressed and denigrated party, was an historical contingency, a fact of usurped power, not a truth about its essential relationship to English Protestantism.

IV

It would be misleading to suggest that Morrice's history of the Puritans was entirely clerical. He had an encyclopedic knowledge of, and a great deal to say about, the Puritan gentry. There was a sociology implicit in his treatment of the laity, for he was acutely aware that movements and beliefs are underpinned by social power. Puritanism was an inheritance entailed upon successive generations in the leading families of the shires. It was sustained not so much through formal institutions, but through kinship, patronage, print, and household piety.[49]

Often Morrice breaks off from his chronological place and follows a family down from Elizabethan to present times. For example, he traces the Gells of Hopton in Derbyshire down to the current 'worthy gent Sir Philip Gell'. There is an admiring family portrait of the Armynes of Osgodby Hall, an island of godliness through several generations, notably Sir William, a redoubtable Parliamentarian in the Civil War, his house sacked by the Royalists, a son killed in battle, his wife, Lady Mary, a brave harbourer of ejected ministers in the 1660s. The account of the Bromleys

---

[47] RM MS, G 583, H 280(12), I 657(8), J 1641(8). Morrice applauded John Selden's *History of Tithes* (1618) for its refutation of the claim that the clergy had a divine right to tithes: G 653.

[48] RM MS, G 731-5, I 499(2), J 1644(12).

[49] These themes are echoed in J.T. Cliffe's trilogy (which makes use of RM MS, H-J), *The Puritan Gentry: The Puritan Families of Early Stuart England* (London, 1984); *Puritans in Conflict: The Puritan Gentry during and after the Civil Wars* (London, 1988); *The Puritan Gentry Besieged, 1650-1700* (London, 1993). See also Jacqueline Eales, 'A Road to Revolution: The Continuity of Puritanism, 1559-1642', in Durston and Eales (eds.), *The Culture of English Puritanism*.

begins with Sir Thomas, Lord Chancellor in the 1580s, who would not 'sacrifice his judgement and reason entirely to the archbishop's pleasure'; turns to his son, Sir Henry, MP, 'a very religious and able patriot'; and thence to Lady Margaret in the 1630s, who sheltered nonconformists persecuted by Laud and gave them opportunities to minister.[50] Morrice does not often refer to women, and when he does it is generally to extol the 'pietas domestica'. Lettice, countess of Leicester, 'had two sermons every Lord's day, and public prayers in her family, twice every day, her servants constantly catechized openly together'. Frances, countess of Warwick, supported the education of 'hopeful youths for the ministry'.[51] Some families, however, fell from grace. The ancestors of Sir Henry Wroth, who died about 1673, were godly and zealous, but he was conspicuous for 'debaucheries, vices, and for persecuting nonconformists'; there follows an account of his vindictive terrorizing of nonconforming households as justice of the peace in Hertfordshire in the 1660s.[52]

Morrice had a keen eye for Puritan networks. His own world depended upon an alliance between Puritan clergy and sympathetic godly laymen of wealth and influence, and he himself was successively chaplain to Denzil, Lord Holles, and Sir John Maynard. Though he sometimes expresses doubts about the propriety of lay patronage of clerical livings, he was keenly aware of the role of the Puritan aristocracy and gentry as a counterweight to prelatical power at court. In 1587 the earl of Huntingdon settled the vicarage of Ashby de la Zouche on the redoubtable Arthur Hildersham, despite prosecutions against Hildersham. In 1582 Sir John Heigham and eleven other Suffolk gentlemen petitioned on behalf of oppressed nonconformists. Morrice records those Elizabethan counsellors who sympathized with the Puritans, such as Sir Walter Mildmay, Sir Francis Walsingham, Sir Nicholas Bacon, and the earl of Leicester. When he turns to James I's reign there is a further recitation of lay protectors of Puritans: Sir Francis Hastings, John Holles, Sir Francis Barrington, Oliver St John, Sir Henry Yelverton, Sir William Morrice.

Morrice was ambivalent about Parliaments. He was struck by their fickleness and avarice, in the 'past as well as in the present century', by their capacity to betray the reformed religion at the beck of monarchs.[53] His hatred of the Cavalier Parliament of 1661-79 colours his perspective on its predecessors. Parliaments, like bishops, must be judged individually. The Parliaments of 1571-72 gave great countenance to the Puritans, notwithstanding the queen's threats. He had no difficulty in identifying a distinctive Puritan phalanx in those Parliaments: the Wentworth brothers, Sir Francis Knollys, Sir Anthony Cope, William Strickland, Thomas Norton. Norton is singled out: he helped Foxe prepare the *Book of Martyrs*, helped

---

[50] RM MS, I 373(20), 395(23), 697.
[51] RM MS, I 417(4), J 1628(16). See Jacqueline Eales, 'Samuel Clarke and the "Lives" of Godly Women in Seventeenth-Century England', *Studies in Church History* 27 (1990), pp. 365-76.
[52] RM MS, L86-8.
[53] RM MS, D 9.

Thomas Sackville write his masterpiece of political theatre *Gorboduc*, and wrote a reply to Whitgift's articles of 1585.[54]

When Morrice arrived at the early Stuart period, he gave increasing emphasis to secular politics. His account of early Stuart Parliaments is recognizable as what we now call the 'Whig interpretation of history'. It is an interpretation that would remain remarkably stable in English historiography until the twentieth century. Morrice dwells on moments at which Parliament asserted its privileges against the crown, in 1604, in 1627-8; on the passage of the Petition of Right; on the assertion of a right to consider grievances; on the liberty of the subject from arbitrary arrest. Parliaments are bulwarks of 'civil rights' as well as of the Reformation.[55] He points to the growing propensity of the Caroline clergy to preach up the king's authority. Samuel Harsnett 'made as bold with our property, as he had before with our religion', reading Christ's injunction to 'render unto Caesar' as if the right of taxation was inherent in the crown. Robert Sibthorpe's notorious book, *Apostolike Obedience* (1627), was a 'promoting of arbitrary power', making 'the king original proprietor of all we had, and left our lives, liberties and estates precarious'. Religion, Morrice contends, remained the lodestone of politics—the contest in Parliament in 1628 was between 'the patrons of the prelatical and Puritanical party'[56]—yet under James I and Charles I religious and secular concerns coalesced. The cause of true religion became enmeshed with the cause of English liberty. James's provocations to Parliament, his use of Bancroft to coerce the church, and the strength of the Spanish faction, began to amount to an assault on temporal as well as spiritual interests.

> Hereupon many subjects thought themselves obliged and necessitated the more to insist upon the securing of their religion, and endeavouring a further reformation which they believed to be true and necessary, and of their laws, liberties, properties, and privileges of parliament. And many more subjects of all qualities the more to insist upon the securing of the said civil right. For as we must justly say many in England predominantly love their religion, so we may without breach of charity say, many more predominantly love their estates, both these parties united in the joint defence of these their rights...thereupon the controversy which was begun between the king and the parliament made great advances in this reign, and in the next growed to such a height, that no decision could be made thereof but by the sword, which ordinarily is the worst as well as the last remedy.[57]

Accordingly, by the 1620s the 'Puritan party' was defending both 'true reformed religion and civil rights'.[58] Morrice's history becomes dominated by the gathering storm of civil war. His is a reading of the 'Whig interpretation' that would tally with those of S.R. Gardiner in the 1880s and

---

[54] RM MS, F 377, 389, 391, G 479, H 243(2).
[55] RM MS, G 549.
[56] RM MS, J 1630(2-4), U 31, G 813.
[57] RM MS, G 629.
[58] RM MS, G 667, 775.

William Haller in the 1930s. If the Civil War finally became a lawyer's war to preserve the 'ancient constitution' and a gentleman's war to preserve property, it was in origin the godly's war to save religion. In sum, it was a Puritan Revolution. Morrice felt able, by the 1690s, to say what had been unsayable throughout the Restoration: that the Civil War was, for all its tragedy, a necessary and noble defence of religion and rights. If, for us, the 'Whig interpretation' amounts to a cliché, it is important to say that Morrice was present practically at its birth.

There is, of course, a paradox in all this. Those historians who have urged a 'horizontal' treatment of Puritanism have provided one of the mainsprings of revisionism against the 'Whig interpretation' during the past thirty years. They have sought to insist that Puritanism is not to be construed as an engine of revolutionary opposition against crown and church. For all that there are tensions within Morrice's approach, he had a clear view that his 'horizontalist' history was compatible with a Whig reading of the Civil War. For him, Puritanism was not in origin a movement of revolution against church and state, because it was interwoven with the very fabric of the magisterial Reformation, yet it had become so by 1640, because monarchs and prelates had by then destroyed the Reformation.

Chapter 3

Charles Leslie and the Political Implications of Theology

Robert Cornwall

Nonjuror divine, polemicist, and Jacobite agent, Charles Leslie (1650-1722) considered religion and politics to be of a piece. According to Leslie, religious heterodoxy played a significant, even causative role in the origins of political disaffection, heterodoxy, and radicalism in England. Socinians, deists, and latitudinarians were, for him, the religious counterparts to Commonwealthmen, Roundheads, and Whigs. Writing in 1695, Leslie asserted: 'There are none of these Latitudinarians that are not Commonwealth-Men: They are against monarchy in heaven or on Earth: And indeed against all government, if they could tell how: that is, all that is not in their own hands'.[1] An apologist for the exiled Stuarts, Leslie offered one of the more explicit defences of traditional divine right monarchy during the Augustan age, strongly affirming the role the church played in sustaining that monarchy. Viewing the Glorious Revolution of 1689 as an attack on the monarchy, he concluded that religious heterodoxy, especially Christological and Trinitarian heterodoxy, provided the theological foundation for this assault on the divinely ordered political state, a state supported and sustained by a divinely ordered episcopal church.

Like Leslie, Jonathan Clark has recently argued that religious heterodoxy was a leading contributor to political disaffection and even radicalism during the eighteenth century.[2] In the first edition of his *English Society* (1985), Clark wrote that the 'problem for the disaffected within a Christian monarchical polity was precisely that of rejecting Trinitarian orthodoxy, the intellectual underpinning of church, king, and parliament'. In the book's second edition (2000), Clark softened this statement, but still insisted that 'doctrinally, the disaffected in the Christian-monarchical polity largely coincided with those who rejected its theological orthodoxy...'.[3] Though he recognizes the existence of disaffection among

---

[1] Charles Leslie, *The Charge of Socinianism Against Mr. Tillotson Considered* (Edinburgh, 1695), p. 32.
[2] J.C.D. Clark, *The Language of Liberty, 1660-1832: political discourse and social dynamics in the Anglo-American World* (Cambridge, 1994), pp. 37-9, 41-5, 303-04; idem, *English Society, 1688-1832: ideology, social structure, and political practice during the ancien regime* (Cambridge, 1985), p. 277.
[3] Clark, *English Society, 1688-1832*, pp. 277, 303-05. In the second edition, Clark backs away from using the term radicalism and replaces it with the much

orthodox Dissenters, Clark insists that it was the heterodox elite that provided the essential leadership for the expression of these grievances.[4] Therefore, in spite of the softening of the language, Clark still assumes that theological heterodoxy provided a significant fountain of political disaffection, while an orthodox church provided a stabilizing force for England's *ancien regime*.

Clark's views, however, are not without their critics. James E. Bradley agrees with Clark that religion played a significant role in eighteenth-century political developments, but he rejects Clark's claim that Christological and Trinitarian heterodoxy provided a primary religious impetus for political disaffection or radicalism. Instead, Bradley believes that church polity provided the theological foundation for political radicalism in England. Therefore, the roots of radical opposition to political oppression can be found in 'the congregational polity, which provided a longstanding and abiding orientation against a hierarchical conception of society'. He points out that orthodox Trinitarian Dissenters were just as likely to oppose the government as heterodox Unitarian Dissenters, since their 'common heritage of a radically separated polity was controlling for both "rational" and orthodox alike'.[5] Whereas Clark argues that it was the heterodox elite that provided the leadership to Dissent's radicalism or disaffection, Bradley argues that this alone cannot account for the

---

softer 'political disaffection,' arguing that the use of radicalism in the eighteenth century is anachronistic; see Clark, *English Society 1660-1832: religion, ideology and politics during the ancien regime* (Cambridge, 2000), p. 320. A.M.C. Waterman argues along similar lines as Clark that heterodoxy and political radicalism correspond, but he seeks to demonstrate this by appeal to Dissenting attitudes toward the *Book of Common Prayer*. He argues that the BCP 'presupposes and inculcates' a '"Catholic" ecclesiology', which he defines as the church being a 'divine society transcending space and time' rather than as 'voluntary, human society'. Therefore, by rejecting the BCP, Dissenters rejected the divine order for church and society. Although Leslie would likely agree with Waterman's assessment of catholic ecclesiology, he did not appeal to the BCP in his writings. There is no evidence, either, that Dissenters rejected the prayer book because of its Trinitarian or Christological orthodoxy. See Waterman, 'The nexus between theology and political doctrine in Church and Dissent', in Knud Haakonssen (ed.), *Enlightenment and Religion: Rational Dissent in Eighteenth-century England* (Cambridge, 1996), pp. 198-9.

[4] Clark, *English Society, 1660-1832*, pp. 322-3.
[5] James Bradley, '"Religion as a Cloak for Worldly Designs": Reconciling Heresy, Polity, and Social Inequality as Preconditions to Rebellion' (Unpublished paper presented to the American Historical Association annual meeting, Chicago, 1995), pp. 1-3, 27. See also James Bradley, *Religion, Revolution, and English Radicalism: Nonconformity in Eighteenth Century Politics and Society* (Cambridge, 1990), pp. 4, 134-5. Bradley would also add anti-clericalism to the foundations of dissenting political radicalism; see James Bradley, 'Anti-Catholicism as Anglican Anticlericalism: Nonconformity and the Ideological Origins of Radical Disaffection', in Nigel Aston and Matthew Craggoe (eds.), *Anticlericalism in Britain, 1500-1914* (Stroud, 2000), p. 68ff.

'expressions of political discontent and calls for political reform' among Dissenters. Instead, he argues that 'it was the presence of hundreds of segregated, potentially seditious religious bodies scattered through the realms of England, Scotland, and Ireland that at length rested the attention of the established churches and government, prompting repression in some cases, accommodation in others, and genuine efforts at reform in still others'.[6] Bradley does recognize that rational Dissent offered a fruitful pathway to radicalism, with its commitment to free inquiry in religion easily leading to the questioning of traditional political boundaries, but it was not the only available pathway to radicalism or even political disaffection.[7] As John Gascoigne points out, the argument between Bradley and Clark focuses on the degree to which the English state could accommodate religious and political pluralism. While Clark focuses on the unity and uniformity of English society, Bradley, in Gascoigne's opinion, believes that 'Dissenter and Anglican might have different conceptions of the way in which society should be ordered but both could work within the framework of eighteenth-century political life, albeit with some inevitable conflict'.[8]

Although much of the debate between Clark and Bradley centres on events and intellectual developments during the latter half of the eighteenth century, the roots of these events can be traced back to earlier debates and crises during the age of Locke, Hoadly, Defoe, and Toland.[9] Fear of republicanism and commonwealth ideology fuelled both Tory and Jacobite polemics at the beginning of the eighteenth century, even as fear of the French and American revolutions fuelled them at the end of the century. For his part, Leslie feared that the Glorious Revolution had ushered in a new and dangerous era that paralleled the earlier English Revolution. He believed that the political and religious principles of this new era threatened to overthrow the divinely ordained monarchy in England and with it an ordered patriarchal society, which he defined in

---

[6] James Bradley, 'The Religious Origins of Radical Politics in England, Scotland, and Ireland, 1662-1800', in James Bradley and Dale Van Kley (eds.), *Religion and Politics in Enlightenment Europe* (Notre Dame, 2001), pp. 188-9.

[7] Bradley, 'Religion as a Cloak', p. 7; Martin Fitzpatrick, 'Heretical Religion and Radical Political Ideas in Late Eighteenth-Century England', in Eckhart Hellmuth (ed.), *Transformation of Political Culture: England and Germany in the Late Eighteenth Century* (Oxford,1990), p. 342. On the origins of rational dissent, see David Wykes, 'The Contribution of the Dissenting Academy to the emergence of Rational Dissent', in Haakonssen (ed.), *Enlightenment and Religion*, pp. 99-139. For a succinct summary of the Clark-Bradley debate see John Gascoigne, 'Anglican Latitudinarianism, Rational Dissent and political radicalism in the late eighteenth century', in Haakonssen (ed.), *Enlightenment and Religion*, pp. 219-23.

[8] Gascoigne, 'Anglican Latitudinarianism', p. 220.

[9] H.T. Dickinson, 'The Precursors of Political Radicalism in Augustan Britain', in Clyve Jones (ed.), *Britain in the First Age of Party, 1680-1750* (London, 1987), pp. 64-5.

terms of Robert Filmer's patriarchalism.[10] Because theological and political heterodoxy were intertwined, both must be stamped out. Despite his fear of Dissent's threat to English society, Leslie found latitudinarianism within the established church an even more dangerous menace to the viability of both church and state. This concern led to his attack on the supposed heterodoxy of the Archbishop of Canterbury, John Tillotson, whose willingness to supplant the deprived Archbishop of Canterbury, William Sancroft, epitomized the dangers of latitudinarianism to the proper order within the church.

I

Leslie was born to be a Tory and supporter of the Stuarts. He was the son of John Leslie, a royalist bishop of the Irish diocese of Raphoe and Clogher who continued his ecclesiastical duties underground during the interregnum. With this background it is not surprising that he became a zealous Tory in his politics and a high churchman in his churchmanship. Though trained to be a lawyer at the Temple in London, lack of success in that profession led him to pursue a career in the church. Ordained in 1681, he returned to Ireland and began a fairly unremarkable career, serving simultaneously as assistant curate in his brother's church at Donagh and as justice of the peace at Connor. He later served as chancellor of the cathedral at Connor and as chaplain to the 2nd Earl of Clarendon. It was Leslie's refusal to take the oaths in 1690, and his subsequent deprival from his government and church positions, that pushed him into nonjury and Jacobitism and then catapulted him into his career as a Tory propagandist and defender of church interests. His paper *The Rehearsal*, which ran from 1704 to 1709, offered strong opposition to Whig interests in church and state.[11] His Jacobite activities and role in the Sacheverell controversy led to an attempted arrest and flight into exile in 1711, after which he served at the court of James III until 1719. Finally, broken by ill health he received permission from the hated Hanoverian government to return home to Ireland in 1719 if he gave up all political activities on behalf of the Pretender, dying on 13 April 1722.[12]

---

[10] Although Leslie was the leading exponent of Filmer's thought, he rarely mentioned Filmer, only doing so to disagree with Filmer's position. However, as James Daly demonstrates, Leslie makes wide use of Filmer's ideas: James Daly, *Sir Robert Filmer and English Political Thought* (Toronto, 1979), pp. 133-4.

[11] Bruce Frank, '"The Excellent Rehearser," Charles Leslie and the Tory Party, 1688-1714', in J.D. Browning (ed.), *Biography in the 18th Century* (New York, 1980), pp. 47-50. William Bruce Frank, 'Charles Leslie and Theological Politics in Post-Revolutionary England' (McMaster University PhD thesis, 1983), pp. 52-4.

[12] Frank, 'Charles Leslie', pp. 50-53, 479-80. See also my article on Leslie in the

For a Tory partisan who had imbibed the patriarchalism of Robert Filmer, the Augustan Age presented both church and state with a significant threat.[13] Leslie believed that king and bishop ruled with divinely ordained authority, with the people called to submit obediently to this authority. His ideology was one of proper order, and after 1689 many high church and Tory partisans, like Leslie, believed that these twin authorities in church and state suffered their greatest setback since the English Civil War. The threat to church and state came from a variety of directions, including Protestant Dissent, Roman Catholicism, deism, erastianism, and Socinianism. High church partisans, such as Leslie, feared the impact of the Toleration Act, comprehension, and an absence of Convocation. Most insidious of all, they believed that the hallowed place of monarchy and episcopacy was threatened from within the established Church of England by the heterodox theological and political opinions of some of the Church's most important leaders. latitudinarians such as John Tillotson, Gilbert Burnet, and later Benjamin Hoadly, were all accused of holding heretical views not only regarding ecclesiology, but also regarding Christology. Jonathan Swift called Tillotson 'the person whom all English Free Thinkers own as their head', and at the Convocation of Canterbury in 1701, Francis Atterbury questioned the orthodoxy of Gilbert Burnet's *Exposition of the Thirty-Nine Articles of the Church of England* (1699).[14] Therefore, post-revolution Tories viewed the events of the day as threatening to destroy England's national church, both from within and from without.[15]

Although there were several Tory propagandists and apologists, few had the single-mindedness and persistence of Charles Leslie, whom Samuel Johnson called 'a reasoner, and a reasoner who was not to be

---

Oxford Dictionary of National Biography (forthcoming).

[13] Gordon Schochet, *Patriarchalism in Political Thought: The Authoritarian Family and Political Speculation and Attitudes Especially in Seventeenth Century England*, (Oxford, 1975), p. 221; Daly, *Sir Robert Filmer*, pp. 133-9.

[14] Jonathan Swift, 'Mr. Collin's Discourse of Free Thinking' (1713), in *The Prose Works of Jonathan Swift*, Herbert Davis and Louis A. Landa (eds.), (Oxford, 1957), IV, p. 47; Richard Nash, 'Benevolent Readers: Burnet's *Exposition* and Eighteenth Century Interpretation of the Thirty-Nine Articles', *Eighteenth-Century Studies* 25:3 (Spring 1992), p. 355. Martin Greig, 'Heresy Hunt: Gilbert Burnet and the Convocation Controversy of 1701', *Historical Journal* 37:3 (September 1994), pp. 571-3. Bennett, *Tory Crisis*, pp. 58-60. John Locke also challenged critics who viewed his *Two Treatises of Government* as being inspired by Socinianism. James Moore, 'Theological Politics: A Study of the Reception of Locke's *Two Treatises of Government* in England and Scotland in the Early Eighteenth Century', in Martyn P. Thompson (ed.), *John Locke and Immanuel Kant: Historical Reception and Contemporary Relevance* (Berlin, 1991), pp. 63-4.

[15] Roy Porter, 'The English Enlightenment', in Roy Porter and Mikulas Teich (eds.), *The Enlightenment in National Context* (Cambridge, 1981), p. 6; Margaret Jacob, *The Radical Enlightenment: Pantheists, Free Masons, and Republicans* (London, 1981), pp. 21-3, 88-9.

reasoned against'.[16] Leslie was already in middle age at the time of the Glorious Revolution and had yet to show any inclination toward publishing, but for the next three decades he was one of the busiest writers of the day. He lent his pen to defend the established orders in church and state, even though he was a pariah in both quarters for refusing the oaths of supremacy and allegiance to William and Mary.[17] Assuming that theological heterodoxy posed a danger to both church and state, Leslie targeted Whigs, latitudinarians, republicans, and Dissenters for attack.[18] As strong a proponent of episcopacy as he was of Trinitarian orthodoxy, he saw the two doctrinal affirmations being intimately related. To question one doctrine usually led one to question the other.[19] Although Leslie played an active role in Tory and Jacobite politics, his contributions to the political and theological debates of the era are often overlooked. The Whig victory during the middle of the eighteenth century and the failure of the Jacobite agenda should not lead us to ignore this important opponent of much better known figures such as John Locke, Benjamin Hoadly, and Daniel Defoe.[20]

Largely quiescent before the Glorious Revolution, William and Mary's decision to deprive the nonjuror bishops and clergy of their places in the church awakened in Leslie a passion for the traditional patterns in church and state. His defense of the divine right monarchy and patriarchalism in society should not be separated from his interest in the fate of the nonjuror movement. Like other nonjuror apologists such as Henry Dodwell and George Hickes, Leslie viewed the state's actions against the nonjuror bishops as part of the Whig-latitudinarian effort to undermine the divine order for human society.[21]

Eighteenth-century England was far from a secular nation. Whether Whig or Tory, religious practice and theology continued to play a major role in the political thinking of most people of that age. Both Daniel Defoe and Leslie believed that theology determined politics, but they differed as

---

[16] James Boswell, *Boswell's Life of Johnson*, George Birkbeck Hill (ed.), (Oxford, 1934), IV, p. 286 n.3.

[17] Frank, 'Charles Leslie and Theological Politics', p. 1.

[18] Leslie would not make the distinction Jonathan Clark makes between the majority of Whigs, who 'shared the chief elements of this dynastic political theology' and the radical Whigs or 'commonwealthmen'. Clark also recognizes that Leslie misrepresented the extreme position for mainstream Whigs, but for Leslie there was no difference except for degree. See Clark, *English Society, 1660-1832*, pp. 324, 347.

[19] Although this essay focuses on the interplay of Christological heterodoxy and political radicalism, Leslie also considered church polity to be influential in the formation of political radicalism. In this, he offers support to James Bradley's contention that polity is the key to understanding the political radicalism of Dissent.

[20] One important treatment of Leslie's role in the Tory response to John Locke and his interpreters is found in Moore, 'Theological Politics', pp. 68-76.

[21] Frank, 'Charles Leslie', pp. 421-2.

to whether the voice of the people (*vox populi, vox dei*) or ecclesiastically sanctioned hereditary monarchy best expressed the divine order of human government.[22] Leslie, following Filmer, argued that hereditary monarchy alone represented God's order for human society. Although his influence waned during the middle of the eighteenth century, by the end of the century, with revolutions in America and France threatening to undermine the political stability in England, Leslie's writings again found an audience. His arguments on behalf of the church and the monarchy clearly influenced Tory writers, such as the Hutchinsonians, William Jones, and George Horne. Jones affirmed that Leslie had planted the seeds that preserved the nation during this period of radical revolution. Jones also included Leslie's 'Short method with the Deists' in *The Scholar Armed Against the Errors of the Times*. Ironically, these Tory partisans were using Leslie's works, designed to defend the Stuart dynasty, to vindicate a Hanoverian monarch.[23]

II

Leslie was a committed Tory, who through political necessity became a Jacobite. As a Tory he offered his talents as a writer to defend Anne.[24] He also served as a contact between English Jacobites and the Stuart court in France. At the heart of his political and theological positions stood his commitment to Robert Filmer's patriarchalism. With Filmer, he insisted that the father's authority, like that of the civil government, was absolute, except where there was a superior authority to control it. Even as a father is subject to his father, so vassal kings are subject to those in higher authority. All authority is received from God, who reigns as the supreme Father over all families and kingdoms.[25] Leslie's affirmation of Filmer's thought underpinned his endorsement of the principles of divine right monarchy, passive obedience, and non-resistance, a conviction that led him to resist strongly James II's ejection from his throne. His strong resistance to

---

[22] Manuel Schonhorn, *Defoe's Politics: Parliament, Power, Kingship, and Robinson Crusoe* (Cambridge, 1991), p. 3. See also Moore, 'Theological Politics', pp. 68-9.

[23] Peter B. Nockles, *The Oxford Movement in Context: Anglican High Churchmanship, 1760-1857* (Cambridge, 1994), pp. 57-8; F.C. Mather, *High Church Prophet: Bishop Samuel Horsley (1733-1806) and the Caroline Tradition in the Later Georgian Church* (Oxford, 1992), pp. 227, 305-6; Clark, *English Society, 1688-1832*, pp. 219-21; James J. Sack, *From Jacobite to Conservative: Reaction and Orthodoxy in Britain c.1760-1832* (Cambridge, 1993), pp. 190-91; J.A.W. Gunn, *Beyond Liberty and Property: The Process of Self-Recognition in Eighteenth-Century Political Thought* (Kingston and Montreal, 1983), pp. 164-5.

[24] Daly, *Sir Robert Filmer*, p. 133.

[25] [Charles Leslie], *The Finishing Stroke: Being a Vindication of the Patriarchal Scheme of Government* (London, 1711), pp. 12-13; Schochet, *Patriarchalism in Political Thought*, p. 221.

contractarian theory and egalitarianism is clear in a 1706 edition of *The Rehearsal*:

> For while the authority of God over the people remains, kings will be the Lord's, and not the people's anointed; and priests will be the priests of God, and not of the people. The opposition to which has led then at last to blasphemy against the Great God of Heaven and Earth; whose authority over them they deny, unless he will accept of it, as derived from them![26]

Leslie conceived of all society, whether familial, political, or religious, under the absolute authority of God. Every form of society had its proper chain of authority, which was ultimately derived from God the Father. He viewed the seeming ejection of James II from his throne and the ascendancy of William and Mary as a humanly designed abrogation of this divinely ordered society. Conceiving of church and state as two divinely ordained and established societies, he insisted that there should be no confusion or meddling between the two societies. Each society had its own purpose and foundation. Therefore, 'the sacred and civil powers were like two parallel lines, which cou'd never meet, or interfere; for these two authorities lie in two distinct channels'. In making this point, Leslie rejected any hint of Erastian domination of the church by the state.[27] However, although each society had independent authority, they should protect and support each other. If one took liberties regarding the church then it seemed logical that one would take seditious attitudes toward the state. 'For those who allow no Divine Right in the Church, can never find it in the state. And whoever set up the power of the people, must extend it to the Church, as well as to the State. These go hand in hand together; for they set up the people in the place of *God*, and then their power can have no limits'.[28] Leslie wrote elsewhere in the *Rehearsal:* 'So closely is Religion and Government link'd together, that the one supports the other, and corruption in a Christian government cannot come in but, by the corruption of religion, and overthrowing those principles which it teaches'.[29] He viewed the Glorious Revolution through this kind of lens, believing that corruption in the church paved the way for political upheaval. A healthy church was a prerequisite to a properly functioning state.

---

[26] Charles Leslie, *The Rehearsal* (Saturday, 11 January 1706).

[27] Idem, *The Case of the Regale and the Pontificate, Stated* (London, 1700), pp. 14-15. For discussions of the 'two societies' doctrine see Robert Cornwall, *Visible and Apostolic: The Constitution of the Church in High Church Anglican and Non-Juror Thought 1688-1745* (Newark, 1993), pp. 73-93; Mark Goldie, 'The Nonjurors, Episcopacy and the Origins of the Convocation Controversy', in Eveline Cruickshanks (ed.), *Ideology and Conspiracy: Aspects of Jacobitism, 1689-1759* (Edinburgh, 1982), pp. 15-35.

[28] Leslie, *The Rehearsal* 248 (Wednesday, 1 October 1707).

[29] Ibid., 147 (Saturday, 12 October 1706).

III

Leslie thought that a healthy church-state relationship depended on orthodox religious foundations, both Christologically and ecclesiologically. Leslie believed that there were destructive forces at work in both church and state that undermined these two vital forms of society. He believed that he could find suspicious links between the political and theological radicalism of the day. Equating Whiggism, republicanism, and Commonwealthism with Socinianism, Dissent, and deism, he wrote that he had never met a true Whig in politics who was not a deist in religion.[30]

Leslie painted the Whigs in radical colours. His definition of Whig included commitments to deism or Dissent in religion and to Commonwealth or republican positions in politics. As such, Whigs despised proper authority and placed government at the feet of the people. In *The Wolf-Stript of His Shepherd's Clothing*, Leslie suggested that religious dissenters stood behind the rebellion of 1641, the Rye House plot, and Monmouth's rebellion. Those churchmen involved in the Monmouth plot were in reality 'Whigs, that is, Republicans; and that is Dissenters, in the lay sense, as it respects the state'.[31] He spoke of republicans and Whigs as 'Jack Presbyter's lay elders'. These elders had two different faces, one each for church and for state: 'rebellion is his lay face, as schism is his ecclesiastical: they are both the same thing, only changing of the object; all the dissenters will agree and join against the common enemy, that is, the church and the crown'.[32] Therefore, the term Whig carried highly negative connotations, connotations that did not describe mainstream Whigs, who located ultimate authority in the combination of king, lords, and commons.[33]

One can see this equation between heterodoxy and political radicalism even more clearly in Leslie's attacks on John Tillotson, archbishop of Canterbury (1691-94), and Gilbert Burnet (1689-1715), bishop of Salisbury. To a high churchman such as Leslie, no two men better epitomized the threats against the old order. Both were well-known defenders of the low church position and were intimately connected with the new regime of William and Mary. In 1695 Leslie wrote a strongly worded pamphlet accusing Tillotson and Burnet of heterodoxy. Though the two bishops insisted upon their theological orthodoxy, Leslie sought to demonstrate that they held heterodox positions on Christ and the Trinity and that Tillotson was a freethinker in both his theology and his politics. For Leslie, Dissent, Whiggism, Socinianism, and republicanism were one piece; even Roman Catholicism could be fit into this mix. He wrote in *The Wolf-Stript of His Shepherd's Clothing*: 'Then for the state, the deposing doctrine, and

---

[30] Ibid., 3 (22 May 1708); ibid., (Saturday, 29 June 1706).
[31] Leslie, 'The Wolf-Stript of His Shepherd's Clothing', in *The Theological Works of the Rev. Charles Leslie* (Oxford, 1832), VI, p. 443 [hereafter: WCL].
[32] Ibid., VI, p. 445.
[33] Dickinson, 'Precursors of Political Radicalism', p. 65; Clark, *English Society, 1688-1832*, 279.

placing the power in the people, is but the spittle of the Papists and the Jesuits, which our whigs and dissenters have licked up'.[34] This pamphlet led to what John Redwood suggests was a decade-long outburst against the alleged Socinianism in the church.[35]

As purveyors of heterodoxy, even Socinianism, these church leaders placed church and state in extreme danger. Though Tillotson might deny his Socinianism, Leslie charged that Socinians were adept at 'altering the meaning of words, so that no words can almost bind them'.[36] According to Leslie, Tillotson's embrace of Socinianism reduced Christianity to little more than a moral prop to ordered government. Socinianism led to Hobbism, by which Tillotson downplayed the spiritual, ridiculed the supernatural, and reduced God to matter. As archbishop, Tillotson now had the opportunity to disseminate this poison:[37] 'Yet these adversaries roar in the midst of our congregations, and set up their banners for tokens. O God, in what condition is this poor church, these miserable misled people of England when such doctrine is taught from the throne of Canterbury!...When these men are made primates and bishops of our church, whom our homilies think not to be accounted as Christian men, but adversaries to Christ and his gospel!'[38] Therefore, Leslie felt it was his duty to warn the nation of this man's principles, beliefs that would 'pervert the whole nation' and possibly lay the axe to the very root of Christianity'.[39]

Socinianism, according to Leslie, not only betrayed the Trinity, but it also denied the doctrine of satisfaction. This doctrine, which states that God requires that humanity make satisfaction for its offence against God's law and honour, was, for Leslie, the foundation of Christian religion, a doctrine that should serve as the criterion for choosing a church. By embracing this doctrine one could steer clear of entanglements with the Socinians, who denied the validity of the doctrine of satisfaction.[40] By equating Socinianism with a rejection of the doctrine of satisfaction, Leslie

---

[34] Leslie, 'The Wolf-Stript of His Shepherd's Clothing', p. 355. Tillotson's sermon on the Trinity, preached prior to the Revolution, gives evidence of an unwillingness to venture into speculative theology. However, he declares himself to be fully in agreement with Trinitarian doctrine: John Tillotson, 'Sermon XLVIII: Concerning the Unity of the Divine Nature, and the B. Trinity, &c.', in *The Works of Dr John Tillotson, Late Lord Archbishop of Canterbury* (London, 1820), III, pp. 409-38. See also Greig, 'Heresy Hunt', pp. 569-92. Harvey Hill, however, notes that Tillotson's writings and sermons can be interpreted in both orthodox and heterodox ways: Hill, 'The Law of Nature Revived: Christianity and Natural Religion in the Sermons of John Tillotson', *Anglican and Episcopal History* 70:2 (June 2001), pp. 170-71.

[35] John Redwood, *Reason, Ridicule, and Religion: The Age of Enlightenment in England 1660-1750* (Cambridge, MA, 1976), p.163.

[36] [Leslie], *The Charge of Socinianism*, p. 3.

[37] Ibid., pp. 13, 16.

[38] Ibid., p. 23.

[39] Ibid., p. 16.

[40] Charles Leslie, 'Short and Easy Method with the Deists', in *WCL*, I, p. 64.

could also use the equation to link John Tillotson to Socinianism. He accused Tillotson of using his sermon on hell to deny that God's justice needed to be satisfied. Rejection of hell and punishment eliminated the need for a satisfaction for sins, which meant that humanity did not need the atoning work of Christ on the cross.[41] Jonathan Clark suggests that this alleged rejection of the doctrine of satisfaction gave credibility to the idea that humanity was benevolent and able to order its own affairs. This was a perspective that ultimately brought into question the need for hierarchical government. If humanity was essentially good then people could choose for themselves the form of government that best suited them. For Leslie, this was an overly optimistic view of humanity, which in the end would lead to the downfall of both church and state.[42]

Leslie did not place great confidence in the judgements of the individual. Distrusting human reason, he believed that it was fallible and insufficient to lead humanity either to heaven or to a properly ordered government. Therefore, humans needed revelation to guide them in both religious and civil matters. Divine revelation alone provided the necessary foundations for true human government.[43] Private judgement, however, led to a 'multiplicity of sects and opinions'. Without an 'umpire' personal prejudices led to animosity, strife, and envy and ultimately to 'all the war of religion'. Needing a judge in matters of religion and politics, humanity found that judge in the divinely ordained societies of monarchy and episcopacy.[44]

Socinianism had entered the church under the guise of 'moderation'. The principle of moderation, which was based on the premise of private judgement, had been espoused by the new leaders of church and state (Tillotson, Burnet, William III), enabling heterodoxy to enter the church. Thus, a Socinian such as Thomas Firmin might remain within the church and be considered an 'excellent Christian'. Leslie glibly pointed out: 'See now, what Moderation can do!'[45]

A Socinian Christology inevitably led to low church principles. By using this line of argument, he was able to link Christology and church polity. Low church precepts included having a 'low regard to the preservation of that society of which they are members'.[46] Once one rejected the church's understanding of God, it was easy to deny God's divinely ordained order first for the church and then for the state. Ultimately, he accused low church partisans of having 'no notion of God's having appointed any order of men to represent him'. Rejection of the necessity of episcopal ordination could be traced to the heretical and

---

[41] [Leslie], *The Charge of Socinianism*, p. 9.
[42] Clark, *English Society, 1688-1832*, 281. Cf. W.M. Spellman, *The Latitudinarians and the Church of England, 1660-1700* (Athens, GA, 1993), pp. 100-102.
[43] Leslie, *The Rehearsal* 125 (Saturday, 27 July 1706).
[44] Charles Leslie, *The Truth of Christianity Demonstrated with a Dissertation Concerning Private Judgment and Authority* (London, 1711), pp. 181-3.
[45] Charles Leslie, *The Rehearsal* 28 (Saturday, 3-10 February 1704/5).
[46] Ibid., 82 (Saturday, 19 January 1705/6).

ambitious presbyter, Arius, 'whose heresy is now revived among us'.[47]

Moderation did have its defenders. One tract, attributed to a James Owen, responded to Leslie's charges by pointing out that the enemies of church and state were not the 'peaceable Dissenters'. Instead they were 'Papists and other disaffected persons' who were 'plotting to dethrone [Queen Anne], and to bring Popery and Tyranny' into England. Owen expressed his wonderment that the defender of the high church cause would be a Jacobite enemy of the current regime.[48] Gilbert Burnet suggested that the charges of Socinianism made against latitudinarians were simply slanderous responses by those unwilling to take the oaths. Burnet charged his opponents with using the same tactics as the 'papists' under James II had used against their latitudinarian opponents.[49] Both sides of the controversy found it easy to point to the problematic company the other side kept; one had to decide who corrupted one more, the Roman Catholic or the Dissenter.

For Leslie, the terms Dissenter and nonconformist represented two different attitudes. While both terms denoted an evil challenge to the true church, they had different connotations. The difference between them was that Dissenters were open about their dissent. latitudinarians such as Tillotson, Burnet, and Hoadly, however, were nonconformists who lived in society but did not conform to the orders of that society. Therefore, latitudinarians were the enemy within the walls.[50] The principles of the latitudinarians ran counter to the safety of ordered society: 'These are they who are call'd Low-Men, and Low-Church, that is, who have but a Low-Regard to the Preservation of that Society of which they are members. And therefore take upon themselves to dispense with the rule and orders of the society'.[51]

Leslie took his linkage of opponents into one politically and theologically heterodox camp a step further. Having linked Latitudinarianism with Whig political doctrine, he declared that all Whigs, whether conformist or nonconformist, were adherents of Commonwealth ideology, by which he meant the republican principles of John Milton and Algeron Sidney, principles that had manifested themselves during the Civil War and Interregnum of a half century earlier.[52] Painting with a broad brush, Leslie charged that 'commonwealthmen' such as Tillotson upheld the right of resistance to kings and opposed the divinely established monarchy both in heaven and on earth:

---

[47] Leslie, 'The Wolf-Stript of His Shepherd's Clothing', VI, p. 357.
[48] [James Owen], *Moderation Still a Virtue: In Answer to Several Bitter Pamphlets* (London, 1704), p. 75.
[49] Gilbert Burnet, *Bishop Burnet's History of His Own Time* (Edinburgh, 1753), IV, pp. 40-41.
[50] Leslie, *The Rehearsal* (Saturday, 26 January 1705/6).
[51] Ibid., 82 (Saturday, 19 January 1705/6).
[52] On the development of republicanism, see David Wootton (ed.), *Republicanism, Liberty, and Commercial Society, 1649-1776* (Stanford, 1994).

There are none of these Latitudinarians that are not Commonwealth-men: They are against monarchy in heaven or on earth: and indeed against all government, if they could tell how: that is, all that is not in their own hands. They cannot bear to be under the discipline of any other. This is the true ground of their quarrel at Religion. It is not the mystery of it, that they would not trouble their head with: nor spend their breath to undeceive those fools (as they call them) who believe it: they would not concern themselves at priest-craft, or care if priests wore fools caps, so they were not under their correction.[53]

Therefore, even as Commonwealthmen had overthrown an earlier king, 'nonconformist' low churchmen were liable to repeat the earlier events and oppose the divinely ordered societies of church and state.

Leslie accused his latitudinarian and nonconformist opponents of libertinism for their opposition to 'priestcraft', which he saw as an attempt to break free from the law. Therefore, in response to this libertinism and attempt to free themselves from priestcraft, Leslie argued that 'religion enforces and strengthens Government; and Government protects and encourages Religion: therefore both are equally obnoxious to these filthy dreamers who defile the flesh, despise dominion, and speak evil of dignitaries, of those things which they know not, Jude 8'.[54] Assuming that all ordered society had been divinely established, he believed that if a person attacked one structure of society, they attacked the others. If one could call orthodox Christian doctrine priestcraft, then one could just as easily challenge the divinely ordained monarchy.

Leslie also viewed deism as an enemy of church and state. Playing loose with labels, he often used Socinianism and deism interchangeably. Even as he linked latitudinarianism to commonwealth principles, he suggested that deism led to contractarian views. Those people who affirmed the ideology that 'all power being in the people, and making them the original of government' will almost of necessity be deists in religion. Thus, he could write that 'throwing off the authority of God as to government, leads naturally to the laying aside of religion too, if that may be call'd Religion which has not God for its author'.[55]

Although both church and state faced significant challenges from the outside, the most dangerous threats to the stability of society came from opponents hiding within these societies. A Tillotson and a Hoadly were much more dangerous to society than a Defoe, as dangerous as Leslie believed him to be. The 'men of moderation' within the church served to give ammunition to the deists, Socinians, and others who threatened the church, by suggesting that 'there is nothing essential in church-government, or any authority of divine appointment in her governours; that she is no otherwise a society, than as the people please to make her;

---

[53] [Leslie], *The Charge of Socinianism*, p. 32.
[54] Ibid. On the issue of 'priestcraft' see, J.A.I. Champion, *The Pillars of Priestcraft Shaken: The Church of England and its Enemies 1660-1730* (Cambridge, 1992).
[55] [Leslie], *The Truth of Christianity*, p.12.

but only a sect of such and such opinions, which are free without hazard, for every man to take up or lay down as he pleases'.[56] For Leslie, low churchmen were nonconformists, differing from true Dissenters only by staying within the church but not conforming to the rubrics and doctrines of the church. Thus, low churchmen or nonconformists were more dangerous to the church than Dissenters; for the low churchman was an 'enemy within my walls, one who is trusted and employed by me', and therefore, 'is worse than 20 open and professed enemies, who fairly besiege me'.[57] Whether from within or from without, heterodoxy threatened the foundations of both church and state.

IV

Leslie's case for equating Christological and ecclesiological heterodoxy with political radicalism was undermined by his continual misrepresentation of the views of his opponents. Most of Leslie's charges against Tillotson, Burnet, and other latitudinarians were unfounded. Latitudinarians, such as Tillotson and Burnet, may have attempted to simplify the Christian faith, but there is little evidence that they held heterodox views.[58] Their adherence to Whig views of the state allowed them in good conscience to embrace William and Mary as monarchs, and neither man ever advocated republicanism. John Redwood points out that even true deists, such as Anthony Collins, were puzzled by Leslie's attacks on what they believed to be solid Anglican apologists.[59] Leslie, using a shotgun approach to respond to his opponents, could not distinguish between theologically orthodox low churchmen such as Tillotson and Burnet and more heterodox and radical churchmen and Dissenters such as Benjamin Hoadly, Matthew Tindal, Anthony Collins, and Daniel Defoe. The writings of these latter four men did have radical implications, and Tindal and Collins were deists, though a case can be made for Hoadly's essential orthodoxy.[60] His judgment of his opponents was coloured in part by his Jacobitism and allegiance to the nonjuror bishops. Tillotson and Burnet had taken a leading part in their deprival and had been appointed

---

[56] Leslie, 'The Wolf-Stript of His Shepherd's Clothing', p. 467.
[57] Leslie, *The Rehearsal* (Saturday, 26 January 1706).
[58] On the orthodoxy of Tillotson and Burnet see Gerard Reedy, 'Interpreting Tillotson', *Harvard Theological Review* 86:1 (January 1993), pp. 81-103.
[59] Redwood, *Reason, Ridicule, and Religion*, p. 211; Greig, 'Heresy Hunt', pp. 570-73; Isabel Rivers, *Reason, Grace, and Sentiment: A Study of the Language of Religion and Ethics in England, 1660-1780, Volume 1: Whichcote to Wesley* (Cambridge, 1991), pp. 26, 34, 87. W.M. Spellman, 'Archbishop John Tillotson and the Meaning of Moralism', *Anglican and Episcopal History* 56:4 (December 1987), pp. 406-7.
[60] Moore, 'Theological Politics', pp. 72-3.

to their sees by the usurpers of James' throne: surely this was evidence of their heterodoxy. Therefore, believing that heterodoxy in one aspect of religion led to errors in another, he concluded that religious heterodoxy in any form ultimately lead to a breakdown of society as a whole.

Nevertheless, like many other Tory partisans, Leslie believed that the connection between heterodoxy and political radicalism did exist. Though he may have been off target in his attempts to link his opponents with radical political ideology, there is some truth to the accusations, especially concerning church polity. Therefore, both Jonathan Clark and James Bradley can both find support for their positions in Leslie's writings. Rejection of episcopacy did have the effect of undermining divine right monarchy. Leslie believed firmly that God stood as the ultimate authority in both church and state, and he considered any attempt to ridicule God's authority in the church would inevitably lead to ridiculing God's authority over the state. Although Leslie painted his opponents with such broad strokes, he failed to recognize or give allowance for theological orthodoxy among opponents of divine right monarchy and episcopacy. His insistence on their equation blinded him from seeing the presence of Christologically orthodox partisans among his opponents. His presuppositions did not allow for them. Only the true church, a church governed by bishops in apostolic succession, could preserve true Trinitarian orthodoxy and therefore offer a secure foundation for a stable church and a stable civil government. God had designed, Leslie believed, for church and state to exist side by side supporting, protecting, and guiding each other under the government of God the Father.

Fearing that Whigs, republicans, Dissenters, deists, and Socinians were attempting to undermine both church and state, Leslie strongly opposed any form of toleration or comprehension of the Dissenters. What is more important, he strongly opposed the practice of occasional conformity. He believed that occasional conformity, which allowed Dissenters to take communion in the established church to qualify for political office, offered the greatest external threat to established society. He feared that the practice of occasional conformity would enable nonconformists and other opponents of the traditional church, including deists and Socinians, to enter government. This would give them a voice in the affairs of the church, thereby undermining the church. Leslie believed that if the church allowed the practice to continue the church would be admitting that the priesthood, the altar, and the sacraments were not essential parts of the church. Therefore, the church could dispense with them if that were the will of the people. In response he made these parts of the church essential to its existence. He concluded that unless one believed in the divinely ordained character of the episcopate and the monarchy it was 'impossible to be a good churchman or a loyal subject'.[61]

God's voice did not resonate from the people. God spoke through scripture, which Leslie believed supported Trinitarianism, episcopacy, and

---

[61] Leslie, 'The Wolf-Stript of His Shepherd's Clothing', pp. 467-8.

monarchy. To undermine either of these two divinely established governments was equivalent to questioning God's Trinitarian existence. To question any of these three doctrines was to challenge God's sovereignty. Leslie could not conceive of any kind of alliance with anyone or any group that called into question this long-settled order in church and state. The willingness of 'moderate' Anglicans (latitudinarians) to relativize the essential nature of the episcopate by trying to comprehend heterodox Dissenters made the latitudinarians a threat to God's providential design for ordering human society. Yet, it may have been their willingness to relativize the church's polity rather than their Christology that made the latitudinarians a threat to the established order in church and state. Tillotson and Burnet were happy with the established forms of the church, but they did not see them as divinely ordained. They were open to comprehending the Dissenters into the church. Later Hoadly would advocate even more sweeping changes.

As compelling as Leslie's argument was, he clearly overreached himself. Burnet and Tillotson, though more given to basing their arguments on reason than tradition, were not heterodox in their Christologies. While rational dissent did offer significant challenges to the political system, so did Trinitarian Dissenters. However, while Bradley appears to be correct that polity was the primary theological catalyst for radicalism, late eighteenth-century defenders of the traditional church-state alliance, such as George Horne and William Jones, turned to Leslie's arguments to support their contention that irreligion and heterodoxy led down the road to the radicalism of the French Revolution.[62]

---

[62] Clark, *English Society* (1985), pp. 219-20.

Chapter 4

Altitudinarian Equivocation: George Smalridge's Churchmanship*

William Gibson

Historians of the Augustan church have tended to use the terms 'low church' and 'high church' with some confidence that they are well-defined homogenous strands in Anglican theology.[1] The two church 'parties' are often compared with, and linked to, the political parties, and an easy assumption is made that their doctrines were as settled as those of the Whigs and Tories. Recent scholarship has begun to question this alignment: W.M. Spellman has asked whether we can identify a single monolithic heterodox connection between low churchmanship, rationalism, deism and Whiggery.[2] Rebecca Warner has suggested that low churchmanship was defined by shared attitudes in a post-Revolutionary context toward key issues such as the relationship of church and state, and attitudes to nonjurors, Catholics, and Dissenters.[3] And John Spurr's study of latitudinarians suggests that their doctrines were close to the orthodox core of Anglicanism.[4] While low church values and tenets have thus been placed into greater perspective, the same has not happened for the high church tendency of Anglicanism. Moreover, Jonathan Clark's alignment of political and religious heterodoxy has resonance in the second half of the eighteenth century, but its application to nonjurors and politically and theologically heterodox groups earlier in the century is less apparent. For while political heterodoxy often implied a radical and reforming ideology during the second half of the eighteenth century, in the century's first two decades it stood as much for ultra-conservativism such as divine right and

---

* A version of this paper was read at the 2002 meeting of the American Historical Association and the American Society for Church History in San Francisco. I am grateful for the comments and views expressed at the meeting, and especially by Professor Jeffrey Chamberlain, the panel commentator.
[1] See, for example, George Every, *The High Church Party, 1688-1718* (London, 1956).
[2] W.M. Spellman, *The Latitudinarians and the Church of England, 1660-1700* (Athens, GA, 1993). This is a view that is explored in William Gibson, *The Church of England, 1688-1832: Unity and Accord* (London, 2001).
[3] Rebecca L. Warner, 'Early Eighteenth Century Low Churchmanship: The Glorious Revolution to the Bangorian Controversy' (Reading University PhD thesis, 1999), chapter 1.
[4] John Spurr, 'Latitudinarianism in the Restoration Church', *Historical Journal* 31:1 (March 1988), pp. 61-82.

patriarchalism. James E. Bradley's response to Clark, that heterodox theology did not always align with radical political opposition, seems a more valid observation.[5] This chapter re-evaluates the nature of the delineation of the two church 'parties' and theological heterodoxy through the views of one of the early eighteenth century's most clearly acknowledged high churchmen, George Smalridge. It argues that, though Smalridge was a Tory, his churchmanship—like a significant number of others—was not exclusively 'high church', and included a willingness to conciliate, compromise, and incorporate heterodox latitudinarianism.

To most historians George Smalridge's orthodox Tory-high church credentials have been clear and incontestable. He was educated at Westminster with Francis Atterbury, of whom he was a close friend and colleague. He proceeded to Christ Church, Oxford, with Atterbury and fellow high church Anglican Henry Aldrich. In 1687, while a student, he published *Animadversions on the Eight Theses laid down in...Church Government*, in which he hotly defended the high Anglican position, and attacked the Popish master of University College, Oxford.[6] In 1698 Smalridge and Atterbury collaborated to oppose the Whig Richard Bentley in the Phalaris debate. In a sermon before the House of Commons in 1701 on the anniversary of the death of Charles I, Smalridge advanced a core high church attitude: 'whosoever did not abhor the execution of Charles I was so ill a man that no good man could converse with him'. In 1705-06 he was closely associated with Atterbury and the Tory-high church lower clergy in the Convocation crisis, and was strong in his desire to prevent the clergy from submitting to the blandishments of Archbishop Tenison. At the core of the Convocation controversy lay the high church view that the clergy was a sacramental body, with rights and privileges that should be safeguarded by Convocation. Two years later Smalridge led the support for Atterbury's candidature for the prolocutorship of the lower House of Convocation. At Oxford Smalridge had spent some years deputizing for William Jane, the Regius Professor of Divinity, but in 1707 was refused succession to the chair, largely because his Tory-high church views were thought by some to be too close to nonjury. Certainly a year later he recommended the use of theological works by the nonjurors Isham and John Kettlewell to Arthur Charlett. Smalridge also composed the epitaph for the tomb of the nonjuror Robert Nelson, and was bequeathed Nelson's Madonna by Correggio. In 1709 Smalridge was at the heart of the Sacheverell campaign, joining with Atterbury and Harcourt in planning

---

[5] J.C.D. Clark, *English Society, 1688-1832: ideology, social structure, and political practice during the ancien regime* (Cambridge, 1985), p. 277; James E. Bradley, *Religion, Revolution and English Radicalism: Nonconformity in Eighteenth-Century Politics and Society* (Cambridge, 1990), pp. 134-5.

[6] Robert Folkestone Williams, *Memoirs and Correspondence of Francis Atterbury DD, Bishop of Rochester* (London, 1869), I, pp. 19-20. Smalridge's undergraduate career was also marked by a brawl following an accusation that Smalridge had opened another student's post. E.G.W. Bill, *Education at Christ Church, Oxford, 1660-1800* (Oxford, 1988), p. 160.

Henry Sacheverell's triumphant protest against his prosecution. The sermon for which Sacheverell was impeached had argued for severe measures to eradicate Dissent and had excoriated low churchmen as fellow travellers with Dissenters. Smalridge was active in encouraging the production of addresses to the Commons in Sacheverell's defence. During the trial Smalridge stood with the defence team in the House of Lords.

In 1710, when the Tories returned to office, Smalridge was appointed chaplain to Queen Anne, whose taste for high churchmen was pronounced and with whom he quickly became a favourite. Thereafter Smalridge and Atterbury worked closely in planning the high church agenda of the lower House of Convocation, which supported the aggressively anti-Dissent Occasional Conformity and Schism Acts passed by the Tory government. Smalridge's career also developed in the wake of the Tory victory. In 1711 he was seriously considered as a candidate for the deanery of Christ Church, Oxford, and was Queen Anne's choice for the post. Atterbury's seniority secured him the deanery, but Smalridge was consoled with the appointment to a canonry of Christ Church and succeeded Atterbury as dean of Carlisle. In 1713 Smalridge succeeded Atterbury as dean of Christ Church and there were rumours that he drank to the Pretender's health in his rooms in Christ Church. Certainly Oxford Jacobites looked upon him as a supporter.[7] Thomas Hearne regarded Smalridge as 'an eloquent ingenious gentleman; a true friend to the Church, resolute and brave, of steady principles and not likely to be turned as ye Party would have'.[8]

In 1714 Smalridge was nominated to the bishopric of Bristol at Queen Anne's express wish and was also appointed Lord High Almoner with direct access to her.[9] Though in 1714 Smalridge was a member of the committee to draft a loyal address to the new King, George I, in September 1715 he opposed a loyal address to the King on the Jacobite uprising because the preamble referred to 'pretended Tory zeal for the Church'. The refusal to sign the loyal address cost Smalridge the post of Almoner and the prospect of future preferment. It also served as a signal to other undergraduates at Christ church to 'see their Dean refuse to sign the abhorrence of the last rebellion...what can their principle be but to be pleased with the rebels?'[10] This did not deter him from strongly defending his Tory-high church principles. In 1717 Smalridge was one of six Tory bishops who voted to acquit Harley at his impeachment. So firm were Smalridge's Tory principles that when, during a visitation in 1716, he

---

[7] C.J. Abbey, *The English Church and its Bishops 1700-1800* (London, 1887), II, p. 27.
[8] Bill, *Education at Christ Church*, p. 43. On the Pretender's birthday he invited noblemen to dine in the Deanery to avoid any disturbance. Hearne later revised his view, claiming Smalridge was 'a man of little prudence or wisdom...he cringes and sneaks...'. Smalridge was also a reforming dean. Ibid., p. 214.
[9] It was claimed that Smalridge had changed his mind about Bristol, but could not get Harley to withdraw the offer from the Queen. Ibid., p. 42.
[10] Ibid., p. 44.

praised the newly-appointed Archbishop of Canterbury, William Wake, it was widely—but erroneously—assumed that Wake must also be a Tory. In the same year he was responsible for leading Wake away from the Whig policy of repeal of the Occasional Conformity and Schism Acts, which largely ended Wake's relationship with the Hanoverian Whigs and led to Wake's eclipse as the Whig church leader. In 1718 Smalridge strongly defended the Test and Corporation Acts, the touchstone of the high church Anglican monopoly on public office, in the Lords. He also opposed the repeal of the Bristol Act, which had applied a religious test for the guardians of the Bristol workhouse.[11]

In spite of this extremely orthodox Tory-high church record, Smalridge was the subject of some speculation by contemporaries. A decade after his death, for example, Lord Perceval recorded that the Duke of Kent told Queen Caroline that Smalridge held heterodox views of the Trinity

> but had not the courage to own it. The Queen replied that if the Bishop thought those notions necessary to salvation he did wrong not to own them and even preach them, but if otherwise, he was to be commended for not disturbing the world with them.[12]

There were other signs in Smalridge's career that he held views that were not entirely congruent with Tory-high church orthodoxy. Some of these were personal matters. Since their time as students at Oxford, Smalridge had disapproved of Atterbury's irascibility. During Atterbury's attack on Arthur Bury, author of *The Naked Gospel*, Smalridge had advised his friend, 'no gruffness, I beseech you—use them civilly and stick to your point'.[13] In 1711 he fell out with Atterbury; the issue appeared to be related to Atterbury's high-handed management of Christ Church. Atterbury told the canons that he intended to appoint college livings himself, rather than allow the chapter to do so. Smalridge also felt that he had inherited difficulties that Atterbury had stirred up at the deanery in Carlisle. And Atterbury insisted on defending Charles Aldrich, the undergraduate nephew of Dean Aldrich, from charges of theft, against the canons' desire to prosecute him. Smalridge complained of his former friend, 'Atterbury goes before and sets everything on fire. I come after him with a bucket of

---

[11] Details of Smalridge's life and career from the *Dictionary of National Biography*; W.R. Ward, *Georgian Oxford: University Politics in the Eighteenth Century* (Oxford, 1958); G.V. Bennett, *The Tory Crisis in Church and State, 1688-1730: The career of Francis Atterbury, Bishop of Rochester* (Oxford, 1975); Norman Sykes, *William Wake, Archbishop of Canterbury, 1657-1737* (Cambridge, 1957); A.J. Ward and A.R. Waller (eds.), *The Cambridge History of English and American Literature, Vol. X: The Age of Johnson*; Geoffrey Holmes, *The Trial of Dr. Sacheverell* (London, 1973). For the Bristol Act see David Bogue and James Bennett, *History of the Dissenters from the Revolution in the year 1688 to the year 1808* (London, 1809), III, p. 141.

[12] Historical Manuscripts Commission, *Diary of the First Earl of Egmont (Viscount Percival)* (London, 1923), I, p. 233.

[13] Williams, *Memoirs and Correspondence of Francis Atterbury*, p. 44.

water'. Smalridge reported his disputes with Atterbury to Harley, and this was probably instrumental in denying Atterbury advancement to the see of Hereford in 1713.[14] Smalridge clearly felt discomfort with one of the psychological badges of high churchmanship: the aggression that marked Atterbury and Sacheverell's contributions to politico-theology.

In the wake of the greatest triumph of the high church party, Sacheverell's trial, Smalridge was also equivocal. In August 1710, after the trial, Smalridge drafted the address of loyalty from the London clergy to Queen Anne. This was one of eleven clerical addresses to the Queen, but it attracted most attention.[15] Benjamin Hoadly read the address with astonishment. Knowing of Smalridge's authorship, Hoadly had expected the address to be full of the usual claims to hereditary right and passive non-resistance, which had marked out the Tory-high church faction. Indeed, Hoadly had refused to sign it because of this expectation. But, wrote Hoadly, 'to my surprise and astonishment I found the address so very ambiguous, the words so artfully chosen...and the whole so equivocally or so inconsistently fram'd'.[16] Smalridge had cast the address so that it asserted the Tory principles of hereditary right and the Queen's 'irresistible authority'; but it also defended the Revolution of 1688 and the Hanoverian succession. Hoadly's *Some Short Remarks*...made great play of Smalridge's inconsistencies. In one telling passage, Hoadly controverted Smalridge's claim to have 'often and freely' preached in favour of the Revolution. Hoadly claimed that members of Smalridge's congregations could never once remember him, in fourteen years, preaching against hereditary right and non-resistance.[17]

In 1711, a year after he had been ejected from his professorship at Cambridge for suspected Arian tendencies, the heterodox William Whiston published *Primitive Christianity Reviv'd* in four volumes. Smalridge wrote to Whiston at that time:

> I did not send for the books sooner because I had rather have them bound than in sheets. I pray God the publication of them may not do that disservice to our Holy Religion, which I am persuaded you are far from intending. It seems to me much more likely that unbelievers should thereby be strengthened in their infidelity than that those whom you suppose mistaken should be induc'd to reform the opinions which you take to be erroneous. There is one suffrage of

---

[14] Bennett, *The Tory Crisis in Church and State*, pp. 144-58. In August 1714, Atterbury approached Smalridge in the House of Lords, took his hand, and asked his forgiveness for the breach. Ibid., p. 186.

[15] See, for example, *The Observator*, August 1710. The other addresses are to be found in *A Collection of the addresses which have been presented to the Queen since the Impeachment of the Revd Dr. Henry Sacheverell* (London, 1713).

[16] *Some Short Remarks Upon the Late Address of the Bishop of London and his Clergy to the Queen. In a Letter to Dr. Sm-l-ge* (London, 1713), p. 4. This tract is ascribed to Hoadly by Samuel Halkett and John Laing (eds.), *Dictionary of anonymous and pseudonymous English literature* (London, 1926).

[17] *Some Short Remarks*, p. 14.

our litany, in which you will heartily join with us, that it may please God to bring into the way of truth, all such as have erred or deceived.[18]

When he had read all four volumes, Smalridge commented that Whiston had 'acted very uprightly' that his quotations were fair and just and that suggestions that Whiston had edited the texts selectively to support his case were unfounded. Smalridge told Whiston, 'God has given you greater judgement than to think that any man has power to alter such sacred laws of the Gospel, and then give good reasons why they have altered them'.[19] In 1713, Whiston published his *Liturgy of the Church of England, reduc'd nearer to the Primitive Standard*. Before he had published it, Whiston had asked Smalridge to read it. He did so, and, claimed Whiston, was satisfied by it. When Whiston's book was moved for censure by the lower House of Convocation, Smalridge made public his intention to defend Whiston by declaring openly that Whiston should not be censured. Whiston recorded 'that Dr. Smalridge in some measure assisted my escape from that Convocation'.[20]

More significant was Smalridge's reaction to Samuel Clarke's book, *The Scripture Doctrine of the Trinity*, published in 1713. The book consisted of a collection of texts bearing upon the doctrine, a statement of the doctrine itself, and a consideration of passages in the Anglican liturgy. Smalridge had been involved with Clarke previously on this issue. In 1712, Smalridge had meetings with Clarke at Thomas Cartwright's house at Aynho. These discussions were described as friendly occasions on which 'good scholars and good Christians' were well treated, and they attracted attendance from leading members of Oxford University:

> The conference between Dr. Smalridge and Dr. Clarke was proposed by the former, in order to the conviction of the latter. And if any person in England was able to convince upon that head, it must have been Dr. Smalridge who...was a thorough master of those original books of Christianity...However he failed of success; and on the contrary, the company were generally satisfied that the evidence on Dr. Clarke's side was greatly superior to the other...[21]

On the publication of his book, Clarke was accused of Arianism by Nelson, Waterland, and others. On 2 June 1714, the lower House of Convocation complained of the book to the House of Bishops and sent them extracts to support their case. In response Clarke made a declaration of his beliefs in orthodox terms, which some felt was evasive. He promised not to preach any more, and stated that he did not intend to write any more on the question. He also denied a report that the Athanasian creed—the

---

[18] Dated 22 November 1711, in William Whiston, *Historical Memoirs of the Life of Dr. Samuel Clarke. Being a Supplement to Dr. Sykes's and Bishop Hoadley's Account* (London, 1730), pp. 171-2.
[19] Whiston, *Historical Memoirs*, pp. 175-6.
[20] Ibid., p. 73.
[21] Ibid., p. 66.

shibboleth of Trinitarianism—had been intentionally omitted in the services at his church. On 5 July the House of Bishops resolved to proceed no further, after ordering that Clarke's papers should be entered in their minutes. But, on 7 July, the lower House voted that Clarke had not recanted satisfactorily, and that the inquiry should not have been dropped.

The matter was almost exactly the same as the Convocation controversy in 1705, in which the lower House of Convocation had confronted the bishops on their refusal to respond to dissent and to censure heterodox theology, and in which Smalridge had so strongly supported the Tory-high church position. In 1714, however, Smalridge played a very different role. When Clarke made his declaration of orthodoxy, Archbishop Wake consulted Bishops Trelawny, Fleetwood, and Smalridge, who he described to Clarke as 'all your very good friends' and told Clarke that they had 'appeared very hearty on your behalf'. Smalridge's advice to Wake was that they should avoid any censure of Clarke or any breach of the peace of the church. Wake told Clarke, 'we promise ourselves that having gone so far as you have done for the peace of the Church, you will not insist upon anything which may endanger it.'[22] Smalridge was undoubtedly the prime mover in acquitting Clarke; he went to Clarke as Wake's emissary and secured the promise from him to let the issue lie. He expressed the view that 'as to [the] other of Dr. Clarke's metaphysical notions about the Trinity, he did not think it necessary to proceed to their condemnation, provided he [Clarke] could truly declare he believed the real eternity of the Son of God'.[23] In 1729, looking back on the occasion, Lord Percival wrote:

> It was the great interest of Bishop Smalridge among his brethren which at that time saved him [Clarke] from some formidable censure, on condition of the promise [not to write on the subject again]...which the Bishop afterward complained to me was not performed...[24]

This was very different from the behaviour Smalridge exhibited during the crisis of 1705 and the Sacheverell trial in 1710, when Smalridge seemed to take the view that orthodox principles were more important than disturbing the peace of church and state. But Smalridge had long been an admirer of Clarke, praising his Boyle lectures as 'the best book on those subjects that had been written in any language.'[25] Whiston explained Smalridge's attitudes:

> Tis true, Bishop Smalridge's regard to modern Church Authority; his dread of the ill-consequences of discovering so great and lasting errors in the Church; the situation he was in at Oxford and in Convocation; with his suspicion of the harm politicians and unbelievers would turn such discoveries to, instead of uniting with good men to correct the errors themselves would not permit him

---

[22] Sykes, *William Wake*, II, pp. 156-7.
[23] Edward Cardwell, *Synodalia* (London, 1842), pp. 786-7.
[24] *Diary of the First Earl of Egmont*, I, p. 8.
[25] Whiston, *Historical Memoirs*, p. 8.

to exert those very great talents which God had given him for the Discovery and Restoration of true primitive Christianity; which true primitive Christianity yet Bishop Smalridge, as I have long thought, was not otherwise less able to discover, and at bottom, not less willing to promote, than any other learned man that ever I was acquainted with...[26]

It could be assumed that Smalridge's response to Clarke's book was the seasoned response of an older man, which contrasted with the fiery actions of his youth; but, as has been seen, after 1714 Smalridge stood firmly on matters of principle. However, the Clarke incident was not the only occasion on which Smalridge abandoned his earlier principles and stood on the side of peace rather than a controversy he had previously embraced.

In 1717, in the wake of Benjamin Hoadly's sermon, 'My kingdom is not of this world', Smalridge took a similarly quietist line. Hoadly's sermon was exactly the kind of theology that threatened to rekindle the flames of the Convocation and Sacheverell controversies, and might therefore have been expected to provoke a strong reaction from Smalridge. Hoadly argued that Christ had not dictated any form of church government, and therefore, by implication the Church of England could not insist that Dissenters accept episcopacy as the price for comprehension within the church. All those who took the Tory-high church line in 1705 and 1710 spoke against Hoadly, indeed even orthodox Whig churchmen, like Edmund Gibson and Lancelot Blackburne, denounced him. But Smalridge's response was extraordinary. Rather than support his fellow bishops and the wholesale condemnation of Hoadly by Convocation, Smalridge and John Potter proposed a means to make the point with less turbulence. Their proposal was that there should be no censure of Hoadly, but that Arthur Ashley Sykes, who had preached a similar sermon about the same time, should be censured in Convocation and therefore the point would have been made without sparking a theological conflict.[27] It was an elegant solution to the problem, and one with which Archbishop Wake sympathized. Nevertheless it was not adopted, as the desire to censure Hoadly was too great, and the great Bangorian pamphlet war ensued.

Some insights into Smalridge's churchmanship can also be found in his sermons. There is much that is the work of an orthodox high churchman. In a sermon on 'Stated Forms of Prayer', Smalridge made a standard orthodox attack on extempore prayer that was characteristic of the high church view.[28] The settled liturgy of the church was strongly valued by high Anglicans, whereas Dissenters tended towards extempore prayer in their services.[29] This represented the differing origins of ecclesiastical authority on liturgy: high church Anglicans holding that it came from the church;

---

[26] Ibid., pp. 126-7.
[27] Sykes, *William Wake*, II, pp. 142-3.
[28] George Smalridge, *Sixty Sermons Preached on Several Occasions* (Oxford, 1724), Sermon VII, pp. 63-72.
[29] For analysis of the dislike of extempore prayer see Gibson, *The Church of England, 1688-1832, passim*.

Dissenters believing that it could be transmitted through the consciences of churchmen. But, paradoxically, in a subsequent sermon on 'Rites and Ceremonies' Smalridge advanced a view of the liturgy that was close to that of the latitudinarians. He argued that the settled liturgy was 'intended only for decency, for order, and for edification, let us use them in such manner as may best minister to those great ends'. But he proceeded further than any high churchman would:

> Let us not lay as great stress upon the Cross in Baptism, which is only a significant rite and symbol of our owning the faith of Christ crucified, as we do upon fighting manfully under Christ's banner against the world, the flesh and the devil. Let us not think the particular posture of body we use in receiving the sacrament of the Lord's Supper a matter of the same importance as we do the posture of soul and disposition of heart wherewith we receive it...in short the kingdom of God is not meat and drink, consisteth not so much in the use, or forbearance of different rites, as it doth in righteousness, peace and joy in the Holy Ghost...[30]

This is a far more latitudinarian position than that taken by Smalridge's high church friend Henry Sacheverell, who raised much dust by insisting that his parishioners stand and kneel at certain points in the Communion service.[31] A greater emphasis on conscience, individual response, and inner piety than on sacramental externals was characteristic of heterodox latitudinarianism rather than altitudinarianism.

In matters of ecumenism, Smalridge stood, in part, with the Tory-high church interest. As Archbishops Tenison and Wake conducted talks with continental Protestants, Smalridge was prepared to encourage their enterprise, but was not prepared, as others were, to compromise in matters of episcopacy.[32] Indeed Smalridge commented that, if the continental Protestants would not accept episcopacy, 'we shall not be obliged to entertain the same charitable opinion of them'.[33] In 1706, when Oxford University responded formally to the strictures of the Geneva professors, Smalridge wrote the response which in turn censured Geneva Presbyterianism for an example to English Dissenters.[34] In his sermon 'Of Obedience to Our Spiritual Guides and Governors', which was a staunch statement of the importance of episcopacy, he made clear that the episcopal government, to which some foreign Protestants and low church Anglicans such as Benjamin Hoadly were indifferent, was a *sine qua non*. 'There is no salvation out of an episcopal communion', he claimed, and argued that those who separated themselves from episcopal church government had

---

[30] Smalridge, *Sixty Sermons*, Sermon VIII, p. 82.
[31] William Fleetwood, *A Letter to an Inhabitant of the Parish of St. Andrew's Holbourn about New Ceremonies in the Church* (London, 1717), *passim*.
[32] Gibson, *The Church of England, 1688-1832*, chapter 5.
[33] Bodleian Library, Oxford, Ballard MSS, 7, f.16, quoted in Norman Sykes, *From Sheldon to Secker* (Cambridge, 1959), p. 137.
[34] Frank H. Ellis (ed.), *Poems on Affairs of State, Augustan Satirical Verse, 1660-1714* (New Haven, 1970), VII, pp. 415-16.

separated themselves from Christ, and that their prayers and sacraments were invalid.[35] This in itself contradicted his moderate and conciliatory response to Hoadly's sermon of 1717. Paradoxically, Smalridge also argued of continental Protestants that 'our pretended disagreement with them is manifestly groundless'.[36] Moreover, Smalridge felt that in comparison with Catholics, Protestants should be more closely united: 'we are members one of another as we are fellow Christians and are still more nearly united to each other as we are fellow Protestants'.[37] This sort of statement brought Smalridge closer to the low church tradition that saw Protestant unity as a greater objective than disagreements over doctrine or liturgy. At the time of the Convocation crisis in 1705 Smalridge preached a sermon before the Queen; he did not use it to advance the high church position, but rather strongly to attack the Catholics and to make a further call for Protestant unity. 'Franciscans and Dominicans, Jansenists and Jesuits, Seculars and Regulars lay aside their mutual quarrels and join their forces against the heretic as a common adversary', he asserted.[38] Smalridge, far from speaking his mind on the Convocation issue, argued that Protestants should show the same unity and cohesion as Catholics.

In theology, Smalridge followed the high church Laudian-Arminian tradition that was in opposition to Calvinism. Moreover Smalridge pursued the Pauline tradition of arguing that,

> some sins in comparison to others [are] so small that according to the gracious dispensation of the Gospel, they will be forgiven if repented...no sins committed by Christians are so great but that, if sincerely repented of and timely forsaken, they will through the merits of Christ be forgiven...[39]

He advanced this in a second sermon, arguing that

> We may conclude that because God is not unrighteous, that is, not regardless of his promises, therefore he will not forget our good works, but will reward us for them with the glories of heaven and happiness everlasting...[40]

Those sermons which Smalridge preached on national or specific occasions also bore the marks of equivocal churchmanship. In preaching to the Aldermen of London on the anniversary of the Martyrdom of Charles I in 1708/9 he advocated the sort of engagement in controversy that had marked his role in the Convocation and Sacheverell controversies, but was in contrast to his dealings with Clarke and Hoadly:

---

[35] Smalridge, *Sixty Sermons*, Sermon XI, p. 112.
[36] Ibid., Sermon IX, p. 87.
[37] Ibid., Sermon XXV, p. 265.
[38] Ibid., Sermon XXXVIII, p. 391.
[39] Ibid., Sermon XXI, p. 213.
[40] Ibid., Sermon LIV, p. 556.

when any actions do both at first view, and also upon farther enquiry, appear very flagitious we should then without any reserve openly and freely speak our minds concerning them...[41]

Similarly in 1711, in a sermon preached to mark his departure from St. Dunstan's Church, London, he warned his congregation, in the words of St. Peter, of 'false teachers among you', which was almost exactly the same text as that used by Henry Sacheverell, 'on the perils of false brethren'.[42]

In 1716 Smalridge preached before the House of Lords on the anniversary of the Restoration of Charles II, quoting Psalm 80 with heavy allusion: God 'brought his vine out of Egypt and planted it among us, having prepared room for it and caused it to take deep root'.[43] In the light of the Hanoverian succession and the recent defeat of the Jacobite rising, Smalridge seemed to be arguing a point of view that Atterbury and Sacheverell would have found horrifying: God had made the ground ready and planted the Hanoverian dynasty in Britain. Moreover at the Surrey Assizes in 1710/11, Smalridge advanced a view of the origin of government that hinted at contract theory, which was held by the rationalist-latitudinarians in opposition to the high church preference for the divine origins of government and monarchy. Smalridge suggested 'protection and obedience are reciprocal duties; that since I receive the benefits of government it is reasonable I should conform myself to the rules of it';[44] of course the implication was equally that without protection from the ruler obedience could be abandoned, a low church doctrine that was anathema to high churchmen.

Perhaps the most enlightening of Smalridge's sermons is that preached on the doctrine of the Trinity, on which Lord Percival and Queen Caroline suspected his views were heterodox. Smalridge's sermon was entitled 'The Uses of Reason in Religion' and, given the emphasis of low church Whigs on rationalism in religion, might be expected to indicate a critical doctrinal stance by Smalridge.[45] Smalridge took as the starting point for his sermon that Dissenters often sought evidence in the Scriptures for episcopacy as a form of church government, and that Arians asked where in the Bible the doctrine of the Trinity was to be found. Smalridge addressed these issues directly:

> Now it is true that the Scriptures are the adequate rule of our faith; but then it is not also true, nor by us confessed, that nothing is to be looked upon as taught us in Scripture, but what is there in so many words delivered...As well

---

[41] Ibid., Sermon XIII, p. 132.
[42] Ibid., Sermon LI, p. 514.
[43] Ibid., Sermon XVI, p. 169. Thomas Hearne had accused Smalridge of being a 'sneaker' in 1715, keen to ingratiate himself with the new Hanoverian regime. *Reliquae Hearnianae: The Remains of Thomas Hearne by Philip Bliss* (London 1869), II, p. 5.
[44] Smalridge, *Sixty Sermons*, Sermon XLIV, p. 459.
[45] The text was on Acts 17:2: 'And Paul...went in unto them and three sabbath days reasoned with them out of the Scriptures'.

what may from thence be proved, as what is therein read, may be believed as an article of faith, and may be requisite and necessary to our salvation. St. Paul...reasoned out of Scripture, and we also may so reason. What is rightly inferred from the Scriptures doth as much challenge our assent as what is literally deliver'd in the Scriptures...

It must be owned that the doctrine of the Trinity, as it is proposed in our Articles, our Liturgy and our Creeds, is not in so many words taught us in the Holy Scripture. What we profess in our prayers, we no where read in Scripture...There is no such text in Scripture as this: that 'the Unity in Trinity and the Trinity in Unity' is 'to be worshipped'...But though these truths are not read in Scripture; yet they may easily be regularly and undeniably inferred from Scripture. If indeed it can be shewn that these inferences are wrong, they may be safely rejected; but they ought not to be rejected for no other reason but this; that they are not plain assertions of Scripture, but bare inferences from it...Our Saviour saith in Scripture that 'he and the father are one'...We declare therefore our belief of their being not only in consent, but they are both one...[46]

While Smalridge's position on the doctrine of the Trinity appears to be a defence of it, it also encapsulates his equivocation. Unlike many high churchmen, who accepted the doctrine of the Trinity as one of the mysteries of faith, founded on revelation and church tradition, Smalridge sought to use the weapons of rationalism applied to scripture (the weapons employed by the latitudinarians) to prove the source and validity of the doctrine. High churchmen sometimes used the language of rationalism and reason: Francis Atterbury certainly did so.[47] But Smalridge went beyond the simple use of rational language, or the defence of a high church position based on reason. The consequence of the use of reason to support the doctrine of the Trinity was Smalridge's extraordinary suggestion that, if the inference from Scripture of the doctrine of the Trinity could be disproved, it would be dispensable, and thus would have been anathema to high churchmen and the reason why high churchmen preferred other arguments, such as church tradition, to support the doctrine against Socinians and Arians. The high church reliance on the traditions and authority of the church as the source of the doctrine of the Trinity is absent from the sermon. Moreover the danger of Smalridge's position was that it opened the Bible to interpretation and inference, and this was at the root of the high church rejection of Dissenting and latitudinarian emphasis on conscience and personal interpretation of the Scriptures.

Whiston claimed that Smalridge agreed with his heterodox views on the Trinity. When discussing the doctrine of the Trinity with Francis Gastrell and George Smalridge, Whiston argued that as far as the Trinity is concerned he 'had no mind to know any modern's opinion upon that head, but only the doctrine of Christ and his Apostles'. Smalridge agreed, saying 'Mr Whiston, you are in the right'.[48] Whiston acknowledged Smalridge to be one of the most learned and excellent persons in the kingdom, and said

---

[46] Smalridge, *Sixty Sermons*, Sermon XXXIII, pp. 338-48.
[47] *Sermons of Francis Atterbury*, T. Moore (ed.), (London, 1734), III, p. 29.
[48] Whiston, *Historical Memoirs*, p. 147.

that if anyone could have convinced him that he was in error, it would be he. Whiston rather flattered himself that he had convinced the bishop of some 'emendanda' in the Athanasian creed. He also believed that Smalridge's mind, cultured though it was, was not really of a speculative turn, and he claimed Smalridge had said, 'with great earnestness, that even if it were as his companion had said, he had no wish to examine it and to find that the church had been in error for so many hundred years'.[49]

The heterodox views that Smalridge was reputed to hold became widely discussed toward the end of his life and beyond. By 1719 there was growing concern in the church about the growth of Arianism and Socinianism and the questioning of the doctrine of the Trinity. In March 1719 the Dissenters split at a meeting at Salters Hall over the issue; in the Church of England Bishop Trelawny of Winchester spoke to Archbishop Wake in the same month, urging him to mount a campaign to combat Arianism. Wake reassured Trelawny that the King intended to mention the importance of the doctrine of the Trinity in his message to Parliament at the end of the current session, and had authorized the Archbishop to circulate an injunction to all the bishops on the importance of orthodoxy in the doctrine.[50] But for Trelawny the suspicion that his old friend George Smalridge might hold heterodox beliefs grew too strong. In the summer of 1719 Trelawny's anxiety was sufficient for him to ask Smalridge directly whether he held unorthodox views. On 23 September 1719, Smalridge replied to Trelawny with a statement of his orthodoxy:

> My very good Lord
> Among the many proofs your Lordship has given me of your favour and friendship to me, none could be greater, or more obliging, than the generous concern you have shewn for my injured reputation; and I am very much surprised to hear that I should be suspected of Arianism, having never given, as I know of, the least ground for such suspicion. I have from the Chair (when I supply'd Dr. James's place) from the pulpit, when I have preached at the new Chapel; and here at Oxon, on Christmas Day was Twelvemonth; and on the same day at court, when I was Almoner; the first Christmas after the King's accession; and in Convocation, when a censure was passed on Mr Whiston's doctrines (whilst I was presbyter, and a member of the Lower House) and upon all other proper occasions, expressed my sentiments about the divinity of our Lord and Saviour, in opposition both to the Socinians and Arians. I did on Sunday last ordain some clergymen, and I examined them particularly betwixt the Catholic Church and the Arians, and said what to me seemed proper to confirm them in the Catholic faith, and to arm them against the objections usually brought by Arians. I have read over more than once, and as well as I was able, have considered Dr. Waterland's late book, and have in conversation

---

[49] *Dictionary of National Biography.*
[50] M.G. Smith, *Fighting Joshua: Sir Jonathan Trelawny 1650-1721* (Redruth, 1985), p. 151. It was a call taken up by William Stephens in *The Several Heterodox Hypotheses concerning both the Persons and the Attributes of the Godhead...A Sermon Preached at the Visitation of the Rt Revd Father in God Lancelot, Lord Bishop of Exeter...at St. Andrews, Plymouth...28 August 1724* (Oxford, 1725). Trelawny had appointed Stephens to his benefice.

signified by approbation of it, and recommended it to my friends, as a substantial vindication of received doctrines and confutation of Arianism.[51]

Trelawny's need to vindicate Smalridge was sufficient for him to have copies of the letter made for circulation within the church.[52] Four days after he wrote the letter to Trelawny, Smalridge died. William Whiston, having read Trelawny's copy of the letter asked 'why the Bishop of Winchester should suppress those parts of Bishop Smalridge's letter, which declar'd the regard he had for some persons, not of the Athanasian opinion; and his little approbation of at least the damnatory sentences in the Athanasian Creed, which my Lord Nottingham inform'd me were in that letter, I do not well understand'.[53] Nevertheless in the same month Arthur Charlett commented that Smalridge was 'always ready to forgive, willing to promote any public business, rarely out of humour, seldom complaining, severe sometimes upon himself and friends, generally very candid, not easy to believe the worst of any, too apt to believe the better of some than they deserved'.[54]

Bishop Smalridge's protestations did not convince other contemporaries. Bishop Goodwin told Lord Percival in 1729: 'no man was more of Dr. Clarke's notions in these matters [of the Trinity] than Smalridge, but that being one of the heads of the high church party, he would never discover his opinion'.[55] In spite of Smalridge's last minute repudiation, Lord Percival firmly believed that Smalridge was heterodox: after his conversation with Queen Caroline, mentioned earlier, he wrote in his diary, 'I told her Bishop Smalridge said to myself that he could pardon everything in Dr. Clarke but his calling the three persons in the Trinity three beings, which made too great a distinction in the unity of the Godhead'. In short, Smalridge had no quarrel with Clarke's Arian suggestion that Christ was not co-eternal with God. Perhaps the Queen's comment on the matter was significant; she simply replied of Smalridge: 'he did not say true'. Whiston concluded

> Bishop Smalridge seems always to me readily enough to give up the Athanasian Creed; only he loved to put it upon another foot than I should have done; I mean, that it should be given up to the clamours of the Dissenters, who are still making its damnatory sentences an objection against conformity with the Church of England. I was also informed by an eye-witness, Sir Robert Clarke, that when he was once at Bristol Cathedral, on an Athanasian Creed Day, and not believing that Creed himself, had nothing else to do but to watch

---

[51] Whiston, *Historical Memoirs*, pp. 172-3.
[52] A copy of the letter is in Christ Church, Oxford, Wake MS, XXI, f. 161 [hereafter: Wake MS]. Trelawny's circular letter was headed: 'This is a true copy of part of the Bishop of Bristol's Letter to me; and without going deeper into it, is a sufficient vindication of him from the damnable, but thriving heresy of Arianism'.
[53] Whiston, *Historical Memoirs*, p. 174.
[54] Wake MS, XVI, f. 66: Charlett to Wake, 10 October 1719.
[55] *Diary of the First Earl of Egmont (Viscount Percival)*, I, p. 8.

Bishop Smalridge's behaviour, he took notice that he did not repeat that Creed any more than himself.[56]

Smalridge's inconsistent and equivocal position in matters of churchmanship seems puzzling; he moved from open confrontation with low churchmanship and heterodoxy during the Convocation and Sacheverell debates to conciliation of heterodoxy in the cases of the latitudinarians Whiston, Clarke, and Hoadly. In much of what he wrote and preached he was the archetype of altitudinarian views, but in a number of cases he reached deep into latitudinarian dogma and methodology. How should Smalridge's variegated churchmanship be explained?

Smalridge may be more representative of clergy in the early eighteenth century than historians have hitherto recognized. The idea that churchmen were homogenously and exclusively high or low church, heterodox or orthodox, in doctrine and practice is a misunderstanding of the traditions. High and low churchmen may have been associated with the Tories and Whigs respectively, but the traditions in the church were not hard and fast parties. They were, rather, tendencies or collections of theological preferences, which were not mutually exclusive. High and low churchmen moved between positions and doctrines relatively easily. Clergy who were clearly identified as low churchmen, like Simon Patrick, Edward Stillingfleet, Gilbert Burnet, Benjamin Hoadly, William Whiston, and William Powell adopted some high church views. William Talbot, long held to be a decided low churchman, advocated firm belief in the divinity of Christ and consistently called for frequent celebration of Holy Communion, both doctrines usually associated with high churchmen.[57] Gilbert Burnet was an avowed latitudinarian, yet he held the high church view that the church and state were independent of each other.[58] Noted high churchmen, like Edmund Gibson, John Sharp, Henry Compton, Daniel Waterland, Robert South, and William Sherlock also incorporated some latitudinarian views.[59] Gibson and Wake shared the high church reverence for ancient authorities: they were canonists and believed in church discipline. But they were also Erastians and disagreed with the sacerdotal view of the priesthood held by Atterbury. Atterbury and Sacheverell were rare in consistently maintaining high church views. Fielding's fictional portrait of Adams as a high church parson is interesting because Fielding, no stranger to theology, puts praise for Hoadly's *Plain Account of the Lord's Supper* into Adams's mouth. Thus a high churchman

---

[56] Whiston, *Historical Memoirs*, pp. 174-5.
[57] William Talbot, *The Divinity of Christ Asserted, A Sermon Preached before the Queen, at St. James's on Christmas Day, 1702* (London, 1702). William Talbot, *A Letter from the Bishop of Durham, With a Charge to the Clergy of his Diocese, Anno 1722* (London, 1722).
[58] Warner, 'Early Eighteenth Century Low Churchmanship', p. 49.
[59] Gibson, *The Church of England, 1688-1832*, chapter 2.

praises the most extreme statement of low church attitudes to the Eucharist in the century.[60]

The circumstances of the church between 1688 and 1714 changed so radically to and fro, that it would be astonishing if churchmen were able to hold to one doctrinal position irrespective of the circumstances of the moment. Gilbert Burnet himself wrote:

> Why are the words tossed about with so much fury of High and Low church? Is there any ground for infusing the conceit of a diversity among us, that is so much laboured by some incendiaries. All believe the same doctrine, and practice the same worship, they all acquiesce in the same Constitution, and profess obedience to the same government?[61]

Evidence that churchmen of differing parties held similar opinions emerged during the Bangorian debate of 1717. Hoadly was censured by a committee of Convocation, including Thomas Sherlock, a high churchman. But Arthur Ashley Sykes suggested that Sherlock shared Hoadly's views. Sykes claimed that Sherlock had preached exactly Hoadly's views in a sermon before the Lord Mayor of London on 5 November 1713. Sherlock had indeed concluded his sermon with the words:

> 'tis just reasoning, I think, to infer from the spiritual nature of Christ's Kingdom, and the spiritual powers of his ministers on earth, that temporal punishments are not proper to enforce the laws and edicts of Christ's Kingdom.[62]

Sykes published passages of Hoadly's sermon alongside those of Sherlock's and concluded, 'can the position in your sermon escape the same censure if the Bishop must be censured?'[63] It was a devastating technique, the historian Thomas Lathbury conceded: 'in my opinion, Sykes succeeded in proving that inconsistency of Sherlock, for I cannot perceive any difference between the views of [Sherlock's] sermon on the 5th November and those of the Bishop of Bangor'.[64] Charles Norris's *A Dialogue between Dr. Sherlock, Dean of Chichester and Dr. Sherlock, Master of the Temple*, published in 1718, made similar fun of Sherlock.[65] Sherlock responded weakly that secular

---

[60] Treadwell Ruml, 'Henry Fielding and Parson Adams: Whig Writer and Tory Priest', *Journal of English and Germanic Philology* 97:2 (April 1998), p. 230.

[61] Gilbert Burnet, *A Sermon Preached before the Rt. Honourable the Lord-Mayor of London...at St. Sepulchres Church on Easter Monday, 1706* (London, 1706), p. 17.

[62] Thomas Sherlock, *A Sermon Preached before the Rt. Hon. The Lord Mayor, Aldermen and Citizens of London...5 November 1712* (London 1712), p. 8.

[63] Arthur Ashley Sykes, *A Letter to the Revd Dr. Sherlock, one of the Committee of Convocation* (London, 1717), p. 22.

[64] Thomas Lathbury, *A History of the Convocation of the Church of England* (London, 1842), p. 457.

[65] Norris claimed ingeniously to have solved the Bangorian controversy in *The Reconciler: or the Bangorian Controversy* in 1718. He claimed that both the high and low Church parties held similar views: the high Church party stubbornly

punishments *could* be added to spiritual punishments, but he made the fatal mistake of claiming that he should not be judged by a single sermon.[66] Sykes was quick to reply that Sherlock had been quick to condemn Hoadly on the basis of one sermon.[67] Similarly, while Hoadly attracted great opprobrium for his stout defences of the right of resistance to authority, John Conybeare, Bishop Gibson's favoured orthodox preacher, advanced identical views in his sermon 'Providence Concerned in the Revolutions of Government'.[68]

As far as the Clark-Bradley debate is concerned, it is clear that Smalridge's equivocal Toryism went hand in hand with his equivocal theology. But two issues arise for the historian: first, do the terms 'high church' and 'low church', orthodoxy and heterodoxy, have a precise and functional meaning? Were they as much, or perhaps predominantly, cultural and psychological, rather than just theological descriptors?[69] It is clear that Smalridge's equivocal high churchmanship was influenced by friendships with Atterbury, Whiston, and Clarke. Equally personal *animus* motivated responses to Hoadly, Atterbury, Sacheverell, and others; and in the case of Hoadly and Sherlock, cited above, personality principally seems to have divided them. Second, if high and low churchmanship were collections of theological tendencies, how should we define them? If the central tenets of churchmanship, such as the use of reason in scripture, the frequency of communion, the nature of church authority, the church's response to Dissent and other Protestants, and the doctrine of the Trinity, cannot be used to differentiate low and high churchmen, what is the value of such terms? Smalridge's views encapsulate the inconsistencies and reversals in churchmanship that many clergy experienced. The significance of Smalridge's views is that he demonstrates that when historians write of low or high churchmanship as single monolithic and consistent positions, they fall into error.

---

   defend Church authority, but when they explain what it is, they reach the same views as Hoadly expounded.
[66] Thomas Sherlock, *An Answer to a Letter sent to the Revd Dr. Sherlock* (London, 1717), p. 6.
[67] Arthur Ashley Sykes, *A Second Letter to the Revd Dr. Sherlock* (London, n.d.), p. 37.
[68] John Conybeare, *Sermons by John Conybeare DD Late Bishop of Bristol and Dean of Christ Church, Oxon* (London, 1757), II, p. 311.
[69] This is an idea Mark Knights advanced at the eighth History of Parliament Conference ('Parliament and Dissent') at Dr. Williams's Library, London, in July 2002.

Chapter 5

How Heterodox was Benjamin Hoadly?

Guglielmo Sanna

Historians praise Benjamin Hoadly (1676-1761) as an able political controversialist, but, at the same time, they castigate him as a scandalous cleric. This hardly surprises. Since his own day, the great defender of the Revolution settlement was vociferously blamed as a pluralist, nepotist, and absentee. Indeed Hoadly's preferment from Bangor to Hereford, Salisbury, and finally to Winchester, seemed to most of his contemporaries a reward for his support of the Hanoverians, rather than for promoting the interest of the Church. Additionally, Hoadly had a reputation for heresy. Many of his brethren would condemn him as an impostor, a fifth-columnist of Dissent with theological opinions dangerously close to those of the Arians, Socinians, even Deists.

As to the first charge, recent research reveals that Hoadly was far less negligent than his eighteenth-century adversaries committed us to believe.[1] But when Hoadly's theology is considered, the old altitudinarian judgment still dominates the scene. High church polemicists returned a verdict of heresy to discredit Hoadly: nineteenth- and twentieth-century scholars subscribed to it because it fitted the ideal of modern liberal society. This essay suggests that Hoadly's involvement in Arianism, Socinianism, or deism is more passively maintained than unquestionably proved. Although Hoadly's political works have been studied in detail, no serious attempt has been made to compare his religious writings with the Anglican apologetics of the period. Texts like the *Preservative on the Principles and Practices of the Nonjurors* (1716) and the *Nature of the Kingdom or Church of Christ* (1717) did arouse the historian's interest. They precipitated the harsh ideological conflict of the Bangorian controversy, and it was owing to the storm they raised that the Church of England lost the Convocation of

---

[1] The legend of Hoadly never visiting Bangor was disproved by Norman Sykes, *Church & State in England in the XVIII Century* (Cambridge, 1934), p. 362. For further evidence that Hoadly was not the worst conceivable bishop under the circumstances of his day, see R.K. Pugh, 'Bishop Hoadly: a Plea in Mitigation', *Proceedings of Hampshire Field Club and Archaeological Society* 41 (December 1984), pp. 243-52; and William Gibson, '"A happy fertile soil which bringeth forth abundantly": the diocese of Winchester, 1689-1800', in Jeffrey S. Chamberlain and Jeremy Gregory (eds.), *The National Church in Local Perspective: The Church of England and the Regions, 1660-1800* (Woodbridge, 2002), pp. 99-120.

Canterbury in 1717. Yet, the *Preservative* and the *Kingdom* form but one chapter of a larger body of work. Hoadly produced a defence of episcopal ordination, four extensive treatises on conformity, eighteen discourses concerning the terms of acceptance with God, and other sermons. He also left three charges to his diocesan clergy, not to mention two early disquisitions relating to prophecies and miracles and one short invective against the freethinkers. Notwithstanding this, religious historians remember Hoadly exclusively as a 'latitudinarian traitor'. Such an approach is misleading, especially given that the vicissitudes of the Bangorian controversy itself remain largely untold.[2] To appreciate the theological prose of Benjamin Hoadly still demands the right sort of attention.

Among Hoadly's religious writings, *A Plain Account of the Nature and End of the Sacrament of the Lord's Supper* occupies a prominent position. It was published anonymously in 1735, but there was never any secret about its authorship, which was openly acknowledged by its earliest reviewers, so that nobody wondered when in 1773 Hoadly's son inserted the treatise in the collected edition of his father's works.[3]

As soon as it appeared, the *Plain Account* created considerable theological excitement. Thomas Brett, Edmund Gibson, John Johnson, William Law, Conyers Middleton, Daniel Waterland, and William Whiston are only few of the several divines who responded to Hoadly's views. What caused so warm a reaction? Put succinctly, the *Plain Account* explained Eucharistic worship as merely symbolic in character. In the opening of his book, Hoadly enunciated his intention of representing the Lord's Supper 'in its original simplicity'. Holy Communion, he contended, was not a human creation: it was an institution of Christ. It followed from this that the meaning of the Eucharist could not be grasped except by resorting to the words of Jesus. Believers should attach no importance to what others, since the time of the evangelists, had said. The passages in the New Testament which related to Christ's institution were 'the only authentick declarations, upon which we of later ages can safely depend', Hoadly urged. Such accounts were written by the apostles, who were either witnesses to the institution itself or instructed in it by those who were. In both cases, scripture was the only source to be regarded.[4]

---

[2] The best accounts of the controversy remain John Hunt, *Religious Thought in England* (London, 1870-73), III, pp. 31-51; and Leslie Stephen, *English Thought in the Eighteenth-Century* (London, 1902), II, pp. 152-67. On Hoadly's religious opinion at the time of the Bangorian controversy, see also Henry D. Rack, '"Christ's Kingdom not of this World": the Case of Benjamin Hoadly versus William Law Reconsidered', in Derek Baker (ed.), *Church, Society and Politics* (Oxford, 1975), pp. 275-91. Regrettably no comprehensive study of Hoadly has been produced yet. William Gibson's forthcoming biography, *Enlightenment Prelate: Benjamin Hoadly (1676-1761)* is therefore particularly welcome.

[3] *The Works of Benjamin Hoadly* (London, 1773), III, pp. 843-924 [hereafter: *WBH*].

[4] Ibid., pp. 845, 847-8. On the theology of the Eucharist in late Stuart and early Hanoverian Anglicanism, see W. Jardine Grisbrooke, *Anglican Liturgies of the Seventeenth and Eighteenth Centuries* (London, 1958). See also Kenneth W.

For Hoadly, none of the original prescriptions was more indicative of the nature and end of Holy Communion than Christ's invitation to eat the bread and drink the wine 'in remembrance of him'. Hoadly erected his Eucharistic doctrine on the latter part of Luke 22:19. St. Paul's epistles—which Hoadly revered as no less divinely inspired than the Gospels and the Acts—confirmed that the Lord's Supper presented no sacrificial connotations. By receiving the elements, the faithful did not partake of the body and blood of Christ, but commemorated his redemptive suffering. Bodily presence was a medieval superstition. As Hoadly commented on I Corinthians 11:24, Jesus could not physically attend a feast designed to celebrate his death on the cross. Only in spirit would Christ assist mankind until his second coming.[5]

Such a memorialist approach had far-reaching implications. According to Hoadly, Christ's words at the Last Supper were words of thanksgiving, not consecration. The evangelist Luke wrote of the bread 'He gave thanks' instead of 'He blessed'—and so did St. Paul in I Corinthians 11:24. Of course there was contrary scriptural evidence. The *Plain Account* drew so heavily upon the Bible that Hoadly did not shut his eyes to what might disturb his exposition. Both Matthew 26:26-27 and Mark 14:22-23 reported that Christ 'blessed' before breaking the bread and 'gave thanks' before offering the cup. But the synoptic context allowed Hoadly to evade the difficulty. Following St. Chrysostom and Theophylact, he stated that in the Gospel language of the Eucharist 'to bless' was synonymous with 'to give thanks'. This could be demonstrated by observing the discrepancy between Mark 14:22 and Matthew 26:26. While the latter averred that Christ's words at the institution of the bread were 'He blessed it', the former recited 'He blessed'. How could Mark's version make sense if 'to bless' signified 'to consecrate'? The *eulogesas* before the bread, then, had to be identical in meaning with the *eucharistesas* before the cup. Since the evangelists were error-free, the pronoun 'it' in Matthew 26:26 had to be the mistake of a translator from the Greek, if not a malicious addition purposely calculated to introduce a perverse understanding of the Lord's Supper.[6]

If Hoadly's construction was accepted, and if the *eulogesas* absorbed the *eucharistesas* totally, Holy Communion would designate a general thanksgiving service, not a propitiatory oblation. The due performance of such a rite did not require priestly consecration of the elements. Indeed, the Eucharist needed no altar. As Hoadly pointed out, the Paschal Supper itself (the Jewish archetype of the Christian Communion) was distinct from the sacrifice of the lamb, 'and after it'. There were tables but no altars in the Jewish houses. Accordingly, St. Paul, in his account of the institution of the Eucharist, told that Jesus required his disciples, in times to come, and as

---

Stevenson, *Covenant of Grace Renewed* (London, 1994); and Michele Cassese, *Holy Communion. La Santa Cena anglicana* (Genoa, 1996).

[5] WBH, III, p. 853.
[6] Ibid., III, p. 849. It is worth noticing that while the authorized version of the Bible translated *eulogesas* by 'He blessed it', the revised version translates 'He blessed'.

soon as his suffering should be over, to celebrate another sort of feast in honour of a greater deliverance. Christ required the apostles to eat and drink in a thankful remembrance of him, substituting the Lord's Supper and the Communion table for the Jewish supper and table.[7] Hoadly assailed popish notions of the priesthood. If Jesus was not victim and priest, but only victim (though in a very peculiar way, given that his crucifixion was not wanted, and yet self-willing), how could a poor clergyman confer the host any special value?

This radical anti-sacerdotalism was not the most striking aspect of the *Plain Account*. There was nothing new in Hoadly's assertion that the liturgy of the Eucharist was not the repetition of Christ's sacrifice, but a memorial of it. The Anglican doctrine of Holy Communion was never dominated by either a single reformer or a particular confessional agreement. Nevertheless, the Church of England held that Christ's sacrifice was 'offered once for all', and thus it could not be repeated. In crying out against the Roman Catholic notion of the mass, therefore, Hoadly was only keeping to the Protestant line. If the Eucharist was a sacrifice, then bodily eating was a means of grace; and if bodily eating was a means of grace, then salvation was put at everyone's disposal, since it was possible for believers and unbelievers alike to take the host.

Similarly, Hoadly's solution to the dilemma, 'How can we make sure that true faith in God does not turn into idolatrous faith in the sacrament', was typically Anglican. The *Plain Account* asserted the principle of the worthily partaking, and claimed that whatever service the Eucharist was of, it rested primarily on the faithful communicant, and only secondarily on the consecrated elements. This was the dominant position within the Church of England until the Oxford Movement. In the 1730s, advocates of the receptionist theory could appeal to Anglican forebears such as Cramner, Hooker, and Bramhall. However, Hoadly did not content himself with attacking the *opus operatum*. In the last proposition of his treatise, Hoadly parted company with his co-religionists and affirmed that no promise of salvation was immediately annexed to the receiving Holy Communion, even for the worthy partaker. For Hoadly, the benefit of the Eucharist was to bring to mind Christ's example. Only in this sense could the Lord's Supper be the 'nourishment of the soul', since it was by following the teachings of Christ daily, rather than by observing externals occasionally, that the believer reached eternal life:

> This peculiar remembrance of him, and of these benefits, is...one, (and but one) mean of procuring them; not at the very time of the due performance of this rite, but after it: not by necessary or instantaneous effect upon Christians, but as it may lead and help them, to such thoughts, and resolutions, as may confirm them in that universal obedience which alone can entitle them to the promises of Christ.[8]

---

[7] Ibid., III, pp. 859-61.
[8] Ibid., III, p. 893. For the origins and character of the receptionist understanding of Holy Communion in the Church of England, see Cyril C. Richardson, *Zwingli and Cranmer on the Eucharist* (Evanston, 1949); Clifford W. Dugmore,

Such an overt denial of direct value of the Sacrament was a desertion of the Anglican canon. Hoadly's insistence that even worthily partaking of the Lord's Supper was as effective as any act of obedience to the will of God could not be reconciled with the high notions of the Eucharist nor with the low view of the Whig clerics. For most Anglican Latitudinarians of the early eighteenth century, to assert the commemorative character of the Eucharist was to confirm the self-sufficiency of Christ's death. From this anti-Catholic perspective, the memorialist approach could be embraced by many: the High Churchman Daniel Waterland himself hailed John Lewis's *Bread and Wine in the Holy Eucharist not a Proper Sacrifice* (1714). Lewis's book (a ferocious answer to Nonjuror and High Church divines like Hickes, Leslie, and Johnson) became a classic on the subject, and when Lewis reiterated his opinions from the pulpit in 1717, Archbishop Wake rewarded him with the mastership of Eastbridge Hospital in Canterbury.[9]

Hoadly, then, was not alone in his view that the Eucharist did not make present the sacrificial action of Christ's redemptive offering to God. Yet few Anglican clergy abjured their faith in the sacraments as effectual signs of grace. In this respect, Hoadly's *Plain Account* differed markedly from the latitudinarian sentiment of the 1710s. On the one hand Hoadly showed tremendous respect for the sacrament of Holy Communion. Throughout his lengthy treatise, he always referred to the Lord's Supper as a solemn engagement binding every Christian. He held the Eucharist was not a common meal, 'an ordinary eating and drinking', but a particular rite appointed by Jesus. On the other hand he made clear that Christ was not spiritually received unless the partaker resolved to reform his manners and follow virtue instead of vice. It was not enough for men that the elements were devoutly taken, or to trust in the mercy and greatness of God through Christ. Men had also to believe that they were followers of Jesus, thereby adopting rectitude as a rule for their lives. Only the practice of virtue would lead to eternal happiness. In Hoadly's view, salvation was not the fruit of any ceremony. Salvation depended entirely on the choice between good and evil. The externals of religion might encourage probity, but did not represent a substitute for human merit. In the last resort, Holy Communion was a matter of conscience. It was characteristic of Hoadly's doctrine that no prescribed liturgy was either advantageous or detrimental to the spiritual health of the communicant. Place, time, and position reflected order and decency, not the intrinsic effectiveness of the sacrament.[10]

Even the duty of self-examination was of secondary importance. St. Paul's exhortation 'Let a man examine himself' (I Corinthians 11:28) was explained by Hoadly as to allow every honest Christian to sit at his

---

The Mass and the English Reformers (London, 1958); Peter N. Brooks, *Thomas Cranmer's Doctrine of the Eucharist* (New York, 1965); Olivier Loyer, *L'anglicanism de Richard Hooker* (Paris, 1979), I, pp. 475-542.

[9] *Dictionary of National Biography*.
[10] *WBH*, III, pp. 866.

master's table. For Hoadly, self-examination was not a requirement of the Lord's Supper, nor was it spoken of by St. Paul as necessary to one's due partaking of it. It was a laudable initiative, helping the well-disposed to be rendered more perfect in the practice of all that was praiseworthy. Everyone was the best judge for himself. Why, then, should anyone be told when was most convenient for him to inquire into his conduct? No earnest believer should be uneasy at performance of Holy Communion because he had not previously undertaken self-examination. Similarly, the Eucharist was so powerful a means of edification that nobody could argue that he did not come to the holy table because he had not had enough time for inspecting his past actions. For Hoadly, every Christian who ate and drank with a sincere and solemn remembrance of Christ as his Lord could eat and drink to the end of Holy Communion. Only receiving the bread and wine and remaining a habitual sinner would be certainly condemned. But even then 'for the disobedience of his life in those points which are indispensably necessary to salvation' the wicked would be deprived of eternal life.[11]

Where did Hoadly's doctrine stem from? Some of Hoadly's critics catalogued the *Plain Account* as the work of a Quaker.[12] Quakers, who identified Christ's last supper with the Mosaic Passover, believed that the words of the Saviour at the institution of the bread were directed exclusively to the apostles then present. Only the Twelve, therefore, were required to eat and drink, until the Saviour's return, in remembrance of him. Other disciples were to follow internal light: the elements were never appointed to signify remission of sin, as communion with Christ was spiritual. But the number of those linking Hoadly with the Friends was not large. Socinianism was a much better charge. Socinus's assertion that the due performance of the sacraments did not convey grace, which rested on faith in God alone, was the direct consequence of a most extreme heterodoxy on the Trinity. By associating Hoadly with the Socinians, then, it became possible to present the *Plain Account* in the worst conceivable light. Indeed, a cohort of pamphleteers charged Hoadly with paving the way to the Racovian catechism. Thomas Bowyer, vicar of Martock in Somersetshire, compared every single point of it to the tenets of Socinus, Crellius, Smalcius, and the other big framers of the *Bibliotheca fratrum Polonorum*.[13]

---

[11] Ibid., III, pp. 867-71.

[12] Anonymous, *The Sacrament of the Altar* (London, 1735), p. 1.

[13] Thomas Bowyer, *A True Account of the Nature of the Sacrament of the Lord's-Supper* (London, 1736). The list of writers tarring Hoadly with the same brush of Socinus includes Richard Biscoe, *Remarks on a Late Book, Entituled, A Plain Account...* (London, 1735), pp. 21-2; D'Blossiers Tovey, *The Winchester Converts: or, a full and true discovery of the real usefulness and design of a late seasonable and religious treatise, entitled, A plain account...In three dialogues* (London,1735), pp. 25-7; Thomas Brett, *A True Scripture Account of the Nature of the Eucharist* (London, 1736), p. 5; Philip Skelton, *A Vindication of the Bishop of Winchester* (London, 1736), pp. 68-9; Richard Warren, *An Appendix to the Answer to a Book Intituled A Plain Account* (Cambridge, 1736), p. 58; Charles Wheatly, *Christian*

To this flood of accusations, the echo of which even crossed the Atlantic,[14] Hoadly replied with indignation. In his visitation charge of 1736, he protested his loyalty to the Thirty-Nine Articles to the clergy of Winchester diocese. Socinianism, he claimed, was alien to him. And he also explained that if he ever embraced any new confession, he would first 'give up all the temporal advantages, great as they appear, which I have reaped from [the Church of England]'.[15]

It was not the first time that allegations of anti-Trinitarianism were levelled at Hoadly.[16] In the heat of the Bangorian controversy the suspicion of heresy was reinforced by the fact that many supporters of the latitudinarian bishop—Thomas Herne, John Jackson, Arthur Ashley Sykes, for instance—were notorious denigrators of the Athanasian Creed. Indeed, Hoadly had to guard against those enthusiastic backers. He had been criticized when Toland lauded him in the introductory essay of the *Nazarenus*.[17] Thomas Mangey, rector of St. Nicholas's, Guildford, Surrey, blamed Hoadly for being a professed enemy of religion, and asked him to decline such inopportune commendation, 'unless he thinks his case to be the same with Fabius Maximus [in Livy], whose estate was particularly spar'd by Hannibal, when he destroy'd the lands of the other citizens, in order to expose him to suspicion'.[18] Thomas Dawson, one of the proctors in Convocation for the diocese of Salisbury, was even more brutal, and presented Hoadly and Toland as men of the same despicable persuasion.[19]

No commentator observed that many earnest Trinitarians—such as Gilbert Burnet the younger—were supporting Hoadly with as much liveliness as the revilers of the Athanasian Creed. Indeed, Toland's panegyric is no evidence for a successful prosecution. Nevertheless, the imputation of apostasy on the Trinity has so influenced all later reflection on the author of the *Plain Account* that it is a matter of particular importance to try to evaluate the grounds for it.

Here historians of Hoadly face the most perplexing question. Firstly, Hoadly never entangled himself with Christological quarrels. This

---

Exceptions to the Plain Account (London, 1736), pp. iii, 25-9; William Law, *A Demonstration of the Gross and Fundamental Errors of a late book, called A plain account...* (London, 1737), pp. 99-100. Henry Card, *An Essay on the Eucharist* (Worcester, 1814), p. iv, carried Hoadly's reputed association with Socinianism well into the nineteenth century.

[14] John Nichols, *Illustrations of the Literary History of the Eighteenth Century* (London, 1817-58), IV, pp. 299-300 [hereafter: *Literary Illustrations*].

[15] WBH, III, pp. 491-2.

[16] See Anonymous, *Justice Done to the Sacred Texts* (London, 1717), p. 16; Anonymous, *The Layman's Humble Address to the Bishops and Clergy in Convocation* (London, 1717), p. 9; John Cockburn, *Short Review of the Bishop of Bangor's Sermon* (London, 1718), p. 23; and John Potter, *A Defence of the Late Charge Deliver'd to the Clergy of the Diocese of Oxford* (London, 1720), pp. 16, 80.

[17] John Toland, *Nazarenus* (London, 1718), p. xxiv.

[18] Thomas Mangey, *Remarks upon Nazarenus* (London, 1718), p. 4.

[19] [Thomas Dawson], *An Introduction to the Bishop of Bangor's Intended Collection of Authorities* (London, 1718), p. ii.

contrasted with the religious climate of the day. Since the 1690s, England had become the scene of fierce discussions on Christ's nature. The principle of 'scripture alone' could lead Protestant divines to heterodox conclusions. The Bible nowhere mentioned the Trinity, and the sole passage in the authorized version which referred to the Athanasian symbol, I John 5:7-8, was rejected as a spurious interpolation by the French Oratorian Richard Simon in 1689. The Athanasian Creed itself was suspected to be a medieval forgery. In 1685 Edward Stillingfleet quoted the fragments sent by Nicholas Faber to Baronius as a proof that the Athanasian Creed was first spoken of in the eleventh century.[20] In 1688 William Cave reckoned that he could not find any trace of it before 794, and asserted that it was only at the Constantinople disputation of 1233 that the Athanasian symbol had established itself as an article of faith.[21] By the beginning of the eighteenth century most British antiquaries were persuaded that the Athanasian Creed was a late composition. Even those Anglican divines who would insist that the Athanasian Creed had come into existence before the schism between East and West, discounted Athanasius's authorship. Joseph Bingham agreed with Pascal Quesnel that the Athanasian symbol had emerged as early as the fifth century, and that Virgilius Tapsensis, not Athanasius, was its framer.[22] Trinitarian orthodoxy could be upset by such discomforting investigations. Both clergy and laity were divided on the issue. But Hoadly never took sides in the altercation.

Secondly, Hoadly left almost no manuscripts to help us to grasp his private views. In 1764, when preparing new critical editions of the *Spectator* and the *Guardian*, Thomas Percy asked Hoadly's son to pass him any unpublished writing which might be of use.[23] But, as Hoadly's son would repeat to the new bishop of Winchester, John Thomas, in 1765, 'my father destroyed most of his unnecessary papers, and I did the same after his death'.[24] That Hoadly took the utmost care to conceal his sentiments is confirmed by his uneasiness at hearing, not many years before he died, that Lady Sundon (mistress of the robes to Queen Caroline) had preserved his letters to her.[25] Those letters contained nothing compromising, but when a certain Mr. Case appropriated them, with an eye to making some money out of it, Hoadly grieved for weeks, until John Green, the bishop of Lincoln, and Thomas Chapman, the master of Magdalen College, Cambridge, (both of whom had read the letters) assured him that there was nothing to worry about.[26]

Thirdly, the very few times that Hoadly mentioned the Trinity, he did so in contradictory terms. That Hoadly was a Socinian, we can safely

---

[20] Edward Stillingfleet, *Origines Britannicae* (London, 1685), pp. 227-30.
[21] William Cave, *Scriptorum ecclesiasticorum* (London, 1688), p. 146.
[22] Joseph Bingham, *Origines ecclesiasticae* (London, 1715), pp. 118-20.
[23] *The Correspondence of Thomas Wharton*, David Fairer (ed.), (Athens, GA, 1995), pp. 174, 181-2, 187.
[24] John Nichols, *Literary Anecdotes of the Eighteenth Century* (London, 1812), IX, p. 786 [hereafter: *Literary Anecdotes*].
[25] *WBH*, I, pp. v-vi.
[26] *Literary Illustrations*, III, p. 298.

discount. There is no evidence beyond some accidental similarity of conclusion that he borrowed from Socinus. Despite the large body of accusations, Hoadly never mentioned the Racovians. On the contrary, he distanced himself from them in too many aspects of his thought. Hoadly believed in the pre-existence of Christ as a distinct person, and put the cross at the very centre of his religious vision. Hoadly would never agree with Socinus that the forgiveness of God was neither *propter Christum* nor *per Christum*, but *gratuito*. For the Socinians, Christ's sacrifice redeemed mankind only because God was willing to accept it. Hoadly advocated a far more active role for Christ. As he stated in a late 1730s sermon on Luke 17:10, it was the atoning death of the Son which restored us to the favour of the Father.[27]

Arianism was a more serious affair. Arianism, rather than Socinianism, was the prevailing heresy of England in the first half of the eighteenth century. And Hoadly, like other latitudinarian divines, had contact with some of its expounders. In 1730 William Whiston wrote of a group of clerics who used to meet in London to discuss Christian dogmas and Church reform in the light of recent scholarship on the Bible. Whiston was a participant in these talks, together with Samuel Clarke, and Hoadly was also a prominent figure.[28] However, there was never an Arian party with a single defined programme. Arianism covered a broad range of theology. Whose particular influence did Hoadly fall under? The eccentric Whiston was of too authoritarian a temper to please him. Whiston's endeavours at restoring the severe discipline of the Apostolical constitutions induced Hoadly's brother to esteem him as 'one desirous of bringing persecution into the church'.[29] The two men distrusted each other, particularly after Hoadly was consecrated bishop, so that when the *Plain Account* appeared in print, Whiston branded it as 'a most unjudicious and unlearned treatise'.[30]

Hoadly's links with Samuel Clarke were much closer. Indeed, it is a commonplace of historical writing that Hoadly was in entire sympathy with the semi-Arian Christology of the *Scripture Doctrine of the Trinity* (1712). Such a long-established historiographical tradition has solid foundations. Hoadly himself never concealed his admiration for his old schoolmate at Cambridge. In 1719 he wrote to the duchess of Marlborough, 'You know, Madam, how exact all Dr. Clarke's notions are'.[31] And the tone of the biographical sketch he pictured in 1730 was highly supportive of the great philosopher.[32] Unsurprisingly Hoadly 'wished to be distinguished

---

[27] WBH, III, p. 827.
[28] William Whiston, *Historical Memoirs of the Life of Dr. Samuel Clarke* (London, 1748), pp. 10, 20.
[29] Ibid., p. 21.
[30] William Whiston, *Memoirs of the Life of William Whiston* (London, 1749), p. 244.
[31] British Library, Add. MS, 61464, f. 164r: Hoadly to Sarah, duchess of Marlborough, 11 August 1719.
[32] *An Account of the Life, Writings, and Character of Samuel Clarke, D.D. Rector of St. James's Westminster* (1730-1), in WBH, III, pp. 453-69.

after his death by no higher title than friend of Dr. Clarke'.[33] Like Clarke, Hoadly sought to approach revelation in a reasonable manner, adopting human intellect as a counterpoise to unthinking biblicism and unthinking historical precedent. Moreover, both Hoadly and Clarke stood in the orbit of Arminian soteriology in their refusal of any sort of moral necessity in intelligent creatures. For Hoadly, God's omnipotence did not detract from the freedom of human beings to accept or resist grace. It was God who had endowed the spirit of men with reasoning to recognize what was praiseworthy. But although faith and reason were gifts of God, and although the gates of Heaven could only be reopened by the sacrifice of Christ, mankind achieved salvation through a life of good works. *Sine actionum humanorum libertate nulla religio potest esse*: religion can do nothing without free will. The choice between good and evil was what gave Christianity its most intimate significance. This was the argument Hoadly so consistently employed in favour of the Dissenters in the Bangorian controversy. And it was to free will again that Hoadly turned when crossing swords with the Deists. As he argued in his *Queries Recommended to the Authors of the Late Discourse of Free-Thinking* (1713), no human being could pursue virtue if his actions and thoughts were the necessary effect of matter and motion.[34]

Whether Hoadly aligned with Clarke on Trinitarianism is unclear. Hoadly complimented Clarke on his method of inquiring into the Christian truth by searching all the texts of scripture, regardless of both dogmas and tradition. And he resented that the results of such an erudite effort had not been met with toleration. But on the basic question, whether the Father and the Son were exactly of the same substance while being two distinct persons, he declined to render his opinion. For Hoadly, the *Scripture Doctrine of the Trinity* had two merits. In the first place, Clarke's book had displayed a huge collection of texts of the New Testament on which to decide what to believe about the matter. In the second place, it had demonstrated 'how widely the most honest enquirers after truth may differ, upon such subjects'.[35]

Here Hoadly was adopting a typical latitudinarian stance. The Trinity, some Anglicans contended, was not against reason: it was above it. And what God had thought fit not to reveal or to render intelligible to human understanding, men were bound to leave undetermined. Hoadly's rationalism should not be exaggerated. Shortly before his elevation to the Episcopal bench, Hoadly warned his parishioners against the dangers of 'implicit subjection' to human authorities and human decisions: in a 1713 sermon on I Thessalonians 5:21, he claimed that 'the Christian religion itself desired...all men to examine into the proofs upon which it stood'. At the same time, Hoadly admonished the boldest not to make the contrary mistake of infidelity 'under pretence of examination'. The several prophecies and miracles of both the Old and the New Testament bore

---

[33] *Literary Anecdotes*, IX, p. 427.
[34] *WBH*, I, p. 151.
[35] *An Account of the Life, Writings, and Character of Samuel Clarke*, pp. 461-2.

witness to the fact that God could call upon his creatures 'in any method, which may seem best to his [inapprehensible] wisdom'.[36]

From this point of view, appealing to reason was just bringing to mind the Protestant principle of individual access to the divine truth. For Hoadly to appeal to reason meant also to remember that religion should persuade rather than compel: genuine Christians, Hoadly insisted, must not have recourse to force, whose only consequence was the turning away of too many from the faith. To follow reason had one last meaning. It was 'to imitate God', and therefore 'to practise virtue'. Even pleasure, when pursued with moderation, 'so as to preserve, and not destroy life and health', did not detract from the spiritual welfare of mankind, but rather added glory to the Father.[37]

In short, Hoadly exalted reason as 'God's original light', the 'primary revelation of his will', more important even than the scriptures, which, in comparison to reason, were a secondary source. However, the correct use of the rational faculties by any man could but confirm the great plan of Christianity as purged of all the undesirable interferences of both tradition and philosophy. As Hoadly outlined in a 1732 sermon on Galatians 2:18:

> The religion of nature is not the opinion...of this or that philosopher...but it is truly that law of God, which may justly be collected, by his reasonable creatures, from the immutable reasons, and relations of things; and is the same law, as one of the heathen writers well observes, at Rome and at Athens; that is, in other words, at all places, from one end of the world to the other.[38]

Faith and reason were twins. Indeed, Hoadly never hesitated to admonish his parishioners that those who reviled the Gospel while 'having opportunity to hear it proposed to them' incurred certain damnation.[39] Human reason was limited. It was only the reflection of divine perfection. Men had to accept such a restriction. By their reason, weak as it was since the Fall, they were required to judge the Gospel, not to worry about those things that God had left out of it.

From this perspective, Hoadly agreed with St. Jerome that the apostles were not so proficient in metaphysics as to understand the eternal generation of the Son from the Father. Hoadly also advanced that by 'the son of God' the apostles did not signify anything but the Messiah sent into the world by God. Following Lactantius, he observed that the name 'Christ' was a name of power and dominion, indicating him to be a sovereign, regardless of any implication as to its relationship with the other persons of the Trinity.[40] By these references to patristic knowledge Hoadly did not aim at denying either the co-eternity or the co-substantiality of the Saviour. He rather wanted to affirm that the Trinitarian enigma could not be represented in so detailed a manner as High Churchmen maintained.

---

[36] *WBH*, I, pp. 152-8.
[37] Ibid., I, pp. 45, 55; III, p. 725.
[38] Ibid., III, pp. 748-9.
[39] Ibid., p. 601.
[40] Ibid., II, p. 932.

Indeed, Hoadly never refused to subscribe to the Athanasian Creed. In 1761 John Jones reported that Hoadly had once confided to him that 'he had constantly, whilst a parish-minister, observed the rules prescribed; and, amongst other injunctions, that he had never omitted the Athanasian Creed, when ordered to be read in the church':

> But you...are, I see, of much the same mind with my late excellent friend Dr. Clarke...I leave you to God, and to your own judgment and conscience: for I never go farther.[41]

This suggests that on Christology Hoadly was at variance with Clarke. Hoadly conformed to article VIII, and in all probability he conformed with a good conscience. According to Jones, Hoadly's subscription to the Athanasian Creed did not rest on mental equivocation. Few clerics in Clarke's circle believed that they could lawfully comply with ecclesiastical forms in any sense as long as it was agreeable to the Bible. After Daniel Waterland's *Case of Arian Subscription* appeared in 1721, clerics objecting to the Athanasian Creed would either refuse preferment or abandon the Church. Hoadly remained, and in 1734 he received the rich see of Winchester, one of the greatest prizes of the Anglican communion.

At the same time Hoadly wished those who scrupled 'more liberty, as really due to them by the laws of Nature, and of Gospel'.[42] He despised the enemies of freedom, and on occasion he ridiculed the Athanasian Creed itself. In his mordant *Dedication to Clement XI* (1715), Hoadly inveighed against the attempts of the theologians at giving the notion of the hypostatic union geometrical expression:

> We have one very common, and very scandalous representation, in multitudes of our churches...and that is, of the trinity in unity, figured in a triangle, and generally inclosed in a circle, over our altars...This is justly esteemed the most inexplicable, and unintelligible, mystery of our faith. And yet it is suffered, by those who so esteem it, to be set forth, even to men's eyes, by a mathematical figure; which always supposeth the clearest, and fullest ideas possible.[43]

Historians refer to this passage as the best evidence of Hoadly's Arianism. Indeed, the *Dedication* amused the enemies of the Athanasian Creed. As late as 1732, Hoadly himself recalled 'the excesses of joy with which Dr. Clarke then received it'.[44] Yet, ironic statements against the pretensions of Athanasians do not prove commitment to anti-Trinitarianism. It was in its French edition that Hoadly's pamphlet had serious heterodox connotations. In the introductory essay to the book, François de la Pillonnière—the translator from English, a converted French Jesuit who served Hoadly as the private tutor of his sons—eulogized the Racovians as

---

[41] *Literary Anecdotes*, III, pp. 747-8.
[42] Ibid., III, p. 747.
[43] *WBH*, I, p. 541.
[44] Ibid., I, p. 534.

an admirable example of Christian 'moderation'.⁴⁵ Hoadly's adversaries did not wait too long to exploit such an opportunity, and treated him as if he was the inspirer of the excerpt.⁴⁶ But Hoadly never propounded an alternative explanation of the hypostatic union. For Hoadly, any endeavour to settle the Trinitarian question in positive terms represented an offence to God and mankind. It was an offence to God in that it exceeded what the Omnipotent had made knowable to human reason or directly exposed by revelation. And it was an offence to mankind because it troubled human conscience to no purpose. The more the theologian entered the territory of darkness, the more the faithful was afflicted, particularly those low-born people whose intellectual capacities were not so refined as to allow them to tread the same tortuous path.

Hoadly regretted that Christians made salvation depend on puzzling tests of loyalty. Although he subscribed to the formulas adopted by the Church of England, his interpretation of the atonement prompted him to render eternal life accessible to all. From this soteriological postulation, Hoadly wondered how the low-born could escape the damnatory clause of the Athanasian Creed. The unlearned could not assent if they did not understand what the Athanasian symbol meant. Assent without understanding would not acquire any merit either, since Christianity was a matter of individual choice between good and evil, not of acquiescence to authority or decision.⁴⁷

It is clear why Hoadly was so ambivalent towards the Arians. For Hoadly the *credenda*, or matters absolutely necessary to be believed, did not include Athanasius's formulations. It was not the design of the Gospel to disclose the deep things of God. The Bible affirmed the generation of the Son from the Father, but it did not enter into details. And since scripture left the question open, diversity of opinions had to be allowed. Even the subscribers to the Athanasian Creed should recognize the liberty of those who dissented to adhere to other formulas. It was from this latitudinarian point of view, rather than from any commitment to heterodoxy, that Hoadly defended the right of private judgment for all Protestants as far as Christological issues were concerned. His *Letter to a Friend in Lancashire*, published anonymously in 1714, opposed all prohibitions of speculating about the Trinity. It took self-possession to advance such an unpopular opinion. George I's *Directions for the Preserving of Unity in the Church* had been issued only four days before to put a stop to the flood of Trinitarian writings. Many Anglicans were angered by Hoadly's impudence. A few years later, Archbishop Wake would censure it as 'a libel upon the King himself'.⁴⁸

---

45   *Epitre dedicatorie au Pape Clement XI* (London, 1717), p. 15
46   Anonymous, *Mr. Pillonnière's Preface to his Translation of Steele's Epistle* (London, 1717), pp. 15-16.
47   *WBH*, II, p. 899.
48   Christ Church, Oxford, Wake MS, 241, no. 67, f. 2r: Miscellaneous reading notes of William Wake.

At the same time, Hoadly feared the consequences of theological speculation. So thin was the path of Christological orthodoxy that even the author of the *Plain Account* thought clerics had to be careful as to what they said both from the pulpit and in print. Such an anxiety could but grow stronger when Hoadly rose to the order of prelacy. Bishops were the guardians of the Church: it was a fundamental part of their duty to preserve order and decency. No wonder, therefore, that in the charge delivered to the clergy of the diocese of Salisbury, at his visitation of 1726, Hoadly should recommend conformity in uncompromising words. Ten years later he repeated to the clergy of the diocese of Winchester:

> In matters plainly determined by authority, I shall expect from all under my inspection the most exact conformity to the rubrics and rules they have solemnly promised to observe.[49]

These were not empty threats. Both his friend Clarke and John Jackson, his supporter at the time of the Bangorian controversy, were refused preferment because of their unwillingness to subscribe to the Athanasian Creed. Jackson's affair is illuminating. In 1724 Clarke recommended him for a prebend at Salisbury. It was unclear whether subscription was necessary for holding this kind of benefice. Jackson himself was already prebendary of Wherwell, and was also confrater at Wingston's Hospital in Leicester. But Hoadly remained inflexible: he knew that by making heterodox appointments he could bring conflict within the Church. The fact that he pressed to remove doctrinal barriers does not imply that he was ready to breach them. Peace and unity were too precious a gift to run the risk of anarchy and confusion.[50]

Did Hoadly betray his Arian associates in exchange for ecclesiastical promotion? There is evidence that he did. Even the bishop's son was convinced that his father assented to the Christology of Clarke and that he avoided to profess this openly because 'he knew how to distinguish between a private opinion and the practice of the Church'.[51] Yet, doctrinal inquiries did not attract Hoadly very much. Hoadly's priority was the unity of all English Protestants. Such a political and religious ideal was particularly widespread at a time when the Protestant interest was under threat. In the 1700s Hoadly voiced the Whig yearning to fight France until Louis XIV had been silenced; after 1714 Jacobite manoeuvres kept Hoadly's anti-Catholicism well alive. The great champion of the revolution settlement did not wait until his appointment to Bangor to stand up as a supporter of national concord. Even before becoming a bishop, his main purpose had been to persuade Dissenters to communicate with the Church of England. In order to accomplish this, he was prepared to accept a reform of the Anglican liturgy, even to abandon strict religious uniformity. But he also knew that the unity of English Protestants could not be achieved at the

---

[49] WBH, III, pp. 473, 492.
[50] *Biographia Britannica* (London, 1766), VI, part II, p. 108.
[51] Ibid., p. 102.

expense of the Anglicans only. Therefore, he demanded that the Dissenters renounce some of their claims as well. Early in his career, Hoadly had quarrelled with Edmund Calamy, the Presbyterian minister. It was on account of the Nonconformist's obsession with the externals of religion that English Protestantism was affected by internal schism. Although Hoadly upheld freedom of conscience, he sharply distinguished between the liberty of the lay people and that of the Christian ministers. While the first were not scholars of the Bible, and therefore should be the object of charity rather than reproach, the second were responsible for the spiritual welfare of the unlearned, and thus must not encourage divisions. As he wrote in his *Reasonableness of Conformity* (1703), it was better to leave the ministry rather than to sow the seed of discord among the followers of Christ.[52]

On that very occasion Hoadly pointed out that nobody could refuse subscription to the Athanasian Creed who had both the historical opportunity and the intellectual capability to know it agreeable to the word of God.[53] The Anglican clergyman, no less than the Dissenting minister, had to ponder this. In many senses, Hoadly's arguments were fundamentally consistent both before and after his consecration. Hoadly heartily wished the faith of the Church of England might be restored to scriptural simplicity, and that the Athanasian Creed might be taken out of the Anglican liturgy, or reserved for occasional use. This would have made the English Church more comprehensive. But no reform should be implemented at the cost of new divisions. The fate of English Protestantism counted for more than theological conjecturing.

Indeed, Hoadly's position was not so heterodox as it has been assumed. Trinity in unity was revealed, as a matter above human understanding. The word of God, therefore, was sufficient to command assent. But the doctrinal consequences of the Trinitarian article were not equally certain. Hoadly objected to the Athanasian Creed in so far as it puzzled believers. The Athanasian Creed contradicted the Reformation as to the sufficiency of the rule of scripture. Additionally, it was so worded that most people understood it in a sense favouring of either Sabellianism or Tritheism—neither of which was consistent with the Bible. Hoadly regretted that enemies of Christianity should take advantage of diverging interpretations. Above all, he deplored the fact that the Athanasian Creed made the terms of Christian communion straighter than Christ and his apostles had done. However, no alternative explanation of the Trinitarian article was ever propounded by the author of the *Plain Account*. Although Hoadly's religious thought was not orthodox by the standards of the altitudinarians, neither was it markedly Arian, let alone Socinian. Hoadly's approach to theology owed much to William Chillingworth, Jeremy Taylor, John Tillotson and the rest of the English latitudinarians. Hoadly may well have fallen short of the expected Trinitarian orthodoxy, he may have been a subordinationist like Clarke in some moments of his life. But theological speculation was not his main concern. In Hoadly's mind, the design of the

---

[52] *WBH*, I, pp. 251-4.
[53] Ibid., p. 361.

Gospel was not to fill men's heads with useless suppositions, but to possess their hearts with the love of piety and virtue, and to excite them to the practice of those God-like graces by which only they could resemble the glorious author of their being. Our Lord, Hoadly contended, did not come into the world to set up a school of virtuosos and disputants in it; Christ came into the world to renew the minds and to reform the manners. As Hoadly commented on Colossians 1:12, Christianity was designed to 'make us meet to be partakers of the inheritance of the saints in light'. Trinitarian problems could but be met with agnosticism by Hoadly.

Insistence on doctrinal norms as the only interpretative prism has proved a serious hindrance to the emergence of a proper understanding of Benjamin Hoadly. Hoadly's intellectual life can be explained as a uninterrupted tension between the two ideals of liberty of conscience and religious peace. Within such a framework, there was no place for theological subtleties. Hoadly was an admirer of Clarke, but, as an advocate for Protestant union, he was also persuaded that clergymen had to abstain from raising questions which could foment discord among Christians. The *Plain Account* followed on Clarke's footsteps in that it affirmed the validity of Biblical sources exclusively, not in that it sympathized with anti-Trinitarian thought. The Eucharistic doctrine of Hoadly did put a strong accent on Christ as a 'moral exemplar'. But this, sympathetic though it seemed, had nothing to do with the Racovian catechism and with the other texts of the *Bibliotheca fratrum Polonorum*. Hoadly's emphasis on the pedagogic value of the Gospel was just an affirmation that by following the moral teachings of Christianity daily the believer could reach eternal life more safely than by adhering to the human—therefore uncertain and disputed—requirements of worship occasionally.

Such a vision was relatively consistent with Arminian soteriology. Indeed, Hoadly tried hard never to depart from the Anglican tradition. Even the notion that the Messiahship of Jesus was the fundamental article of Christianity was always referred by him to Anglican pillars like Hooker, Taylor, Tillotson, Patrick, etc., and never to Locke. The *Plain Account* betrayed Anglicanism. Heterodoxy, however, was not the only available option outside the province of codified doctrinal norms. The religious rationale of Hoadly's most extreme tract is better understood when related to what Jaroslav Pelikan has termed the 'crisis of orthodoxy'.[54] The convulsions of the Reformation and Counter-Reformation had left Christians with a strong impression that devotion could not mean acceptance of articles of faith exclusively. If religious peace was to be attained, devotion had also to mean one's determination of virtuously following the example of Christ. Hoadly's *Plain Account* shared the attitude of his age. It claimed that subscription to an orthodox creed would not atone for an un-Christian practice; that 'thinking rightly' was the mere consequence of 'doing rightly'; that holiness of life was the great point to be

---

[54] Jaroslav Pelikan, *Christian Doctrine and Modern Culture* (Chicago, 1989), pp. 9-59.

regarded. As Hoadly commented on Heb. 11, faith could not be a mere internal disposition: it had to be a 'vital active principle'.[55]

There is no reason to doubt Hoadly's contention that in sketching the *Plain Account* he did not turn to Arian or Socinian sources, but to scripture alone. At the same time Hoadly could not be unaware that his Eucharistic treatise was far removed from the Anglican canon. Why, then, did he publish it? The most plausible explanation is that Hoadly aimed at fostering religious unity once again. Hoadly had always regretted that English Protestants should divide over something which was the memorial of Christ's highest act of love for mankind. Indeed, the basic themes of the *Plain Account* had been long anticipated. As early as 1703 Hoadly had declared:

> Christ's institution of the Eucharist, was only, eat this bread, and drink this wine, in remembrance of me: not in this particular posture, any more than at this particular time; the gesture being no more a part of the institution, than the time.[56]

Even closer to the *Plain Account* was a sermon on St. Paul's discourse to Felix (Acts 24:24-25) preached before George II in February 1730. Christian virtues, not the elements, were 'the means of grace':

> Thus the believing in Christ...and the remembrance of him...are...subservient, to one and the same great end; the engaging us to abhor all immorality, and to proceed to the highest perfection we can, in every instance of morality.[57]

In the early 1730s, Hoadly had good reasons for restating his ideas on Holy Communion. The *Plain Account* appeared in print in 1735, but the better-informed among contemporaries knew that it had been completed long before.[58] It is possible that Hoadly wrote it in 1732-33, as a reaction to the campaign of the Dissenters for the repeal of the Test and Corporation Acts. By the autumn of 1732 it had become evident that such renewed pressure from Dissent might embarrass the Whig administration. Any endeavour at levelling the barriers between Anglicans and Nonconformists aroused Tory fury, and the privileged status of the Church was of paramount importance for the Whigs themselves. So, to lessen political tension, the leading minister Robert Walpole asked Hoadly to convince Dissenters to procrastinate their requests until the general elections of 1734 had passed off without any major incidents. At first Hoadly hesitated. He had supported Walpole on many occasions, but he had so often asserted 'the unreasonableness of these laws in the social light, and the profaneness of them theologically' that he could not serve him again with an easy mind. In

---

[55] *WBH*, III, p. 555.
[56] Ibid., I, p. 188.
[57] Ibid., III, pp. 737-8.
[58] Romney Sedgwick (ed.), *Some Materials towards Memoirs of the Reign of King George II, by John, Lord Hervey* (New York, 1970), II, p. 499 [hereafter: *Lord Hervey's Memoirs*].

the end Hoadly yielded to ministerial entreaties. His reputation at court was declining: in 1730 he had been denied preferment to the diocese of Durham, and, as if disfavour with the administration was not enough, George II detested him. By helping Walpole to keep Dissenters quiet, Hoadly could strengthen his position both in Church and state. Besides, Hoadly was persuaded that by raising such a problematic issue, his 'long-oppressed friends' could incur something more unpleasant than the legal disabilities they were trying to get rid of. The prospect of an 'universal toleration' was so frightful to so many that supplementary restrictions could suddenly materialize if the Dissenters persisted in their intentions.[59]

Hoadly may have conceived his *Plain Account* as a part of a strategy to discourage Nonconformists from crusading for the repeal of the Test and Corporation Acts. Such a low view of the Lord's Supper could have been intended by Hoadly to show the Dissenters that they were in the wrong to make a difficulty of conforming to a rite so indifferent in its nature. Christ had given the apostles no rules. It followed from this that the Eucharist could be celebrated in many different ways, the one as worthy as the other. The Dissenter, Hoadly inferred, had no title to censure the kneeling position of the Anglican as a sinful adoration of the host. As Hoadly had already told the Presbyterian minister Edmund Calamy in 1703, 'your constant use of any posture, (whether it be standing, or sitting) is as much a reflection upon the defectiveness of Christ's institution, as your constant use of kneeling could be; it being the use of what is as much an addition to Christ's institution, as kneeling is'.[60] The Lord's Supper was only a commemoration. It needed the consecration of no kind of clergy; it required no special preparation in order to receive it; it conveyed no immediate benefits. Why, then, did the Dissenter refuse to communicate with the Anglican? Was not causeless separation as uncharitable and unchristian as High Church bigotry was? The Lord's Supper was tailor-made for the united profession of the faith in Christ. As Hoadly put it, only by receiving the bread in communion with all other Christians, the faithful declared himself 'to be under Christ's governance and influence' as a fellow member 'of that same body of which [Christ] is the head'.[61] If Nonconformists realized how lawful the occasional attendance at Anglican Communion under the political circumstances of the day was, qualification for civil office would be achieved with less political agitation. Full civil rights could be demanded at a more seasonable time.

In September 1734, Walpole rewarded Hoadly with the bishopric of Winchester. It was only then that he decided to publish his *Plain Account*. Double-edged as it was, the *Plain Account* could be now presented to the world as a call for 'further toleration' of Dissent. Christ annexed no spiritual benefit to those receiving Holy Communion: how could men attach to it the profit of a worldly office? Besides, as Hoadly had repeatedly maintained both in print and from the pulpit, Nonconformists were loyal

---

[59] Ibid., I, p. 125-6.
[60] *WBH*, I, p. 188.
[61] Ibid., III, p. 862.

English subjects, they had always sustained the dynasty as well as the administration. Why, then, did Anglicans continue to discriminate them? But although the general elections of 1734 had passed, no minister of the crown would endorse such a discomforting policy. At court things went even worse. The *Plain Account* infuriated George II. The king rebuked Hoadly for disturbing the government 'with impertinent disputes that nobody of any sense ever troubled himself about'.[62]

In the eyes of George II, it was as if Hoadly had kept his most perverse inclinations secret until he had secured himself the richest see of the Church of England. Once again, Hoadly was accused of damaging his allies no less than his opponents. But in spite of the King's disdain, the author of the *Plain Account* knew very well whose side he was on. In 1737 he took up another Walpole commission, and managed to dissuade Prince Frederick from distressing the court by stirring up the Dissenters. As Hoadly pointed out on that new occasion, the security of the dynasty counted for more than the repeal of the Test Act.[63] He may appear as a political gambler. But in the eighteenth century Church and state were so closely related that the welfare of the former could not be promoted but by advancing the interest of the latter. For Hoadly, the Hanoverian succession was the best safeguard for Protestant liberties. If London should ever fall into the hands of Paris—so he feared—Canterbury would immediately return under the tyranny of Rome.

---

[62] *Lord Hervey's Memoirs*, II, pp. 499-500.
[63] Ibid., III, pp. 794-5.

Chapter 6

The Jacobite Failure to Bridge the Catholic/Protestant Divide, 1717-1730

Jeffrey S. Chamberlain

Religion was the bane of the Stuarts. Since they first came to power in England in 1603, they could not seem to find a formula that worked. From James I and Charles I, who alienated Puritans, to James II, who alienated Anglicans and thereby lost his throne, religion was an intractable problem. After James II was deposed, he at first resolutely tried to pursue goals that favoured Catholicism. But it became clear the longer he was in exile, that he could not win back a Protestant country by surrounding himself with doctrinaire Catholic advisors and pushing a Catholic agenda. Therefore he set out on a policy of accommodating Protestants and Catholics alike.[1] As he made clear in 'His Majestie's Most Gracious Declaration' in 1693, 'We likewise declare, upon our royal word, that we will protect and defend the Church of England, as it is now established by law...We further declare, we will not dispense with, or violate the Test'.[2] Thereafter he never varied from this approach: declaration after declaration promised support of the Church of England.

His son, the 'Old Pretender' (who styled himself James III), had learned this lesson early. He, too, promised protection of the Church in his declarations.[3] Though devoutly Catholic himself, James III welcomed

---

[1] According to Daniel Szechi, there was a seismic shift in the Jacobite court in 1693. The 'noncompounders', or those who did not want to compromise with non-Catholics, lost out and James II issued a declaration that he would uphold and protect the Church of England 'as it is now established by law'. Thereafter, the Jacobite court became more and more accommodating—even radical. See Szechi, *The Jacobites* (Manchester, 1994), pp. 12-30, and idem, 'The Jacobite Revolution Settlement, 1689-1696', *English Historical Review* 93 (July 1993), pp. 610-28, especially p. 623ff.

[2] As quoted in Szechi, *The Jacobites*, p. 144.

[3] 'We do likewise renew & confirm all the promises...to protect, support & maintain our subjects of the Church of England and Ireland in the full & free exercise of their Relligion, & to secure the say'd Churches as by law establish'd...As to dissenters from the foresay'd Church establish'd by law, as it is not our intention that any of our subjects shall suffer persecution under our government for Conscience Sake, so we referr it to our first Parliament to grant such indulgence to truly tender consciences as they in their wisdom shall think fit'. 'His Majesty's Most Gracious Declaration', 31 March 1719: Royal

followers from all Christian camps. From the beginning of his 'reign', he showed toleration and acceptance. Indeed, Stuart attitudes became the most liberal and accommodating of almost any regime of the time. As James admitted to Father Gaillard, his mother's confessor, 'I am Catholic, but I am a king, and subjects of whatever religion they may be, have an equal right to be protected...the Pope has himself told me that I am not an apostle...I am not bound to convert my subjects otherwise than by my example'.[4] As a visitor to his court observed, James was 'very far from any sort of Bigotry, and most averse to disputes and distinctions of Religion'.[5] James even employed Protestant chaplains.[6]

Such an ecumenical temperament was very rare in Protestant England at the time. In fact, most recent historians have pointed to the connection between deep-seated fears of Catholicism as fundamental to the development of English identity.[7] Because of the long and notorious history of Catholic intrigue (and imagined Catholic intrigue)—the Ridolfi Plot, Babington Plot, Gunpowder Plot, and Popish Plot, *inter alia*—Catholicism itself represented a serious foreign threat.[8] In the face of the threat of Catholicism, Englishmen minimized differences between Anglican and Dissenter. Therefore, as England entered the eighteenth century, there was

---

Archives, Windsor Castle, SP 43/16 [hereafter: RA]. See also RA, SP 150/43/16. See, also, RA, SP 5/61: 'His Majesty's Most Gracious Declaration', 1715.

[4] Historical Manuscript Commission, *Calendar of the Stuart Papers* (London, 1912), V, p. 515 [hereafter: *CSP*]. The Stuart Papers are used by the gracious permission of Her Majesty the Queen. See also George Hilton Jones, *The Mainstream of Jacobitism* (Cambridge, MA, 1954), p. 134; and Bryan Bevan, *King James the Third of England: A Study of Kingship in Exile* (London, 1967), pp. 106-7.

[5] From the manuscript *An English Traveller at Rome*, cited in Peggy Miller, *James* (London, 1917), p. 261.

[6] Ibid., p. 126. There is at least one dissenting view. The anonymous author of *A Letter from a Gentleman at R. to a Friend at L.* (London, 1718), who labelled himself as Protestant, said that James's 'unhappy Zeal for another Religion' 'knew no Bounds'. The 'gentleman' claimed to have witnessed the 'Excess of his Zeal for the Catholick Religion': pp. 4-5. However, the pamphlet then accuses James of giving in to the earl of Mar's desire to advance all of his Scottish friends, never once acknowledging that most of them were Protestant.

[7] Linda Colley, *Britons: Forging the Nation, 1707-1837* (New Haven, 1992), pp. 18-54; and Colin Haydon, '"I love my King and Country, but a Roman catholic I hate": anti-catholicism, xenophobia and national identity in eighteenth-century England', in Tony Claydon and Ian McBride (eds.), *Protestantism and National Identity: Britain and Ireland, c. 1650-c.1850* (Cambridge, 1998), pp. 33-52. J.C.D. Clark, 'Protestantism, Nationalism, and National Identity, 1660-1832', *Historical Journal* 43:1 (March 2000), pp. 249-76 reviews the literature on Protestantism and the formation of the British national identity.

[8] William Gibson, *The Church of England 1688-1832: Unity and Accord* (London and New York, 2001), 216-19, Colin Haydon, *Anti-Catholicism in Eighteenth-Century England* (Manchester, 1993), especially pp. 117-29; and idem, '"I love my King and Country"', pp. 33-8. See also Paul Hopkins, 'Sham Plots and Real Plots in the 1690s', in Eveline Cruickshanks (ed.), *Ideology and Conspiracy: Aspects of Jacobitism, 1689-1759* (Edinburgh, 1982), pp. 89-109.

toleration for wide variations in Protestantism, but there was more of a gulf than ever between Protestantism and Catholicism.[9] Whigs and Tories alike decried popery, and broadminded attitudes bridging the gap between Protestantism and Catholicism would have to wait until much later in the century, and no official toleration for Catholics would be granted until well into the next century.[10] Keenly aware of this, James and the Jacobite court clearly tried to separate religion from national identity. James argued that he was much more English than George I, despite the latter's Protestantism. In a declaration made after the South Sea Bubble burst and precipitated new opportunities for the Jacobites, James averred:

> ...no people can be happy under ye yoke of a foreigner; lett his professions be what they will, lett his intentions be what they will, yet innate love to his native Country will always subsist and be prevalent, and indeed ought to do so, for what virtue is either so natural to a Prince or so commendable in him as affections for his own people. As our Birth was English so is our heart entirely English, and although driven from our cradle to wander an Exile in foreign Countrys our education has also been truly English, we have made the constitution of our Country our first study, and in that search have been delighted to find that our ancient laws have provided everything that a just and reasonable Kind can desire....[11]

Jacobites never failed to point out how foreign the reigns, first of William of Orange, then of George of Hanover, were. They sometimes even argued that Catholics and Protestants could be united around the religious-political doctrine of *jure divino* monarchy. How could a foreign Lutheran protect Anglicanism? Better to have an English Catholic, who was divinely appointed to rule, than a foreign stranger who was set on the throne for convenience.[12]

---

[9] Gibson, *The Church of England*, pp. 217-19.
[10] Colley, *Britons*, p. 19.
[11] RA, SP 49/48a: Declaration, 12 October 1720.
[12] *A Letter to the People of Great Britain* argues that the 'Protestant Succession' will not preserve the Church of England, but will, rather, tend towards 'atheism and infidelity', because it violates 'the essential spirit of Christianity' which includes obedience: RA SP40/110, ff. 10-13. Compare also 'A Prophetick Congratulatory Hymn to His Sacred Britannick Majesty King James III' (Public Record Office, Kew, SP 35/40/60): 'Our Constitution's spoilt, our Church supress'd/Religion's lost, and we are slaves at best/And shall we under such oppressions rest?; Let us but arm our Business is done/For I am sure that we are six to one/True Englishmen the English king that own'. Jacobite agents were known to make the same arguments to people to persuade them to align with the Pretender. It was reported, for example, that Christopher Layer said that 'the land was enslaved, and the People obliged to be Slaves; that though the Pretender was a Papist, there was no Difference between a Papist and a Lutheran King...' *A Report from the Committee Appointed by Order of the House of Commons to Examine Christopher Layer, and others. 1722.* Reprint in *Reports from Committees of the House of Commons*, (1803) I, p. 175.

The court of James III, then, should have been the most ecumenical of courts. In fact, the nature of the Stuart enterprise to regain the throne virtually dictated that James and his courtiers be precocious in developing religious tolerance across the Catholic-Protestant divide. English Whigs were known for their 'latitude' and toleration, but they could not envision a society where Catholics and Protestants were equal.[13]

Catholic and Protestant Jacobites in England as abroad were not immune to religious rivalries, and did not always like working with each other.[14] Nevertheless, whether or not they accepted James's reasoning that national identity was not based on religion, they usually had the grace to work closely with people who were on the other side of the Catholic-Protestant divide from themselves. Even the most ardent and dedicated Anglican churchmen worked with Catholics to restore James.[15] The latter, of course, was on the assumption that James would protect the Church of England as by law established, but it meant that they would, at least, accept a Catholic king. How the Catholics in the Jacobite camp could accept James's promise that he would keep the Test Act in place is more difficult to explain.

In theory, then, James III and his followers were closer to a genuine ecumenism than the majority of other Englishmen. Most historians have, accordingly, assigned blame for the fractiousness and ineffectiveness of the

---

[13] It is important to note, however, that popular attitudes about Catholics in English society could vary. The official rhetoric might remain shrill, but some regions were able to be more relaxed and tolerant. Some parishes watched Catholics very carefully, while others seemed quite tolerant. See Jeremy Gregory and Jeffrey S. Chamberlain, 'National and local perspectives on the Church of England in the long eighteenth century', in idem (eds.), *The National Church in Local Perspective: The Church of England and the Regions, 1660-1800* (Woodbridge, 2003), p. 24. Especially note the contrast between the parishes of Hereford (pp. 216-19) and Durham (pp. 230-34).

[14] Haydon, *Anti-Catholicism in Eighteenth-Century England*, p. 124. One illustration of this was Philip Neynoe, who was employed as a copyist during the Atterbury Plot. Neynoe was an Irish Anglican clergyman, and he participated readily with his Anglican priest friend George Kelly in the plot. However, as he testified later, he refused to endorse Catholic arguments for a Stuart restoration: when he was asked to copy a document encouraging French assistance to the Jacobites, he instead threw the document in the fire since 'the author was a Papist, and he wrote to a Cardinal, [and] most of his Arguments turn upon the Hinge of holy Church'. *Reports from Committees of the House of Commons* (1803) I, p. 266.

[15] Francis Atterbury, for instance, worked with many Catholics (such as Sir Harry Goring) in his Jacobite activity, and was very good friends with the Catholic Alexander Pope. See G.V. Bennett, *The Tory Crisis in Church and State 1688-1730: The Career of Francis Atterbury, Bishop of Rochester* (Oxford, 1975); Rex A. Barrell, *Francis Atterbury (1662-1732), Bishop of Rochester, and His French Correspondents* (Lewiston, 1990); and John Gough Nichols (ed.), 'The Letters of Pope to Atterbury when in the Tower of London' in *The Camden Miscellany* IV (1859), pp. 1-22.

Stuart court to incompetence, personality conflicts, and divided loyalties.[16] These clearly played significant roles, but the situation was more complicated than this. As this chapter will demonstrate, religious tensions also were not insignificant factors. Try as they might to be accommodating, the Stuarts continued to find religion to be their bane. James himself maintained that there was no genuine religious rift, but that enemies of his used religion as a pretext to stir up discord and create problems for his court. This was undoubtedly true to some extent, but such 'enemy' schemes could only work if, in fact, there were religious fissures that could be wedged open. Thus, though the Stuarts had done marvelously well in becoming more genuinely tolerant than virtually any other English 'court', denominational attachments and prejudices were still strong enough among adherents that they caused unavoidable conflicts. Religion may not have been, in itself, the chief cause of problems, but it was a genuine contributing factor that was not overcome. Very often the difficulties in the Jacobite court arose because of James's 'factious friends'—those who disputed over religious issues—not, as the Pretender preferred to believe, because of insidious, 'real enemies'.[17]

This chapter will not try to demonstrate these complications comprehensively, but will take several episodes—case studies, if you will—and try to discern the role of religion in those episodes. The players in these dramas are not important in and of themselves (though they could have been, had the Stuart cause been more successful), but they demonstrate in their actions and attitudes that a true ecumenism would have been very difficult to implement in the early eighteenth century. Though James III was forward thinking, his cause was hindered by religious rivalries. Had he achieved power, it is likely that these rivalries would have been magnified. The British Isles were simply not ready for easy working relationships between Catholics and Protestants. It was not, therefore, just the Whig fear of Catholicism as a foreign element that precluded tolerance across the Protestant/Catholic divide: religious

---

[16] The culprits vary, but almost always the main problem is seen as jealousy, scheming, and ineptitude. Peggy Miller argued that James 'was incapable of choosing wise or helpful advisors and more than once he placed his trust where it was lightly valued': Miller, *James*, pp. 235-6. See also Bevan, *King James the Third*, p. 86, and his characterization of various Jacobite servants; also Bennett, *Tory Crisis*, pp. 223-57. Henrietta Tayler, *The Jacobite Court at Rome in 1719* (Edinburgh, 1938) portrays the court virtually as a soap opera. The earl of Mar has come in for the most criticism. Edward Gregg, 'The Jacobite Career of John, Earl of Mar', in Eveline Cruickshanks (ed.), *Ideology and Conspiracy: Aspects of Jacobitism, 1689-1759* (London, 1982), pp. 179-200. Some older analyses are kinder, but these have lost influence. See, for instance, Maurice Bruce, 'The Duke of Mar in Exile, 1716-32', *Transactions of the Royal Historical Society* XX (1937), pp. 61-82.

[17] *The Lockhart Papers: Containing Memoirs and Commentaries upon the Affairs of Scotland from 1702 to 1715, by George Lockhart, Esq. Of Carnwath, His Secret Correspondence with the Son of King James the Second from 1718 to 1728, and his other political Writings* (London, 1817), II, pp. 265-6.

identities went too deep and could not quite yet be reconciled, even when there was strong motivation to do so.

This analysis will be focused around James III's marriage to Maria Clementina Sobieski. More than anyone else, Clementina proved to be a lightning rod for Catholic/Protestant rifts in the court. It could, in fact, be argued that, other than her crucial contribution of producing male heirs, Clementina created more difficulties for the Stuart cause than she solved. We begin in 1717, when the Jacobite court had moved to Urbino. James had been exiled from France, and, much to his dismay, found that few even of the Catholic courts of Europe wanted to harbour him. He was particularly disappointed that his uncle, the duke of Modena, whose daughter he had fallen in love with, refused to let him stay. John Erskine, the earl of Mar (created duke of Mar by James) who had failed miserably in his Scottish command during the '15, had become James's Secretary of State. Mar was clearly a problematic choice, since his loyalties were questionable.[18] Nevertheless, it did not immediately appear that Mar would create problems. Mar was accused of creating a 'Protestant party' which he used to advance his own partisans and get rid of important Catholics, including the Queen Mother and others.[19] But some saw this attempt at power redistribution by Mar as an effort to be more inclusive in order to win broader support.[20] This latter view has a lot to recommend it.

Religion was a topic of consideration when James decided to wed. Contrary to the view of some historians, however, it was not a stumbling block. James did not dictate the religion of his future wife.[21] Indeed, he seems to have been open to ladies of all persuasions. Political and diplomatic gain was far more important than religion, as is clear from the excitement about the possibility of marrying one of Peter the Great's daughters or nieces, who would, of course, have been Russian Orthodox.[22] And Mar, despite his reputation for pushing a Protestant agenda, argued that it was not advisable to seek a Protestant wife. James Murray wrote to him and recommended that he encouraged James to marry a Protestant because 'it would in all human probability reconcile the discontented Whigs to his [James's] interest...'[23] Mar understood the point, but did not

---

[18] Gregg, 'The Jacobite Career of John, Earl of Mar', 179-200.

[19] Ibid., p. 186. Gregg seems to base some of this on *A Letter from a Gentleman at R. to a Friend at L*. It is true that the pamphlet accuses Mar of advancing his Scottish countrymen, but it does so while maintaining that James was a bigoted Catholic. This discrepancy is never explained.

[20] J. Robethon reported to Lord Polwarth in May 1718 that 'Lord Mar, who governs all at the Pretender's court, has given him to understand that if he wishes to increase his following in England, he must no longer employ any papist....' Historical Manuscripts Commission, *Report on the Manuscripts of Lord Polwarth* (London, 1911), I, p. 496.

[21] Peggy Miller, *A Bride for the Pretender* (London, 1965), p. 22, claimed that it was a requirement that the bride be Catholic, but I have found no documentary support for this.

[22] See the correspondence in *CSP*, VI, pp. 222, 227, 270, 311.

[23] Ibid., V, p. 328: Murray to Mar, 14 December 1717.

accept the conclusion. Eligible Protestant women, he noted, were not in great supply. It was simply not that high a priority to worry about. A Catholic would, therefore, be fine.[24]

Another indication that Mar was not anti-Catholic is that he, evidently at James's instructions, commissioned an Irish Catholic—Charles Wogan—to search for an appropriate bride.[25] Wogan was a veteran of the '15, and had escaped from the Newgate prison shortly before he was to have been tried. Once he made his way to the continent, Wogan served James as an agent/spy in Lyons. After Wogan received James's commission, he traveled throughout the Holy Roman Empire for months looking for a woman who would make a good match for James III. He had to keep his mission quiet since the emperor was now under the influence of the elector of Hanover. He visited a number of princely courts, but did not find a woman he thought was worthy of James until he went to the Sobieski court in Ohlau (Silesia). The Sobieskis were now out of power in Poland, but Prince James Sobieski was the son of the great Jan Sobieski, who had rescued Vienna in 1683. The family was thus wealthy and illustrious, if not powerful, which made an alliance with the Sobieskis quite desirable. At the court in Ohlau, Wogan found the charms of the youngest daughter of Prince James to be irresistible.[26] Wogan liked Maria Clementina immediately, but he lingered at the court for some weeks making sure that she was interested.

Wogan's interactions with Murray and Mar indicate something about the religious climate at the Stuart court. Though at this point Wogan seemed to work well with Mar and James Murray (son of Viscount Stormont and brother-in-law of Colonel John Hay, who was in charge when Mar was gone), there was always awareness of religious differences. He wrote to James Murray a telling comment about his treatment as he passed through the city of Trent. He was held up and interrogated by the governor there. When he explained his difficulty to Murray, he felt compelled to note that it was Trent, 'whose Council, you know, has utterly condemned you and yours'.[27] Despite the fact that they worked together, there was clearly an awareness of religious difference, and he seemed to take this opportunity to rub the Protestant's nose in it.

After Wogan was successful in his quest for a suitable bride, he expected that James would commission him to return to the Sobieski court to make a marriage contract, but Wogan waited in vain for the call. Instead, Mar seems to have convinced James that it would be better to send James Murray. This does not appear to have been a partisan move. Murray had a higher rank than Wogan and was an appropriate person to send.

---

[24] Ibid., V, p. 483: Mar to Murray, 16 February 1718.
[25] Ibid., V, pp. 234-5: Mar to Wogan, 25 November 1717.
[26] In a letter to Mar 14 February 1718 (*CSP*, V, pp. 468-74), he reported the deficiencies of the princesses in Rastatt, Furstemberg, Durlach, etc. In a letter to Mar 6 February 1718 (*CSP*, VI, pp. 93-6), he sang the praises of the Sobieski women, especially Clementina.
[27] Ibid., VII, p. 607: Wogan to Murray, 5 December 1718.

Furthermore, since the Sobieski court was solidly Catholic, it would not hurt for James to send a Protestant in order to demonstrate his equanimity. Wogan, of course, could not understand this, and reacted strongly—he blamed the duke of Mar, and said that it was his prejudice against Irish Catholics that caused him to lobby for a fellow Scottish Protestant to be the representative. Mar does not seem to have had anything personal against Wogan, though Wogan took it that way, and would continue to have a respectful working relationship with him later. In fact, Mar was not always close to his Protestant Scottish brethren: in fact, he had a particularly rocky relationship with Murray. Indeed, Mar's chief ally amongst the Jacobite exiles was Wogan's fellow countryman, General Arthur Dillon.[28] But none of this mattered to Wogan: he was convinced that Mar had it in for Irish Catholics, and he was so disturbed that he tried to drown his disappointment in ale. He started a barroom brawl in Urbino shortly after the decision was made, for which he duly apologized to the Pretender.[29] Even he understood—if he did not accept—the stated rationale for the choice, however. Though still smarting and feeling slighted, he wrote: 'But the duke of Mar...knew how to change the king's intention, making him understand...what harm' appointing an Irish Catholic would 'create to the English in general, and how much offense they would take of this, should his Majesty use an Irish Catholic in such an important matter'.[30] This was just the beginning of the religious rift in the Jacobite court because of Clementina.

Murray returned with a marriage contract, but subsequent events were to put the match in doubt. Clementina and her mother made arrangements to travel from the Sobieski court in Ohlau to Italy to meet James. Once again he chose a Protestant—John Hay—to assist. Hay was to escort the women through the territories of the Holy Roman Empire to Italy. It was a dangerous venture, since the elector of Hanover was determined to stop the match at all costs. George had tried to lure other suitors by offering to

---

[28] Gregg, 'The Jacobite Career of John, Earl of Mar,' pp. 183-4.
[29] *CSP*, VI, p. 72: Wogan to Mar, 22 July 1718.
[30] In his memoirs, Wogan wrote: 'Mais le duc de Mar, son sécretaire d'etat, seigneur Esossois de beaucoup d'adresse et d'intrigue, sut détourner le roi de ce dessein, en lui faisant comprendre (avec plus de ruse que de vérité) le tort qu'il se pourroit faire auprès des Anglois en général, et l'ombrage que ceux-cy en prendroisent necessairement, si S.M. se servoit dans une affaire si importante de l'entremise d'un Catholique Irlandois. Aussi gagnat-il sur le roi d'envoyer à la place du chevalier le sieur Murray, Ecossois aussi et Protestant, par un excès de raffinement et de politique; ce qui auroit eu des suites très facheuses pour S.M. si elles n'eussent été prevenues et rendues sans effet dans la suite par l'adresse et l'intrepideité de ce même Catholiuie Irlandois, don't ce ministre avoit fait un point d'état de frustrer l'attente': 'Narrative by Charles Wogan', in John Thomas Gilbert, *Narratives of the Detention, Liberation and Marriage of Maria Clementina Stuart, styled Queen of Great Britain and Ireland* (Dublin, 1894), p. 39. James was clearly convinced that Murray would be more 'agreeable to my friends in England' than Wogan: *CSP*, VI, p. 564: James III to Ormonde, 23 June 1718.

add £10,000 to Clementina's dowry, and, failing success here, he had demanded that the emperor Charles IX arrest the Sobieskis before they could cross the border into Italy. The additional dowry attracted attention, but did not succeed in its objective. Finally, cowed by George I, Charles ordered an arrest and the wedding party was stopped and held captive in Innsbruck.

After months of complaints, protests, and negotiations, Clementina was still captive and James was despondent. He was beginning to seek other alternatives for a bride when Charles Wogan approached him and requested permission to attempt a rescue. James acquiesced as, evidently, did Mar. Soon his adventure began as he traveled back to the Sobieski court, with a false passport by Pope Clement issued in the name of Count Cernes, attempting to gain support and assistance. He had several setbacks in this process—not least of which was getting the vacillating father of the bride to back the venture—but he finally managed to put together a small rescue party, made up mostly of Wogan's relatives and soldier friends. All were his co-religionists. If anybody was being exclusive here, it was Wogan. The rescue attempt, exciting as it was, need not detain us here. Suffice it to say that Wogan and his small band of Irishmen were successful. The larger point is that Wogan was, once again, an active emissary of James and Mar. In fact, his effusive reports went directly to Mar, and Mar gave him all of the support he possibly could.[31] In fact, the relationship seemed cordial until Wogan arrived with Clementina. Then new problems arose.

First, since James was away in Spain, a proxy marriage in Bologna was arranged. James had designated James Murray to stand in for him at the altar, which he did. Jealousies undoubtedly arose from this. Wogan himself fails to mention the proxy marriage in his narrative, which seems to suggest that he resented the choice of Murray. It is certainly clear that Wogan was emotionally attached to Clementina, and that this complicated things immensely.[32] People were, of course, eager to get close to the

---

[31] There are many detailed letters about the preparations and rescue from the end of 1718 until the summer of 1719. It must be acknowledged that Wogan had to deal with James's Secretary of State. Further, James himself was unavailable since he had left for Spain on the hopes that the latter would sponsor another invasion attempt of England. For the letters between Wogan and Mar, see, for example, RA, SP 40/58; RA SP 41/46; RA, SP 41/113, etc. For the fullest print account of the rescue, see Miller, *A Wife for the Pretender*, and for Charles Wogan's own account, see Gilbert, *Narratives*, pp. 38-108.

[32] Charles always spoke of Clementina with affection. After his initial meeting with her, he wrote that she 'is the darling of the family by advantage she has over the others in point of sense, discretion, evenness of temper and a very becoming modesty...light brown hair, very pretty black eyes and genteel little features, with a good shape and a behaviour already as much formed, as regular and becoming as can arise from good education and good sense: very devout and no manner of airs or variety of humour. She has a good mixture of haughtiness in her composition, but cunning enough to disguise it upon occasion. But in the main I think I do not exaggerate, when I say that she may

celebrated Clementina, but she herself was uncomfortable. She trusted few people other than the Pretender or Wogan. James Murray had been put in charge of the king's affairs, but Clementina was not entirely comfortable with him. She insisted that Wogan remain with her, despite the fact that James had ordered him to Spain in case an expedition could be put together. Numerous disputes and jealousies arose over Murray's management of the affairs, but religious bias was not, for once, alleged as the reason, undoubtedly because complaints against Murray were made primarily by his countrymen and co-religionists.[33]

Did religion figure into these disputes? Some of it seems to have developed because of jealousies and personality differences. Murray, who seemed unprepared for the clamoring of people to receive an audience with Clementina and with the insistent applications to serve her, waved virtually everyone off. Lord Nithsdale was so angry that he told Murray that he 'had treated the Lords and Gentlemen like Footmen'.[34] But there may have been more to it than this. Clementina seems to have been overwhelmed by the number of people who wanted to get her attention. Naturally, she was far more comfortable with the people who had rescued her since she had spent so much time with them and had depended on them so completely. Given Wogan's suspicion of the Protestants in James's service, it is not unlikely that there was some effort to keep Clementina surrounded mainly by Catholics. It was reported that Clementina even despised Murray, and encouraged her rescuers to make fun of him when they were in her company.[35]

Then there was fear that Clementina was allowing herself to be influenced by extreme Catholic proselytizers. Murray wrote to James that there were 'caballs and projects' to woo Clementina into the camp of the Jesuits. Murray continued: '…by the means of a certain busy little lady two Jesuits were in the complot, and…it was a part of the scheme to have given Andrew [i.e. Clementina] a confessor of that order'.[36] The 'busy little lady' appears to have been the Countess of Nithsdale, who after Clementina arrived at Rome, contrived to gain the Queen's affections and monopolize

---

well be the most desirable wife in Europe for a Prince': *CSP*, VI, pp. 95-6. After he had brought her safely to Rome, he wrote to James that 'our admirable, I cou'd allmost say adorable Queen has given my Endeavours that blessing they have mett with, by her firmness, her prudence & a Constancy in all situations without example; your majesty was highly in the right, as to the judgment you form'd of her, where you hoped allways so much from her conduct and steadyness: they are indeed beyond anything that can be imagined in her age and sex, and not to be equalled but by her extreme affection for your person': RA, SP 43/12220 June 1719: and years later (ironically just when Clementina was in process of leaving her husband to reside in a convent), he requested permission to name his firstborn daughter after her.

[33] *The Jacobite Court at Rome*, 'Lord Pitsligo's Narrative', Scottish Historical Society, 3rd series, XXXI, pp. 59-68.
[34] Ibid., p. 60.
[35] Ibid., p. 95.
[36] RA, SP 43/123: Murray to James, 20 June 1718.

her time.[37] As late as October 1719, Lady Nithsdale was still influential with the Queen and was still pushing the Jesuit agenda. As James wrote, 'the Lady is always coming into the Queen's closet. She has no privacy'.[38] Lady Nithsdale's influence and her Jesuit connections were perceived both by Murray and James as dangerous and destructive. It is likely that the fear was that if Clementina fell under sway of the Jesuits, that she would become intolerant of James's Protestant courtiers, and the court would be in peril of religious division. James clearly took steps to wean Clementina away from the Jesuits, and wrote that the 'curbing of' Lady Nithsdale's 'project of Jesuits' would 'be no unpopular thing'. It is unclear how long this struggle over Clementina's confessors went on, but it would not be the last time that conservative Catholics would pressure and influence the Queen.

Well-wishers of the Jacobites cheered when Clementina delivered a healthy baby boy, Charles Edward, on 31 December 1720. After the successful union of James and Clementina and then the birth of their first son, the Stuarts finally seemed to have fortune on their side. There was another cruel defeat in England with the failure of the Atterbury Plot and the banishment of the Bishop of Rochester, but trouble closer to home was brewing too. Just a few months after the birth of their second son, Henry, in 1725, Clementina quarreled with James and left in a huff for a monastery, where she took up residence and remained until nearly 1730. James's and Clementina's relationship had not always been harmony and light, but this was a particularly bitter blow. The earl of Mar had recommended employing General Dillon's sister-in-law, a Mrs. Sheldon, as governess for Prince Charles. Clementina liked the idea because Mrs. Sheldon was a good Catholic, and she quickly became as much a confidante to the queen as a governess to Charles. She undoubtedly hoped that Mrs. Sheldon's Catholic influence would help tame Charles, who had already shown such an independent streak that he had refused to bow down to Pope Benedict XIII when he was presented to him shortly after his election.[39] James, on the other hand, decided in 1724 that he wanted Charles to have a balanced education, and so appointed his old Protestant minister James Murray, now earl of Dunbar, as governor. He counterbalanced this with a Catholic under-governor, Sir Thomas Sheridan, but this appointment did not placate Clementina or Mrs. Sheldon. To make things worse, James then appointed John Hay, now earl of Inverness, as his Secretary of State. Clementina had struggled with Hay in the past, and now she took these

---

[37] *Jacobite Court at Rome*, pp. 172-3: James Murray to James, 10 August 1719. The earl of Nithsdale had been persecuted for his Catholicism and his connection to the Jesuits (see *DNB*, s.v. Maxwell, William, fifth earl of Nithsdale), and, given this account, it is most likely that the countess followed suit. Peggy Miller assumes that the countess was a Protestant and was opposed by Clementina on that account. This is unlikely. Miller, *James*, p. 275.
[38] *Jacobite Court at Rome*, p. 183.
[39] Miller, *James*, p. 274.

appointments as personal affronts. She demanded that James dismiss the Hays, and when he refused, she left in a huff. As she wrote to her sister:

> Mr. Hay and his lady are the cause that I am retired into a convent. I received your letter in their behalf, and returnd you ane answer, only to do you a pleasure and to oblige the King, but it all has been to no purpose, for instead of making them my friends [sic], all the civilitys I have shown them have only served to render them the more insolent. Their unworthy treatment of me has in short reduced me to such ane extremity, and I am in such a cruell situation, that I had rather suffer death than live in the Kings palace with persons that have no religion, honour, nor conscience, and who, not content with having been the authors of so fatall a separation betwixt the King and me, are continually teazing him every day to part with his best freinds [sic] and his most faithful subjects. This at length determined me to retire into a convent, there to spend the rest of my dayes lamenting my misfortunes, after having been fretted for six years togather [sic].[40]

James, of course, maintained that this was a device of his enemies to divide and confound the Jacobite court. As was reported by the publisher of *The Memorial of The Chevalier de St. George, On Occasion of the Princess Sobieski's Retiring into a Nunnery*:

> Immediately upon the Princess's Retiring into the Nunnery of the *Benedictine* Nuns of St. *Caecilia*, she wrote a Letter to the Pope, and another to Cardinal *Paolucci*, Secretary of State, to give 'em Notice of it; and to inform 'em, that her Reason for so doing was, because the Chevalier had appointed the Earl of *Dunbar*...who is a Protestant, Governour to their eldest Son; by which his Religion was endanger'd, and heretical Notions might be infus'd into him. This was a very specious Pretence, and made her more grateful to the zealous Catholicks.[41]

It was a 'specious Pretence' that had been manufactured by those that desired to destroy James. He wrote: 'It is some time since the King suspected that his enemies and pretended friends, finding that they could not impose upon his Majesty, were endeavouring by malicious insinuations to animate the Queen against His Majesty's most faithful servants...'.[42] Likewise Lord Inverness wrote: 'A Protestant being put about the Prince has been made great use of on this occasion to enflame the people of this country...'.[43] And it may well have been true that people fanned the flames of discord—it was reported that Cardinal Alberoni was spending a good deal of time with Clementina and had been encouraging her in her demands.[44] Alberoni had been counsellor to Philip V in Spain, and had helped orchestrate the alliance with the Jacobites and abortive

---

[40] *Lockhart Papers*, II, pp. 265-6.
[41] *The Memorial of The Chevalier de St. George, On Occasion of the Princess Sobieski's Retiring into a Nunnery* (London, 1725), pp. iii-iv.
[42] *Lockhart Papers*, II, p. 243: Letter, 13 November 1725.
[43] *Lockhart Papers*, II, p. 252: Letter, 24 November 1725.
[44] Miller, *James*, p. 279.

invasion of 1719, had fallen from grace in Spain and was trying to ingratiate himself with the new pope Benedict XIII. In order to do this he had been focusing on the inappropriateness of the papacy supporting a Jacobite court that encouraged Protestantism. He pressed hard on James to oust the Protestants, but when he could get no hearing from the king, he sought out the queen, who was prone (as demonstrated by the previous episode of allowing Jesuit counsel) to conservative Catholic suggestion. Whether it was all Alberoni's doing or not is debatable, but whatever prompted it, Clementina was resolute. She left the Palazzo Muti and took up residence at the convent of Santa Cecilia.

Here again was another dispute in which religion played a central part. This one especially hurt James because, in the wake of Clementina's departure, Pope Benedict withdrew his financial support for the Jacobite court. In fact, it created many problems for him. Without papal subsidies, James had to retreat to Bologna where the cost of living was less. James was between a rock and a hard place—he resolutely refused to bow to Clementina's will in what he considered his prerogative, but he also had to try to regain the goodwill of the pope. In 1727, he resorted to bringing his eldest son to an audience with Benedict and had Charles recite his catechism to prove his fidelity to the faith. Benedict was impressed, but it did not end the schism. In fact, it took nearly five years and a new pope (Clement VII, who succeeded Benedict in February 1730) until Clementina finally agreed to end the dispute and take up residence with James again at the Palazzo Muti.[45]

Interestingly, when a visitor to Rome had an audience with the queen soon after her return, he found her ecumenical in tone, just as she had seemed before her departure.[46] He wrote that 'though she is heartily attached to her own religion, she has no rancour against those who differ from her in opinion, but would fain reclaim them by her good example and good nature'.[47] This seems to be a comment designed for public consumption much more than a genuine belief. Underneath Clementina seems to have had as much trouble being ecumenical—or even tolerant—as any eighteenth-century person.

Despite James's best efforts, he could not create a genuinely ecumenical court. It is undoubtedly true that there were other causes than religious for the difficulty in presenting a unified front. But the point stands nonetheless: religion was a good device to use to divide because it was still a powerful force that could not be entirely ignored. Try as they might to minimize the differences, most of the players found themselves motivated more by religion than they wanted to admit. Clementina had tried to adopt her husband's policy of toleration and ecumenism, but, in the end, it was impossible.

In fact, in subsequent years the court seemed to favour Protestants more and more. The duke of Wharton and the earl of Inverness converted

---

[45] Ibid., pp. 279-90.
[46] Ibid., p. 263.
[47] Ibid., p. 289.

to the Church of England in 1731.[48] Later Prince Charles himself would convert. It was simply too difficult to get any ecumenical balance in this day and age. Though the Stuart experiment was born out of exigency, it was nevertheless too liberal for its time. Catholics in particular seem to have been disappointed by this.

Charles Wogan, still clearly attached to James's interest, made some significant observations about religion when he wrote to Jonathan Swift. He apologized for closing one letter 'as folks generally do in their drink', with grousing about the ways men used religion, but the topic animated him so much that he couldn't help himself. He was disgusted and fed up with the way the people used religion to advance their own self-interest. Religion had been used over and over to justify 'vile and cruel rogeries'. In particular he seems to have been referring to the way that Catholics were treated by the English, and even in the Pretender's court. Here he was undoubtedly thinking of the way that Mar had ill-treated him. This constant abuse so incensed him that, he blurted, 'if my creed did not determine me to be a Catholic, I hereby own that I should be troubled with' no religion.[49] But this was just the point—Wogan knew that religion should not be a divider, but he himself could not entirely give it up. And because he could not, he acted in ways—undoubtedly sometimes unconsciously—that favoured Catholicism. He wanted James to marry a Catholic, not a Protestant (indeed, he seemed peeved by the efforts to ally the Stuarts with the Romanovs); he wanted a Catholic (preferably himself) to negotiate the terms and to chaperone Clementina; and he wanted James to have ministers who would favour the Catholic subjects of a Catholic king. He could not escape his own Catholicism any more than Clementina could escape hers, or any more than Mar could escape his Protestantism.

Religion had come a long way under the Jacobites. They had formed one of the first truly and openly ecumenical organizations. But religion was still an irritant and, ultimately, a divider. It is unlikely that, had religion not stood between them, they would have been so unified that they would have been able to regain the throne of England, but they certainly would not have had as many pretences for division. James did not like to admit it, but religion was a real cause of problems in his court.

It is interesting to speculate how things would have been different had the Stuarts regained the throne of England in the early eighteenth century. Would the English have had a different national identity from that which coalesced around anti-Catholicism? Would Catholicism have slowly gained ground such that the issue of religion did not divide the British from the French or Spanish? Or would the development of the English identity have been retarded? Regardless of what might have been, however, one thing can be said: given the difficulty that the progressive Stuart court had in keeping religious peace and harmony, it is very unlikely that any regime

---

[48] Ibid., p. 290.
[49] Quoted in J.M. Flood, *The Life of Chevalier Charles Wogan, An Irish Soldier of Fortune* (Dublin, 1922), p. 148.

could at this time have bridged the Catholic/Protestant divide in the British Isles.

Chapter 7

William Warburton, Divine Action, and Enlightened Christianity[*]

Robert G. Ingram

The English Enlightenment was not an irreligious moment. 'Atheism, if it existed at all, was marginal', Mark Goldie notes.[1] Neither was England's Enlightenment necessarily a secular moment.[2] J.G.A. Pocock and Brian Young have recently demonstrated its clerical, conservative nature,[3] confirming Sheridan Gilley's argument that '"enlightenment" found a home *within* the Christian churches' in the Anglo-American world.[4] Even those, like the late Roy Porter, who locate the origins of 'modernity' during the period, readily acknowledge 'that Enlightenment goals...throve in

---

[*] I thank the Center on Religion and Democracy in Charlottesville, Virginia, for supporting the research into Warburton and the staff of the Harry Ransom Humanities Research Center in Austin, Texas, for allowing me to examine the Warburton manuscripts housed there. I am particularly grateful to Bill Gibson, Pat Griffin, Paul Halliday, and Jill Ingram for their valuable advice in the preparation of the chapter. All mistakes are mine alone.

[1] Mark Goldie, 'Priestcraft and the birth of Whiggism', in Nicholas Phillipson and Quentin Skinner (eds.), *Political Discourse in Early Modern Britain* (Cambridge, 1993), p. 211. Cf. David Berman, *A History of Atheism in Britain: From Hobbes to Russell* (London, 1988); Jonathan I. Israel, *Radical Enlightenment: Philosophy and the Making of Modernity, 1650-1750* (Oxford and New York, 2001), especially pp. 599-627; and Margaret C. Jacob, *The Radical Enlightenment: Pantheists, Freemasons and Republicans* (London, 1981) for more radical strains of enlightened thought in England.

[2] Callum G. Brown, *The Death of Christian Britain: Understanding secularisation, 1800-2000* (London and New York, 2001). But cf. Blair Worden, 'The question of secularization', in Alan Houston and Steve Pincus (eds.), *A Nation Transformed: England after the Restoration* (Cambridge, 2001), pp. 20-40.

[3] J.G.A. Pocock, 'Post-Puritan England and the problem of the Enlightenment,' in Perez Zagorin (ed.), *Culture and Politics from Puritanism to the Enlightenment* (Berkeley and Los Angeles, 1980), pp. 91-112; idem, 'Clergy and Commerce: The Conservative Enlightenment in England', in R. Ajello, E. Contese, and V. Piano (eds.), *L'età dei Lumi: Studi storici sul settecento europeo in onore di Franco Venturi* (Naples, 1985), I, pp. 523-62; idem, 'Conservative Enlightenment and Democratic Revolutions: The American and French Cases in British Perspective', *Government and Opposition* 24:1 (1989), pp. 81-105; B.W. Young, *Religion and Enlightenment in Eighteenth-Century England: Theological Debate from Locke to Burke* (Oxford, 1998).

[4] Sheridan Gilley, 'Christianity and Enlightenment: An Historical Survey', *History of European Ideas* 1:2 (1981), p. 104. Emphasis in the original.

England *within* piety'.[5] We now recognize eighteenth-century England for what it was—a country whose people and culture were still decidedly Christian.[6]

Yet if the late seventeenth and early eighteenth centuries did not usher in the putative secular 'Age of Reason', they did witness innovative intellectual developments, particularly in natural philosophy, whose effect on orthodox Christian belief we do not fully appreciate.[7] This is attributable, in part, to scholarly neglect.[8] The tendency of modern scholars to privilege heterodoxies over orthodoxies has also distorted our perspective.[9] The historiography of freethinking and unbelief continues to burgeon, while that of mainstream Christian thought remains thin on the ground. Yet orthodoxy is not synonymous with irrelevancy, and, if we are to chart the topography of the eighteenth-century English intellectual and religious landscape accurately, we need to pay as much attention to Thomas Sherlock, William Warburton, and Thomas Church, as to John Toland, the earl of Shaftesbury, and David Hume. Finally, the conceptual model for understanding intellectual and theological development during the eighteenth century has a whiggish clash between new and old as its central theme. Heterodoxy and orthodoxy, reason and revelation, private conscience and church authority all skirmish one another in the larger war

---

[5] Roy Porter, 'The Enlightenment in England', in idem and Miklaus Teich (eds.), *The Enlightenment in national context* (Cambridge, 1981), p. 6. Emphasis in the original. This is a theme given fuller treatment in idem, *The Creation of the Modern World: The Untold Story of the British Enlightenment* (New York, 2000), especially pp. 96-129.

[6] For English culture, see, Jeremy Gregory, 'Christianity and Culture: Religion, the Arts and Sciences in England, 1660-1800', in Jeremy Black (ed.), *Culture and Society in Britain, 1660-1800* (Manchester and New York, 1997), pp. 102-23; W.M. Jacob, *Lay people and religion in the early eighteenth century* (Cambridge, 1996); Vladimir Jankovic, *Reading the Skies: A Cultural History of English Weather, 1650-1820* (Chicago and London, 2000), pp. 55-77. But see, for instance, John Brewer, *The Pleasures of the Imagination: English Culture in the Eighteenth Century* (London, 1997).

[7] For the purposes of this chapter, 'orthodox Christianity' has as its core the belief in the revealed, triune Christian God; the 'orthodox' are those who believed in the revealed, triune Christian God. The use of religious labels for the eighteenth century—and particularly for the mid-century period—is fraught with difficulties. For this, see William Gibson, *The Church of England, 1688-1832: Unity and Accord* (London, 2001), especially pp. 1-27; Robert G. Ingram, 'Nation, Empire, and Church: Thomas Secker, Anglican Identity, and Public Life in Georgian Britain, 1700-1770' (University of Virginia PhD dissertation, 2002), pp. 24-5; John Walsh and Stephen Taylor, 'Introduction: The Church and Anglicanism in the "long" eighteenth century', in John Walsh, Colin Haydon, and Stephen Taylor (eds.), *The Church of England, c.1689-c.1833: From Toleration to Tractarianism* (Cambridge, 1993), pp. 29-45.

[8] See, for instance, J.A.I. Champion, *The Pillars of Priestcraft Shaken: The Church of England and its Enemies, 1660-1730* (Cambridge, 1992), p. 4.

[9] B.W. Young, 'Religious History and the Eighteenth-Century Historian', *Historical Journal* 43:3 (September 2000), pp. 849-68 explores the secularization of the historiography of eighteenth-century England.

between modernity and pre-modernity.[10] In this conflict, deists, Arians, Socinians, unitarians, atheists, and other heterodox figures are the enlightened harbingers of modernity while the orthodox are the blinkered opponents of progress.

Among the most influential proponents of this view is Margaret Jacob, who argues that the 'new science from Descartes to Newton offered a radically altered picture of nature' in which a 'vision of order and harmony, God's work, replaced biblical texts and stories, God's word'.[11] 'Gradually, highly educated Protestants and Catholics thought more about God's work as revealed by science than by his biblical Word', she contends.[12] The enlightened jettisoned their belief in miracles and divine interventions in favour of a natural theology, 'a rather cerebral religion'. This 'Newtonian Christianity' (or 'liberal Christianity') posed a 'threat to the metaphysics of Orthodox Christianity [that] was real and immediate'.[13] The orthodox feared the new learning, imaging 'a slippery slope that began with Newton's natural philosophy, leading its adherents to tumble in the direction of antitrinitarianism, winding up caught on the ledge of deism, or plunging into the abyss of atheism. For the orthodox, Newtonian science presented a no-win alternative'.[14] Someone forgot to tell that to orthodox Christians in the mid-eighteenth century. Indeed, Jacob's interpretative schema fails to help us understand someone like William Warburton (1698-1779), for whom orthodox Christianity and Newtonian natural philosophy were mutually supportive, rather than mutually exclusive.[15] This chapter anatomizes Warburton's providential theology, considering in turn his understanding of miracles, prodigies, and particular providences in human affairs. In illustrating just how one enlightened, orthodox Christian understood and explained his religious beliefs in light of the new science, it takes heed of J.G.A. Pocock's salutary reminder that orthodoxy 'is not a mere rejection of tensions or an attempt to freeze or deny them; it is a particular way of responding to tensions and seeking to recombine them' in order to maintain 'durable and traditional positions'.[16] Warburton's providential theology did not reject the new science, but rather found that

---

[10] This view pervades even works that take orthodoxy seriously. See, for instance, Roger D. Lund (ed.), *The Margins of Orthodoxy: Heterodox Writing and Cultural Response, 1660-1750* (Cambridge, 1995).

[11] Margaret C. Jacob, *Scientific Culture and the Making of the Industrial West* (Oxford, 1997), p. 74.

[12] Margaret C. Jacob, *The Enlightenment* (Boston and New York, 2001), p. 18.

[13] Jacob, *Scientific Culture and the Making of the Industrial West*, pp. 75, 79.

[14] Betty Jo Teeter Dobbs and Margaret C. Jacob, *Newton and the Culture of Newtonianism* (Atlantic Highlands, NJ, 1995), p. 100.

[15] J.C.D. Clark, *English Society, 1660-1832: Religion, ideology and politics during the ancien regime* (Cambridge, 2000), p. 29; Gregory, 'Christianity and Culture: Religion, the Arts and Sciences in England, 1660-1800', p. 112.

[16] J.G.A. Pocock, 'Within the margins: the definitions of orthodoxy', in Lund (ed.), *The Margins of Orthodoxy*, p. 35.

it strengthened traditional orthodox Christian beliefs regarding God's sovereignty over his creation.[17]

William Warburton—memorably described by Leslie Stephen as having 'led the life of a terrier in a rat-pit, worrying all theological vermin'—was one of the most visible and vituperative orthodox apologists of his day.[18] Though he rose to the office of bishop in the Church of England, Warburton himself reckoned that his most important work 'in the service of religion' had been polemical, rather than pastoral: 'In defending Revelation, and the established church of this land, against the rude attacks of ribald writers of all denominations, atheists, deists, libertines, freethinkers, bigots, and fanatics'.[19] Elsewhere, he characterized his life as 'a warfare on earth; that is to say, with bigots and libertines, against whom I have denounced eternal war, like Hannibal against Rome, at the altar'.[20] Part of his work 'defending Revelation' required Warburton to explain the mechanics of providence, for it was through acts of providence that the

---

[17] There were ultra-trinitarian Christians who did reject Newtonian natural philosophy. In *Moses's Principia* (1724-47), John Hutchinson argued that the original Hebrew Bible contained not just religious truth, but also the only true system of natural philosophy. The Hutchinsonians, however, were never more than a fringe group. G.N. Cantor, 'Revelation and the cyclical cosmos of John Hutchison', in L.J. Jordanova and Roy S. Porter (eds.), *Images of the Earth: Essays in the History of the Environmental Sciences* (Chalfont St. Giles, 1978), pp. 3-22; John C. English, 'John Hutchinson's Critique of Newtonian Heterodoxy', *Church History* 68:3 (September 1999), pp. 581-97; C.B. Wilde, 'Hutchinsonianism, Natural Philosophy and Religious Controversy in Eighteenth Century Britain', *History of Science* 18:1 (March 1980), pp. 1-24; and Young, *Religion and Enlightenment in Eighteenth-Century England*, pp. 136-51 provide useful introductions to Hutchinson and the Hutchinsonians.

[18] Leslie Stephen, *History of English Thought in the Eighteenth Century* (London, 1902), I, vii:2. John Selby Watson, *The Life of William Warburton, D.D.* (London, 1863); A.W. Evans, *Warburton and the Warburtonians: A Study in Some Eighteenth-Century Controversies* (London, 1932); Robert M. Ryley, *William Warburton* (Boston, 1984); R.W. Greaves, 'The Working of the Alliance: A Comment on Warburton', in G.V. Bennett and J.D. Walsh (eds.), *Essays in Modern English Church History: in memory of Norman Sykes* (Oxford, 1966), pp. 163-80; Stephen Taylor, 'William Warburton and the Alliance of Church and State', *Journal of Ecclesiastical History* 43:2 (April 1992), pp. 271-86; Young, *Religion and Enlightenment in Eighteenth-Century England*, pp. 167-212; and David Sorkin, 'William Warburton: The Middle Way of "Heroic Moderation"', *Dutch Review of Church History* 82:2 (2002), pp. 262-300 provide useful introductions to Warburton and his thought.

[19] Quoted in Young, *Religion and Enlightenment in Eighteenth-Century England*, p. 168. John Redwood, *Reason, Ridicule and Religion: The Age of Enlightenment in England, 1660-1750* (London, 1976); Isabel Rivers, 'Responses to Hume on Religion by Anglicans and Dissenters', *Journal of Ecclesiastical History* 52:4 (October 2001), pp. 675-95; and Brian Young, 'Theological Books from *The Naked Gospel* to *Nemesis of Faith*', in Isabel Rivers (eds.), *Books and their Readers in Eighteenth-Century England: New Essays* (London and New York, 2001), pp. 79-104 usefully introduce the culture of religious debate during the period.

[20] Quoted in Stephen, *History of English Thought in the Eighteenth Century*, I, vii:2.

triune Christian God revealed himself to man. Likewise, Christians believed that the omnipotent God continued to govern the 'moral universe' providentially. As the orthodox saw it, the question they needed to address was less *whether* God intervened than *how* he intervened. And as we shall see, Newtonian natural philosophy provided Warburton with the ability to explain the mechanics of divine action in a language even those who were not his co-religionists could understand.

I

Providence is the longstanding Christian doctrine regarding God's sovereignty over his creation. It is premised on the notion that God is not simply a cosmic watchmaker who created the universe and then left it to run unattended. Rather, the omnipotent, omniscient, and eternal God who created and sustains the universe for supremely good purposes has a plan for mankind. In the very way he designed and ordered the universe, he ensured that many of these good purposes would be achieved—this is his general providence. At other times, though, God intervenes directly in natural and human events to secure his divine designs. These interventions come through fulfilled prophecies, through miracles, and through other non-miraculous acts—this is his particular providence.

Providence was an important language of causation in early modern England.[21] And it remained so well into the eighteenth century, though 'most accounts of this period tend to pass over it very quickly, if indeed it is acknowledged at all'.[22] Eighteenth-century English men and women understood divine action rather differently from their forebears in the sixteenth and seventeenth centuries, though. In the post-Reformation mental world in which providence figured so prominently, few found God's general and particular providences contradictory. Yet a few vocal religious sceptics during the 'long' eighteenth century questioned how to reconcile the watchmaker God who created the seemingly immutable laws that guide nature, with the interventionist God of the Bible who worked miracles and fulfilled prophecies. Was God only generally provident? Did he merely create the world and regularize the mechanisms that governed it? Or, was he instead specially provident? Did he intervene in the natural

---

[21] Alexandra Walsham, *Providence in Early Modern England* (Oxford, 1999) is now the standard treatment of its subject for the post-Reformation period. Alister McGrath, *Reformation Thought: An Introduction* (Oxford, 1988), pp. 86-93 examines providential theology's central importance for the magisterial reformers, particularly Calvin.

[22] Bob Harris, *Politics and the Nation: Britain in the Mid-Eighteenth Century* (Oxford, 2002), pp. 290-95, at p. 290. See also, Clark, *English Society, 1660-1832*, pp. 107-12 and D. Napthine and W.A. Speck, 'Clergymen and Conflict, 1660-1763', in W.J. Sheils (ed.), *The Church and War*, Studies in Church History XX (Oxford, 1983), pp. 238-46.

order of things to warn humans and fulfil prophecies to instruct them?[23] Orthodox Christians believed God was specially provident, and it fell to orthodox apologists to explain why and how God minutely governed his creation. This chapter examines the arguments and languages Warburton used to explain three types of providential action—miracles, prodigies, and divine interventions in human events.

Protestants had always suspected Roman Catholic miracles, but freethinkers assaulted the very concept of the miraculous, questioning revealed religion's necessity and the historical credibility of miracle reports.[24] In his defence of the miraculous, Warburton offered a twin-prong response, arguing from Scripture why miracles were necessary and from Newtonian natural philosophy how they occurred. His most sustained defence of Christian miracles came in *Julian, or a discourse concerning the earthquake and fiery eruption, which defeated the emperor's attempt to rebuild the Temple at Jerusalem* (1750).[25] 'I have taken upon me to defend a Miracle of the fourth century; and to enquire into the nature of that evidence, which will demand the assent of every reasonable man to a miraculous fact,' he announced at the work's outset.[26] He began writing sometime in the spring of 1749. 'I have been a little diverted upon an important subject: viz. in writing a Discourse to prove the miraculous interposition of Providence in defeating Julian's attempt to rebuild the Temple at Jerusalem', he confided to Philip Doddridge in June 1749. Three sections were to comprise the discourse: the first, 'to establish the truth by human testimony, and the nature of the fact'; the second, 'An Answer to Objections'; and a final part, to enquire 'into the nature of that evidence which is sufficient to claim a rational assent to the miraculous fact'.[27]

---

[23] Redwood, *Reason, Ridicule and Religion*, p. 145 suggests that this was 'the great debate of the new age'.

[24] Israel, *Radical Enlightenment*, pp. 218-29 provides a useful introduction to the deistic critique of miracles. For English deism in particular, see also James A. Herrick, *The Radical Rhetoric of the English Deists: The Discourse of Skepticism, 1680-1750* (Columbia, SC, 1997), pp. 145-79.

[25] This is a work infrequently studied by Warburton scholars, but one which contemporaries thought significant. Montesquieu, for instance, praised *Julian*: Richard Hurd, 'A Discourse, by way of a general preface to the quarto edition of Bishop Warburton's Works, containing some of the Life, Writings, and Character of the Author', in *The Works of William Warburton, Lord Bishop of Gloucester. In Seven Volumes* (London, 1798), I, pp. 65-6 [hereafter: *WWW*].

[26] *Julian*, in *WWW*, VII, p. 362. See Harry Ransom Humanities Research Center, Austin, Texas, Warburton MSS, Letter 3: Warburton to Thomas Balguy, 7 February 1751 for Warburton's thoughts on whether miracles should be considered singly and as a group [hereafter: Warburton MSS].

[27] *Letters to and from the Rev. Philip Doddridge, DD late of Northampton: published from the originals: with notes explanatory and biographical*, edited by Thomas Stedman (Shrewsbury, 1790), p. 206: Warburton to Doddridge, 10 June 1749. Warburton never completed the third of these sections. It is worth noting, as well, that Warburton intended to defend orthodox Christianity, rather than orthodox Anglicanism: 'My chief design in writing is in behalf of our common

Julian interrogates the circumstances surrounding the failed rebuilding of the Temple at Jerusalem in the mid-fourth century AD.[28] The Roman emperor Julian (the Apostate) had encouraged the Jews of Jerusalem to rebuild their Temple in 363, but the project was abandoned after an earthquake at the site killed a number of builders and after the emperor himself died in June of that year. Warburton aimed to prove that the earthquake which brought the construction to a close was wrought directly by God.

David Hume (1711-76) was one of Warburton's targets in *Julian*. Warburton loathed Hume. 'He is an atheistical Jacobite, a monster as rare with us as a hippogriff', he inveighed upon the publication of Hume's *History of England* (1754-63).[29] And none could dissuade him from these views. 'You have often told me of this man's moral virtues', he wrote Andrew Millar, Hume's publisher. 'He may have many, for aught I know; but let me observe to you, there are vices of the mind as well as of the body: and I think a wickeder mind, and a more obstinately bent on public mischief, I never knew'.[30] Warburton eventually succeeded in getting Hume's 'Of Suicide' and 'Of the Immortality of the Soul' banned, and his opposition compelled Hume to tone down *The Natural History of Religion* (1757).[31] When he was writing *Julian*, Warburton had in mind Hume's *Essay concerning Human Understanding* (1748), in which Hume assaulted the very foundations of religious belief and in which he attacked the miraculous in particular. But Warburton was unsure whether the Scot was worth challenging explicitly. To Richard Hurd, he confided, 'I am strongly tempted too to have a stroke at Hume in parting. He is the author of a little book called Philosophical Essays. In one part of which he argues against the Being of God, and in another (very needlessly you will say) against the possibility of miracles'. Warburton wanted 'to do justice on his argument against miracles, which...might be done in very few words'. But, he worried, this might actually gain Hume a wider readership: 'But does he deserve notice? Is he known amongst you? Pray answer me these questions. For if his own weight keeps him down, I should be sorry to contribute to his advancement to any place but the pillory'.[32] In the end, Warburton made only passing reference to Hume in *Julian*.

Christianity, and not to support or discredit the particular doctrines of this or that church or age': Warburton, *Julian*, p. 362.

[28] For the historical background to this incident, see Polymnia Athanassiadi, *Julian: An Intellectual Biography* (New York, 1992; reprint of 1981 edition), pp. 163ff; G.W. Bowersock, *Julian the Apostate* (London, 1978), pp. 120-22; and Robert L. Wilken, *John Chrysostom and the Jews: Rhetoric and Reality in the Late Fourth Century* (Berkeley, 1983), pp. 134-5, 140-45. I thank Jackie Maxwell for these references.

[29] Francis Kilvert (ed.), *A Selection from the Unpublished Papers...of William Warburton* (London, 1841), p. 257: Warburton to Joseph Atwell, 8 January 1755.

[30] Ibid., pp. 309-10: Warburton to Millar, 7 February 1757.

[31] Young, *Religion and Enlightenment in Eighteenth-Century England*, pp. 210-11.

[32] *Letters from a late eminent prelate*, pp. 10-11: Warburton Hurd, 28 September 1749. See also, *Letters to and from the Rev. Philip Doddridge*, pp. 207-9: Warburton

It was actually a heterodox Anglican cleric, rather than the Scottish sceptic, that was Warburton's primary target in *Julian*. Indeed, he took up his pen in early 1749 to rebut Conyers Middleton's *Free Enquiry into the miraculous powers which are supposed to have existed in the Christian Church through several successive ages* (1748), a work that challenged the reliability of miracles from the patristic age, though not miracles generally nor biblical ones in particular.[33] Worried about 'the conclusions which licentious men are apt to draw from Dr. Middleton's book, against Revelation', Warburton aimed 'to prove a miracle recorded in Ecclesiastical history: and to shew that these miracles stand on a different footing from those recorded in the Gospel'.[34]

Conyers Middleton (1683-1750) was an Anglican cleric who spent his entire career at Cambridge. Denied elevation to the episcopal bench because of his theological heterodoxy, Middleton produced work that was 'finely balanced between thoroughgoing latitudinarianism and disbelief'.[35] He accepted the possibility of miracles, but he insisted that one needed a litmus test to distinguish between real and false miracles. His tests were those of the deists. Neither necessary nor reliably reported, the miracles of patristic age were suspect, he contended. Because he voiced these kinds of views from within the Church, Middleton drew down upon himself the full weight of orthodox polemic, particularly from Thomas Sherlock's circle.[36] Warburton disagreed with Middleton on miracles, but was fond of

---

to Doddridge, 19 June 1749, in which Warburton speculated that an attack on Hume to end the second section of *Julian* might actually help assuage some of the book's potential critics: '...and as the subject of the second part may be a little ticklish, perhaps it may be prudent to conciliate warm tempers by such a conclusion'.

[33] Evans, *Warburton and the Warburtonians*, p. 171; Hurd, 'A Discourse', p. 63. *Literary Illustrations*, pp. 99-101: Warburton to Birch, 6 April 1739 suggests that Warburton's interest in Julian the Apostate dated back at least a decade before he began writing the discourse. Hume actually believed that his *Enquiry* had been overshadowed by Middleton's work: 'On my return from Italy, I had the mortification to find all England in a Ferment on account of Dr. Middletons Free Enquiry; while my performance was entirely overlooked and neglected', he groused. Quoted in John Valdimir Price, 'The reading of philosophical literature', in Isabel Rivers (ed.), *Books and their Readers in Eighteenth-Century England* (Leicester, 1982), p. 171.

[34] John Nichols, *Illustrations of the Literary History of the Eighteenth Century* (London, 1817), II, pp. 160-61: Warburton to Nathaniel Forster, 13 December 1749 [hereafter: *Literary Illustrations*].

[35] John Gascoigne, *Cambridge in the age of the Enlightenment: Science, religion and politics from the Restoration to the French Revolution* (Cambridge, 1989), p. 139. While there is no modern biography of Middleton, John Hunt, *Religious Thought in England from the Reformation to the End of Last Century* (London, 1873), III, pp. 60-70 and Stephen, *English Thought in the Eighteenth Century*, I, vi:66-83 serve as useful introductions to his thought.

[36] Edward Carpenter, *Thomas Sherlock, 1678-1761* (London, 1936), pp. 305-10.

him personally.[37] And, in an uncharacteristic move, he revised *Julian*'s introduction to soften his criticism of Middleton.[38]

Warburton countered the arguments against miracles first by attempting to prove why they happened. God involved himself in the world through acts of particular providence, such as miracles, because he was responsible for both the natural and moral government of the universe. God, 'the moral Governor of the universe, whose essential character it is, not to leave himself without a witness, doth frequently employ the physical and civil operations of the natural system, to support and reform the moral', Warburton argued. It followed that if God really were to govern the moral universe, 'he must manifest his dominion in whatever world he is pleased to station and to exercise his accountable and probationary creatures. In man's state and condition here, natural and civil events are the proper instruments of moral government'.[39]

Deists refused 'to make God the moral, that is, the close, the minute and immediate inspector of human actions' because they thought this role both degraded the creator of the universe and defied reason.[40] Warburton rejected this out of hand, arguing that reasonableness is not the appropriate criteria to judge God's actions.[41] Rather, the appropriate touchstone of the miraculous was necessity. A miracle was 'of so high importance as to be even necessary to Revelation, and to the religious Dispensation to which it belongs'.[42] Elsewhere he explained, that when a miracle is 'performed by the immediate power of God, without the intervention of his servants', it must meet one of two criteria: 'either that an inspired servant of God predicted it, and declared its purpose beforehand...or that it be seen to interpose so seasonably and critically as to cover and secure God's moral government from inevitable dishonour'.[43] The miracle of the fiery eruption that halted the construction on the Temple at Jerusalem in 363 was the kind 'necessary to secure God's moral government from dishonour'. For in the Bible, God had providentially linked the Temple's destruction and the rise of Christianity: '...the truth of Christianity must stand or fall with the ruin or restoration of the temple at Jerusalem; for if that temple should be rebuilt for the purpose of Christian worship, Christianity could not support its pretensions; nor the Prophets, nor Jesus, the truth of their predictions'.[44]

---

[37] *Letters from a late eminent prelate to one of his friends*, p. 6: Warburton to Richard Hurd, 6 August 1749.
[38] *Literary Illustrations*, II, p. 168: Warburton to Nathaniel Forster, 5 February 1750; *Letters from a late eminent prelate*, pp. 28-30: Warburton to Hurd, 10 February 1750.
[39] William Warburton, *Natural and civil events the instruments of God's moral government. A sermon preached the last public fast-day, at Lincoln's-Inn-Chappel* (London, 1756), p. 4.
[40] Warburton, 'God's Moral Government' (1752), in *WWW*, V, p. 30.
[41] Warburton, 'On the Resurrection', in *WWW*, V, pp. 484-5.
[42] Ibid., p. 474.
[43] Warburton, *Julian*, p. 513. See also, idem, *The Divine Legation of Moses*, p. 670.
[44] Ibid., pp. 363-74 at pp. 373-4.

Having proven *why* God could not allow the Temple to be reconstructed, Warburton turned to explain *how* he had stopped the construction through a miracle. He acknowledged that God's operations were often beyond human comprehension. 'The ordinary Dispensations of Providence are dark and perplexing, and have ever wore a double Face', he conceded, 'from which, with equal Force, may be drawn contrary Conclusions, according to the Humour or Interest of the Contemplator'.[45] Nonetheless, he thought it possible at times to discern the mechanisms of divine action.

In the section 10 ('Of Miracles') of his *Enquiry*, Hume defined a miracle as 'a violation of the laws of nature' and as 'a transgression of a law of nature by a particular volition of the Deity, or by the interposition of some invisible agent'. By this definition miracles were impossible: 'as a firm and unalterable experience has established these laws, the proof against a miracle, from the very nature of its fact, is as entire as any argument from experience as can possibly be imagined'.[46] Warburton disagreed wholly with Hume's definition. Miracles, he argued as far back as 1727, did not violate nature's immutable laws. Rather, a miracle 'is the giving new laws to those Portions of Matter within the Sphere of the Miracle, which carry with them the equal Marks of stupendous Wisdom and Power'.[47] Later he held that '[t]he agency of a superior Being on any part of the visible creation lying within the reach of our senses, whereby it acquires properties and directions different from what we hold it capable of receiving from the established laws of matter and motion, we call a Miracle'.[48] Miracles came in three varieties. First are those 'where the laws of nature are suspended or reversed' (e.g., Jesus raising Lazarus from the dead); second are 'those which only give a new direction to its Laws' (e.g., water pouring forth from stone); and third are those which 'compounded of the other two, where the laws of nature are in part arrested and

---

[45] Warburton, *A Critical and Philosophical Enquiry into the causes of prodigies and miracles*, p. 122.

[46] David Hume, *An Enquiry concerning Human Understanding*, edited by Tom L. Beauchamp (Oxford, 1999), p. 173. Like Middleton, Hume also assailed the veracity of historical testimony of miracles. The secondary literature on Hume's critique of miracles is voluminous. R.M. Burns, *The Great Debate on Miracles: From Joseph Glanvill to David Hume* (London and Toronto, 1981), especially pp. 131ff.; J.C.A. Gaskin, 'Hume on religion', in David Fate Norton (ed.), *The Cambridge Companion to Hume* (Cambridge, 1993), pp. 313-34; M.A. Stewart, 'Hume's historical view of miracles', in idem and John P. Wright (eds.), *Hume and Hume's Connexions* (University Park, PA, 1994), pp. 171-200; and David Wootton, 'Hume's "Of Miracles": Probability and Irreligion', in M.A. Stewart (ed.), *Studies in the Philosophy of the Scottish Enlightenment*, pp. 191-229 provide useful introductions to his thought.

[47] William Warburton, *A Critical and Philosophical Enquiry into the causes of prodigies and miracles, as related by historians. With an essay towards restoring method and purity in history...In two parts* (London, 1727), p. 127.

[48] Warburton, *Julian*, p. 504.

suspended; and, in part only, differently directed' (e.g., the Biblical flood).[49] Either God immediately effected these miracles himself or he worked through one of his messengers, such as the Apostles.

Warburton's understanding here of divine action and the miraculous evidenced his debt to contemporary natural philosophy. Like many, he found support for his religious beliefs in science.[50] Bacon, Boyle, Locke, and Pascal were among 'the great Masters of science' who held a 'warm attachment to Revelation'.[51] The nascent field of geology, for instance, spoke to the truth of Christianity. 'In natural philosophy', Warburton wrote, 'more exact enquiries have been made into the contents of the superior covering the terraqueous Globe; the peculiarities of whose arrangements give the strongest evidence of the Mosaic account of the Deluge'.[52] Similar fossils, he noted, were found across the earth and in varying types of soils: 'Had these adventitious fossils not been found in every quarter of the Globe, we would not conclude the Deluge to have been universal'. However, he continued, 'when we see them spread over every climate, and yet only in such soils as are proper for the preservation of foreign bodies, we rightly conclude them to be the deposit of a Deluge of waters which covered the whole face of the Earth'.[53] Science and religion effortlessly supported one another in instances like these.

The star that shone brightest among the scientific firmament for Warburton and his contemporaries was Isaac Newton. Now Warburton did read Newton's biblical scholarship with a wary eye. Of *Observations upon the Prophecies of Daniel, and the Apocalypse of St. John* (1732), he commented, 'though he was a prodigy in his way, yet I never expected great things in this kind...from a man who spent all of his days looking through a telescope'.[54] Warburton expressed great interest in Newton's scientific writings, though, and Newtonian natural philosophy informed his understanding of divine action in the natural world.[55] 'And the

---

[49] Ibid., pp. 504-8.
[50] Nigel Aston, *Christianity and Revolutionary Europe, c.1750-1830* (Cambridge, 2002), p. 114 rightly notes that during this period, '[w]hatever the individual's precise religious outlook, he could look to the advance in the natural sciences for its justification'.
[51] Warburton, 'The Influence of Learning on Revelation', in *WWW*, V, pp. 195, 196. See also, idem, 'The Rise of Antichrist', in ibid., V, p. 469.
[52] Warburton, 'The Influence of Learning on Revelation', p. 195.
[53] Ibid., p. 196. Roy Porter, *The Making of Geology: Earth Science in Britain, 1660-1815* (Cambridge, 1977) surveys the different theories of the earth during the period.
[54] *Literary Illustrations*, II, p. 21: Warburton to William Stukeley, 10 February 1733. See also, *The Divine Legation of Moses* Book IV, section v, in which refutes Newton's *Chronology of Ancient Kingdom's Amended* (1728).
[55] Warburton MSS, Letter 4: Warburton to Robert Taylor, 23 December 1729, finds Warburton asking Taylor to buy him a copy of Henry Pemberton's *A View of Sir Isaac Newton's Philosophy* (London, 1728). It was clear that Warburton knew large parts of Newton's natural philosophical work, for Thomas Birch published Warburton's thoughts on Newton's theories of the solar system and

immortal Theory of Newton absolutely demonstrates that intimate relation which Moses speaks of, between the Creator and his work', Warburton argued.[56] The portion of Newton's 'immortal Theory' he found especially useful concerned the distinction between matter and activity. Newton theorized that matter was wholly inert and had activity imposed upon it by a God who was immanent in the world.[57] Likewise, Newton distinguished between causes, so that the physical laws governing nature were but second causes created and put in place by God, the first cause. He also held that God ruled the world providentially, not just through the general mechanical laws of nature that governed his creation, but also through particular voluntary actions.[58] The Boyle lecturers annually popularized and more explicitly Christianized Newton's natural philosophy.[59] Warburton was parroting the Boyle lecturers when he drew the connections for his audiences at Lincoln's Inn between Newtonian natural philosophy and God's governance of the universe. When we examine the universe 'on the unerring experience of the Newtonian physics', Warburton argued, it is evident 'that God is intimately present to every particle of Matter, at every point of Space, and in every instance of a Being':

> For a *vis inertiae*, or resistance to the change of its present state, being an essential quality of Matter, and inconsistent with any motive force, or power in that Substance, all those effects commonly ascribed to a certain essence residing in it, such as gravity, or attraction, elasticity, repulsion, or whatever

---

of colours in his *Life of Newton: Literary Illustrations*, II, pp. 89-90: Warburton to Thomas Birch, 17 June 1738.

[56] Warburton, 'The Influence of Learning on Revelation', p. 196.

[57] P.M. Heimann and J.E. McGuire, 'Newtonian forces and Lockean powers: concepts of matter in eighteenth-century thought', *Historical studies in the physical sciences* 3 (1971), pp. 233-306; P.M. Heimann, 'Voluntarism and Immanence: Conceptions of Nature in Eighteenth-century Thought,' *Journal of the History of Ideas* 39:2 (April-June 1978), pp. 271-83; Simon Schaffer, 'Natural philosophy,' in G.S. Rousseau and Roy Porter (eds.), *The Ferment of Knowledge: Studies in the Historiography of Eighteenth-Century Science* (Cambridge, 1980), pp. 58-71; C.B. Wilde, 'Matter and Spirit as Natural Symbols in Eighteenth-Century British Natural Philosophy', *British Journal of the History of Science* 15:2 (July 1982), pp. 99-115; and John W. Yolton, *Thinking Matter: Materialism in Eighteenth-Century Britain* (Minneapolis, 1983), pp. 90-105 explore eighteenth-century British understandings of matter and their theological implications.

[58] For this, see David Kubrin, 'Newton and the Cyclical Cosmos: Providence and the Mechanical Philosophy', *Journal of the History of Ideas* (July-September 1967), pp. 325-46 and Ayval Ramati, 'The hidden truth of creation: Newton's method of fluxions', *British Journal of the History of Science* 34:4 (December 2001), pp. 417-38.

[59] Henry Guerlac and M.C. Jacob, 'Bentley, Newton, and Providence (The Boyle Lectures Once More)', *Journal of the History of Ideas* 30:3 (September 1969), pp. 307-18; Margaret C. Jacob, *The Newtonians an the English Revolution, 1689-1720* (New York, 1976), pp. 162-200; and John Gascoigne, 'From Bentley to the Victorians: The Rise and Fall of British Newtonian Natural Theology,' *Science in Context* 2:2 (Autumn 1988), pp. 222-6 discuss the influence of the early Boyle Lectures.

other tendencies to Motion are observed in Matter, are not powers naturally belonging to it, or what can possibly be made inherent in it. So that these qualities, without which, Matter would be utterly unfit for use, must needs be produced by the immediate influence of the first Cause, incessantly performing, by his almighty finger, the minutest Office in the Material Oeconomy; working still near us, round us, within us, and in every part of us.[60]

The distinction between matter and activity and between first and second causes, then, provided the intellectual foundation of Warburton's explanations of God's providential interventions in the natural world.[61] Nowhere is this more evident than in *Julian*.

Construction in 363 on the Temple at Jerusalem was brought to a halt by a series of extraordinary natural occurrences, all of which, Warburton argued, could be traced directly to God's hand. Collating, examining, and comparing the patristic testimony regarding the abandoned Temple reconstruction,[62] Warburton identified the chain of natural events that together led authorities to abandon the Temple reconstruction. 'The first signs the Almighty gave of his approaching judgement, were the storms, tempests, and whirlwinds', he wrote. 'These instruments of vengeance performed their office, in the dispersion of loose materials'.[63] Shortly thereafter, lightning appeared. 'The effects of this produced were, first, destroying the more solid materials, and melting down the iron instruments: and secondly, impressing that prodigious mark on the bodies and garments of the assistants...'. The lightning was prelude to an earthquake which 'cast out the stones of the old foundations...it shook the earth into the new-dug foundation...and it overthrew the adjoining buildings and porticos'. Then followed a 'fiery eruption, which destroyed and maimed so many of the workmen and assistants; and at length forced the undertakers to give over the attempt as desperate'. Finally, there appeared 'a lucid cross in the heavens, circumscribed within a luminous circle'. This, Warburton noted, was a fitting symbolic end to the chain of events: 'Nature, put so suddenly into commotion by its Creator, was, on the despair and dispersion of its enemies, as suddenly calmed and

---

[60] Warburton, 'God's Moral Government', pp. 33-4.
[61] Stephen D. Snoblen, '"God of gods, and Lord of lords": The Theology of Isaac Newton's General Scholium to the *Principia*', *Osiris* 16:1 (2001), pp. 169-208 argues that while the *Principia*'s physics were 'consistent with revealed religion', Newton was trying, in this work, to 'corrupt Trinitarian hermeneutics'. This was not an aspect of Newton's theological programme of his contemporary Christian admirers, like Warburton, were aware. Larry Stewart, 'Seeing Through the Scholium: Religion and Reading Newton in the Eighteenth Century', *History of Science* 34:2 (June 1996), pp. 123-65 examines the later reception of Newton's religious thought.
[62] The considerable attention Warburton devoted in *Julian* to the vindicating the truth of patristic testimony tempers the conclusions of G.V. Bennett, 'Patristic Authority in the Age of Reason', *Oecumenica* (1971/2), pp. 72-87.
[63] Unless otherwise noted, all quotations that follow in this paragraph are drawn from Warburton, *Julian*, pp. 448-51.

composed....And what could be conceived so proper to close this tremendous scene, or to celebrate this decisive victory, as the Cross triumphant, incircled with the Heroic symbol of conquest?'.

Warburton pointed out that a number of these phenomenon could be explained scientifically. The encircled cross in the sky, for instance, 'was neither more nor less than one of those meteoric lights, in a still and clouded sky, which are not unfrequently seen in solar or lunar halos', he averred.[64] The crosses were also phosphorific: 'They shown at night, and were dark, and smokey-coloured by day...the very property...of Phosphori'.[65] Likewise, the lightning that attended the fiery eruption was subject to scientific explanation. Air 'put into a violent motion, always produces lightning, when it abounds with matter susceptible of inflammation,' he explained. 'And those columns of air, which lie over places that labour with convulsive throws to cast out an inkindled matter from its entrails, must needs be impregnated with vast quantities of sulphurous particles, which the earth...exudes from its pores, and which the solar heat draws upwards'.[66]

Where natural philosophy and orthodox theology converged was in Warburton's explanation of what set these natural events in motion. Having examined the evidence, Warburton concluded 'that the mineral and metallic substances (which, by their accidental fermentation, are wont to take fire and burst into flames)...would have slept, and still continued in the quiet innoxious state in which they had so long remained had not the breath of the Lord awoke and kindled them'. Having 'miraculously interposed to stir up the rage of these firey elements, and yet to restrain their fury to the objects of his vengeance, he then again suffered them to do their ordinary office'. For, he noted, 'Nature thus directed would, by the exertion of its own laws, answer all the ends of the moral designation'. For this reason the effects which attended the fiery eruption in 363 'would be the same with those attending mere natural eruptions'. In the end, Warburton concluded that

> ...the specific qualities of the fermented elements, which occasioned the frightful appearances, though they were natural or enflamed matter under certain circumstances, were yet, by the peculiar pleasure of Providence, given on this occasion; and not left merely to the conjunction of mechanic causes, or the fortuitous concourse of matter and motion, to produce. And my reason is, because these frightful appearances, namely the cross in the heavens, and on the garments, were admirably fitted, as moral emblems, to proclaim the triumph of Christ over Julian...[67]

Newtonian matter theory helped explain *how* God had intervened miraculously in fourth-century Jerusalem, while necessity proved *why* God

---

[64] Ibid., p. 431.
[65] Ibid., pp. 435-6.
[66] Ibid., p. 433.
[67] Ibid., pp. 506-507. See also, Warburton MSS, Letter 91: Warburton to Thomas Balguy, 1766 regarding the 'immediate Agent' for the Temple miracle.

had no choice but to effect the miraculous fiery eruption that brought the Temple's reconstruction to an end.

II

Warburton wrote *Julian* in 1749 to defend orthodox understanding of miracles. The book's publication in the late spring of 1750 was, inadvertently, timed for maximum impact, for it followed a series of earthquakes that had shaken London.[68] A minor earthquake struck London on 8 February 1750. When a more violent tremor rumbled under London exactly a month later, the concerned reactions of February turned to widespread panic, especially when a mad soldier predicted that God would destroy London a month later on 8 April with a third earthquake.[69] Many who were able to do so fled London, hoping that distance from the capital would ensure their safety when the next earthquake hit. 'This frantic terror prevails so much, that within these three days 730 coaches have been counted passing Hyde Park Corner, with whole parties removing into the country', Horace Walpole reported on 2 April.[70] The third earthquake never materialized, but the seismic activity of that winter and early spring unnerved both ordinary Britons and their nation's leaders. Most believed that the London earthquakes were divinely caused. But were they miracles? Warburton thought not. Instead, the London earthquakes—and the calamitous earthquake that struck Lisbon on 1 November 1755—were prodigies. 'The prodigious', William Burns notes, 'was a loosely bounded category', bordered on one side by the miraculous and other by 'those phenomena which were merely odd or remarkable'.[71]

As with miracles, Warburton sought to explain both why God produced these prodigies and how he effected them. The London and Lisbon earthquakes were not miraculous, he argued, because they met neither of the 'two necessary occasions' for miracles: 'to attest and support the truth of a new Religion coming from God' or 'to administer a Theocratic government'.[72] God intended them nonetheless as warnings to a

---

[68] G.S. Rousseau, 'The London Earthquakes of 1750', *Cahiers d'mondiale* 6 (1968), pp. 436-51 and T.D. Kendrick, *The Lisbon Earthquake* (London, 1956), pp. 1-23 provide useful descriptive surveys of the London earthquakes.

[69] See, for instance, *A Series of Letters between Mrs. Elizabeth Carter and Miss Catherine Talbot from the year 1741 to 1770...in the Possession of the Rev. Montagu Pennington* (London, 1809), I, p. 332: Catherine Talbot to Elizabeth Carter, 3 April 1750; *Secret Comment: The Diaries of Gertrude Savile, 1721-1757*, Alan Savile (ed.), (Devon, 1997), p. 291.

[70] *The Yale Edition of Horace Walpole's Correspondence*, W.S. Lewis et al. (eds.), (New Haven and London, 1937-83), XX, pp. 136-7: Walpole to Horace Mann, 2 April 1750.

[71] William E. Burns, *An Age of Wonders: Prodigies, politics and providence in England, 1657-1727* (Manchester and New York, 2002), pp. 2, 3.

[72] Ibid., p. 9.

sinful nation, a belief expressed in nine out of ten publications in Britain occasioned by the London and Lisbon earthquakes.[73] Providentialism likewise informed the government's decision, in the wake of the Lisbon earthquake, to call for a day of public fast and humiliation in Britain and Ireland on 6 February 1756.[74] 'Whereas the manifold Sins and Wickedness of these Kingdoms, have most justly deserved heavy and severe Punishments from the Hand of Heaven', read the English proclamation, '...[we] send up our Prayers and Supplications to the Divine Majesty, to avert all those Judgements which We most justly have deserved'.[75] Only a national reformation of manners, Warburton preached in his fast sermon, could avert Britain's imminent punishment at God's hands: 'A sincere, a speedy and a thorough reformation will not fail to avert the anger of the Lord, now gone out against the sinful inhabitants of the earth'. Party politics, luxury, and greed had corrupted the nation, and it was now being punished by God for that corruption. The only solution was 'a reformation of the general manners, where each of us, in our several stations, may concur to heal the breaches made in our excellent constitution by our party-follies; to oppose the enormous progress of avarice and corruption; to check the wasting rage for displeasure and amusement; to shake off those unmanly luxuries crept in to domestic life, some for the gratification of our appetites, but more for the display of our vanities'.[76]

Warburton adopted this line of argument because he believed that God punished nations for their sins.[77] 'The temporal punishments, which God inflicts upon iniquity, have three objects. Particulars; a People; and a State or Government', he explained. 'The punishment of the first two Objects, I hold to be for the crimes of men; the latter...for the crimes of the state'.[78] God punished nations collectively instead of their inhabitants individually because states were moral agents: 'A society is an artificial man, having like the natural, all those essential qualities, which constitute a moral agent; the

---

[73] See Robert G. Ingram, '"The trembling Earth is God's Herald": Earthquakes, Religion, and Public Life in Britain during the 1750s' (forthcoming).
[74] James Joseph Caudle, 'Measures of Allegiance: Sermon Culture and the Creation of a Public Discourse of Obedience and Resistance in Georgian Britain, 1714-1760' (Yale University PhD thesis, 1996), pp. 262-3; and Roland Bartel, 'The Story of Public Fast Days in England', *Anglican Theological Review* 37:3 (June 1955), pp. 190-200 explain the mechanisms of public days of fast and humiliation.
[75] 'The Proclamation for a General Fast [6 February 1756]' (London, 1755), p. 1. I thank Adrian Jones of the Society of Antiquaries, London, for providing me with a copy of this fast proclamation.
[76] Warburton, *Natural and civil events the instruments of God's moral government*, p. 14. The following analysis vitiates William Burn's contention that by 1727, Warburton 'was able to treat past belief in the providential prodigy as self-evidently absurd. By his time, the realms of politics, religion and science were no longer connected through prodigies': Burns, *An Age of Wonders*, p. 187.
[77] Napthine and Speck, 'Clergymen and Conflict, 1660-1763', pp. 231-2 discusses the eighteenth-century understanding of corporate sin.
[78] Warburton, 'A Defence of the preceding Discourse' (1746), in *WWW*, V pp. 236-7.

discernment of good and evil; A will to chuse, and a power to put its choice into execution'. For that reason, 'the hand of Heaven distributes good and evil to Societies, according to their merit or undesert'.[79] During the middle third of the eighteenth century, the Anglo-Spanish war of 1739, the Jacobite rebellion of 1745-46, and the ongoing hostilities with France gave Warburton, the English, and their government ample reason to feel as if God were punishing England. Despite these internal and external threats to the nation's security, Britain somehow survived. Warburton, like many of his contemporaries, discerned a clear message from this deliverance: this 'preservation of us, at every important crisis, when human power and policy...seemed combined to our destruction' indicated God's 'election of us for the instruments of his glory'.[80] But elected to do what? 'It is possible we may be selected by Providence...to preserve the memory of civil liberty amongst a slavish world, as the house of Israel was formerly, to keep alive true religion amidst an universal apostasy'.[81]

Having explained the reasons for prodigies, Warburton turned to explain how they occurred. He was clear that they were not miracles and, thus, were not the result of God suspending, reversing, redirecting, or compounding the mechanical laws of nature. Prodigies did, however, have 'natural effects; whose causes we being ignorant of, we have made them ideal creatures of a distinct species, but rank with all other natural effects'.[82] Prodigies were not, in other words, part of God's particular providence, but were, instead, part of his general providence. They were the 'pre-established direction of natural events' where 'the stated laws of physics, while they are promoting their own purpose, are, at the same time...contrived as to support, invigorate and inforce the sanctions of religion'.[83] God had pre-ordained 'the circumstances of the natural and moral systems, so to make the events of the former serve the regulation of the latter'.[84]

III

Prodigies were instruments of warning or punishment that required God to preset the operation or confluence of nature's immutable laws in a certain way, at a certain time and place, and in a certain manner. This belief

---

[79] Warburton, 'The nature of national offences truly stated...A sermon preached on the general fast day, appointed to be observed December 18, 1745' (1746), in *WWW*, V, p. 228.

[80] Warburton, 'A sermon preach'd on the thanksgiving appointed to be observed the ninth of October, for the suppression of the late unnatural rebellion' (1746), in *WWW*, V, p. 258.

[81] Ibid.

[82] *Letters from a late eminent prelate*, pp. 80-81: Warburton to Hurd, [1752].

[83] Warburton, *Natural and civil events the instruments of God's moral government*, pp. 9, 10.

[84] Ibid., p. 6.

jibed easily with the natural philosophical distinction between first and second causes. For Warburton to explain how divine action shaped human historical causation, however, required him to leave science behind and venture into territory few of his orthodox contemporaries wished to visit. In so doing, it highlights the explanatory limits of Newtonian natural philosophy for orthodox Christians during the mid-eighteenth century.

Now Warburton agreed with most orthodox that God interposed himself directly in human events, just as he did in the natural world. 'Indeed, all who believe the moral government of God, how much soever they may differ concerning his mode of administering it among Particular, and how obscure soever his ways may appear in the tracts of private life, yet concur to acknowledge and to revere his visible interposition in the revolutions of States and Empires', he wrote.[85] These interpositions enabled God to govern the moral universe: 'Civil commotions have the same use, in the moral world, that stormy and tempestuous seasons have in the physical', he contended. 'In the stagnation of a continued calm, the best system sickens and decays; but these periodic agitations stifle corruption in the seed, give new vigour to the languid Constitution, and enable the vital Principles of it to perform their destined operations'.[86]

The tricky issue, as the orthodox saw it, was not *whether* God intervened in human events, but *how* he intervened. In their jeremiads of the eighteenth century, few clergymen discussed the means of God's interposition in human affairs.[87] Warburton himself offered conflicting explanations of divine action upon mankind. In a 30 January sermon to the House of Lords in 1760 commemorating Charles I's death, he argued that God does not actually control human affairs. 'The System of Nature has the Providence of God to curb the blind violence of stubborn matter, which else, in the impetuosity of its course, would soon reduce itself to its former Chaos', he wrote. The 'Political System', though, has only the 'Providence of Government to sustain it against its own fury, from falling into Anarchy'. Because the 'Providence of Government is weak and bounded' it requires 'all the assistance of good subjects to strengthen its hands, and enforce obedience to its insulted Authority'. Regicide and republicanism resulted from the failure of the English in 'this salutary duty' during the 1640s.[88] Where politics were concerned, then, there was no check on free will.

Elsewhere, though, Warburton contended that God does actually directly shape human actions. In the *annus mirabilis* of 1759, he preached that God had fought 'our battles', proving that Britain was the 'sole remaining Trustee of Civil Freedom, and so of the great Bulwark of Gospel

---

[85] Warburton, 'A sermon preached before the Right Honourable House of Lords, January 30, 1760', in *WWW*, V, p. 302.
[86] Ibid., p. 317.
[87] See Napthine and Speck, 'Clergymen and Conflict', *passim*.
[88] Warburton, 'A sermon preached before the Right Honourable House of Lords, January 30, 1760', p. 317.

Truth'.[89] How had God fought and won them on Britain's behalf? God 'governs the material world, has immediate access to the minds of men, and manages and turns them as rivulets of water'. Consider 'what a multitude of thoughts shall come uncalled and unforeseen' into your mind, 'and how suddenly without design, and even against our will, they shall dart from object to object'. Sometimes only a 'trifling incident' will set in motion 'a train of ideas with which are connected events of the last consequence to our own comfort, and the happiness of those around us. Can we fail to conclude that God is within over-ruling the mind?' Warburton asked. 'And in what instance does this influence and direction more remarkably appear than in the thoughts that guide and give efficacy to the conduct and events of war? the rise, the rebuke or revolution of great enterprises?' God, then, tinkers with our very thoughts when he finds it necessary to do so. The 'noblest genius, and the most sanguine expectations of princes' are no match for God when he chooses to do so.[90] It is easy to see why some might have been loath to make such an argument, robbing man, as it does, of free will and the unimpeded use of his rational faculties. At best, it was an argument unlikely to persuade sceptics.

IV

William Warburton lived in a world whose unfolding history was shaped and governed directly by God. Indeed, he could barely contemplate a world in which God's fingerprints on events were not evidently visible. When Conyers Middleton died, he could not help but wonder why Middleton could rejoice in being confident that 'he had given the Miracles of the early ages such a blow as they would not easily recover'. He failed to 'see how the mere discovery of Truth affords such pleasure':

> If this Truth be, that the Providence of God governs the moral as well as natural world; and that, in compassion to human distresses, he has revealed his will to mankind, by which we are enabled to get the better of them, by a restoration of his favour, I can easily conceive the pleasure that, at any period of life, must accompany such a discovery. But, if the Truth discovered be that we have no farther share in God than as we partake of his natural government of the Universe; or that all there is in his moral government is only the natural necessary effects of Virtue and Vice upon human agents here, and that all the pretended Revelations of an hereafter were begot by fools, and hurried up by

---

[89] Warburton, 'Sermon preached at Bristol, November 29, 1759. Being the day appointed for a public thanksgiving for victories obtained by the British armies', in WWW, V, p. 406.

[90] William Warburton, A People's Prayer for Peace. A sermon preached at Northampton, February 13, 1761, the day appointed for a General Fast (London, 1761), pp. 21-2.

knaves; if this, I say, be our boasted discovery, it must, I think, prove a very uncomfortable contemplation, especially in our last hours.[91]

When something horrible, like the Lisbon earthquake, occurred, Warburton could find comfort in the belief that it was God's doing. 'It is indeed a dreadful thing to suppose these disasters the vengeance of our offended Master', he wrote Joseph Atwell, 'but it is ten times more terrible to believe we have our precarious being in a forlorn and fatherless world. In the first case, we have it in our power to avert our destruction by the amendment of our manners; in the latter, we are exposed without hopes of refuge to the free range of matters and motion in a ferment'.[92] Just as the nation girded itself against the threats to its security by identifying itself as God's chosen people, as a latter-day Israel, so too did Warburton ground his identity and his faith in God's providence.

This God-infused worldview is not one that modern liberal scholarship would have us believe was prevalent during the eighteenth century. Those, like William Warburton, who retained their belief in an interventionist God are supposed to be credulous, pre-modern figures untouched by enlightened thought and, thus, on the fringe. Margaret Jacob scoffs at scholars who believe otherwise as 'historian adherents of high-church orthodoxy'.[93] One need not adhere to 'high-church orthodoxy' to recognize that in mid-eighteenth-century England, orthodox Christianity and the new science were, more often than not, mutually supportive systems of thought.[94] The new science did not shift 'the emphasis from an interventionist God to one whose greatest gift to human kind was natural reason'.[95] Instead, as Warburton's example shows, it could provide an effective language for orthodox Christians to explain how God intervened providentially in the natural world and in human events. Newtonian natural philosophy was not monopolized by the orthodox, and the new science was, in the hands of many freethinkers, used to support the view of a creator-less universe. Neither was Newtonianism of unlimited explanatory use to the orthodox. It failed, for instance, to explain how God might effect the outcome of human events such as wars, and many

---

[91] *Literary Illustrations*, pp. 179-81: Warburton to John Jortin, 30 July 1750.
[92] Kilvert (ed.), *A Selection from the Unpublished Papers...of William Warburton*, pp. 257-8: Warburton to Joseph Atwell, 9 December 1755. See also, *Letters from a late eminent prelate*, p. 149: Warburton to Hurd, [December 1755].
[93] Dobbs and Jacob, *Newton and the Culture of Newtonianism*, p. 100. She is referring to Jonathan Clark.
[94] This is a theme I have explored more broadly in '"The trembling earth is God's Herald": Earthquakes, Religion, and Public Life in Britain during the 1750s'.
[95] Patricia Bonomi, *Under the Cope of Heaven: Religion, Society and Politics in Colonial America* (New York and Oxford, 1998), p. 98. See also, Burns, *An Age of Wonders*, pp. 185-7; Porter, *The Creation of the Modern World*, p. 100; Michael P. Winship, *Seers of God: Puritan Providentialism in the Restoration and Early Enlightenment* (Baltimore, 1996), pp. 138-52.

contemporaries recognized that Newton himself was anti-trinitarian.[96] The point of this chapter, though, has not been that the essence of orthodoxy during the eighteenth century was a kind of Newtonianized Christianity. Rather, it has been that the orthodox could maintain their traditional and durable belief in the triune, revealed, interventionist Christian God, yet explain the mechanisms of his interventionism in new ways. Far from undermining orthodoxy, the new learning enlivened and strengthened it.

---

[96] Scott Mandelbrote, 'Newton and eighteenth-century Christianity', in I. Bernard Cohen and George E. Smith (eds.), *The Cambridge Companion to Newton* (Cambridge, 2002), pp. 409-30.

Chapter 8

James Boswell and the Bi-Confessional State[*]

James J. Caudle

The bi-confessional polity of Georgian Britain was fundamentally different from uni-confessional polities with which *ancien régime* studies lump it. In the political theory of a classic monist confessional realm, there juridically is (or ought to be) only one king, one faith, and one law. Transparently in Britain after 1689, and even after the Union of England and Scotland into Great Britain in 1707, that was not the case. In Great Britain 1707-1800, there was certainly one king, but juridically speaking there were two faiths, and two laws. Actually, in light of the refocus of attention on the survival of Jacobitism 1689-1789, we might as well claim two kings, two faiths, and two laws and complete the parallel.

The Church of Scotland, as by law established after 1689, did not behave as a 'Dissenting' church in its relations with its neighbour to the south, nor was it treated on its native soil as a Dissenting church. The elite who worshipped in the Church of Scotland did not have the same

---

[*] Several colleagues read this chapter in draft, including Pamela Edwards, Johnny Wink, Mark Spicer, Gordon Turnbull, Joe Levine, and Brian Cowan. Others heard an early version of it delivered as a conference paper at the MACBS in New York City and offered comments at that point, including Jeremy Gregory. Bill Gibson greatly aided in the task of shortening a much longer version of this essay to fit within the bounds of this volume. Marlies K. Danziger, editor of the 'German' and 'Swiss' Grand Tour volume in the Yale Research Edition of Boswell's Journals, kindly allowed me to consult her careful transcriptions of Boswell's French documents to Rousseau from 1764 which form an important part of my evidence. Certain of the letters used as background for Boswell's youth appear in the Hankins and Caudle edition of *General Correspondence of James Boswell, 1757-1763* in the Boswell Editions Research series. All material from the Yale Boswell Editions, manuscript, proof/transcript, or printed volume, has been quoted according to the conventions of fair use, but has been made available for quotation through the generosity of the Yale Editions of the Private Papers of James Boswell; these materials remain under copyright. In this chapter, 'Yale MS' refers to those Papers of James Boswell housed in the Beinecke Rare Book and Manuscript Library at Yale University. The numbering system of the documents in that collection which have been quoted in this essay is explained more fully in Marion S. Pottle, Claude Colleer Abbott, and Frederick A. Pottle, *Catalogue of the Papers of James Boswell at Yale University*, 3 vols. (New Haven, 1993).

obviously subordinate or dependent relation to the Church of England elite as did the ruling ascendancies in Wales and Ireland, where the established church was a semi-detached dependency on the Church of England's hierarchy and clergy. This subordination to Canterbury was less the case in Ireland, which had its own primate and archbishops, but more true in Wales. Religiously, Scotland's Established Church had for the most part held its own and maintained its independence against the aggressive cultural annexation by England.

The two nations' churches were separate and, except in the larger context of Great Britain and access to the power of Westminster and the Court, roughly equal in their ability to impose belief and penalties for unbelief in their own spheres of influence. This situation led to some anomalies. A Church of Scotland communicant in Edinburgh was a member of the church by law established, but if he crossed the border into England he was a dissenter of sorts and vice versa. I stress the point 'a dissenter of sorts' because, as I wish to point out, Church of England and Church of Scotland congregants were juridically and socially different, even off their home turf, from true Dissenters.

Therefore, the study of 'amphibians', those who moved between those two Ascendancy cultures in the years 1707-1828, should be undertaken with at least some regard to that situation. Such has not been the case with work on James Boswell, particularly in the justifiably famous set-piece biographical work by Frederick Pottle.[1] Despite its age, Pottle's biography remains important because the early chapters of so many subsequent biographies of Boswell are chiefly pastiches of it. Since Pottle wrote from a self-confessed American Episcopalian point of view, his concept of Boswell's choices between the churches of England and Scotland were discussed mostly in terms of his choice between 'Episcopalianism' and 'Presbyterianism'. In America, the competition 1740-75 was generally between Anglican versus *Congregational* established churches; there were no 'presbyterian' colonial establishments. Furthermore, in the United States, disestablishment began in Boswell's lifetime, and took place state by state from 1775-1833, whereas in the British Isles, disestablishment only became a serious agenda in the 1840s, with the Church of Ireland disestablished in 1869 and the Church of Wales disestablished in 1914-1920: the Churches of Scotland and England remain established, though weakened. Both Pottle and Mary Margaret Stewart read 'Boswell's Denominational Dilemma' in terms of the social place of Protestant denominational preferences in the United States of the Eisenhower-Kennedy-Johnson era, in which,

---

[1] Frederick A. Pottle, *James Boswell: The Earlier Years: 1740-1769* (New York,1966).

despite lingering class prejudices about religion, the choice between becoming Episcopalian or Presbyterian was often construed as similar to the choice between buying a Ford or a Chevrolet.[2] Admittedly, the psychological, emotional, and aesthetic reasons for religious decision which Pottle and Stewart emphasized were present in Boswell's decisions of churchmanship. They are indeed so important that they are discussed at length in this essay, and were unqualifiably stated in his own diaries and letters. However, Boswell's religious choices were always contextually conditioned and shaped by consideration of the power of the Establishment and of the Church as an element in sociopolitical power *wherever* he lived. It would be as dangerous to consider James Boswell as characteristic or typical as it would be imprudent to interpret Samuel Johnson's spiritual eccentricities as the key to religion in the 'Age of Johnson'. Nonetheless, Boswell's *cuius regio eius religio* stance towards established church and conformity is more characteristic in terms of the vast majority of people in both kingdoms than Johnson's conforming crypto-nonjurant worldview. The spiritual, like the personal, was political. National identity was religious identity.

I

The life of James Boswell (1740-95) is an unusually well-documented instance of a confessional 'amphibian'. About forty-two years of Boswell's

---

[2] Mary Margaret Stewart, 'Boswell's Denominational Dilemma', *PMLA* 76:5 (December 1961), pp. 503-11; idem, 'James Boswell and the National Church of Scotland', *Huntington Library Quarterly* 30:4 (August 1967), pp. 369-87; idem, 'Boswell and the Infidels', *Studies in English Literature 1500-1900* 4:5 (Summer 1964), pp. 475-83; idem, 'James Hervey's Influence on Boswell', *American Notes & Queries* 4:8 (April 1966), pp. 117-20. A considered review of Boswell's relations with three Church of Scotland Men (John Dun, Andrew Crosbie, and John Maclaurin) is Richard B. Sher, 'Scottish Divines and Legal Lairds: Boswell's Scot's Presbyterian Identity', in Greg Clingham, (ed.), *New Light on Boswell: Critical and Historical Essays on the Essays on the Occasion of the Bicentenary of 'The Life of Johnson'* (Cambridge, 1991), pp. 28–55. A bare recital of Boswell's attendance at churches from 1762–1776 may be found in Samuel J. Rogal, 'James Boswell at Church: 1762–1776', *Historical Magazine of the Protestant Episcopal Church* 41:4 (December 1972), pp. 415–27. There is only one book-length study of the topic, to my knowledge, and it takes the form of a spiritual biography: Sharon Lee Priestley, 'The Navigation Of A Soul: The Spiritual Autobiography Of James Boswell' (University of Nevada at Reno Ph.D. dissertation, 1995) which claims that Boswell was a 'devout skeptic...who often chose to engage in entirely secular behavior', and falls into Pottle and Stewart's error in considering the churches of England and Scotland as two among 'four Christian denominations', in her case the national churches of Scotland and England, Roman Catholics, and Friends.

life were spent in Scotland (1740-62, 1766-85) and about thirteen in England (1762-63, 1785-95), not counting 'jaunts' in 1760 and from 1766-85, which he construed as holidays rather than residences.

It is unarguably true that Boswell rebelled, especially in his early twenties, against the Church of Scotland and what he believed it to represent. He argued in a series of brief autobiographical sketches[3] that his entire family had been burdened by strict religious upbringings for at least three generations. Thus he rewrote the drama of his personal struggle against the national church into an epic of the entire Boswell (and Erskine and Cochrane) family's relation to the Kirk.[4]

Boswell's objections to Church of Scotland practice as it affected his own life began with his perceptions of the role it had played in discolouring and souring what he perceived was his Rousseauistic childhood innocence. He was particularly displeased with the emphasis that the more zealous members of the Church of Scotland, including his mother, placed on childhood conversions. This took the form of encouraging children to demonstrate the signs of salvation and sanctification: 'She hurried [pressured] me a great deal to surrender to the Operations of the Grace of God, and she put into my hands a little book in which I read of the conversions of very young children. I remembered that one of them was [converted when] three years old'.[5]

He objected to the emphasis placed in catechistical education on rote memorization of the doctrines of the Westminster Confession of Faith. The young Boswell was catechized on Sunday evenings: 'At night I was made to say my Catechism'.[6] Boswell (at least as of 1764) found these methods of religious instruction unsuitable; his objections were partly pedagogical and psychological: 'My Catechism contained within it the blackest of doctrines'.[7] However, much of his animus was less a credal critique of the Kirk's system of 'blackest' doctrines than emotional remembrances of a youth spent under a burden of understanding, or at least memorizing by heart, the 107 questions and answers of the Shorter Catechism. As he explained to Rousseau, 'From my earliest childhood I

---

[3] Yale MSS L 1107-1112. The translations into English from Boswell's French are my own, and vary from those previous translations printed in *Earlier Years* pp. 1-6 and Frederick Pottle (ed.), *Boswell on the Grand Tour: Germany and Switzerland* (New York, 1953), pp. 234-5.

[4] Yale MS L 1107, Ebauche de ma Vie: Final Copy 5 December 1764; Yale MS L 1108 Ebauche de ma Vie, unfinished first draft; Yale, MS L 1109 Ebauche de ma Vie, outline. Future references to these variants of the 'Ebauche' are by the Yale manuscript numbers solely.

[5] Yale MS L 1107.

[6] Ibid.

[7] Ibid.

was taught the most abstract dogmas. The Fall of Man, Original Sin,[8] and the Incarnation of Jesus Christ[9] were painstakingly repeated to me. By the end I was able to repeat them myself, but with such ideas'.[10]

However, it was not the Fall, Adam's Sin, or Jesus' Incarnation which first impressed him, but rather hell.[11] As he intended to explain to Rousseau, 'My Imagination was terrified by the first grand idea, of Eternal Punishment—it was sensible [to me] like a fire...How I trembled at it. How the fire was something of which I had a very material [concrete] idea'.[12] When Sir David Dalrymple in late 1764 threatened to tell William Robertson that Boswell thought the established worship was evocative of hell, it was a threat based on Robertson's not knowing Boswell's secret opinion. Dalrymple needled Boswell by asking, 'Shall I tell Dr. Robertson that he is a Calvinist who cannot be pleasing in the sight of God, and that his prayers and sermons put you in mind of hell?'[13]

By contrast, he felt that his catechistical education was nearly entirely lacking in references to the allure of heaven.[14] Indeed the major merit of heaven was not that it was heavenly or paradisiacal, but only that it did not entail suffering in the fires of hell. 'I thought little of the blessedness of heaven, because I had no idea of it...I should not have ever hoped to go to heaven, if it had not been a means to escape hell. I imagined that the Saints passed all Eternity in the humour of People recently saved from a Fire who consoled themselves on being in safety while they heard the lugubrious cries of the tormented [perishing in the flames]'.[15] If we credit Boswell's memory of events from a decade or more

---

[8] The fall of man and the doctrine of Adam's original sin was taught in *Sum of Saving Knowledge* (Head I: 'Our woeful condition by nature, through breaking the covenant of works', Points II-III; compare to Westminster *Shorter Catechism*, Questions 13, 15-20).

[9] The description of the Incarnation occurred in *Sum of Saving Knowledge* (Head II: 'The remedy provided in Jesus Christ for the elect by the covenant of grace', Points I-III; compare to Westminster *Shorter Catechism*, Questions 21-2, 27).

[10] Yale MS L 1108.

[11] As for the doctrine of the eternality of punishment, it was a brief component of *Sum of Saving Knowledge* (Head IV: 'The blessings which are effectually conveyed by these means to the Lord's elect, or chosen ones', Point II; compare to the Westminster *Shorter Catechism*, Question 19; see also the *Larger Catechism* Questions 29, 86, 89). With their emphasis on the somatic sufferings of the physical body after the Judgement, it is not surprising that Boswell thought of hell in a very literal fashion as the equivalent of an earthly house afire.

[12] Yale MS L 1109, 1107.

[13] Pottle (ed.), *Boswell on the Grand Tour: Germany and Switzerland*, pp. 242-6: Sir David Dalrymple (Lord Hailes) to James Boswell, 10 October 1764.

[14] The blessedness of heaven, a doctrine which Boswell complained was omitted in the hellfire preaching of the traditional Scots, was dealt with in *Sum of Saving Knowledge* (Head IV: 'The blessings which are effectually conveyed by these means to the Lord's elect, or chosen ones', Point II; compare to the *Larger Catechism*, Questions 86, 90).

[15] Yale MS L 1107.

previous, then Scots' religious teachings offered a great deal of stick, and precious little carrot, to believers. Such discussions of heaven and hell also presented (as did all orthodox Christian teaching of the era) a sort of survivor's guilt for those who believed themselves saved from hell and damnation as they confronted the obvious implication that many (most?) around them were damned from before the beginning of all time. Under those conditions, horrified relief was an understandable reaction. Importantly, one of the few *sensual* ideas he had of heaven was intuitive, somatic, and pre-sexual: at the age of twelve, while rubbing up against a tree while climbing it, he 'thought of heaven', a thought which returned whenever he climbed the tree or felt himself fall from the high branches in 'ecstasy'.[16] Only when his tutor John Dun presented to him post-Moderate and Pelagian visions of a heaven was he *cerebrally* intrigued by heaven. In Dun's heaven, good works in life were rewarded by a happy afterlife of conversations with Great Men and Dear Friends, accompanied by beautiful music, and access to the civil and polite 'sciences sublimes'.[17] That vision of heaven appears in his untitled religious poem thought to have been composed in 1758-62.[18] The sublime sciences of John Dun's heaven played a strong role in that vision: 'That mystic time, when in the World above,/Th'enraptur'd Soul with adoration mix'd,/And Gratitude profound shall humbly trace/The mazy lab'rynths of the ways of *God*.' If this heaven is still close to the Westminster Standards theology of Boswell's catechistical education, it is strongly flavoured with Addison's 'Spacious Firmament on High' and Pope's 'Universal Prayer'. He also felt heavenly notions after attending the Church of England services in a Qualified Chapel with his friend John Johnston of Grange. The vision of heaven offered at 'Grants' was also 'chearing', focused on the 'state of bliss' in a 'world above'.[19]

It was pointless to argue with Boswell, as Sir David Dalrymple tried, that the Kirk Moderates such as Dr. Robertson offered a new style of Calvinism which adopted a Tillotsonian strategy of emphasizing the comforts and rewards of faith rather than the sufferings of the sinful.[20] Boswell's vivid memory of old-school Kirk hellfire teachings was as

---

[16] Yale MS L 1109.
[17] Yale MS L 1107.
[18] Bodleian Library, Douce MS 193, f. 39r, transcribed liberally in Jack Werner, *Boswell's Book of Bad Verse (A Verse Self-Portrait) or 'Love Poems and Other Verses by James Boswell'...Now First Published from the Original Autograph MS* (London, 1974), pp. 102-3.
[19] *The Correspondence of James Boswell and John Johnston of Grange*, edited by Ralph S. Walker (New York, 1966), pp. 17-8: James Boswell to John Johnston of Grange, 27 October 1762.
[20] *Boswell on the Grand Tour: Germany and Switzerland*, pp. 242-6: Sir David Dalrymple (Lord Hailes) to James Boswell, 10 October 1764.

hardwired as his devotion to the memory of the unhappy royal family of Stewart or his fear of ghouls and ghosts ('frightened terribly of spirits').[21] None the less, as Dalrymple's 1764 letter implied, the new Moderate viewpoints of men like William Robertson had softened the old hellfire sermonizing in the Scottish Kirk in favour of more encouragement of good works; a new style of piety more based on gentle hopes for divine clemency and less reliant on dire warnings of divine justice.

Various discussions by Pottle and others about how Boswell might have salved his upsets about predestination and hell by abandoning 'presbyterianism' for 'episcopalianism' or Roman Catholicism are peculiar at best. At least doctrinally, the Church of England was as keen on frightening people with the burning torments of hell as was the Church of Scotland. The doctrines of hell and predestination remained present in the Thirty-Nine Articles of the Church of England (viz. Articles 3, 9), and were preached even in the Age of Enlightenment. Furthermore, few people would imagine that by becoming Catholic in the era of the Tridentine settlement, one could avoid thinking about the eternality of hell or questions of free will or divine foreknowledge. Indeed, Boswell's eccentric personal views of free will, the efficacies of prayers for and by the dead, and the general non-eternality of punishment went beyond the orthodoxies of Westminster, Canterbury, and Trent into Socinian or Pelagian territory.

However, he failed to mention to Rousseau in 1764 one of his greatest disagreements with Church of Scotland Orthodoxy: the question of Calvinist and Knoxian notions of predestination.[22] After his child's fear of becoming a sinner in the hands of an angry God had been confronted, a Boswell who was university-aged (i.e., 13-16) grew to fear the doctrine of predestination and limited election. It took some time for young Boswell to figure out what predestination actually *meant*. Predestination was not dramatically representable in terms of concrete and sensual images, in the manner that the scorching heat of the fires of hell or the soporific drone of the chanting of metrical Psalms in the Court of heaven were to him. Therefore, such a comprehension had to wait for his capacity for abstraction to mature. Once he understood it, the doctrine of inevitability frightened him. Even the contemplation of secular philosophical doctrines of inevitability and necessity as exposited in a philosophy

---

[21] Yale MS L 1109.
[22] Predestination in the context of the Elect, their fore-ordination to effectual calling and salvation, and the necessity of their accepting an irresistible divine grace, was pervasive in the *Sum of Saving Knowledge*, viz. Question 20. One may possibly over-emphasize its relative importance in actual Church of Scotland doctrine. None the less, it was one of the core teachings of Calvin's interpretation as developed by the Scottish and 'Westminster' divines.

professor's classes was capable of causing him to become melancholy. Sir David Dalrymple wrote sympathetically to prevent Boswell from being 'infatuated with Fatality',[23] and Samuel Johnson attempted, without success, to ease Boswell's anxiety about the moral consequences of necessity.[24] However, Boswell also wrote a poem in defence of providential decrees.[25] That poem, thought to have been written during the period 1758-62, counselled humble acceptance of 'Æternal Providence'. Although the poem does not present a rigid Calvinist predestinarianism, it does argue the unknowability of 'Heav'n's supreme Decrees', described as 'darkness all' and 'veil'd in thickest clouds/ From mortal eyes'. The speaker of the poem suggests that one not try to be wise 'Beyond what *He* ordains'.

Whatever compromises he had arrived at on divine foreknowledge and predestination in 1764, he pointedly asked Rousseau on paper the reasons for burdening a young mind with abstruse doctrines. Such fine points of theology undoubtedly had made sense to the Westminster Assembly of Divines but were none the less so complex that they could not be made plain to children.[26]

Implicit in this critique of catechizing was a view of natural innocence of children which was in harmony with Rousseau's views, but in opposition to the Kirk teachings that children were born into innate sinfulness. Boswell's vision of children was that they had a clean heart, and a manly joy at learning the moral truths of the universe. Instead of enjoying such an edenic virtue, after his religious upbringing he complained that he was 'broken-spirited, without any noble hopes'.[27]

To some extent, his kicking against the established church was a revolt against the burden of systematic theology. Boswell recalled an instance of an encounter with the printed religious confession of his nation: 'I remember perfectly how my mother promised to make me a present of a Confession of Faith of the Church of Scotland, provided that I read it from beginning to end...I therefore read as quickly as I could that collection of absurd unintelligibility, but my mind did not receive the least impression from it. Election and Reprobation and Irresistible Grace

---

[23] Yale MS C 1430, as translated in *Boswell in Holland 1763-1764: Including His Correspondence with Belle de Zuylen (Zélide)*, edited by Frederick A. Pottle (London, 1952), pp. 90-92: Sir David Dalrymple (Lord Hailes) to James Boswell, 2 December 1763.
[24] Journal 26 October 1769: *Boswell in Search of a Wife, 1766-1769*, Frank Brady and Frederick A. Pottle (eds.), (New York, 1956), pp. 330-33.
[25] MS Douce 193, f. 39r, transcribed liberally in Werner, *Boswell's Book of Bad Verse*, pp. 102-3.
[26] Yale MS L 1108.
[27] Yale MS L 1109.

were to me as unknown as the systems of the votaries of Vistnou [Vishnu], Eswara [Ishvara/Shiva], and Brahma in the East Indies'.[28]

His sense of childhood deprivation was liturgical as well as doctrinal. He repined against what he considered to be the dourness, homely plainness, and canting of the Kirk: the 'whole vulgar idea of the Presbyterian worship'.[29] His major objections were to the way in which the clergy, their lengthy sermons, spontaneous prayers, metrical Psalms, and catechism and obsession with sin combined into a grim and boring stew.[30]

Although he was not universally condemnatory of all clergymen, he did have harsh words for the Kirk's clergy as a class: 'Oh men in black! Oh Preachers! O Ministers! how have you acquired over us so great an Influence. How your decisions are able to make us tremble'.[31] His description of the man who was his tutor from 1752 until he departed for university was a thinly-veiled indictment of the Establishment rigorist: 'a strongly honest man, but hard and without any knowledge of the human spirit...He was a dogmatist without even doubting. He felt and acted by System'.[32] The implication was that clerical Scots Calvinism was a monkish system of pure logic and geometric rationale which lacked any emotion except grim seriousness: diligent drudgery at books for the sake of learning the art of diligent drudgery.

Likewise, the patience and piety of Church of Scotland congregations were tested by the torrent of spontaneous prayers. In the Roman *Missal* or the English *Book of Common Prayer*, rituals which ordained standard set printed forms of prayer, the prayers were governed if not limited by the approved forms. By contrast, the *Westminster Directory* only provided an outline of some suggested themes rather than an upper limit of words to be spoken.[33] Indeed, open-ended directions encouraging spontaneous effusions of prayer typified the *Directory*'s divergence from the *Book of Common Prayer*. Boswell noted that such unpredictable and potentially rambling 'extempore prayers...made me very gloomy'.[34]

---

[28] French Theme, 29-30 January 1764, adapted from translation by Elizabeth Manwaring.
[29] Journal 15 May 1763.
[30] Yale MS L 1109
[31] Ibid.
[32] Yale MS L 1107.
[33] *Westminster Directory*, 'Of Publick Prayer before the Sermon'.
[34] Journal, 15 May 1763. All citations from Boswell's 1759-63 journals in this chapter are quoted from the forthcoming volume of Boswell's Earliest Journals which I am currently editing. Thanks is due to the Yale Editions for permission.

Boswell also found the chanting of the Psalms, in the official Metrical Psalms of the 1650 Scottish Psalter[35] sung by the congregation without instrumental accompaniment, to be provocative of gloom. His perception was that the Psalms were simply another incentive to drag out an already long Scottish Sabbath by 'a great number of chanted Psalms' in church followed by evening recitations of Psalms in the family home.[36] The goal of Scottish psalmody was not Rococo elegance nor Baroque beauty, but plain melody of voices without instruments based on a carefully translated text which stayed mostly unaltered until 1929.

As Boswell from a very early age wanted to be a poet, and three of his early known poems are Psalms paraphrased into Anglo-Scots verse, it is not surprising that he quite early had an aesthetic critique of the national psalter as having been rendered 'in the lowest sorts of verse'.[37] The Common Metre of the Scottish Psalter (stanzas of four lines, alternating lines of iambic tetrameter and iambic trimeter) was deliberately in 'vers...basses', the culturally low metres of basic song. By contrast, Boswell's renditions of the Psalms, thought to have been written some time in 1758-62, were in the high style of Thomson or Gray, not that of Francis Rous nor his sturdy sagacious improvers.[38] In adapting each of his Psalms, he employed a genteel though sentimental Anglo-Scots style of poetry which, although it was not always perfectly apposite to the rendering of Hebrew verse, was a suitably respectable contribution to the Scottish social verse of the era.

Boswell's own early experience of the congregational chanting of metrical psalms as the chief national medium of praise of God was so underwhelming that he thought that if heaven chiefly consisted of the Saints singing the *Psalms of David in Meter* that he would gladly forego the experience: 'I had heard that in Heaven one would be praising God without ceasing, and I imagined that [this meant that] one would be chanting Psalms [in heaven] as [the congregation did] at church and such a thing did not inspire me'.[39]

It is, however, erroneous to assume that what Boswell believed to be the peasant vulgarities of Common Metre Psalm-singing was a peculiar custom limited to Scotland. Admittedly, by the eighteenth century, the Church of England had largely exchanged the 1562 'Old Version' of

---

[35] *The Psalms of David in Meter...Allowed by the Authority of the General Assembly of the Kirk of Scotland, and appointed to be sung in Congregations and Families*, 1650 et seq. to 1929.
[36] Yale MS L 1107.
[37] Ibid.
[38] Bodleian Library, Douce MS 193, ff. 40r-42r, transcribed liberally in Werner, *Boswell's Book of Bad Verse*, pp. 99-101.
[39] Yale MS L 1107; Yale MS L 1109.

Sternhold and Hopkins[40] for the more modern and graceful 1696 'New Version' of Brady and Tate with its wider and more sophisticated variety of metres.[41] However, the Church of England in 1740-95 was still mainly reciting the psalms without music in the over two-hundred-year old (1539) Coverdale translations offered in the *Book of Common Prayer*, or singing them in Common Metre verses a half-century or more old.

The thoroughgoing rigour of the Knoxian/Melvilleian Sabbatarian Sunday was troublesome to Boswell throughout his life. Even during his allegedly happy interval from 1748-52, he hated Sundays: 'Ages eight to twelve...I was happy except on Sundays when I was made to remember the Terrible Being which was referred to as God'.[42] As his verses read,

> Th' approach of Sunday still I can't but dread,
> For still old Edinburgh comes into my head,
> Where on that day a dreary gloom appears,
> And the kirk-bells ring doleful in your ears.
> Enthusiasts sad, how can you thus employ
> What your Redeemer made a day of joy?
> With thankful hearts to your Creator pray,
> From labour rest, be cheerful and be gay.
> Let us not keep the Sabbath of the Jews;
> Let generous Christians Christian freedom use.[43]

The burden of the Lord's Day in Scotland was for Boswell emblematic of the hard and unremitting nature of the Kirk and its dour Calvinism.[44] In the evenings he had to say his catechism, and repeat Psalms from the metrical version. Most demanding of all, especially for an individual who is sometimes considered to be among the many founders of the modern concept of the self, was the almost Buddhist negation of self required by the orthodox Sabbath: 'I was obliged by my religion "not to do my own work, nor speak my own words, not think my own thoughts on the Lord's Day. I tried in all honesty of heart to conform myself to this [demand]; above all to not think my own thoughts'.[45]

Of course the English version of the Sabbath, while somewhat less dramatically restrictive, was none the less rigorous. Studies of the rise of the English Sunday have noted that the sabbatarianism which crescendoed in the 'puritan' or 'Victorian' eras was none the less a distinct and restrictive presence in the Georgian age. English law and royal

---

[40] *The Whole Book of Psalms Collected into English Metre By Thomas Sternhold, John Hopkins, and Others*, eds. 1562 et seq.
[41] *A New Version Of The Psalms Of David Fitted to the Tunes Used In Churches By N[icholas]. Brady, D.D and N[ahum]. Tate, Esq.* , eds. 1696 et seq..
[42] Yale MS L 1107.
[43] Ten Lines a Day, 23 October 1763.
[44] Yale MS L 1110, Ebauche de ma Vie—outline 2.
[45] Yale MS L 1107.

proclamations of 1740-95 set fairly strict norms for the Sabbath, and indeed George III gave sabbatarianism a new respectability.

Boswell's generic early-life horror of the Kirk was not restricted to any one segment of the establishment. A meeting with the son of a leader of the 'high-flying' party of the Kirk 'brought into my mind some dreary Tolbooth Kirk ideas, than which nothing has given me more gloomy feelings. I shall never forget the dismal hours of apprehension that I have endured in my youth from narrow notions of religion while my tender mind was lacerated with infernal horror'.[46] Having been offended by the high (Webster) and the moderate (Robertson), it was only left for Boswell to be displeased by the dissent from the Kirk tradition: for example, his relative Dr. John Boswell's Glassite/Sandemanian independent Calvinism: 'He talked, too, something about Jesus Christ's being his friend. I was quite provoked at this. "My dear Doctor," said I, "you would bring your religion into everything. I believe you will make it mend your breeches and sole your shoes by and by."'[47]

However, there was at least one great alternate model of a Church of Scotland clergyman and Scottish Establishment religion. It was John Dun: 'My Governor spoke to me now and then of Religion, but in a simple and agreeable manner. He told me that if I comported myself well while I lived, I should be happy in the Other World. There [in heaven] I should hear beautiful Music. I should learn the sublime knowledge which God will accord to the just, and there I should meet all of the Great Men of whom I had read, and all the dear Friends whom I had known. At last my Governor had made me love Heaven, and some hope mixed in with my Religion'.[48]

John Dun, a fairly obscure albeit worthy minister in Scottish history, is crucially important because he represents the sort of clergyman of whom Boswell could approve, a category which included the young minister William McQuhae, a close friend with whom he fervently corresponded in the early 1760s. The relative number of such clergy was likely on the increase during the period 1740-95, although it would be dangerous to equate the Moderate party in the Church of Scotland with the trend towards a gentler and easier style of religiosity. Recognition that the prevalent tradition of the eighteenth-century church remained the 'high Kirk' or strong orthodox Knoxian/Melvillean theology with a strict doctrine and discipline is essential to understanding Boswell's personal revolt in its broader context. Notwithstanding the continuing power of the 'High Kirk', the general revolution in sensibility and

---

[46] Journal, 22 December 1762.
[47] Journal, 19 July 1763.
[48] Yale MS L 1107.

civility which some perceive in 'Enlightenment' Scotland in the period 1700-1800 was led by and responsive to changes in the personalities of the clerical intelligentsia, whatever their churchmanship; indeed, the Scottish Enlightenment was among the most clerically driven of all the European Enlightenments.

At the age of sixteen, he began his religious experimentation in the hopes of finding an acceptable alternative to the Kirk. In the wake of studying logic and metaphysics at university, he turned *'methodist'*. However, the nature of his links to the small numbers of Methodists in Scotland is highly speculative. It is not even clear whether he does not simply use the term as a shorthand for an enthusiastic and emotional piety. By 1760 he was admiring Samuel Foote's savage satires of the methodistical type. None the less, he retained in his life a vocabulary of the emotional religion of the heart which was quite similar to the focus in methodistical discourse on the heart being divinely warmed.[49]

Even more shadowy is his vegan Neo-Pythagoreanism.[50] It is unclear precisely which doctrines his master the Old Pythagorean of Moffat taught, besides vegetarianism. However, Boswell from his youth was highly sensitive to the deaths of animals such as birds and lambs. His poems include laments on destruction of small animals and a strongly sensibility-infused love of nature and its creatures, as in 'October': 'With soft humanity; teach them to show/Compassion mild ev'n to the animals/O'er whom Th'Allmighty has appointed man'.[51] This form of nature-pantheism was a natural byway for him. Nonetheless, the author of the 'Ode to Gluttony' and eager recorder in his journals of his consumption of delights such as roast beef could not long remain a vegan.

His most politically and socially daring deviation from Church of Scotland teaching was in his experimentation with Roman Catholicism in 1758-60, which despite decreasing anti-Catholic animus was still denounced by the more traditional elements of the Establishment as Popery. It is likely significant that his major engagement with Catholic faith and worship occurred during a set of years when he was enthralled by theatre, visual spectacle, drama, and musical pomp. These were all elements provided only very sparingly in the Church of Scotland's Directory worship, and such things were not very luxuriant either in most Book of Common Prayer services of the Church of England.

---

[49] *The Correspondence of James Boswell and John Johnston of Grange*, pp. 17-18: James Boswell to John Johnston of Grange, 27 October 1762.
[50] Yale MS L1107.
[51] His poem 'October', lines of which were quoted in the main text, contains in one of its drafts a section, 'Cruelty to Animals condemned' in which the amusement of wantonly killing small birds is decried.

At the age of eighteen, he turned Roman Catholic, a decision which he realized was against his father's liking, but also was a form of combat against his earthly ambition and [self-]interest.[52] Within the Establishment system in Britain, Roman Catholicism's prescribed status meant that conversion either required a retreat from civil life into an Epicurean country isolation, or an exile on the continent, as so many of the diaspora of Jacobites had chosen. The professions which Boswell most desired—Army officer, Member of Parliament, courtier, owner and laird of the paternal estate of Auchinleck—and even those for which he expected that he would have to settle—lawyer in Scotland or England, judge (in his father's footsteps)—were all closed to professing Catholics in his lifetime. The only careers which he had pondered which he might have followed as a practicing Catholic were poet, actor, respectable author, or Grub Street writer-for-hire. The growing sense of 'Britons' as Protestants in an Elect Nation from 1588-1788, traced by Linda Colley and many others, was indeed a wall which defended the 'ins' of the national identity, but it was also a wall which shut out from civil rights and civil liberties large numbers of people.

Despite Pottle's industrious examination for the evidence on Boswell's Roman Catholic phase, and his sprightly and often novelistic 'intrepid conjecture'/'pure conjecture' on the matter,[53] the nature and depth of Boswell's involvement remains obscure. He became a Catholic at eighteen, but only 'escaped to London' in March 1760. He thought to become a 'Priest—or Monk',[54] a decision which he realized would mean he would likely have to 'hide myself in some melancholy retreat to pass my life in sadness'.[55]

Another option for a socially controversial and publicly censured religious life was to associate with the known scoffers and heterodox. Often, libertine theology was associated with licentious social and sexual practices, and certainly entailed rebelling against Boswell's orthodox upbringing. Libertines such as Eglinton, Hume, and Wilkes frightened him because in so many ways, he believed or wished he might believe what they had dared to believe.

His most strongly deistical and libertine phases were synchronous, in spring 1760 to late 1762 (and later in 1764). The changes of heart in 1758-60 were under the inspiration of the Earl of Eglinton. 'My Lord —— made me a Deist. I surrendered myself to pleasures without bounds. I was in a

---

[52] Yale MS L 1107.
[53] *Earlier Years*, pp. 45-6, 52-4, and 569-74. Pottle noted, 'The reader is here warned, once for all, that he should accompany this stretch of the narrative with a constant qualification of "perhaps" or "possibly"'.
[54] Yale MS L 1110.
[55] Yale MS L 1107.

delirium of joy'. This phase crescendoed into what Boswell remembered as an absolute self-indulgence and dissipation: 'All of my principles were confounded'. 'My Principles became more and more confused'. The result was less a considered Humean Pyrrhonism or an Epicurean balancing of temperate pleasures than a simple escapist hedonism: 'At the end [of the process] I was a Universal Sceptic. I despised everything, and I had no idea other than to pass agreeably the day that was slipping away'.[56]

Among the more socially respectable forms of deviance he could choose was the 'Qualified' Church of England congregations in Scotland. Boswell's early exposure to Church of England ideas was partially due to the presence of such legal Anglican houses of worship in the metropolis of Edinburgh.[57] In autumn 1762 he recalled pleasant moments shared with Johnston in Church of England services held in Edinburgh: 'You also think of the Church of England Chapels, the decent form of prayer, a well-drest Clergyman and the grand sound of the Organ which lifts the soul to the celestial Regions'.[58] These Anglican congregations in Scotland should not be confused with the native tradition of Scottish Episcopalianism which had in the previous century had its day as the national Church of Scotland. Scottish Episcopalianism was a form of Nonjuring tainted (or ennobled, depending on one's politics) by its quite active association with Jacobitism from 1689-1760. Therefore, the 'Piskies' lay under the burden of impaired civil rights and religious liberties limited by the suspicion that their houses of worship were fronts for Jacobitical revolutionary cells.

One may therefore safely conclude that Boswell's cultural/religious predicament was fully developed by October 1762, by the time of his twenty-second birthday and the brink of his return to London. However, the act of recrossing onto English soil girded with the resolve to live an English life in the Guards (or failing that, to enter as a student of English law at the Inns of Court), significantly altered his situation. For by crossing the border, he ceased to be a conforming churchman, and became a confessional amphibian, a spiritual tourist.

II

Boswell's ability to look southwards for an alternative manner of belief and worship which would (unlike Methodism, Roman Catholicism, or Libertinism) be socially and politically respectable was mainly due to

---

[56] Ibid.; Yale MS L 1110.
[57] *The Correspondence of James Boswell and John Johnston of Grange*, p. xvi; David M. Bertie (ed.), *Scottish Episcopal Clergy, 1689-2000* (Edinburgh, 2001).
[58] Ibid., pp. 17-18: James Boswell to John Johnston of Grange, 27 October 1762.

the bi-confessional state in which he lived. Yet Boswell's ideas of a typical Church of England clergyman on his own home soil seem largely to have been gained from English books. He particularly relied upon the *Spectator* papers which the Rev. John Dun had assigned him as reading in his youth. Thus, when Boswell daydreamed about his friend William Temple becoming a clergyman in 'the Church [of England]', Boswell did not imagine Temple as Laud or Herbert or Ken: instead he predicted, 'He will be just like the clergyman in *The Spectator*'.[59] Furthermore, when he went to Westminster Abbey, he remarked: 'I recalled the ideas of it which I had from *The Spectator*'.[60] The idea of the *Spectator* ethos of sociability, and its strong influence on the lives of the Kirk's Moderate Church of Scotland tradition, was more evident in such an observation than any understanding of the Thirty-Nine Articles.[61]

It has been observed that much of Boswell's interest in the Church of England was in the concept of a middling high liturgy which would be 'decent', 'well-drest', and full of 'grand sound', a theatre of moderately luxurious piety. The 'Church of England Chapels' for him meant 'the decent form of prayer', a 'well-drest Clergyman' and 'the grand sound of the Organ' more than any preference for the Thirty-Nine Articles or government by vestries and bishops. He wanted grandeur, costumes, and instrumental music as much from his church as from the theatre.[62] As a major focus in Boswell's life was the idea of 'romantic' situations—medieval or pseudo-medieval pomps which gave him 'noble' ideas, and the lavishness of imagination of theatre and masquerade—it was those aspects of the eighteenth-century English church which allured him. Indeed, it has not been noted that Boswell's interest in theatre, his interest in the military, and his interest in the Church of England often rose and fell in concert with one another. He associated his piety with his amatory and romantic temperament: 'I have a warm heart and a vivacious fancy. I am therefore given to love, and also to piety or gratitude to God, and to the most brilliant and showy method of public worship'.[63] The aesthetic contrast between the spare Bauhaus masculinity of the Kirk's *Westminster Directory* with its 'homely' sermons and 'extempore' prayers, versus the deutero-Caroline Baroque of the *Book of Common Prayer*, the option for ornate Ciceronian (or at least Tillotsonian) sermons, and a set rota of prayers made Boswell incline

---

[59] Journal, 3 April 1763.
[60] Journal, 29 May 1763.
[61] Sir Alexander Grant, *The Story of the University of Edinburgh During Its First Three Hundred Years* (London, 1884), II, pp. 328-30.
[62] *The Correspondence of James Boswell and John Johnston of Grange*, pp. 17-18: James Boswell to John Johnston of Grange, 27 October 1762.
[63] Journal, 28 November 1762.

emotionally to the southern British confession. Boswell even invented personal liturgies of his own to satisfy his cravings for ceremonial departures from Edinburgh and London: 'at St. Paul's...After service, I stood in the center and took leave of the church, bowing to every quarter. I cannot help having a reverence for it'.[64]

Boswell's churchgoing in London in the residence from 1762-63 suggested that his interest in the Church of England was largely in the access it offered to the world of fashion in the metropolis. On the one hand, his solemn resolve to attend church was suggestive of the degree to which Kirk habits of diligent Sabbath-Day church-going remained: 'I am resolved to be at divine service every Sunday'.[65] On the other, his *modus operandi* of becoming a congregant of the Church of England was peculiar. Rather than 'emparishing' himself in the church to which his lodgings in Downing Street belonged, he treated the church-going as a system of tourism and course of cultural anthropology: 'I took a whim to go through all the churches and chapels in London, taking one each Sunday'.[66] Indeed, the geographical pattern of Boswell's church-going during the period of his 1762-63 London residence is suspiciously indicative of the allure he found in the established Church of South Britain.

He missed church on several days, especially during an extended bout with gonorrhoea in January-February 1763.[67] Hangovers could also be a cause of his missing services,[68] as could oversleeping.[69] He also absented himself from church on days of severe melancholy.[70] But he did not remain away from church only for bodily reasons. He absented himself if enjoying a particularly compelling visit with friends.[71] He did not attend

---

[64] Journal, 31 July 1763.
[65] Journal, 12 December 1762.
[66] Journal, 26 December 1763.
[67] Journal, 1763: 23 January: 'In the afternoon, my brother came. He brought many low old Sunday ideas when we were boys into my memory'; 30 January: 'I regretted much my being kept from divine service'; 7, 13, 20 February: 'This forenoon I read the history of Joseph and his brethren....It is a strange thing that the Bible is so little read. I am reading it regularly through at present. I dare say that there are many people of distinction in London who know nothing about it'; 27 February: 'I had now kept the house five complete weeks...My disorder was now over'.
[68] Journal, 5 June 1763: 'The fatigues of last night rendered me very lazy and disposed to relish ease'.
[69] Journal, 3 July 1763: 'I was too late of rising to go to church'.
[70] 'I was so bad this day that I could not settle to go to public worship' (Journal, 1 May 1763).
[71] Journal, 13 March 1763: 'As I was in rather bad frame, and as it was the last day of the ladies' being in London, I stayed at home from church'. Ibid., 3 April 1763: 'We [Temple and Boswell] were so happy and so pleasingly forgetful of everything but the immediate participation of cordial friendly discourse that we

church while in Oxford, that bastion of Tory high church ritual where melancholy, dislike of academic life, and sour memories of his own university days of 'confinement and other gloomy circumstances' at Edinburgh and Glasgow overcame 'All [his] old high ideas of Oxford'. He loved high church ceremonial, but he detested the monkish, donnish, pinched, and astringent temperament of high churchmen.[72] There are more similarities than differences in his disapproval of the clergymen of the liturgically plain Scottish high Kirk and the liturgically fancy English high church—it was the idea of being cloistered in a sad gloomy retreat, after all, which had helped dissuade him from becoming a Roman Catholic priest or monk.

His choice of churches 1762-63 is hardly a random sample of the houses of worship in the Metropolis, in which plain-vanilla parish churches predominated. During his 1762-3 residence, he selected two royal or palace chapels: Whitehall Chapel and the Chapel Royal of St. James's. Westminster Abbey and St. Margaret's Westminster were both official churches for the Parliament: the Abbey Church for the House of Lords, St. Margaret's for the House of Commons. St. Paul's was not only a cathedral but the church used by the Lord Mayor of London, the site of many of the grand national ceremonies from the reign of Queen Anne. The Temple Church was a centre for the legal world. The high percentage of 'chapels' he frequented were Church of England 'chapels of ease' sited in the 'Court End' or West End of town. These 'chapels' existed so their genteel congregants could have a geographically convenient and economically exclusive alternative to the inconveniently distant or dowdy or declassé parish church to which they technically should have been going. Although most of the parish churches Boswell attended were in the West End, as far as can be discerned,[73] he did work his way eastward and northward into the City churches, though he appears never to have attended church south of the Thames or east of the source of the sound of Bow Bells.

Boswell had a persistent habit of associating various superficially unrelated sentiments into a compound *portmanteau* feeling (e.g., piety and sex, hell and melancholy) and therefore he was especially fond of confounding awe at heavenly majesty and earthly majesty. His behaviour at St. George's is characteristic: even as he was impressed by the sermon,

---

did not go to church, although it was Easter Day, that splendid festival...At night, at home, I read the Church service by myself with great devotion'

[72] Journal, 23-26 April 1763, including Sunday, 24 April.
[73] Some, where the name or place is unique, can be identified beyond a reasonable doubt. On the other hand, selecting between candidates from some of the more generic church names (those which appear in John Roque's Map several times) can only be tentative and based on Boswell's known patterns.

he was busily spying on the Duchess of Grafton. His visit to the Chapel Royal was expressed in the same terms he might have used to describe a night at the Opera House at the Haymarket: 'I had a good seat and saw the King'.[74] Even his contacts with churchmen were expressed in terms of aristocratic circles, access to high life, and procuring a 'good seat': 'St. Paul's. Mr. Cooper, one of the gentlemen of the Chapel Royal, who belongs to the choir of this cathedral and whom I have seen at Lord Eglinton's, gave me a good seat by [i.e. beside] himself'.[75] Perhaps this incident may be brought in as another reason Boswell was not drawn to the Kirk's aesthetic. Although the Church of Scotland was an integral part of the 'people above', quite capable of kowtowing to aristocracy and gentry, and placed under a patronage regime of lay presentation, it was also known for its sporadic insults to noble and royal power.

It was also apparent that the appeal of the ornate and the visual was a major reason for Boswell's fascination with Church of England worship. Even a 'low' church was liturgically, musically, and decoratively lush by Kirk standards, which generally dismissed instrumental music and set prayers as 'popery' or at best puppet shows. At St. Andrew's, Holborn, Boswell remarked on '[A] very fine building. At one end of it is a window of very elegant painted glass.'[76] The *Gesamtkunstwerk* of preaching, set prayer, music, and architecture was particularly vivid for him: 'This [sermon] with the music and the good building put me into a very devout frame...my mind was left in a pleasing calm state'.[77]

Yet although Boswell embraced high church furnishings and architecture, it would be wrong to conclude that the draw of Anglicanism for him was a high church theology of the Johnsonian stamp. Boswell's initial attraction to the theology of the Church of England was to the low church teachings of the 'Latitude-Men'. Whereas Samuel Johnson's Church of England belief was self-lacerating in a Christian Stoic and ascetic tradition redolent of the Desert Fathers, Boswell actually craved a comfortable pew, a church which would cosset him and speak of the beauties of virtue and heaven rather than the horrors of vice and hell. It would be a mistake to argue that he saw all Anglican doctrine as inevitably milder and more lenient than all Church of Scotland doctrine; he dreaded Oxonian black-robed monkishness and Johnsonian water-drinking eremiticism. He had already found some comfort from the Kirk itself, in the form of Church of Scotland clergyman John Dun.[78] Although

---

[74] Journal, 26 June 1763.
[75] Journal, 19 June 1763.
[76] Journal, 22 May 1763.
[77] Journal, 10 April 1763.
[78] Yale MS L 1107.

it cannot be statistically proven, it is likely that as of 1750 the post-Tillotsonian or latitudinarian view was more prevalent in England than in Scotland. An account of 'an excellent sermon...on the comforts of piety' which he heard revealed his leading aspiration for a religious belief: 'I thought [after hearing it] that GOD really designed us to be happy'[79]. Boswell's sermon notes reflect his interest in the idea of a religion of Addisonian comfort rather than Knoxian or Covenanting rigour. His account of one sermon in particular reflects this:

> His text was, 'My yoke is easy'. He showed that although religion might in some respects be called a yoke, as it laid some restraint upon the inclinations and passions of men, yet to a mind properly trained it was easy, nay delightful. The happiness of genuine piety he displayed in elegant language enforced by just and animated action.[80]

It is unusual that in his pursuit of the life of a Church of England man, Boswell did not plunge headlong into the more unique aspects of Church of England practice, whereas he did instinctually seek out the most exotic and 'romantic' aspects of Roman Catholicism. For instance, in Scotland, although occasional (emergency) fasts and thanksgivings were ordered by the Church of Scotland, usually but not always in a rough synchronicity with the Church of England's occasional fasts and thanksgivings, the Scots Kirk did not keep annual holidays as they were thought to be 'popish'. Christmas was euphemized as 'the daft days' and kept in homes rather than conformist churches. This refusal was a matter of Knoxian doctrine rather than specific politics: even Whiggish holidays such as the fifth of November or first of August went largely unobserved. Boswell admittedly faced a major impediment in his first attempt to observe 'the fast' on the anniversary of 'The Martyrdom of King Charles' according to the Anglican rites. Although he professed, 'I could have wished to hear some of the sermons this day', and mourned that 'This tragical event is an indelible stain on the British nation', gonorrhoea kept him from the ceremonies.[81] Boswell's description of Charles as the 'Worthy, though misguided Monarch!' demonstrates that his churchmanship from 1758-63 was not as high as one might imagine from his effusions about church-and-king Toryism and Jacobitical notions. Yet he did retain a particular fondness for the thirtieth of January as a holiday of Toryism.

The second unusual thing about Boswell's move towards conformity with the Church of England is that he was not a communicant from autumn 1762, nor indeed until December 1763, when he first took the

---

[79] Journal, 21 November 1762
[80] Journal, 9 January 1763.
[81] Journal, 31 January 1763.

communion in the Chapel of the British Ambassador to the United Provinces of the Netherlands. On that festival, he observed: 'This is Christmas day. Be in due frame. Only hear prayers at Chapel, but don't take sacrament except you can see Chaplain before'. The day after, he recorded, 'The first time that I received the communion in the Church of England'.[82] He elaborated on the 'affable and decent' treatment which he received. 'Yesterday [Dec. 25] you waited on Mr. Richardson, Chaplain to Sir Joseph Yorke; found him affable and decent. Took you up to his room, told you, "Our Church leaves it to every man". Presented to Ambassador...Took [sacrament] with him. Then Chapel. "Grace and truth": fine sermon. Then received the blessed sacrament solemnly professing myself a Christian; was in devout, heavenly frame, quite happy'.[83] As has been known since the work of Norman Sykes, communion in most of the churches and chapels of the Church of England did not tend to occur more frequently than annually or quarterly. Yet it is somewhat odd that Boswell, who had seemingly attended Qualified Chapels courtesy of Johnston of Grange and William Johnson Temple from the mid/late-1750s, delayed his taking holy communion in the Church of England for six to eight years. His dilatoriness in communicating would be peculiar even by low church standards of annual or quarterly communions.

In addition to a rota of private prayers,[84] Boswell adopted fasting, at least as early as 1764, as a religious practice. This fasting consisted of meatless Fridays, generally, as in the Memorandum for 17 February 1764: 'Fast today, or be only maigre by having two rolls at breakfast'.[85] His ten-lines-a-day poem for 17 February remarked, 'The great Apostles bid us often fast;/And think you, Christians, that its use is past?....For me, whose gen'rous and aspiring mind/Is now to solemn piety resign'd,/I shall keep Friday as a holiday [alternate line supplied: 'I shall at seasons set apart a day']/And as the Church directs me, fast and pray'.[86]

Boswell's revolt against confessional respectability and conformity—his personal struggle against the sort of Scoto-Calvinism sanctioned by state, confession, and the cult of Ayrshire and Edinburgh neighbourliness—deepened during his stays in England 1762-63 and the United Provinces of the Netherlands 1763-64, and during his 'Grand Tour' on the Continent 1764-66. In all of these locales, the Church of Scotland was not the established church, but merely one option.

There is not sufficient space in this chapter to trace Boswell's various church-goings in the United Provinces of the Netherlands 1763-4, nor his

---

[82] Memoranda, 25-26 December 1763.
[83] Memoranda, 26 December 1763.
[84] E.g. Memoirs, 13, 14, 18 February 1764
[85] Memoranda, 17 February 1764, in *Boswell in Holland 1763-1764*, pp. 152-3.
[86] Ten Lines a Day, 17 February 1764, *Boswell in Holland 1763-1764*, pp. 152-3.

encounters with arch-sceptics as well as various denominations of Protestant. Furthermore, the loss of the majority of the Netherlands journal in Boswell's own lifetime means that the detailed portrait which exists of Boswell's attendance at worship and reflections on church-going and theology which we have in abundance for September 1762 to July 1763 is largely missing for August 1763 to June 1764. However, the patterns set in 1758-63, which have been explored in detail, provide the key to the understanding of Boswell's trials of faith on the Continent in 1763-64, and by extension during the 'Grand Tour' 1764-66.

III

The remainder of Boswell's church-going life from 1764 until his death in 1795 is complex, and not within the limited compass of this essay which has stressed his piety from 1745-64 in the context of national confessional identity. However, some provisional conclusions may be made on the basis of a close reading of the later journals, especially those of Boswell's life in Edinburgh and Ayrshire.[87]

First, Boswell maintained his religious eccentricities and his ecclesiastical tourism and gourmandizing until the end of his life. He continued in his London jaunts his custom begun in 1760 of going to the Roman Catholic ambassadors' chapels, particularly the Bavarian Chapel, to hear Mass. And yet he did not assertively seek out Catholic congregations elsewhere in Britain than in London, although they were indeed operating less covertly as the respectability of the 'Catholic Relief' agenda advanced in 1778-81.[88] What Boswell called his 'superstition' and 'devotion' continued to be balanced by what he referred to as his 'enthusiasm', as his curious attendance at Friends and Methodist meetings and respect for certain Seceder and Independent Scots practitioners demonstrated.

Boswell's relative openness to a variety of religious experiences was another manner in which he was an inveterate collector of sensations and characters. His pursuit of differing personalities often seems to be a form of butterfly collection, in which Boswell strove to collect a cabinet of

---

[87] Particularly those from 1775-76 published in *Boswell: The Ominous Years, 1774-1776*, edited by Charles Ryskamp and Frederick A. Pottle (New York, 1963).

[88] Roughly, from the Roman Catholic Relief Act of 1778 until the University Tests Act of 1871. The University Tests Act ended religious tests theretofore binding on candidates for university degrees, whether they were Dissenters or Catholics.

'types' or 'species' of religious believers who would evoke certain memories, feelings, and associations in him. His journals and letters show him seeking out the company of those whose beliefs challenged his own. He slotted his friends and relations into those various categories, and allowed them the power to conjure up their various humours in him on his visits with them.

The confessional width of Boswell's circle of heterodox and orthodox friends leads us to a conclusion about the nature of human life and the ways in which human relationships altered the seemingly adamantine abstractions of the bi-confessional polity of Georgian Britain. Further discussion of the cultural wars of the denominations in the eighteenth century must always keep in view the existence—even within that conflictive age of confessional and sectarian battles of orthodox and heterodox—of the mitigating and mollifying influence of catholicity, visits to alien forms of worship, intra-denominationalism, fellowship, and friendship. It is, admittedly, important to understand that religious doctrine and creed mattered a great deal to people in Georgian Britain. Yet as a corrective, one must at the same time realize that outside a small percentage of hard-core isolationist zealots in Scotland and England, the effects of sociability, society, friendship, and love crossed and re-crossed the denominational lines. Study of the circles of friends and relatives of Boswell, and even Johnson, demonstrates this fact abundantly. Boswell's personal doubts about the rights and wrongs of orthodoxy and orthopraxis in the national churches of Scotland and England were fuelled by the considerable number of his friends and relatives who were Seceders, Glassites, Scots Episcopalians, 'Qualifiers', Protestant Dissenters, Roman Catholics, and Socinians—even louche sceptics or 'infidels'. He could not bring himself to believe those articles of the Thirty-Nine Articles or the Westminster Confession which would destine mechanized humans into an eternity of punishment based on a sin of two people whom they had never met. Therefore, Boswell's wobbliness on the doctrines of hell and purgatory, predestination and election and grace, were conceived of in his passions more than in his reason. He became a crypto-Socinian, pseudo-Pelagian, proto-Universalist, and a devotional high-liturgical Catholic not from a rigorous study of theology, but from affective and sentimental feelings about those whom he knew. Outside of a small cadre of doctrinaire theologians, one suspects that this was the case for the majority of people in Georgian Britain: that the influence of relatives, friends, local custom, and emotional sense of rightness trumped strictness of doctrine. This was especially true in the 'age of sentiment' in which Boswell lived.

Yet this leads to the second conclusion. Despite his eccentricity, despite his denominational wanderings and eclectic range of friends and worship styles, Boswell was essentially a conformist, both socially and religiously. He retained the association of ideas between the English liturgy and the grandiose thoughts which England, and London in particular, inspired in him. Thus, attending the English liturgy was a method of culturally affiliating himself with the English, and particularly the London power elite whose churches he favoured. Whereas one might be excused for claiming *ad silentium* that Johnson was a Nonjuror, the earth is littered with Boswellian accommodations to the status quo: from his earliest burgess tickets, through the oaths he took to qualify for the two nations' legal professions. He had one famous qualm when he worried that the anti-Catholic 'Formula' Oath might be applied to him, but was able, like most Scots in England, to swear the necessary oaths in both countries when and as needed.

Arguably, Boswell was a *religious* conformist because he was a *social* conformist. His years of attendance at the Edinburgh New Kirk, one of the most prestigious congregations of the Church of Scotland conformist elite, were sometimes positive, but occasionally marked by a sullenness and resentment of the Knoxian style of worship. However, he repeatedly stated that he attended Kirk worship while he was living in Scotland in order to gain his father's approval and forbearance, which in turn would help secure the estate of Auchinleck for his inheritance. He also did so to placate his wife, to normalize the lives of his children, and to gain a better chance of success as a lawyer, and as an aspirant to the bench, or to a Crown post, or to the Commons. He rationalized to Temple that 'The General Assembly is sitting; and I practise at its' bar. There is *de facto* something low & coarse in such employment, though *upon paper*, it is a *Supreme Judicature*. But Guineas must be had'.[89] Yet in a public article he wrote for the *London Magazine*, he spoke more highly of the General Assembly. For the London press, he wrote that it was a 'Supreme Judicature' and 'perhaps the most learned assembly of men that now meet for deliberation as a court, or tribunal, or legislative body', and boasted that 'THE Church, or, as it has been called, *Kirk* of Scotland exhibits an example of one of the most regular and best-contrived Republics that has ever existed', whose constitution was one which 'the greatest lovers of liberty and equality must admire'.[90] Boswell was not loath to dine at HM High Commissioner's Table in 1777, 1780, and 1782, and in 1782 dined at the 'Minister's' table of the Commissioner's ceremonial purse-bearer.[91]

---

[89] *The Correspondence of James Boswell and William Johnson Temple, 1756-1777*, Thomas Crawford (ed.), (New Haven and London, 1997), VI, pp. 379-81: James Boswell to William Johnson Temple, 3 June 1775.

[90] *London Magazine* 41 (1772): 'A Sketch of the Constitution of the Church of Scotland', pp. 181-7, and 'The Same Continued', pp. 237-42.

[91] *Private Papers of James Boswell from Malahide Castle in the Collection of Lt.-Colonel Ralph Heyward Isham* (privately published, 1931, 1932), XII, p. 196; XIV, p. 87; XV, p. 83.

Even after becoming Laird of Auchinleck, Boswell chose to remain bound by his duty in a conventional sense of post-1712 Kirkmanship based on Boswell's own peculiarly Patriot/Tory vision of Crown, aristocratic, and gentry patronage of the parish clergy. He did not, as he had threatened his father he might, join the growing ranks of socially acceptable Qualifiers. Nor did he hire an episcopal chaplain for his home or build a Qualifying Chapel of Ease for himself. As laird, he played the expected role of Kirk patron of Auchinleck and Heritor of Ochiltree, Mauchline, and other Ayrshire kirks without much kicking against the various pricks of Ayrshire society. Despite his fears of presbyterianism as vulgar and undignified, his Tory feelings of the thrill of paternalism were stoked in Mauchline Kirk: 'I gave a guinea to the poor. I sat in the front of the loft belonging to my family, and looked with great satisfaction on my tenants ranged behind me'.[92] Boswell took an active interest in the supply of ministers to the pulpit of Auchinleck. Peculiarly, rather than choosing 'Court Party' or 'Moderate' ministers of the sort whose preaching he preferred, he presented to his church a member of the evangelicals/popular party/high-flyers/zealots faction of the sort his grandfather and father had preferred.[93] He even laid the foundation stone for the new Ochiltree parish kirk. Boswell apparently considered such religious conformity to the customs of the country to be an outward sign of good lairdship as much as his meetings with the estate managers.

Boswell's distancing of himself from his national confessional state was never merely a 'denominational dilemma' in the way Frederick Pottle and Mary Margaret Stewart stressed it. The Kirk tradition of Knox, Melville, and Carstares was not, to be sure, all of Scotland, anymore than the church of Cranmer, Hampton Court, the Clarendon Codes, and Gibson was all of England. Revolt and Dissent were possible and culturally vital forces in both countries. Having said that, the Kirk in its state as a church by law established from 1690 and 1712 was a reflection of the wider Scottish culture as much as a shaper of it. Those Kirk traditions by the year of Boswell's birth in 1740 were so tangled up in issues of Scottish national identity, both official and popular, that they formed part and parcel of his dance of acceptance and rejection of his own Scottishness.[94] Boswell was embarrassed, especially when in

---

[92] Ibid., XV, pp. 127-8.
[93] John Lindsay [served 1793-1818], acc. Stewart, 'James Boswell and the National Church of Scotland', p. 384.
[94] A dance studied in Roger Craik, *James Boswell: 1740-1795: The Scottish Perspective* (Edinburgh, 1994); Kenneth Simpson, *The Protean Scot: The Crisis of Identity in Eighteenth-Century Scottish Literature* (Aberdeen, 1988), chapter 5; Gordon Turnbull, 'James Boswell: Biography and the Union' in Andrew Hook (ed.), *The History of Scottish Literature, 1660-1800* (Aberdeen, 1987), pp.

England, by most of Lowlands and Urban Scots culture: its heavy accents, its allegedly 'impure' grammar and pronunciation, its hard drinking, its coarse table manners and unrefined country dishes, its bawdy jokes and songs, its zealous Whiggery, and its brutal tradition of humiliating and devouring its own kings. He felt all the worse about them because throughout much of his life he enjoyed them. His mixed feelings about the lack of dignity and devotion in the Scottish church were wrapped up in his general aesthetic fear that Scots culture was itself lacking in dignity and devotion.

Thus, for Boswell to consider rejecting the Kirk was not simply a 'denominational' quandary of abandoning the Westminster Confession and the Kirk worship. Nor was his grousing submission to its authority in marriage, baptisms, and burial solely due to materialistic concerns of inheriting the land (to which qualified Anglicanism would not have been a bar) or even placating his 'presbyterian' father and wife. Certainly after his father died and he became Laird of Auchinleck in 1782, and after his wife died in 1789, he could have freed himself from many of the confines. He lived in the second half of the century when short of Covenanting scrupling or Roman Catholicism or Jacobitism, he could have lived in whichever confession he pleased and still remained a lawyer and a laird and even an M.P. (if he could be elected). Yet he did not change his religious affiliation, nor did he ever become a fully assimilated Englishman.

The third conclusion is that Boswell's experience, while unusually (some would say dauntingly) well-documented, was likely not an exceptional one, despite Boswell's obvious eccentricities. Many more eighteenth-century diaries and letters record such matters of conformism and churchmanship. A balanced account of 'typical' behaviour in church in the eighteenth century should include them.

If we base our accounts of religious belief solely or even mainly on the great champions of resistance to the status quo—whether high church/high Kirk, or Covenanter, or Seceder, or Jacobite/nonjuror, or urban Painite dissident, or Dissenter, or sceptical rationalist—the view we get of conformity and accommodation in the eighteenth-century churches will be a very warped and distorted one indeed. The typical excuse used for avoiding a more broadly-based account is that 'conformity

---

157–74; Andrew Noble, 'James Boswell: Scotland's Prodigal Son', in T.M. Devine (ed.), *Improvement and Enlightenment* (Edinburgh, 1989). See especially Boswell's *Edinburgh Journals 1767-1786*, edited by Hugh Milne (Edinburgh, 2001, revised edition 2003). Milne has performed invaluable service in restoring the emphasis on Boswell as chiefly a resident of Edinburgh (or Auchinleck) and a Scot rather than simply a would-be Londoner and Englishman.

writes in invisible ink', i.e., that it leaves less capacious records than refusals and riots and martyrdoms do. Yet Boswell's case suggests quite the opposite: that many conformists left records of their encounters with and accommodations to the churches established by law. Hopefully, as accounts of eighteenth-century piety which situate it as the continuance of a 'Long Reformation' from 1500 onwards absorb some of the methods and interests of Reformation Studies, there will be more examinations of the ways in which religious believers accommodated their lives and doubts to a world where the alliance of church and state still intruded itself into a vast array of aspects of everyday life. Certainly we would be unwise to presume that British society 1700-1800 was 'secular' in any meaningful sense.

The fourth and final conclusion is that any model of credal and confessional ascendancy in Georgian Britain must include the unique arrangement of the bi-confessional state as one of its basic assumptions. A Little Englander's account of the 'Confessional Old Regime' which omits or at best marginalizes Scotland and the peculiar institution of the Kirk by Law Established is as eccentric and as flawed an account of Britain as would occur if one tried to write a history of Canada without reference to Quebec. Likewise, to mis-conceptualize Scotland's role in British history as that of an exotic 'Celtic Fringe' (as peripheral Looking-Glass-World of not-England mirroring and reversing England's historiographically-assumed normality and centrality) ignores the dialogue and debate and the mutual influences shared between the two Protestant national churches and their adherents from 1689-1800—especially among the 'amphibians' such as Boswell whose travel and immigration within the bi-confessional Old Regime became more frequent and more easy as the eighteenth century progressed. The Church of Scotland was an Establishment, not an optional 'denomination' of 'presbyterianism' subject to rational consumer choice, but a persuasive foundation and expression of the elite, the populace, and the governing structures. The Kirk must be replaced at the centre of studies of religion and society in Britain in 1750-1800, even (especially?) when discussing the 'Enlightenment'. The numerous worthy studies of the minoritarian experiences of the waning (albeit bravely struggling and enduring) subcultures of Scottish Jacobite Episcopalianism and Roman Catholicism are well worth undertaking, but not at the expense of ignoring the centrality in Scottish life in the latter half of the eighteenth century of the dominant and established majoritarian national Church of Boswell's lifetime which successfully defended its traditions against the threat of English assimilation. Scotland and its confessional auld regime may have been the smaller star in the binary pair of Episcopalian and Presbyterian establishments, but it exerted a strong and significant gravitational pull on the lives of Britons

1712-1832 none the less. Boswell's conflictive youth was a living proof of its strength.

Chapter 9

'In the Church I will live and die':
John Wesley, the Church of England, and Methodism

Jeremy Gregory

One of the central dilemmas, and perhaps the most worked-over issue, in eighteenth-century religious history is the question of John Wesley's relationship with the Church of England. How far did he remain a devout and sincere member of the church, and how far was his religious identity quintessentially bound up with that membership? Conversely, how far was Wesley's religious allegiance increasingly outside the church, so that statements such as the one used in this essay's title might be no more than a wilfully deceptive smokescreen to hide the emergence of a new religious movement that effectively stood outside (and even against) it? One of Wesley's correspondents reprimanded him in 1761: 'did you not betray the Church, as Judas his Master, with a kiss?',[1] and someone who might be thought to have had inside information, Thomas Adam, the rector of Wintringham and a former friend of Wesley's, eventually turned against him, accusing Wesley and the Methodists of acting 'under a lie'.[2] We might also ask how far Wesley had a consistent and coherent position towards the established church. Did his attitude towards it change over time, or was it rather that external circumstances altered, which made it seem that Wesley had modified his allegiance? Moreover, what was the nature of that change? Can we discern a linear development, or was it a more confused trajectory? How far were the details of his own biography—the influences upon him, his relationships with members of his family (particularly his mother and younger brother Charles) and friends, and external stimuli, such as the reaction of the established church to his ministry—responsible

---

[1] John Wesley to the editor of the *London Magazine*, in *The Letters of the Revd. John Wesley, M.A.*, John Telford (ed.), (London, 1931), IV, p. 122. It may, of course, be that Wesley fabricated this correspondent. There are several editions of Wesley's works. Unless otherwise stated, I shall use the 'standard' editions: *Letters*, Telford (ed.) and *The Journal of the Revd. John Wesley, A.M.*, Nehemiah Curnock (ed.), (London, 1909-16). In writing this I have benefited greatly from talking to Peter Nockles and Gareth Lloyd, the custodians of the Methodist Archives in the John Rylands University Library of Manchester [hereafter: JRULM], and from the comments of John Walsh and Henry Rack, all of whom would have written a much better essay than this.

[2] *Letters*, V, p. 98: John Wesley to Thomas Adam, 19 July 1768.

for causing changes to his religious position, or how far were changes the result of his own choosing? It is, for example, sometimes argued that the more vociferous Methodist lay preachers pushed Wesley in a direction in which he was reluctant to go, and that some of his actions were the result of outside pressures.[3] Other scholars have suggested that Wesley's stance, and in particular his decision to ordain ministers in 1784 for America (then for Scotland, the West Indies, and finally England in 1788), which is conventionally seen as the point where he had ceased to belong to the church, was more radical than the bulk of the lay preachers and rank and file Methodists wanted, and there are debates about how far separation was a real possibility in Wesley's mind nearly forty years earlier.[4] What caused Wesley to form a movement that would eventually stand outside the church? Was it his own sense of destiny, his sheer determination and egocentric will, or a pragmatic response to events? Was it an accident, or was it God's plan?

Questions such as these (and especially the last) concerning Wesley's religious identity and motivation are probably impossible to answer. Can we ever know what moved people in the past, and in any case, even when, as with Wesley, we have a large amount of available autobiographical information, how far are individuals good judges of what spurs them on? An individual might be unreliable (both consciously and subconsciously) about their own motivation—as scholars have shown in their readings of St. Augustine's *Confessions*, the classic religious autobiography (which Wesley admired).[5] But these may still be questions worth asking since issues surrounding Wesley's religious identity have implications for more than the biography of an individual. Perhaps more than any other modern religious movement, the emergence of Methodism has become associated

---

[3] Norman Sykes, *Church and State in England in the XVIIIth Century* (Cambridge, 1934), p. 394. Wesley himself hints this: *Letters*, VIII, p. 79: John Wesley to Mrs Ward, 2 August 1788; and there are references by Charles of his brother's being pressurized by the preachers: JRULM DD/WES/4/64: Charles Wesley to Sarah Wesley [n.d, 1785?]. Charles also blamed the more extreme of John's advisors: Charles Wesley to Samuel Walker, 21 August 1756, in Frank Baker, *Charles Wesley as Revealed by his Letters* (London, 1948), p. 95, and he commented on his brother's 'indecisiveness' and 'weakness': JRULM, Charles Wesley's Papers 7/2/53: Charles Wesley to Sarah Wesley, 2 March 1760.

[4] Gareth Lloyd, 'Charles Wesley: A New Evaluation of his Life and Ministry', (University of Liverpool PhD thesis, 2002), *passim*. Dr. Lloyd's important thesis transforms our understanding of Charles and is highly significant for those interested in the relationship between Methodism and the Church of England. Sociologists of religion might see the drift of the Wesleyans from the Church as a movement outside Wesley's personal control, and just another example of the inevitable trajectory by which new religious movements shed their original status as ginger-groups and hardened into new churches; see Eileen Barker, *New Religious Movements: A Perspective for Understanding Society* (New York, 1982). I owe this observation to John Walsh.

[5] St. Augustine, *Confessions*, translated by Henry Chadwick (Oxford, 1991). For Wesley's admiration of the *Confessions*, see *Letters*, II, p. 60: John Wesley to 'John Smith', 30 December 1745.

with a single personality. This means that, although during the 1740s and early 1750s Wesley was but one of several who jostled for leadership of the movement, nevertheless, because of his eventual supremacy, he is effectively seen by scholars as the dominant voice of the emerging denomination. Wesley has thus become synonymous with Methodism and the ways in which his own relationship with the established church is conceptualized has influenced how scholars have viewed the relationship between Anglicans and Methodists in the eighteenth century more generally. Was this essentially a separatist association, paving the way for nineteenth-century differences (encapsulated in the church/chapel divide)? Or was it a more all-encompassing relationship, anticipating, perhaps, recent moves towards ecumenism, leading some scholars to suggest that discerning where Wesley really stood on this issue has implications for present-day Anglican-Methodist relations.[6] What I want to do in this essay is to use Wesley's own relations with the Church of England to illuminate the broader problem of the relationship between Methodism and Anglicanism in Georgian England. This of course begs the issue of the extent to which Wesley himself can be seen to be a representative Methodist figure—which, given his very unusual role in the movement, means that on most issues he was not simply typical.

In many ways this is very well-trodden ground. No biographer of Wesley has been able to ignore these questions, since, at a certain level, Wesley's life, at least as revealed through his publications, Journals, and letters, can be said to have had his relationship with the established church as its major theme. Given that these questions have long been mulled over, even from the earliest days of the movement, it might reasonably be asked how far it is worth rehearsing them again. I certainly do not have any fresh material to bring to the problem and therefore it might be thought that nothing new could be said about the topic. But there may be some justification for another look at the evidence. A volume on eighteenth-century religious personalities which omitted some discussion of Wesley would look decidedly lop-sided given that Wesley was arguably the most significant single individual in eighteenth-century religious developments. And the wealth of surviving documentation—there is perhaps more autobiographical material for Wesley than for any eighteenth-century figure—allows some consideration of the possibilities and difficulties involved in exploring an individual's religious identity, so that the issues broached by examining the question of Wesley's religious affiliation might shed light on the wider questions raised by this collection of essays.

I should state at the outset that in exploring Wesley's religious identity I am going to concentrate more on what Wesley said than on what he did. This might be thought to be stacking the cards unfairly on one side of the equation since it has often been argued that Wesley's statements are an unreliable source of evidence, and that a surer way into his religious

---

[6] Albert C. Outler, *The Christian Tradition and the Unity We Seek* (New York and Oxford, 1957); John Munsey Turner, *Conflict and Reconciliation* (London, 1985).

position would be to examine his actions rather than his words.[7] A common reading of what he did presents us with a Wesley, who despite his own protestations, showed how little he cared for the church. The development of the Methodist societies, the use of lay preachers, and the disregard for parish boundaries challenged the Anglican parish system, and his ordination of ministers proves that he wanted to establish a rival church. Even the way in which he came to justify ordaining others, through selective citations of Lord King and Edward Stillingfleet on church orders, has been seen as a convenient and pragmatic justification for something that he had already decided to do.[8] Furthermore, some scholars have suggested that what he said, as revealed in his writings, and especially the *Journals*, are very misleading guides to what Wesley actually believed, and that they should be seen at best as propaganda for the new religious movement and at worst an exercise in dissimulation.[9] The *Journals* were written up some time after the events they describe, and on several occasions Wesley's version can be shown to have been highly partial.[10] How useful are Wesley's written words as a window into his religious identity and allegiance, and in what sense can we regard the *Journals* as a religious autobiography? W.R. Ward, in his masterly introduction to the *Journals*, suggests that in terms of seeking out Wesley's religiosity, his written words will not take us very far since the *Journals* were essentially records of actions and deeds and not of religious thoughts.[11]

It may be, however, that we can be too dismissive of the *Journals* as evidence of Wesley's religious position. The charge that the *Journals* are somehow unreliable could be very well made about Augustine's *Confessions* and Newman's *Apologia* too,[12] but no one has doubted that these texts are not exceptionally important sources for understanding their authors' religious views. Ward's comments suggest that in comparison with, say, Augustine, Bunyan, and Newman, Wesley, for all the talk of the religion of the heart, leaves us very little to go on. There are, it is true, few sustained and extended passages of spiritual self-reflection. But we should not take introspection as the only model for religious experience. Religious identity can be formed as much from a communal and a social encounter as from a private one. To a large degree, Wesley's religious identity seems to have come from his interaction with others. In this he was very much a child of his age, and the stress on 'clubbability' which has been seen as a

---

[7] Henry Rack, *Reasonable Enthusiast: John Wesley and the Rise of Methodism* (London, 2002; 2nd edn.), p. 303.
[8] Ibid., pp. 292, 295.
[9] Richard P. Hietzenrater, *Wesley and the People Called Methodist* (Nashville, 1995), pp. 117, 211, 261, 208.
[10] Rack, *Reasonable Enthusiast*, pp. 292-5.
[11] W.R. Ward, 'Introduction', *The Works of John Wesley*, vol. 18, *Journal and Diaries*, R.P. Heitzenrater and W.R. Ward (eds.), (Nashville, 1988), I, p. 29. The extended entry for 24 May 1738 (*Journal*, I, pp. 465-7), when Wesley's heart was 'strangely warmed', can be placed within a tradition of conversion narratives, but was one of the few pieces of sustained writing in this manner.
[12] See Peter Brown, *Augustine of Hippo: a biography* (London, 1967).

hallmark of the century,[13] has some resonance with Wesley's religiosity (he famously remarked that the Bible knows nothing about solitary religion).[14] As Frederick Dreyer has shown, Wesley envisaged the Methodists as making up a 'society', or even a club where membership was based on mutual consent and reciprocity.[15] There is nothing in Wesley, or perhaps in any other eighteenth-century writer, which conceives of religiosity in John Henry Newman's supremely individualistic statement that there were 'two only absolute and luminously self-evident beings, myself and my Creator'.[16] Instead Wesley's religious highs came through contact with others rather than through inward soul-searching. Time and again, the *Journals* reveal his delight in being in a religious meeting with others and it is then that he records that he is truly happy. For instance, in June 1790, nine months before he died, he visited Newcastle upon Tyne for the last time, poignantly noting 'in the evening I took a solemn leave of this lovely people, perhaps never to see them more in this life'.[17] For someone whose own personality might have made him appear highly egotistical, Wesley does seem to have depended on constant human interaction (although of course this begs the question of the extent to which interaction with others was more an exercise in authority). Nevertheless, the importance of belonging to a group may be a key to his religious sensibility, and may explain why he did not want to sever his ties to the church (which was the group in which he had been brought up), or to the Methodists (the group of which he became the effective leader).

There is another sense in which Wesley's *Journals* can give us an insight into his religious affiliation. The very fact that Wesley intended his *Journal* for publication means that his statements were intended to be read by as wide an audience as possible, and they would not, of course, be seen merely by his critics, but were widely consulted by his supporters. In this, they can be seen not only as a record of his religious position but also as instructions to his followers. Viewed in this way, the *Journals* can be seen as a repeated warning to Methodists not to leave the church. He noted in 1783, a year before his first ordinations, that 'in my Journals, in the Magazine, in every possible way, I have advised the Methodists to keep to the Church. They that do this most prosper best in their souls; I have observed it long. If ever the Methodists in general were to leave the Church, I must leave them'.[18] So even if, as some suggest, his printed words are misleading representations of his own thoughts, the effects of his repeated pronouncements in print should not be minimized. From start to

---

[13] Peter Clark, *British Clubs and Societies, 1580-1800: the Origins of an Associational World* (Oxford, 2000).
[14] Quoted in G. R. Cragg, 'The churchman', in J.L. Clifford (ed.), *Man Versus Society in Eighteenth-Century Britain* (Cambridge, 1968), p. 65.
[15] Frederick Dreyer, 'A "Religious Society under Heaven": John Wesley and the Identity of Methodism', *Journal of British Studies* 25:1 (January 1986), pp. 78-80.
[16] John Henry Newman, *Apologia pro vita sua: being a history of his religious opinions*, Martin J. Svaglic (ed.), (Oxford, 1967), p. 18.
[17] *Journal*, VIII, p. 70 : 9 June 1790.
[18] *Letters*, VII, p. 163: John Wesley to Joseph Taylor, 16 January 1783.

end, the *Journals* were adamant about the necessary relationship between Methodism and the church. In 1748, for example, he advised the Welsh Methodists 'not to leave the Church, and not to rail at their ministers'[19] (and to strengthen this sentiment he wrote *A Word to the Methodists*, which he had translated into Welsh).[20] He later noted—almost as an admonition to his readers—the loss which the Irish Methodists had felt when some of them left the Church of England.[21] During his almost annual visits to Newcastle (he visited 48 times between 1742 and 1790) his *Journal* showed him to be a conscientious attendee at one or other of the parish churches. On his second visit to the city in November 1742, having preached to his followers at 5 a.m., he went to All Saints Church, 'where [there were] such a number of communicants as I have scarce seen but in Bristol', and in 1743 he was impressed by the 'useful' and 'practical' sermons he heard preached at St. Nicholas's and St. Andrew's.[22] On 10 March 1745 he claimed he was much 'refreshed' by both the Anglican sermons he heard that day, and declared that he was 'united in love both to the two preachers and to the clergy in general'.[23] In 1755 he was dismayed to find that 'many were on the point of leaving the Church, which some had done already—and, as they supposed on my authority'. He thus set about demonstrating that he was very much a member of the church, being careful that, having preached at 8 a.m. at Gateshead Fell, he had returned before the service at St. Andrew's began.[24] At the Sacrament there he noted that many 'found an uncommon blessing and felt God has not left the Church. In the following week', he continued, 'I spoke to the members of the society severally and found far fewer than I expected prejudiced against the Church'.[25]

A key way of demonstrating the Methodists' allegiance to the church was the decision which Wesley kept to throughout his life not to have Methodist meetings at the same time as church services. In 1786 he recorded in the *Journal*: 'We fixed both our morning and evening service all over England, at such hours as not to interfere with the Church, with this very design—that those of the Church, if they chose it, might attend both the one and the other. But to fix it at the same hour is obliging them to separate, either from the Church or us, and this I judge to be not only inexpedient, but totally unlawful for me to do'.[26] Wesley also liked to

---

[19] *Journal*, III, p. 335: 26 March 1748
[20] Ibid.
[21] *Journal*, V, p. 211: 15 June 1767.
[22] *Journal* (Heitzenrater and Ward), V, p. 301: 14 November 1742; *Journal*, V, p. 4: 6 November 1743.
[23] *Journal*, VI, p. 55: 10 March 1745.
[24] *Journal* (Heizenrater and Ward), X, p. 11, 13-18: May 1755.
[25] Ibid.
[26] *Journal* (Heitzenrater and Ward), XXIII, p. 422: 22 October 1786. In the last few years of his life Wesley did not defend his selective allowance of service in Church hours. Nevertheless we should take seriously his apparently paradoxical assertion that this was to prevent, not to further, separation. What he was doing was making minimum concessions in the small number of places where the pressure for separation was greatest. By making the concessions he

portray himself in the *Journals* as someone who was stopping the more radical Methodists from leaving the church altogether. In these instances he was the loyal churchman standing firm against those who wanted Methodism to slide into nonconformity. In 1787 he reported that,

> I went over to Deptford; but it seemed I was got into a den of lions. Most of the leading men of the society were mad for separating from the Church. I endeavoured to reason with them, but in vain; they had neither sense nor even good manners left. At length, after meeting the whole society, I told them: 'If you are resolved, you may have your service in Church hours, but remember, from that time you will see my face no more'. This struck deep; and from that hour I have heard no more of separating from the Church.[27]

But despite such public statements against separation, in investigating Wesley's relationship to the Church of England, scholars have, unsurprisingly perhaps, highlighted the contradictory and ambiguous nature of his position. Nearly a century ago, Nehemiah Curnock, the editor of the 'standard' edition of Wesley's *Journals*, noted that 'it cannot be denied that Wesley's views were slowly perhaps but seriously modified', and he lamented that '[b]oth his enemies and admirers have quoted words and deeds of his during this long transition period that seem to justify the charge of inconsistency'. But, so Curnock assured his readers, 'it was the inconsistency of a man emerging out of darkness into light, and who saw men as trees walking'.[28] What this actually means other than to suggest that the seeming inconsistency was in fact explicable and understandable is slightly unclear, although, as a prominent late Victorian Methodist scholar, Curnock was keen to defend the integrity of Wesley's position. Over thirty years ago, Frank Baker dedicated a whole volume to Wesley's relations with the Church of England.[29] His general interpretation was that in many respects Wesley was 'a bundle of contradictions', and having reviewed most of the pertinent evidence, concluded that Wesley was motivated by two competing visions of the church—the apostolic church on the one hand, which led Wesley to side with the establishment, and on the other, the church as a primitive society of believers, which encouraged him to stray beyond the confines of the Church of England.[30] It was these competing visions of what was meant by the church that, according to Baker, led to Wesley's inconsistencies and ambiguities, although Wesley himself did not necessarily see the two impulses as contradictory. In 1758 he maintained that the Church of England and the Church of Christ went

---

staved off formal secession and kept Methodism united. I owe this observation to Henry Rack.

[27] *Journal*, VII, p. 232: 2 January 1787.
[28] *Journal*, III, p. 230, fn.
[29] Frank Baker, *John Wesley and the Church of England* (London, 1970).
[30] John Wesley, *The Works of John Wesley*, XXV, *Letters*, I, Frank Baker (ed.), (Nashville, 1982), p. 3; Baker, *Wesley and the Church of England*, p. 137.

hand in hand and 'that we need not separate from the Church, in order to preserve our Allegiance to Christ, but may be firm members thereof.'[31]

It may, of course, be that the whole effort to find coherence in an individual's beliefs and behaviour is itself a misguided undertaking. Quentin Skinner, for example, has warned us of the fallacy of authorial consistency, and has argued that attempts to find a coherent narrative from people's words are fruitless. In order to understand the meaning of any utterance (written or spoken) we need to pay attention to issues of genre, context, and authorial intention, as well as to the response of the reader/hearer.[32] A related solution would be to take a post-modernist approach to the question of Wesley's (and indeed to everyone else's) religious identity. According to this view, it is useless—and distorting—to expect to find a single, coherent personality. Rather, individuals have multiple, and even perhaps contradictory, identities. From this perspective, the inconsistencies we can find in Wesley are inconsistencies which, no doubt writ large, we could find in everyone.

Nevertheless, in this essay I want to make the case for taking Wesley's statements about his relationship with the church more seriously than some of his contemporaries and some later scholars have been prone to do. In writing on Wesley, it often seems almost to be forgotten, or treated as a rather embarrassing or unimportant fact, that Wesley, the son of an Anglican cleric, was until his death an ordained member of the church, and that whatever anyone else might have accused him of he never joined another body (as did the erstwhile Anglican cleric, Theophilus Lindsey), or converted to another denomination, as did several nonconformist ministers who in the early eighteenth century took orders within the church. Although his 'conversion' on 24 May 1738 has become one of the defining moments of eighteenth-century history, this was, unlike most conversions, firmly within the church to which he belonged (he had after all already been ordained for nearly ten years) and not from one church to another, and he remained adamant that he never left it. On 17 June 1746 (his birthday), Wesley wrote to the aptly named Thomas Church, the vicar of Battersea and a future prebendary of St. Paul's, who had accused him of leaving the Anglican fold, affirming his membership of the church: 'I dare not renounce communion with the Church of England. As a minister, I teach her doctrines; I use her offices; I conform to her rubricks; I suffer reproach for my attachment to her. As a private member I hold her

---

[31] John Wesley, *A Preservative against unsettled notions in Religion* (London, 1758), p. 169.

[32] For Skinner's approach, see James Tulley (ed.), *Meaning and Context: Quentin Skinner and his Critics* (Cambridge, 1988). For some of the issues for biography and identity raised by post-modernism, see James A. Holstein, *The Self We Live By: Identity in a Post-modern World* (New York and Oxford, 2000), and James M. Glass, *Shattered Selves: Multiple Personality in a Postmodern World* (Ithaca, NY and London, 1993).

doctrines; I join in her offices; in prayer, in hearing, in communicating'.[33] He concluded:

> nothing can prove I am no member of the Church, till I either am excommunicated or renounce her communion, and no longer join in her doctrine and in the breaking of bread and in prayer. Nor can anything prove I am no minister of the church till either I am deposed from my ministry or voluntarily renounce her, and wholly cease to teach her doctrines, use her offices, and obey her rubrics for conscience' sake.[34]

Using this criteria, it is clear that the church did not ever excommunicate him (and some consideration of why not will be undertaken later). Wesley's statement is also useful for revealing not only what he himself saw as criteria for membership, but for his (perhaps wishful) understanding of the low common denominator for church membership; note that his membership as a priest rested on not completely stopping to use the Anglican formularies, which to his contemporaries could be seen as at best a minimal condition and at worst as a breach of the canonical requirements. And his justification for potentially giving up the Anglican formularies altogether, 'for conscience' sake', was a defence he would use on repeated occasions to account for what others considered innovations in his practice. The case for John Wesley as Church of England man rests then on his own statements, and the fact that he did not actually join another church. He saw himself as a member of the church even if others did not.

There are various reasons why the Anglican Wesley has been downplayed. The development of a separate Methodist church in the decades after his death has meant that our perspective on the eighteenth-century situation has been through the lens of the nineteenth. Because Victorian Methodism saw itself as largely apart from the established church, it is tempting to believe that those who were considered to be the founders of the movement—and above all Wesley—would have approved of this development, although it is arguable that it was Thomas Coke (who himself had been ordained into the church) and Jabez Bunting rather than Wesley who were the real founders of a separatist Methodist church.[35] Related to this is the fact that most who have examined Wesley's relationship with the Anglican church have, in varying degrees, been either self-proclaimed Methodist scholars, working in Methodist-affiliated institutions (US exponents include Frank Baker, Richard Heitzenrater, and Ted Campbell) or British academics who were brought up within the Methodist tradition (such as Gordon Rupp, John Kent, John Walsh, W.R.

---

[33] *Letters*, XII, p. 240: John Wesley to Thomas Church, 17 June 1746.
[34] Ibid., p. 244.
[35] Charles Wesley certainly blamed Coke: see JRULM, DD/WES/4/69: Charles Wesley to Sarah Wesley, 29 July 1786, calling him the leader of the 'dissenting party'. On Coke see Gareth Lloyd, *The Papers of Thomas Coke. A Catalogue. Bulletin of the John Rylands University Library of Manchester*, 76 (1994). On Bunting, see W.R. Ward, *Religion and Society in England, 1790-1850* (London, 1972).

Ward, and Henry Rack).[36] To point this out is in no way to criticize the extraordinarily high level of scholarship on Wesley that they and others have undertaken—revealed most obviously in the superb Abingdon edition of Wesley's works—but it is to propose that at a subliminal level their own religious affiliation depended on ensuring that Wesley's religious identity was not unlike their own. They are all, to a greater or lesser extent, Methodist insiders. It is then worth suggesting that their own churchmanship has played not a small part in how they have viewed Wesley's relationship with the church. Even while understanding the complexities of the eighteenth-century situation, historians from within the Methodist tradition have nevertheless tended to assume that the natural and inevitable trajectory of the relationship between the established church and Methodism was the denominational division between the two that became dominant (although not exclusive) during the Victorian period. The fact of that eventual demarcation has encouraged these historians to see in Wesley's statements and actions what they considered to be the precursors of, or the necessary steps on the path to, that split, and in doing so their judgements often echoed that of the much quoted nineteenth-century commentator who described Wesley as being 'like a good oarsman [who] looked one way and rowed another'.[37] Some have seen Wesley moving in an almost unbroken journey from what appeared to be a firm and unshaken commitment to the Church of England in the 1730s to the position in the last decade of his life where he enjoyed being the leader of a virtual alternative religious body while only nominally being a member of the church. But this begs the question of how fixed and defined those positions actually were, and in any case smacks of a teleological view which seriously misjudges the relationship between Hanoverian Anglicanism and Methodism.

Just as Methodist historians have been anxious to see Wesley as the father of the Methodist church, historians of the Church of England have traditionally been reluctant to claim Wesley as one of their own. By and large, they have accepted the idea of a necessary divide between Methodism and Anglicanism and Wesley has been placed firmly on the Methodist side of the fence. For many nineteenth-century churchmen, keen to dwell on the inadequacies of the eighteenth-century church against which they measured nineteenth-century successes, Wesley's Methodism was seen as an explicable, if regrettable, reaction against the prevailing lethargy of the age.[38] It is true that Norman Sykes (an Anglican cleric and later dean of Winchester), who in the first half of the twentieth century developed a more positive portrayal of the eighteenth-century Church of

---

[36] It might be worth noting that Walsh and Rupp are from the Wesleyan Methodist tradition, while Rack, Kent, and Ward come from the Primitive Methodist tradition. I owe this insight to Henry Rack.
[37] Quoted in Rack, *Reasonable Enthusiast*, p. 291.
[38] See, for example, C.J. Abbey and J.H. Overton, *The English Church in the Eighteenth Century*, 2 vols. (London, 1878), II, pp. 57-9.

England, was broadly sympathetic towards Wesley.[39] And the studies of Wesley by V.H.H. Green in the 1960s were seminal in that they were fairly favourable interpretations written by an Anglican academic, although it has to be said that the most original aspects of Green's work were on Wesley's Oxford and so-called Anglican years before 1738.[40] Significantly, the revisionist approach to the church which has gathered pace over the last twenty years or so, and which has provided us with a much more upbeat view of the pastoral practices of the eighteenth-century church, has seldom brought Methodism into its purview, except to argue that Wesley's criticisms of the shortcomings of that institution were frequently exaggerated, and to suggest that in many parts of the country the emergence of Methodism was rather later, and the number of adherents rather smaller, than a triumphalist Methodist reading would have it.[41] One of the 'revisionist' studies which did pay some attention to Wesley was J.C.D. Clark's *English Society*. Clark, however, was more interested in Wesley's Toryism and in demonstrating that the individual who attacked the spiritual and pastoral shortcomings of the established church nevertheless shared many of its social and political assumptions. According to Clark this meant that Wesley could be regarded as part of, rather than apart from, the Anglican hegemony which, he argued, made Hanoverian England into a 'confessional state'.[42] Clark's interpretation was, however, criticized by David Hempton (brought up outside the Methodist tradition) who was keen to emphasize Wesley's radicalism and the conditional nature of his submission to the Georgian polity in both church and state.[43]

Historians of both Methodism and the church have then generally not wanted to emphasize Wesley's Anglicanism, and this is suggestive of the ways in which the assumptions of historians can affect the way in which we label people in the past. But if both 'Methodist' and 'Anglican' scholars have been reluctant to explore Wesley's Anglican identity, his contemporaries were also concerned about his allegiance to the church. As early as 16 April 1739, less than a year after Wesley had felt his heart

---

[39] Sykes, *Church and State in England*, pp. 392-6.

[40] V.H.H. Green, *The Young Mr Wesley: A Study of John Wesley and Oxford* (London, 1963), and idem, *John Wesley* (London, 1964). As a personality, Wesley comes out of Green's interpretation as a mildly unpleasant and self-obsessed individual. There is also the disappointing popular study: Garth Lean, *John Wesley, Anglican* (London, 1964).

[41] See, for example, the essays by Jeremy Gregory, William Gibson, Colin Haydon, and William Jacob in Jeremy Gregory and Jeffrey S. Chamberlain (eds.), *The National Church in Local Perspective. The Church of England and the Regions, 1660-1800* (Boydell and Brewer, 2003).

[42] J.C.D. Clark, *English Society, 1688-1832: ideology, social structure, and political practice during the ancien regime* (Cambridge, 1985), p. 235-44. See also his 'England's Ancien Regime as a Confessional State', *Albion*, 21:3 (Fall 1989), pp. 450-74.

[43] David Hempton, 'John Wesley and England's *Ancien Régime*', in his *The Religion of the People. Methodism and Popular Religion c.1750-1900* (London, 1996), pp. 77-90.

'strangely warmed', and a few days after he had begun to preach in the open, his elder brother Samuel, a staunch high churchman, informed Wesley of their mother's fears that the Methodists were heading towards a split with the church and advised him to give up extemporary exposition of the scriptures and extemporary prayer.[44] Samuel later wrote to their mother about his brothers: 'They design separation...they are already forbid all the pulpits in London, and to preach in that diocese is actual schism. In all likelihood it will come to the same all over England if the bishops have courage. As I told Jack, I am not afraid the Church should excommunicate him...but that he should excommunicate the Church'.[45] During the next fifty years Wesley was pressed hard by his siblings and others on the matter of his relations with the church and he attested to the ways in which he saw himself as a member of the established church, professing, 'My affection for the Church is as strong as ever; and I can clearly see my calling; which is to live and die in her communion';[46] 'I believe I shall not separate from the Church of England till my soul departs from my body'; and 'In the Church I will live and die, unless I am thrust out'.[47] These statements (from 1758, 1786, and 1788) demonstrate that Wesley, however sharply critical he might be of current church practice, from beginning to end portrayed himself as a member of the established church (and at times an extremely ardent one). What is also clear is that Wesley certainly did not have a linear trajectory marked by increasing disillusionment with Anglicanism. Some statements in his later life were in fact very fulsome in their praise of the Anglican church. In 1780, for instance, he wrote to Sir Harry Trelawney—admittedly something of a religious maverick whose own religious odyssey enabled him to move from Anglicanism, through nonconformity, to Catholicism, and whom Wesley no doubt wanted to retain for the Church of England: 'Having had an opportunity of seeing several of the Churches abroad, and having deeply consider'd the several sorts of Dissenters at home, I am fully convinced that our own Church, with all her blemishes, is nearer the scriptural plan than any other in Europe'.[48] And, surprisingly for someone who is often seen as the church's sternest critic, as late as 1787 he could preach: 'It must be allowed that ever since the Reformation, and particularly in the present century, the behaviour of the Clergy in general is greatly altered for the better...Insomuch that the English and Irish Clergy are generally allowed to be not inferior to any in Europe, for piety, as well as for knowledge'.[49]

---

[44] JRULM, DD WF/5/15: Samuel Wesley to John Wesley, 16 April 1739.
[45] Quoted in Baker, *Wesley and the Church of England*, p. 58.
[46] Quoted in Rack, *Reasonable Enthusiast*, p. 291; John Wesley, *Reasons against a separation from the Church of England...with hymns for the preachers among the Methodists (so called) by Charles Wesley* (London, 1760), p. 12.
[47] *Letters*, VII, p. 321: John Wesley to Samuel Bardsley, 4 March 1786.
[48] *Letters*, VII, p. 27: John Wesley to Sir Harry Trelawney, 27 August 1780.
[49] 'On attending the Church Service', in *The Works of John Wesley, Sermons*, III, Albert C. Outler (ed.), (Nashville, 1986), p. 470. This sermon is a defence of the efficacy of the Church, even when clergy might be deemed unworthy.

But in counterpoint to phrases and statements such as these, Wesley's letters and *Journals* reveal right from the earliest days of the movement some sharply critical views of the *practice* of the established church. Is there any way out of making sense of these seemingly divergent opinions other than to take the post-modernist line that we are all a bundle of contradictions? In Skinnerian fashion, we need to recognize that one of the matters that needs to be taken into account is the identity of Wesley's audience, and paying attention to this helps to iron out some of the seeming contradictions in his pronouncements. He could be critical of the church when dealing with a member of the establishment, particularly clergy and bishops, flagging up 'abuses' such as pluralism and non-residence ('O what a curse in the poor land are pluralities and non-residence'),[50] and being disparaging of university education as a criteria for Anglican ordination ('[but] how many have a university education and yet no learning at all?').[51] Conversely, with those Methodists urging separation, or with nonconformists, he was more likely to stress the positive features of the church. In 1745, for example, under pressure from his brother-in-law Westley Hall to leave the church, he emphasized the importance of the Apostolic succession and the hierarchy of orders. He continued, revealingly, 'Do you not here quite overlook the circumstance which might be a key to our whole behaviour? We no more look upon these filthy abuses which adhere to the church as part of the building than we look upon any filth which may adhere to the walls of Westminster abbey as part of the structure'.[52] In saying this, Wesley could well see himself as an Anglican reformer, aiming to clean up the existing church, rather than being the creator of a new church.

And instead of viewing Wesley's religious affiliation as ambiguous and inconsistent, it may be more profitable to see his religious position as his response to the rich and varied inheritance he had in religious matters. This inheritance can be seen in two forms, first, from his family and, secondly, from the wider church in which he was brought up. In terms of family background, there was certainly a complex mixture. On his father's side, Wesley's religious and political heritage reveals a broad spectrum. His father Samuel was firmly a establishment clergyman[53] who was proud to be elected to Convocation, but his paternal grandfather (also John) had been a minister during the Interregnum (a fact recalled later in Wesley's life when his brother accused him of recanting the churchmanship of his father to resurrect the 'schismatick' tradition of his grandfather).[54] But whatever the complexities of his paternal heritage, biographers have emphasized the

---

[50] *Journal*, VII, p. 173: 25 June 1786.
[51] *Journal*, IV, p. 373: 20 March 1760.
[52] *Journal*, III, p. 230: 27 December 1745.
[53] There is a suggestive essay by Gordon Rupp, 'Son of Samuel: John Wesley, Church-of-England Man', in Kenneth E. Rowe (ed.), *The Place of Wesley in the Christian Tradition* (Metuchen, N.J), 1976, pp. 39-66. See also Luke Tyerman, *The Life and Times of the Rev. Samuel Wesley, MA*, 3 vols. (London, 1866).
[54] JRULM, DD/WES/4/64: Charles Wesley to Sarah Wesley (n.d.?1785).

dominant weight of his mother, Susanna, on Wesley's development, seeing in her not only a formidable influence (accounting for the fact that John seemed to be happier amongst women than men), but an independence in religious matters which, it can be argued, was a precursor of her son's religious position.[55] As the daughter of a prominent Presbyterian family, she was converted to the Church of England at the age of nearly thirteen, through her own reading, and came to embrace some high church views (and even Jacobite leanings, which John seems to have shared in his twenties). She took both her own religious life and her role as clergy wife seriously, so that, famously, when her husband was away in 1712 on Convocation business, she held services in her kitchen, defending her action on the grounds that she was making up for the inadequacies of the curate and that in any case, she claimed, the result was that it brought more people to the parish church. It was precisely this kind of defence of what others perceived to be innovations, but which John would defend in terms of aiming to shore up the church, which would be a repeated line throughout his life.

Given this religious background, it is not then surprising that the Wesley household reared children who were peculiarly sensitive to the religious issues of the day, and the family letters preserved in the John Rylands Library indicate how far Wesley's own religious development was as much an event in family history as it was in the history of religion. Wesley's correspondence with his siblings (and not just in the well-documented letters with his brother Charles) continually returned to the issue of his relationship with the church. In 1740, for example, his sister Emily quizzed him on where Methodists stood on infant baptism and she noted that she could not understand why the Methodist preachers (who at that time were ordained Anglican clergy) needed to preach in the open air.[56] She wrote to him the next year, saying how pleased she was that he disagreed with Whitefield about predestination, but urged him to steer clear of what she considered to be other false religious models such as the 'Romish errors of confession and bodily austerity', Quaker notions of absolute perfection, and above all exorcism as practised by the French Prophets.[57] But it is clear that even within the context of the Wesley family, John had a peculiarly heightened sense of the importance of religion. Emily, suffering from poverty after the breakdown of her marriage, rebuked him for his constant questions about religious matters, asking 'how any woman, who owes two years rent, and expects daily to have her home taken away, can consider the state of the Church in Germany?'[58] And in what to twenty-first-century readers appears extraordinarily insensitive, Wesley told his sister Martha, whose children had all died of fever, that she

---

[55] On the 'femininity of Wesley's early environment', see Green, *The Young Mr Wesley*, pp. 51-3. See also Charles Wallace, 'Susanna Wesley's Spirituality: the freedom of a Christian woman', *Church History* 22 (1983-4), pp. 158-73.

[56] JRULM, DDWF/6/10: Emily Wesley to John Wesley, 4 August 1740.

[57] Ibid., DDWF/11: Emily Wesley to John Wesley, 17 June 1741.

[58] Ibid., DDWF/9: Emily Wesley to John Wesley 24 November 1738.

should be pleased they had died, because she was always complaining what a handful her children were, and that she would now have more time to devote to religious concerns.[59]

Apart from his family, the Church of England provided Wesley with his religious heritage. One of the features of Wesleyan scholarship has been the attempt to place him within one or other of the traditions which have been considered to be increasingly displaced within the Georgian church. We have had a 'high church Wesley',[60] and a 'Puritan Wesley',[61] and we have even had a Wesley linked to the latitudinarians of the seventeenth century.[62] But it is important to note how far high church and Puritan tendencies could exist within eighteenth-century Anglicanism, and how there were some areas of overlap between these positions—both for example, drew on ideals of the 'primitive Church' which Wesley admired.[63] If Wesley had 'Puritan' or 'high church' leanings it was not because they stood outside mainstream Anglicanism, but because they were part and parcel of it.[64] It was also a distinctive feature of eighteenth-century Anglicanism that individuals could hold these seemingly contradictory positions in tandem, whereas before 1660 and after 1830 the differences were more likely to have been enshrined into distinct parties, and people were more likely to have belonged to one party or another. Something of this rich and varied inheritance can be found in Wesley's *Christian Library*, which he once described as being made up of 'extracts from the ornaments

---

[59] *Letters*, II, Baker (ed.), pp. 90-91: John Wesley to Mrs Martha Hall, 17 November 1742.

[60] For a 'high church Wesley', see [L.P. Holden], *John Wesley in Company with High Churchmen. By an Old Methodist* (London, 1869); John Walsh, 'Origins of the Evangelical Revival', in G.V. Bennett and J.D. Walsh (eds.), *Essays in Modern Church History* (London, 1966), pp. 138-48; and Baker, *Wesley and the Church of England*, p. 251, see the trajectory of Wesley's churchmanship as a move from an early high church to a later low church position.

[61] Robert C. Monk, *John Wesley, His Puritan Heritage. A Study of the Christian Life* (London, 1966). See also, John Newton, *Methodism and the Puritans*, Friends of Dr. Williams' Library Lectures 18 (1964) and his *Susanna Wesley and the Puritan Tradition in Methodism* (Epworth Press, 1968).

[62] John C. English, 'John Wesley and the Anglican Moderates of the seventeenth century', *Anglican Theological Review* 51 (1969), pp. 203-20.

[63] See Ted A. Campbell, *John Wesley and Christian Antiquity: Religious Vision and Cultural Change* (Nashville, 1991), and Eamon Duffy, 'Primitive Christianity revived: religious renewal in Augustan England', in Derek Baker (ed.), *Renaissance and Renewal in Christian History*, Studies in Church History 14 (1977), pp. 287-300.

[64] See Jeremy Gregory, *Restoration, Reformation, and Reform, 1660-1828. Archbishops of Canterbury and their diocese* (Oxford, 2000), pp. 60, 100, 241, 289. It might also be noted that what Outler notes as Wesley's distinctive 'plain style' was not just a 'puritan' inheritance but was very much a feature of mainstream Anglican sermonising: *Sermons*, I, Outler (ed.), pp. 21-2; C.H. Smyth, *The Art of Preaching. A Practical Survey of Preaching in the Church of England, 747-1939* (1940), pp. 90-166.

of the Church of England',[65] and which included works from across the religious spectrum.

In seeing Wesley as coming from within eighteenth-century Anglicanism, rather than merely reacting against it, we also need to recognise that the church in the long eighteenth century was not as static as scholarship has traditionally implied. Despite the fact that Wesley was accused of making 'innovations' in religious matters, it may be that his critics and even Wesley himself exaggerated the extent to which the developments associated with him were entirely new. On a number of occasions Wesley admitted to some novelties—such as the creation of the Methodist societies, the reliance on lay preachers, field preaching, and the use of extemporary prayer. But at least some of these initiatives can be seen to have emerged from late seventeenth and eighteenth-century Anglicanism, with Wesley building on, rather than going against, recent pastoral trends. The Methodist societies, as John Walsh and Henry Rack have shown,[66] drew on the Church of England's sponsored religious societies which are frequently given credit for nourishing parish piety in the fifty years after 1680, where the more religiously committed of the parish could find a spiritual outlet and which could be regarded as an optional addition to, rather than a subversion of, parish Anglicanism. This, it can be argued, is how Wesley envisaged his own societies. In similar fashion, the great Anglican missionary enterprise of the late seventeenth and eighteenth centuries, embodied by the Society for the Promotion of Christian Knowledge (founded 1698), the Society for the Propagation of the Gospel (founded 1701), and the societies for the reformation of manners, anticipated Wesley's own concerns to effect religious and social change.[67] One of his most noted innovations—open air preaching—did not necessarily subvert the Church of England. It did not (as he himself observed) go against the canons,[68] and Wesley received some high church establishment support for the practice from George Horne, dean of Canterbury, and later bishop of Norwich who occasionally preached outside the chapel while president of Magdalen College, Oxford, the better, he said, to emulate John the Baptist.[69] Despite the fact that Wesley was

---

[65] *Letters*, IV, p. 122: John Wesley to the editor of the *London Magazine*, 12 December 1760. Wesley cites extracts from Archbishop Leighton and Bishops Taylor, Patrick, Ken, Reynolds, and Sanderson.

[66] John Walsh, 'Religious Societies: Methodist and Evangelical, 1738-1800', in W.J. Sheils and Diana Wood (eds.), *Voluntary Religion*, Studies in Church History 23 (1986), pp. 279-302; Henry Rack, 'Religious Societies and the origin of Methodism', *Journal of Ecclesiastical History* 38 (1987), pp. 583-95.

[67] Craig Rose, 'The Origins and Ideals of the SPCK, 1699-1716', in John Walsh, Colin Haydon, and Stephen Taylor (eds.), *The Church of England, c. 1689-1833: From Toleration to Tractarianism* (Cambridge, 1993), pp. 172-90.

[68] See Gerald Bray (ed.), *The Anglican Canons 1529-1947* (Woodbridge, 1998), esp. pp. 341-3.

[69] Magdalen College, Oxford, MS 655 (b), p. 214. The mutual regard between Wesley and Horne is one of the relationships which traditional stress on divisions between religious 'parties' can obscure. Wesley, for example, praised

accused of breaking down the parish system, in some ways this had already happened. Certainly the ideal of an incumbent for each parish was not a reality in the eighteenth century (only in the late nineteenth century was it so),[70] and pluralism ensured that, where an incumbent held two contiguous parishes, some of the boundaries between parishes were effectively dissolved. Indeed in parts of the country it was almost official policy that parishioners could attend a neighbouring parish for a second service, and, as in other periods, it was not uncommon to sermon-gad.[71] With some justification Wesley could argue on the grounds of both contemporary practice and the rubrics that no law required 'all to attend always on their own parish church'.[72] Wesley's reliance on lay preachers—which he saw as one of the essentials he would never give up and which so perturbed his Anglican contemporaries whose status felt threatened by those they deemed uneducated rivals—eventually became a crucial part of church practice in the late twentieth century (as did his qualified support for women preachers).[73] There was also a kind of logic from within eighteenth-century Anglicanism for lay preachers, although contemporaries would have been reluctant to admit it. Many years ago Norman Sykes observed that a hallmark of Georgian piety was the laicization of religion,[74] where members of the laity, as much as the clergy, had a duty to contribute to and fully participate in religious matters (with Samuel Johnson even writing sermons for clergy to preach).[75] Of course Wesley took these developments much further than mainstream Anglicanism intended, but nevertheless it may be fruitful to see his

---

Horne's *Commentary on the Psalms* (Oxford, 1776) as 'the best that ever was wrote', and Horne once remarked that he would not mind Wesley preaching in his diocese if he were a bishop: *Journal and Diaries* (Heitzenrater and Ward), IV, p. 351. On 14 October 1790 Horne indeed gave Wesley permission to preach at Diss Church in his diocese of Norwich: *Journal and Diaries*, (Heitzenrater and Ward), VII, pp. 193-4.

[70] Frances Knight, *The Nineteenth-Century Church and English Society* (Cambridge, 1995), p. 209.

[71] Gregory, *Restoration, Reformation, and Reform*, pp. 171-3, 256-7.

[72] *Letters*, III, p. 230: John Wesley to Westley Hall, 17 December 1745.

[73] Paul A. Welsby, *A History of the Church of England, 1945-1980* (Oxford, 1984), p. 254; Deborah Valenze, *Prophetic Sons and Daughters: Female Preaching and Popular Religion in Industrial England* (Princeton, NJ, 1985). It is worth noting that in eighteenth-century North America, because of the shortage of ordained ministers, the use of lay readers (who offered the clerical services except for the administration of the sacrament and marriage) was widespread: Frederick V. Mills, *Bishops by Ballot: An Eighteenth-Century Ecclesiastical Revolution* (New York and Oxford, 1978), p. 8.

[74] Sykes, *Church and State*, p. 379. See also Jeremy Gregory, 'Homo religious: masculinity and religion in the long eighteenth century' in Tim Hitchcock and Michèle Cohen (eds.), *English Masculinities, 1660-1800* (London, 1999), pp. 85-110.

[75] M.J. Quinlan, *Samuel Johnson: A Layman's Religion* (Madison, 1964), p. 13. See also Chester Chapin, *The Religious Thought of Samuel Johnson* (Ann Arbor, MI, 1968) and Charles E. Pierce, *The Religious Life of Samuel Johnson* (London, 1983).

initiatives as extending and supplementing existing church practice rather than being totally novel.

Wesley's brand of Methodism can then be profitably seen as an add-on to the church rather than as a rival to it. In providing an additional level of spirituality to that formally offered by the church, there were plenty of precedents in earlier English religious history. In this, Wesley's Methodism can be seen to have been the heir to the Puritans of the late sixteenth and seventeenth centuries who, as Patrick Collinson and others have shown, were figures within rather than outside the establishment,[76] and who should be considered to be both Anglicans and Puritans rather than as a distinct group apart from mainstream Anglicanism. Like these Anglican Puritans, with their interest in prophesyings, exercises, and sermon-gadding, Wesley envisaged his own societies as spiritual extras to the established church. If Elizabethan and Jacobean Puritans were the 'hotter sort of Protestants',[77] then Wesley's Hanoverian Methodists might well be described as the 'hotter sort of Anglicans'. John Walsh has brilliantly viewed Wesley as a 'both/and' rather than an 'either/or' personality, encompassing, for example, both Puritan and high church elements, both elite and popular cultural values, and both enlightenment and counter-enlightenment systems of thought.[78] This 'both/and' categorization might usefully be applied to the ways in which we should see Wesley's understanding of the relationship between the church and Methodism: he was both a churchman and a Methodist and he saw no contradiction in that. In 1786 he wrote to Henry Brooke: 'We are members of the Church of England, we are no particular sect or party...we love those of the Church wherein we were brought up...in some unessential Circumstances we vary a little from the usual modes of worship, and we have several little prudential helps peculiar to our selves, but still we do not, will not, dare not separate from the Church till we see other reasons than we have yet'.[79]

It may, however, be that Wesley's commitment was increasingly to the add-ons rather than to the original structure. In 1738, at the start of the movement, he was clear about the priorities: 'Are we members of the Church of England?', he asked James Hutton. 'First then, let us observe her sacraments, and then the bye-laws of our Society',[80] but by 1774 Charles Wesley claimed that John's first love was to the Methodists and secondly to the church, while his own (Charles') allegiances were the other way round.

---

[76] Patrick Collinson, *The Religion of Protestants: The Church in English Society, 1559-1625* (Oxford, 1982); Peter Lake, *Moderate Puritans and the Elizabethan Church* (Cambridge, 1983); idem, *Anglicans and Puritans? Presbyterianism and English Conformist Thought from Whitgift to Hooker* (London, 1988).

[77] Patrick Collinson, *English Puritanism* (London, 1983), p. 8. See also Patrick Collinson, John Craig, and Brett Usher (eds.), *Conferences and Combination Lectures in the Elizabethan Church, 1582-1590*, Church of England Record Society 10 (2003), p. xliii, where a Puritan itinerant is called a 'proto-John Wesley'.

[78] John Walsh, *John Wesley, 1703-1791. A bicentennial tribute*, Friends of Dr. Williams' Library Lectures, 48 (1993), p. 12.

[79] *Letters*, VII, p. 333: John Wesley to Henry Brooke, 14 June 1786.

[80] *Letters*, I, p. 276: John Wesley to James Hutton, 1 December 1738.

The younger Wesley accounted for these differences in their judgement of people: 'his all hope; mine all fear',[81] although by this date Charles seems to have had a vested interest in presenting himself as the staunch Anglican against his wayward brother. Nevertheless Wesley's commitment to the church remained central to his mission and he continued to be convinced that his message was to the 'lost sheep of the Church', telling his sister Martha in 1742 that 'my belief is that the present design of God is to visit the poor desolate Church of England, and that therefore neither deluded Mr Gambold'—who had left the church—'nor any who leave it will prosper'.[82] Time and again he said that the Methodists did good precisely by being in the Church. They were to 'leaven the lump', as Archbishop Potter is supposed to have encouraged them to do.[83] And looking back on the previous forty years, Wesley observed to Thomas Taylor in 1786, 'I believe if we had...left the Church we should not have done a tenth of the good which we have done'.[84]

Wesley's attachment to the church was thus deep. When asked in 1739 where he differed from the church, he replied: 'To the best of my knowledge, in none. The doctrines we preach are the doctrines of the Church of England; indeed the fundamental doctrines of the Church, clearly laid down both in her Prayers, Articles, and Homilies'.[85] He even maintained—perhaps in a manner typical of other 'reformers', including Luther, who claimed that they were merely faithful adherents of a tradition that had gone awry—that he was being truer to the church than some other clergy in holding that Justification and Sanctification were distinct occurrences, and that Justification was not conditional on the performance of good works.[86] But it also needs to be stressed that his was never a blind or unconditional devotion. As early as 1738, he informed James Hutton: 'The National Church to which we belong, may doubtless claim some, though not an implicit obedience from us',[87] and in 1739 he exclaimed: 'I love the rites and ceremonies of the Church. But I see well pleased, that our great Lord can work without them'.[88] In 1745 he told Westley Hall that 'we profess that...we will obey all the laws of the Church (such we allow the Rubricks to be, but not the custom of the ecclesiastical courts), so far as we can with a safe conscience'.[89] He went on to say that 'we will obey, with the same restriction, the bishops as executors of those laws, but their bare will,

---

[81] JRULM, Charles Wesley's Papers I/1/64: Charles Wesley to John Horton, 19 June 1774.
[82] *Letters*, II, p. 12: John Wesley to Martha Wesley, 17 November 1742
[83] For Potter's phrase see, JRULM, DD/WES/4/43: Charles Wesley to Benjamin Latrobe, 30 July 1786. John Wesley used a similar phrase about the purpose of the movement; see, *Letters*, VI, p. 326: John Wesley to Miss Bishop, 18 October 1778.
[84] *Letters*, VII, p. 316: John Wesley to Thomas Taylor, 21 February 1786.
[85] *Journal*, II, p. 274: 13 September 1739.
[86] Ibid.
[87] *Letters*, I, p. 276: John Wesley to James Hutton, 1 December 1738.
[88] Baker, *Wesley and Church of England*, p. 57
[89] *Letters*, I, p. 274: John Wesley to James Hutton, 27 November 1738.

distinct from those laws, we do not profess to obey at all'.[90] Statements such as these were again reminiscent of early modern Anglican Puritans, who believed that the contemporary church was but 'halfly reformed', and who were also concerned about the church courts and the powers of bishops. The distinction that they, and other churchmen, made between divine and human laws was one that Wesley echoed. In 1746 he admitted to Thomas Church: 'I cannot have a greater regard to any human rules than to follow them in all things, unless where I apprehend there is a divine rule to the contrary'.[91] Wesley was clear that elements of the established church were human constructs, and if the church went against divine law, as he understood it, then he would not obey it.

In seeing Wesley as a churchman, it is necessary to understand what he conceived the church to be. This was based on his reading of the Thirty-Nine Articles. 'Our twentieth article', he observed, 'defines a true Church as "a congregation of faithful people, wherein the true word of God is preached"'. He continued: 'According to this account the Church of England is that body of faithful people (or holy believers) in England among whom the pure word of God is preached. Who then are the worst dissenters from the Church?; unholy men of all kinds; swearers, Sabbath-breakers, drunkards, fighters, whore-mongers, liars, revilers, evil-speakers; the passionate, the gay, the lovers of money, the lovers of dress or of praise, the lovers of pleasure more than lovers of God; all these are Dissenters of the highest sort, continually striking at the root of the Church, and themselves in truth belonging to no Church, but to the synagogue of Satan'.[92] To this list he added those who were unsound in faith (by denying justification by faith alone) and those who 'unduly' ministered the sacrament.[93] This is a crucial passage and helps perhaps explain why Wesley could see himself as being within the church when others thought that he had left it, and we need to recognise that Wesley's understanding of what was meant by the church differed from that of some of his contemporaries. His view of what was necessary for church membership rested on doctrine and behaviour. Other definitions of the Church of England viewed it as an institution and organization established by God and by Parliament, as evidenced in the 1662 Act of Uniformity, one where episcopacy, and attachment to the 1604 canons, the Thirty-Nine Articles, and the Book of Common Prayer were central. Wesley's definition of the church was not just establishment for its own sake.

In tracing Wesley's—and the broader Methodist relationship to the church—it is worth noting that the issue of separation from the church was raised, only to be dismissed, at the first Methodist Conference in 1744,[94] and for the rest of the 1740s this became the party line. During the early 1750s, Wesley, along with other leading Methodists, pledged on several occasions

---

[90] *Letters*, II, p. 240: John Wesley to Thomas Church, 17 June 1746.
[91] Ibid.
[92] *Journal*, II, p. 335: 6 February 1740
[93] Ibid.
[94] Quoted in Rack, *Reasonable Enthusiast*, p. 293.,

never to leave the church without the consent of the others.[95] But the period between the mid-1750s and the early-1760s witnessed something of a crisis point. Two main issues were at stake which potentially threatened both Wesley's and the movement's relations with the church: the desire of a very small minority of the lay preachers to administer the sacrament, and the hard-line attitude of some Anglican clergy towards the lay preachers. When in 1754 it was discovered that Edward and Charles Perronet, Joseph Cownley, and Thomas Walsh had administered the sacrament, Wesley observed: 'We have in effect ordained already'.[96] But the tone here, it seems to me, was not boastful, but almost resigned and regretful, and the matter was discussed, alongside the issue of separation, at the 1755 Conference in Leeds, where Wesley was clear that lay preachers could not administer the sacrament.[97] And although Wesley held fast to the church, he was irritated by the church's attitude towards the preachers and complained that Bishop Sherlock of London (who had initially seemed supportive of the movement) was insisting that lay preachers needed to be licensed as Dissenters in order to preach. He noted to Charles that the 'point will be speedily determined concerning the Church...actum est'.[98]

In the same year Wesley wrote an extended letter to Samuel Walker, the evangelical vicar of Truro, which discussed several of the pertinent issues, and, as with his correspondence with Thomas Church, raised the issue of the legality and expediency of remaining in or separating from the church. Again, Wesley stressed the importance of the Anglican liturgy (noting that 'it is one of the most excellent human compositions that ever was'),[99] but, again in a manner reminiscent of some of the Anglican Puritan objections a century and a half before, he viewed the Anglican canons as popish, while he considered the ecclesiastical courts to be the 'dregs of popery': 'too bad', he said, 'to be tolerated not in a Christian but in a Mahometan or pagan nation'.[100] Wesley was also critical of some clergy whom he considered did no good, many of whom, he said, denied the necessity for inward conversion and held misguided doctrines. He concluded that it was indeed lawful to continue in the church, but he raised the concern that 'if the essence of the Church is her "orders and laws"' (here Wesley seems to be quoting Walker back at him) and not in her worship and doctrines, then those who separated from it were on stronger grounds. He told Walker that 'duty' compelled him to preach outside his parish, to use extempore prayer, to found societies, and to use lay preachers and 'we should judge it our bounden duty rather wholly to separate from the Church than to give up any one of these points'.

---

[95] JRULM, DD/CW/8/3: copy of agreement, 10 March 1752 ; ibid., DD Pr 2/1/8: May 1754, copy of agreement.
[96] *Letters*, III, p. 131: John Wesley to Charles Wesley, 23 June 1755.
[97] *Journal*, IV, p.115 : 6 June 1755.
[98] *Letters*, III, p. 131: John Wesley to Charles Wesley, 23 June 1755.
[99] Ibid., III, p. 143: John Wesley to Samuel Walker, 24 September 1755.
[100] Ibid., III, p. 144.

'Therefore', he concluded, 'if we cannot stop a separation without stopping lay preachers, the case is clear—we cannot stop it at all'.[101]

In interpreting statements such as this, it is important to remember who Wesley was addressing. Walker was a prominent Anglican Evangelical, and Wesley may well have been pushing his case, perhaps even with a touch of bravado, to make his position clear. It is within the context of talk of separation, the fact that some of the lay preachers had been administering the sacrament, and the attitude of some members of the church to lay preachers that we need to read Wesley's *Reasons against a separation from the Church of England*. This was originally published in 1758 as part of his *A Preservative against unsettled notions in Religion*, with a separate edition in 1760, printed with some of Charles' hymns.[102] Wesley noted in *Reasons* that one good reason not to separate from the church was that 'it would be a contradiction to the solemn and repeated Declarations which we have made in all manner of ways, in Preaching, Print, and Private Conversation'.[103] The early gestation of this tract was an address to the Conference in 1755 and it is worth looking at in some detail because not only is it Wesley's most fully developed statement about Methodism's relationship with the established church, expanding on points he had made to Church and Walker, but it was also something that he urged his followers to read, so it seems that he treated it as his definitive statement on this issue.

Reasons began with the statement that whether it was lawful or not to separate from the church (and this, of course, annoyed some churchmen, for whom it was patently not lawful), it was not expedient, because this would prejudice people against the movement, it would cause people to leave Methodism (indicative of the fact that it was precisely because Methodism was commonly viewed as being part of the church that it had attracted members), and that separation would engender strife at a time—so said Wesley with perhaps a touch of exaggeration—when all was quiet in church-Methodist relations.[104] Moreover, Wesley added, actually to create a new church would take infinite time and care, and besides this experiment had been tried in the past and never worked. Looking back on European history since the Reformation, Wesley observed that 'those men of God' such as John Arndt (an early German pietist) and Robert Bolton (an Anglican Puritan) and who had remained in the churches in which they had been born had achieved great things, whereas those who had left their churches had had limited influence.[105]

Wesley went on to advise his readers not to speak contemptuously of the church and its clergy: 'contempt, sharpness, bitterness', he said, ' can do

---

[101] Ibid., III, p. 145.
[102] John Wesley, *A Preservative against unsettled notions in Religion* (Bristol, 1758); Wesley, *Reasons*.
[103] Wesley, *Reasons*, p. A. 3.
[104] Ibid., p. A. 3-4.
[105] Ibid., p. 4.

no good'.[106] He praised contemporary Anglican preaching: 'In almost all the sermons we hear there, we hear many great and important Truths'. And in what might seem to some as a very Freudian statement, Wesley noted that 'In some sense it is the Mother of us all who have been brought up therein and thus we should be tender to the Church in which we belong'.[107] He maintained that it would be good for every Methodist preacher to attend church as often and as they could, observing 'And the more we attend it, the more we will love it'.[108] His recommendation in this publication was not that Methodists should leave the church but that they should go to it more frequently. In describing his feelings about the church, Wesley anticipated, yet complicated, some of the recent discussions of national identity among eighteenth-century historians. He talked of a national loyalty—although, *pace* Linda Colley, he saw national identity as English rather than British: 'We look upon England as that Part of the world, and the Church as that Part of England, to which all we who are born and have been brought up therein, owe our first and Chief Regard. We feel ourselves a strong *synorge*, a kind of Natural Affection for our Country which we apprehend Christianity was never designed to root out or to impair'.[109] And against Colley's insistence on a common Protestantism which bound together both Anglican and Dissenter, Wesley observed that, 'We have a more peculiar concern to our Brethren, for that Part of our Countrymen, to whom we have been joined from our Youth, by Ties of a Religious as well as a Civil Nature…so much so our Bowels yearn for them'.[110]

The process of writing the *Reasons* strengthened Wesley's resolve to stay within the church. In the following year Charles wrote to his wife that John had 'become a champion for the Church' once again.[111] Wesley's stand was shown in 1760 when again it was discovered that some of the lay preachers in Norwich has been administering the sacrament. Wesley showed his disapproval and forbade the practice.[112] During the next decades he also forbid his preachers from baptizing, from talking against the church or the clergy, and from reading church prayers.[113] In 1761 he warned James Knox not to leave the church: 'I advise you steadily to adhere to her doctrines, especially justification by faith and Holiness. But above all, I cannot but earnestly entreat you not to rest till you experience what she teaches; till (to sum up all in a word) God'—and here he quoted from the Book of Common Prayer—'cleanses the thoughts of your heart by the inspiration of His Holy Spirit, that you may perfectly love Him and

---

[106] Ibid., p. 8.
[107] Ibid., p. 9.
[108] Ibid., p. 11.
[109] Wesley, *Reasons*, p. 7. Linda Colley, *Britons: Forging the Nation, 1707-1837* (New Haven, CT and London, 1993).
[110] Ibid.
[111] JRULM, DDWES/4/37: Charles Wesley to Sarah Wesley [n.d.?1759].
[112] *Letters*, IV, p. 99: John Wesley to Charles Wesley, 23 June 1760. See also *Journals* IV, p. 415: 6 March 1760.
[113] See Letters VII, p. 179: John Wesley to John Benson, 19 May 1783, and ibid., p, 213: John Wesley to William Percival, 4 May 1784.

worthily magnify his Holy Name'.[114] In the same year he wrote to John Green, dean of Lincoln and future bishop: 'I quite agree we neither can be better men nor better Christians than by continuing members of the Church of England'.[115] But despite his affection for the church he continued to be dismayed at some of the church's attitudes towards the Methodists, and the issue of registering as Dissenters reached a head in the Rolvenden case, where a Kent magistrate had taken a Methodist lay-preacher to court for not being registered as a nonconformist.[116] Nevertheless, Wesley liked to present himself as one of those who kept the link with the church going. He told his brother in 1768 ' I am at my wits' end with regard to two things—the Church and Christian perfection. Unless both you and I stand in the gap in Good Earnest, the Methodists will drop them both'.[117] What is interesting, however, is that for nearly fifteen years after, the issue of the separation from the church was hardly mentioned. This is particularly surprising given that between 1765 and 1780 was a period of Methodist growth, and a time when Wesley was consolidating his Connexion.[118]

After nearly two decades of relative quiet, the issue of Wesley's relations with the church was dramatically raised in 1784 when he ordained clergy for America (nevertheless still telling preachers not to talk against the church). This seemed to many to prove that he had set up a rival church. His brother Charles tellingly urged him to re-read *Reasons*, and informed John that 'when once you began ordaining in America I knew (and you knew) that your preachers here would never rest until you ordained them'.[119] Charles and others saw his behaviour as complete disobedience to the bishops. Wesley justified his action: 'Some obedience I always paid to the bishops in obedience to the law of the land. But I cannot see that I am under any obligation to obey them farther than those laws require. It is in obedience to those laws that I have never exercised in England the power which I believe God has given me. I firmly believe I am a scriptural *episkopos* as much as any man in England or Europe'.[120] Wesley now thought that the idea of the apostolic succession was false (contradicting what he had said to his brother-in-law forty years before). But this did not, he said, mean he was no longer part of the Church of England. And, as on other occasions, he returned to the question of what is the Church of England, quoting again the twentieth article, which he

---

[114] *Letters*, IV, p. 303: John Wesley to James Knox, 26 June 1761.
[115] *Letters*, IV, p. 144: John Wesley to John Green, 2 April 1761.
[116] For a discussion of the Rolvenden case, see *Journal and Diaries* (Heitzenrater and Ward), V, p. 26, and Gregory, *Restoration, Reformation, and Reform*, pp. 225, 227.
[117] *Letters*, V, p. 88: John Wesley to Charles Wesley, 14 May 1768.
[118] A.D. Gilbert, *Religion and Society in Industrial England: Church, chapel, and social change, 1740-1914* (London, 1976), p. 31; Robert Currie, Alan Gilbert, and Lee Horsley, *Churches and Churchgoers: patterns of church growth in the British Isles since 1700* (Oxford, 1977), p. 40.
[119] *Letters*, VII, p. 284: John Wesley to Charles Wesley, 19 August 1785, prints Charles' letter.
[120] Ibid.

viewed as 'a true logical definition, containing both the essence and properties of a Church'.[121] He maintained to his brother that he was no more separatist than he was in 1758 (when *Reasons* was first published) and considered that there was 'not a hair's breadth' between him and the church.[122] And at the 1786 Conference Wesley refused to ordain a lay preacher for Yorkshire and repeated his warnings to the lay preachers not to administer the sacrament or baptize.[123]

Nevertheless, there is some indication that during the last three years of his life, Wesley was getting more frustrated with the actual practice of the church (perhaps ironically at a time when his own reputation among Anglican clergy was higher than before, and when he was getting an increasing number of invitation to preach in Anglican churches).[124] In 1788 he insisted that he was not a separatist like Benjamin Ingham or Lady Huntingdon, but he did admit that 'a kind of separation has already taken place, and will inevitably spread',[125] significantly blaming this on the church itself. He argued that if someone lived in a parish where the new incumbent neither lived nor preached the gospel, then Methodists would not dare to attend the church.[126] This statement represents a modification of his earlier view that the lifestyle of the minister was not a reason for leaving the church[127] and later that year he did ordain Alexander Mather for England, as a start to remedy the deficiencies of Anglican clergy there.[128] In 1790, less than a year before his death, he was adamant in a letter to Bishop Prettyman-Tomline, who, as adviser to Pitt, could be considered to have some say in ecclesiastical policy, that the issue of making Methodists take licences was a key one in driving them away from the established church. Wesley considered this as the policy of a persecuting church, maintaining that the law was no better than the infamous Act of *de heretico comburendo* (which had allowed for the burning of heretics in the pre-Reformation era), concluding that 'a persecution which is banished in France is again countenanced in England'.[129]

But despite such disaffection with contemporary church practice, Wesley continued to defend the need to remain part of the church. His own write-up of the 1788 Conference recalled that 'one of the most important

---

[121] Ibid., VII, p. 286.
[122] Ibid., VII, p. 287.
[123] JRULM, Charles Wesley Papers II/4/69: Charles Wesley to Sarah Wesley, 2 July 1786.
[124] William Gibson, *The Church of England, 1688-1832: Unity and Accord* (London and New York, 2001), p. 206, quoting Charles Wesley.
[125] *Letters*, VIII, p. 92: John Wesley to 'a friend', 20 September 1788.
[126] Ibid.
[127] *Letters*, VI, p. 326: John Wesley to Miss Bishop, 18 October 1778.
[128] *Journal*, VII, p. 421: 3 August, 1788, fn. The fact that Wesley only made a limited number of ordinations for special cases, and that there is no sign of any intention for a wholesale ordination, suggests that they were a precaution in case they were needed.
[129] *Letters*, VIII, p. 224: John Wesley to the Bishop of Lincoln, 26 June 1790.

points considered...was that of leaving the Church'.[130] Wesley was clear that he had not willingly departed from it in either doctrine or discipline, and that in terms of doctrine his view remained identical. But, he continued, 'we have in a course of years, out of necessity, not choice, slowly and warily varied in some points of discipline, by preaching in fields, by extemporary prayer, by employing lay preachers, by forming and regulating societies, and by holding yearly Conferences. But we did none of these things till we were convinced we could no longer omit them but at peril of our own souls'.[131] The 1789 Conference again discussed separation from the church, but Wesley noted 'we were all unanimous against it'.[132]

After Wesley's death, and in the wake of the French Revolution, as part of a battle over Wesley's religious identity, a number of pamphlets written by self-styled 'members of the Church of England' stressed that Methodism did indeed go hand in hand with membership of the church. In 1793 'a layman of the Church of England' offered some 'disinterested advice' to the Methodists, reminding them of Wesley's affection for the church.[133] In 1795 'a member of the Church of England' argued that contemporaries should not use terms such as 'sect', 'schism, or 'division' to describe Methodism: 'We believe that [Methodism] does not differ in any essential point; and therefore it will be impossible to shew the dissimilarities between the doctrines of Methodism and the doctrines of the Church of England'.[134] The author emphasized the fact that Methodists kept to the Book of Common Prayer and the Thirty-Nine Articles, and quoted Bishop Warburton: 'Methodism signifies only the manner of preaching; not either an old or a new religion; it is the manner in which Mr Wesley and his followers attempt to propagate the plain old religion'.[135] This can, of course, be seen merely as an attempt at Anglican propaganda to keep Methodists in the church. But what is clear is that not all Methodists needed much convincing. The London Methodist Society—arguably Wesley's flagship—remained staunchly pro-church until the 1820s.[136]

---

[130] *Journal*, VII, p. 422: 4 August 1788.
[131] Ibid.
[132] *Journal*, VII, p. 523: 28 August 1789.
[133] [A Layman of the Church of England], *Disinterested Advice to the people called Methodists, concerning the misunderstandings which have arisen among them since the death of the Rev. John Wesley, and also concerning their conduct towards the Church of England. By a layman of the Church of England* (London, 1793).
[134] [A member of the Church of England], *Methodism vindicated, from the charge of ignorance and enthusiasm. Being a reply, to a sermon, preached by the Rev. Samuel Clapham, M.A. at Borough bridge in Yorkshire, September 2, 1794, intitled [sic], How far Methodism conduces to the interests of Christianity, and the welfare of society...By a member of the Church of England* (Margate and London, 1795), pp. 5, 34.
[135] Ibid., p. 26. The author quotes Warburton '"On Grace", p. 168'. William Warburton, *The Doctrine of Grace: or the office and operations of the Holy Spirit vindicated from the insults of infidelity and the abuses of fanaticism* (London, 1763).
[136] George John Stevenson, *City Road Chapel, London and its Associations, Historical, Biographical and Memorial* (London, 1872), p. 153, quoted in Lloyd, 'Charles Wesley: a New Evaluation'. Dr. Lloyd's important thesis argues that Charles

These purportedly Church of England defences of Wesley and Methodism remind us that another way of looking at Wesley's relationship to the established church is to see how that church reacted to him. Both Methodists and Anglicans have been keen to emphasize the negative responses of the church to the emergence of the new movement. There is certainly evidence of hostility from the church (including the stoning to death of one of the early Methodist lay preachers), and the anti-Methodist pamphlet collection at the John Rylands Library contains over 100 tracts, mainly from members of the church, of which Bishop George Lavington's *The Enthusiasm of Methodists and Papists Compared* (1748-52) is the most quoted.[137] In similar vein, and typical of many others, the author of *The Doctrines of Methodism Examined and Confuted by a Presbyter of the Church of England* (1765), fit Methodists into a long line of heretics from the Bible and the seventeenth century, and emphasized the sexual nature of the movement, noting that love feasts 'savour more of the Priests and Devotees of Venus, than of the Ambassadors and Adorers of a pure and holy God'.[138] The writer emphasized that Wesley and the Methodists were a rival to the established church: 'Another mark here given of false teachers is That they separate themselves from the communion of the established Church, as thinking themselves more perfect than any of us. And yet they pretend to be true and Dutiful Sons of our national Church. But if that were so, why do they preach in the Fields, Streets, and private Houses, contrary to the civil and ecclesiastical laws of the realm?'. What was more was that 'the great leader of this sect hath travelled over most Counties in the Nation, to establish new-fangled Societies, and to appoint spiritual Directors among them'.[139]

But although highly quotable, these were not the only responses to the emergence of Methodism. A number of Church of England clergy were supporters of the movement, and this fact has generally been downplayed by both historians of Methodism and historians of the Church of England. But John Walsh has argued that the movement would never have got off the ground without the backing of Church of England clergy,[140] and John Potter ('a great and good man',[141] according to Wesley) and Thomas Secker, both archbishops of Canterbury, can be shown to have given Wesley encouragement and shared at least some of his concerns about the state of

---

Wesley and most of the Methodists displayed an even greater attachment to the Church of England than John.

[137] George Lavington, *The Enthusiasm of Methodists and Papists Compared* (London, 1748-52).
[138] *The Doctrines of Methodism Examined and Confuted by a Presbyter of the Church of England* (London, 1765), p. 11.
[139] Ibid., p. 12-13.
[140] John Walsh, '"Methodism" and the origins of English-speaking Evangelicalism', in Mark A. Noll, David W. Bebbington, and George A. Rawlyk (eds.), *Evangelicalism: Comparative Studies of Popular Protestantism in North America, The British Isles, and Beyond, 1700-1990* (New York and Oxford 1992), pp. 27-8.
[141] Wesley, 'On attending the Church service', p. 478.

the church and the need for reform.[142] So too, Bishop Beilby Porteus, a protégé of Archbishop Secker and later bishop of Chester and London, and Bishop George Horne, gave Wesley support. And although tracts such as Lavington's have been much quoted, rather marginalized from the picture are more pro-Methodist publications from the church-side. Someone purporting to be 'a member of the Church of England' reminded Lavington in an open publication that Justification by faith was 'a doctrine of the pure Church of England: it is the Doctrine of her Homilies, it is the doctrine which all have subscribed to, yet too many of them disregard'.[143] The writer concluded: 'I have sometimes been tempted to wish everyone a Methodist'.[144]

Given the support that Wesley did receive from a number of fairly well-placed Anglicans, it becomes more understandable why the Church of England did not excommunicate him. Some scholars have also suggested that Wesley benefited from the relatively lax and decentralized nature of the church in this period. If the church had been less slothful, it is alleged, then he would have been thrown out.[145] But one of the ironies of scholarship is that while the Laudian church is fashionably condemned for driving those, such as the Anglican Puritans, who considered themselves members of the church, away from it, and the Elizabethan and Jacobean church is currently valued for its moderation and inclusivity,[146] the Georgian church is seen as being somnolent for its moderate position. Yet the general temper of the church in the eighteenth century was for inclusion, with persuasion, not persecution, its hallmark. In its self-presentation, it is noticeable that the church prided itself on being an essentially tolerant and charitable institution, and many Anglican commentators saw persecution and intolerance as the sign of the anti-Christ.[147] It is also difficult to know on what precise grounds the church

---

[142] For Potter's support, see Baker, *Wesley and the Church of England*, p. 59, and *Journal and Diaries* (Heitzenrater and Ward), II, p. 265. For Secker, see Gregory, *Restoration, Reformation, and Reform*, pp. 226-7. On the wider issue of support for reform from within the Church, see Stephen Taylor, 'Bishop Edmund Gibson's Proposals for Church Reform', in Stephen Taylor (ed.), *From Cranmer to Davidson. A Church of England Miscellany* (Woodbridge, 1999), pp. 169-202; and Gregory, *Restoration, Reformation, and Reform*, pp. 5-6, 26, 65-8, 70, 84, 100, 284-6, 287-95.

[143] [A Clergyman of the Church of England], *A Letter to the Right Reverend Father in God George Lord Bishop of Exeter...in defence of the principles of the Methodism, objected to in his Lordship's charge. By a clergyman of the Church of England* (London, 1748), p. 6.

[144] Ibid., p. 20.

[145] Abbey and Overton, *The English Church*, I, pp. 245-50, 353-5, 383-97; II, pp. 92-3, 132-6; Rack, *Reasonable Enthusiast*, p. 305.

[146] See Collinson, *Religion of Protestants*.

[147] Jeremy Gregory, 'Persecution, toleration, competition, and indifference: the Church of England and its rivals in the long eighteenth century', in C. d'Haussy (ed.), *Quand Religions et Confessions se Regardent* (Paris, 1998), pp. 45-60. It is worth asking why legal action was not taken against the Methodists under the Conventicle Act of 1664. David Hempton examines some of the

could have excommunicated Wesley. Not only were the mechanisms difficult for this, but he had no living so he could not be deprived.

Far from wanting Wesley to be excommunicated, a number of Wesley's supporters within the church came up with schemes which, instead of seeking to distance the church from Methodism, actually aimed to harness the movement more effectively to the church. In 1756 Samuel Walker urged that the Methodists be brought closer to the church and those lay preachers who were considered suitable should be ordained.[148] In 1767 James Creighton, the vicar of Annagh, County Caven, informed Charles Wesley of a scheme for making John Wesley a bishop,[149] and in 1775 John Fletcher, the vicar of Madeley, Shropshire, encouraged Wesley to reform the church from within, making Methodism an *ecclesiola in ecclesia*, with the bishops ordaining the lay preachers. As far as Fletcher was concerned, Wesley's position was clear enough: 'You love the Church of England, and yet you are not blind to her freckles, nor insensible of her shackles'. He urged Wesley to follow a path which was highly reminiscent of the aims of Anglican Puritans in the late sixteenth and early seventeenth centuries: 'What Sir, if you used your liberty as an Englishman, a Christian, a divine, as an extraordinary messenger of God? What if with bold modesty you took a farther step towards the reformation of the Church of England?'[150] In 1786 Richard Dillon, an erstwhile Methodist lay preacher who had by now taken Anglican orders—demonstrating that traffic was not just from the church to Methodism but could in fact be the other way round (the church attracting former Methodists through a kind of ecclesiastical osmosis)—recounted his great pleasure that Wesley and the preachers had pledged to remain within the church during Wesley's lifetime. It was, so Dillon claimed, to Wesley's 'immortal honour that to the very end of his life he continued to call the lost sheep of the almost desolate Church of England to an experimental knowledge of God'.[151]

If Wesley's attitude towards the church reveals a qualified, yet at times often grudging admiration, and if at least some members of the church were aware of the good Methodism could do, he was consistently highly suspicious of Dissent. From the perspective of the nineteenth century, where the majority of Methodists would have seen themselves as Dissenters, Wesley's portrayal of Dissent is at times surprisingly bitter and prejudiced and plays on a range of late seventeenth- and eighteenth-century high church Anglican stereotypes of their nonconformist rivals. In certain respects indeed, Wesley's hostility towards Dissent went further than that of several of his Anglican contemporaries whose attitude towards nonconformity, at least by the 1740s, had softened considerably. In some parishes at least there was a rapprochement between the church and

---

issues in 'Methodism and the Law in English society, 1740-1820', in idem, *Religion and the People*, pp. 145-61.
[148] *Letters*, III, p. 193: John Wesley to Samuel Walker, 3 September 1756.
[149] JRULM, DDWES/2/67: James Creighton to John Wesley, 6 October 1767.
[150] *Journal*, VIII, appendix, p. 331: John Fletcher to John Wesley, 1 August 1775.
[151] JRULM, DD/Pr/2/18: Richard Dillon to Charles Wesley, 26 August 1786.

Dissenters, where there is also evidence of Anglicans and Dissenters working together against the common enemies of atheism and secularism.[152] Wesley, in stark contrast, took a hard-line against those who attended rival places of worship (and it is noticeable that he refers to those who do not attend the church as 'dissenters' rather than the milder 'nonconformists'). In *Reasons* he urged his followers not to go to Dissenting houses: 'Either the ministers are New Light men, denying the Lord that bought them and overturning his Gospels from the very Foundations: or they are Predestinarians' and as such teach 'deadly poison'.[153] Against his perception of Dissent as being Calvinist (which of course ignored the General Baptists and other anti-Calvinist nonconformists), Wesley extolled the Arminianism of the church (ignoring some notable Anglican Calvinists such as William Romaine, Henry Venn, and his correspondent Samuel Walker), even agreeing with the expulsion of the Methodist students from Oxford University in 1768 on the grounds that they were Calvinists. He sided with Dr. Nowell (an Oxford spokesperson) against the Calvinist Sir Richard Hill who had criticized the university, and observed that Nowell's defence was enough to clear the Church of England from the charge of predestination.[154]

Wesley caricatured Dissenting services as dull and over-long. He particularly objected to their lengthy prayers, and their singing 'in a slow drawling manner', noting that 'we sing swift, both because it saves Time, and because it tends to awake and enliven the Soul'.[155] In 1778 he informed Miss Bishop that if Church of England sermons were frequently *un*evangelical, they were much preferable to those given by Dissenters which were *anti*-evangelical. 'Few of the Methodists', he told her, 'are now in danger from imbibing error from the Church ministers, but they are in great danger of imbibing the grand error—Calvinism—from some of the Dissenting ministers'.[156] Wesley's loathing of nonconformity allowed him to stress the superiority of Anglicanism. He claimed to 'find more life in the Church prayers than in the formal extemporary prayers of Dissenters', and what may seem surprising given what historians usually say about the Evangelical revival, he noted that 'I find more profit in sermons on either good temper or good works than in what are vulgarly called gospel sermons'.[157]

Wesley's attacks on Dissent need to be taken into account in any assessment of his attitudes towards the church. For Wesley, leaving the church meant that any fixed religious position would be lost, and he

---

[152] Gregory, *Restoration, Reformation, and Reform*, pp. 181-232.
[153] Wesley, *Reasons against a Separation*, p. 9.
[154] Quoted in *Journal*, V, p. 263: 14 May 1768. The relevant publications were Richard Hill, *Pietas Oxoniensis: or, a full and impartial account of the expulsion of six students from St. Edmund Hall, Oxford* (London, 1768); and Thomas Nowell, *An answer to a pamphlet entitled Pietas oxoniensis...In a letter to the author* (Oxford, 1768).
[155] Wesley, *Reasons against a Separation*, p. 10.
[156] *Letters*, VI, p. 326: John Wesley to Miss Bishop, 18 October 1778.
[157] Ibid.

complained of the 'itching ears'[158] of Dissenters which made them move from group to group. In 1784 he blamed the hostility to the church and the desire to separate that was common in some Methodist circles on the fact that an increasing number of Methodists had originally been Dissenters.[159] His *Journal* echoes his hostility to Dissent, and as part of his instructions to his readers, he warns them of the dangers of mixing with nonconformists. The entry for 4 August 1766 records: 'At one I preached at Bingley, but with a heavy heart, finding so many of the Methodists here, as well as at Haworth, perverted by the Anabaptists. I see clearer and clearer, none will keep to us unless they to the Church. Whoever separates from the Church will separate from the Methodists'.[160] For Wesley, then, Methodism prospered hand in hand with the church.

If Wesley's Anglican links deserve more attention than they are usually given, what light do they shed on the broader issue of Methodist-Anglican relations in the eighteenth century? How did Hanoverian Methodists see their religious identity? Because of nineteenth-century developments, it has all too often been assumed that the attraction of Methodism in the eighteenth century was its dissent from the church, but it may have been Methodism's Anglican credentials that allowed it to develop. Not only was the role of Church of England ministers crucial to its early development, but the movement was able to attract to it those who (like Wesley himself) would not want to have been thought of as nonconformists, so that seeing Methodism as a movement from within, rather than from without the church, can, as has sometimes been noted, help explain its early success. Methodist lay preachers could not fulfil certain social roles, such as the rites of passage associated with baptism, marriage and burial which meant that most Methodists would still want to see themselves as members of the church and would want to benefit from its ministrations. In any case, as an increasing number of social historians of religion argue, we should be wary of imposing false boundaries between religious groups. In 1786, for example, the rector of St. Alphege's, Canterbury noted that 'many go to the Cathedral in the morning, to the Presbyterian meeting in the afternoon, and to a Methodist meeting at night',[161] which is suggestive of the flexibility of the eighteenth-century religious landscape. Given that these Kentish parishioners might well have considered themselves to be Anglican, Methodist and Presbyterian, it makes it easier to see how most Methodists could have seen themselves as Anglican too.

It is also becoming clear from local researches, that, on the ground, the relationship between Methodists and Anglicans were fairly fluid, and indeed was more consensual that the emphasis on conflict might suggest. This is, of course, an issue of the sources. There are certainly those that demonstrate clashes, but there are others that show cooperation and integration. As late as 1806, the rector of St. James', Dover reported that the

---

[158] Ibid., VI, p. 268: John Wesley to anon., 7 July 1777.
[159] Wesley, 'On attending the Church service', pp. 470-71.
[160] *Journal*, V, p. 180: 4 August 1766.
[161] Gregory, *Restoration, Reformation and Reform*, p. 273.

Methodists 'are not only punctual in their attendance at church, and at the sacrament, but in the course of twenty three years I have often been called to visit them in sickness'.[162] If, as Wesley pointed out, the establishment of a Methodist meeting sometimes signalled disaffection with the Anglican incumbent, it is clear that the appointment of an Anglican minister who was liked, could ensure that the Methodist meeting withered away.[163] There may also be some wider benefits from seeing Wesley's Methodism as a pastoral addition to the church, which could also help supply its deficiencies, rather than as a rival movement. As a study of eighteenth-century religion in Wales has demonstrated, much of Methodism's early achievements there emerged in places where there had been a vibrant Anglican pastoral culture.[164] The fact that, like Wesley, the majority of Georgian Methodists saw themselves as both Anglican and Methodist means that not only must eighteenth-century historians think outside the box of the church/chapel divide,[165] but more importantly the emergence of Methodism might, in an ironic way, demonstrate the success, rather than the failing of the eighteenth-century church. Wesley's Anglican Methodism reveals that the church could indeed be creative, and that one of its ordained clergy could develop and refine its pastoral strategies to bring the Christian message to those whom he considered to be previously unchurched or who wanted extra spiritual nourishment. Just as some historians have argued that the sixteenth-century Reformation grew out of a dynamic and vital late medieval church,[166] so Methodism might be an important piece of evidence to show that the Georgian church could be dynamic and vital too.

---

[162] Ibid., p. 229.
[163] *Letters*, VIII, p. 92: John Wesley to 'a friend', 20 September 1788. An example of the appointment of a popular Anglican incumbent leading to the decline of a Methodist meeting is Eastchurch in Kent in the 1780s; see Gregory, *Restoration, Reformation, and Reform*, p. 229.
[164] G.H. Jenkins, *Religion, Literature and Society in Wales 1660-1730* (Cardiff, 1978), p. 263.
[165] Gilbert, *Religion and Society*. As a corrective, see Mark Smith, *Religion in Industrial Society: Oldham and Saddleworth, 1740-1865* (Oxford, 1994). See also the discussion in John Walsh, 'Methodism at the end of the eighteenth century' in Rupert Davies and Gordon Rupp (eds.), *A History of the Methodist Church in Great Britain* (London, 1965), I, pp. 277-315.
[166] Eamon Duffy, *The Stripping of the Altars. Traditional Religion in England, c.1400-1580* (New Haven, CT, 1992).

Chapter 10

The Waning of Protestant Unity and Waxing of Anti-Catholicism? Archdeacon Daubeny and the Reconstruction of 'Anglican' Identity in the Later Georgian Church, c.1780-c.1830

Peter B. Nockles

The historiographical consensus on the Church of England in the period of what has become widely accepted as that of the 'long eighteenth century', is that the few decades of church party controversy and division following the Glorious Revolution and culminating in the reign of Queen Anne (1702-14) were succeeded by a long period of comparative religious peace, consensus and 'protestant unity'; a kind of 'ecclesiastical analogue' to the J.H. Plumb thesis of the 'growth of political stability'.[1] The argument for a mid-eighteenth-century Anglican consensus built on the ideal of 'moderation' and unity, and the non-partisan nature of much churchmanship in the period, with high churchmen grudgingly 'accommodated' to the prevailing *ethos* as well as political realities, has been well made and is convincing.[2] However, it becomes less convincing for the period from the 1770s onwards. The argument for eighteenth-century Anglican and Protestant consensus has not always taken sufficient

---

[1] John Walsh and Stephen Taylor, 'The Church & Anglicanism', in John Walsh, Colin Haydon and Stephen Taylor (eds.), *The Church of England, c. 1689-c. 1833: From Toleration to Tractarianism* (Cambridge, 1993), p. 29; J.H. Plumb, *Growth of Political Stability in England, 1675-1725* (London, 1967); Geoffrey Holmes, *Religion and Party in late Stuart England* (London, 1975), p. 30.

[2] See William Gibson, *The Church of England, 1688-1832: Unity and Accord* (London, 2001), especially chapters 1, 6; Jeffrey S. Chamberlain, *Accommodating high churchmen: the clergy of Sussex, 1700-1745* (Chicago, 1997); William Gibson, *The Achievement of the Anglican Church, 1689-1800: The Confessional State in Eighteenth Century England* (Lewiston, 1996); Robert G. Ingram, 'Nation, Empire, and Church: Thomas Secker, Anglican Identity, and Public Life in Georgian Britain, 1700-1770' (University of Virginia PhD dissertation, 2002, especially pp. 24-5.

account of the internal tensions unleashed by the Evangelical Revival and Methodism. Jonathan Clark's masterly analysis in his path-breaking *English Society* of the 'long eighteenth century' Church of England, points up the divisions within Protestantism in terms of Anglican versus heterodox Dissent as well as the tensions between orthodox and heterodox Dissent,[3] which Linda Colley's somewhat broad-brush depiction of Protestantism as the focus for an emerging 'British' identity' in her *Britons* tended to overlook or downplay.[4] None the less, by focusing on the political theology rather than doctrinal or even spiritual content of what he regards as the orthodox Anglican hegemony of the period, Clark incorporates Evangelicalism and Methodism within the embrace of that hegemonic ideology to the curious neglect of the emerging religious tensions and differences between 'Evangelical' and 'orthodox' within the Church's fold from at least the 1790s onwards.[5] Emphasis has also been given by Colley, Haydon, and others to the binding and unifying force within the Church of England of anti-Catholicism,[6] but the fiercely anti-Methodist critique emanating from high church (but also latitudinarian) quarters from the late 1730s onwards should not be overlooked. The Protestant unity scenario also tends to leave out of the picture the later controversies over subscription to the Thirty-Nine Articles in the period 1766-74, as analysed by Brian Young and Grayson Ditchfield,[7] and to overlook the stresses and strains provoked by the growth of Protestant Dissent, anticlericalism, and the challenges of both the American War and French Revolution in the later decades of the period, which Jonathan Clark, James Bradley, and Nigel Aston,[8] have all highlighted. The case for a 'high church' revival in the later

---

[3] J.C.D. Clark, *English Society, 1688-1832: ideology, social structure and political practice during the ancien regime* (Cambridge, 1985), especially ch. 5; idem, *English Society 1660-1832: religion, ideology and politics during the ancien regime* (Cambridge, 2000), especially ch. 4; idem, *The Language of Liberty: political discourse and social dynamics in the Anglo-American world* (Cambridge, 1994), especially chs. 2, 4.

[4] Linda Colley, *Britons: Forging the Nation, 1707-1837* (London, 1992), especially ch. 1. For effective critiques of Colley's broad-brush approach to Protestantism, see Jeremy Black, 'Confessional state or elect nation?', in Tony Claydon and Ian McBride (eds.), *Protestantism and National Identity: Britain and Ireland, c. 1650-c. 1850* (Cambridge 1998), pp. 53-74.

[5] Clark, *English Society, 1688-1832*, pp. 235-46. Clark surprisingly concludes that Evangelicals and Methodists hardly departed from the Anglican mainstream in ecclesiology. Clark, *English Society, 1660-1832*, p. 285.

[6] See Colin Haydon, *Anti-Catholicism in eighteenth-century England: A political and social study* (Manchester, 1993).

[7] B.W. Young, *Religion and Enlightenment in eighteenth-century England: theological debate from Locke to Burke* (Oxford, 1998), pp. 45-80; G.M. Ditchfield, 'The Subscription issue in British Parliamentary Politics, 1772-1779', *Parliamentary History* 7:1 (1988), pp. 45-80.

[8] See especially Nigel Aston, 'Anglican responses to anticlericalism in the "long" eighteenth century', in Nigel Aston and Matthew Cragoe (eds.), *Anticlericalism in Britain, c. 1500-1914* (Stroud, 2000), pp. 115-37; James E. Bradley, *Religion,*

Georgian Church of England has been made by several historians,[9] and it will form the context for this article. What has come under less scrutiny is the evidence for a growing strain in the internal consensus and sense of 'protestant unity' based on theological as well as political differences. It was these theological factors which underpinned and helped to explain the Protestant divisions analysed by Clark; divisions which foreshadowed, even if they never matched, the much more fundamental church party fragmentation of the post-1830 era under the impact of the Oxford Movement.[10]

The question as to how far during the crucial half-century prior to 1832 there was a waning of 'protestant unity' within and without the Church of England, and a partial renewal or recovery into polemical discourse of an earlier, seventeenth-century Laudian sense of self-conscious 'Anglican' identity built on exclusiveness rather than pan-Protestant consensus (defined as a sense of the Church of England being part of a close-knit Protestant family embracing continental Protestant churches), will form a broad theme of this article. Studies of the eighteenth-century Church of England rightly have tended to focus on its administrative organisation, on the local dioceses, and on pastoral practice, its 'success' or 'failure' largely measured by quantitative statistical and numerical criteria. However, at least until recently, the identity of the Church of England in the period has been viewed primarily in terms of its status as a national establishment rather than in terms of its varied and divergent theological character, style, and complexion. There will be an exploration of the tension between the concept of a 'catholic' and a 'national' identity in the later Georgian Church of England which some historians have recently identified.[11] Such questions will be explored through the writings, career, and personality, of one of the most prolific Anglican controversialists of the age, Charles Daubeny (1745-1827), archdeacon of Sarum.

The late F.C. Mather's study of Bishop Samuel Horsley (1733-1806) shows how fruitful a biographical approach can be in contextualizing as well as raising wider questions relating to church and society in this period. Attention will be focused especially on Daubeny's writings against Evangelicalism, Jacobinism, Protestant Dissent, Anglican

---

Revolution, an English Radicalism: nonconformity in eighteenth-century politics and society (Cambridge, 1990).

[9] F.C. Mather, *High church prophet: Bishop Samuel Horsley (1733-1806) and the Caroline tradition in the later Georgian Church* (Oxford, 1992); Peter B. Nockles, *The Oxford Movement in context: Anglican high churchmanship, 1760-1857* (Cambridge, 1994); Nigel Aston, 'Horne and Heterodoxy: The Defence of Anglican Belief in the Late Eighteenth Century', *English Historical Review* 118:429 (October 1993), pp. 895-919.

[10] Peter B. Nockles, 'Church parties in the pre-Tractarian Church of England 1750-1833: the "orthodox"—some problems of definition and identity', in Haydon, Walsh, and Taylor (eds.), *Church of England c.1689-c.1833*, pp. 334-59.

[11] B.W. Young, 'A history of variations: the identity of the eighteenth-century Church of England', in Claydon and McBride (eds.), *Protestantism and National Identity*, p. 125.

Latitudinarianism, and Roman Catholicism, and how far the main thrust of Daubeny's polemic varied in relation to perceptions as to what were the immediate challenges threatening the Church of England at any one time. In particular, Daubeny's controversy with the Anglican Calvinist Evangelicals, John Overton and Sir Richard Hill, following the publication of his *Guide to the Church* (1798) went to the roots of the whole issue of 'Anglican' theological identity in the later Georgian Church, but it hitherto has escaped close historical scrutiny.

Was Daubeny, perhaps merely on account of a notoriously irascible temperament and idiosyncratic personality, the exception to prove the rule of continued Anglican 'moderation'? Was he unrepresentative even among fellow high churchmen? If he was only representative of a particular *type* of high churchman, did his writings and career point to something deeper and reflect a new mood and shift or change of gear in the undulating theological history 'of variations' within the Church of England? Does the example of his career support or weaken suggestions that high churchmen or 'the orthodox party', as they were commonly designated at the time, were by the start of the nineteenth century receiving on a substantial scale the preferment that was apparently withheld from them in the middle years of the eighteenth century? More particularly, how far does Daubeny's career lead us to recognize variations within the spectrum of high churchmanship? How much can it tell us about the history and self-understanding of 'Anglicanism' in the later phase of the 'long' eighteenth century.

The balance of strength between different schools of Anglican churchmanship differed profoundly in the 'long' eighteenth century between 1688 and 1832; shifts that were caused by varying state policy as much as by divergent intellectual trends. If the ejection of 2000 hundred 'Puritan' clergy in 1662 weakened the 'Calvinistic' Reformed tradition, then the departure of about 300-400 Nonjurors after 1689 led in the longer term to a similar weakening of the Laudian tradition within the Church of England. Crown patronage exercized under the first two monarchs of the Hanoverian dynasty led to a significant strengthening of the Low Church and Whiggish (though the terms were by no means synonymous) element in the higher echelons of the Church.[12] State patronage of the Church encouraged the forces of religious 'moderation' as a necessary adjunct of the ministerial goal of political stability. Although during the reign of Queen Anne, high churchmen had taken up the slogan 'No Moderation' against Whig opponents, a cult of religious moderation soon became a self-defining characteristic of the Hanoverian Church in an era of Whig political hegemony. Moderation was part of the legacy of the long shadow cast by the religious convulsions of the seventeenth century born of both Laudian and Puritan excess. That shadow cut both ways and, as we shall see, was to fuel high church reactions to Evangelicalism and Methodism, but it certainly also rendered Whig statesmen, latitudinarian churchmen, and the

---

[12] Walsh and Taylor, 'The Church and Anglicanism', p. 31.

heterodox, sensitive to the least apparent resurgence of what they regarded as Laudian sacerdotalism.[13]

The Evangelical Revival and rise of Methodism under the leadership of John and Charles Wesley and George Whitefield can be viewed as in part a reaction against the latitudinarianism, rationalism, and moderation as well as the emphasis on morality over doctrine, supposedly characteristic of the mid-eighteenth-century Church of England. The Evangelical revivalists of the 1730s and 1740s sought to recover the claims of revelation from the apparent inroads of rationalism. However, so-called 'Evangelicals' had less of a complete monopoly of this doctrinal and spiritual reaction than many later commentators have assumed. Not only are the high church roots of the Wesley brothers well-attested, but High Church and 'orthodox' churchmen were often at one with Evangelical revivalists in exalting doctrinal preaching over merely moral exhortation and in defence of clerical subscription to the Thirty-Nine Articles against latitudinarian critics represented by Francis Blackburne's *The Confessional* (1766) and the so-called 'Feathers Tavern' petitioners in 1772. Anglican Evangelicals and Methodists were as firm as high churchmen in upholding the doctrine of the Trinity against Socinian and Unitarian opponents; as Henry Rack has shown, Methodist visions of the Trinity were common in the 1770s at a time when anti-Trinitarian and latitudinarian forces were challenging Anglican credal orthodoxy.

The 'Hutchinsonians', followers of the anti-Newtonian Hebraist philosopher, John Hutchinson (1674-1737),[14] though commonly regarded as a coterie of high churchmen such as George Horne and William Jones of Nayland, originally also encompassed some Evangelicals such as William Romaine and Thomas Haweis; the group being at least for a time as suspect as Methodists were in the eyes of the 'orthodox' Anglican mainstream, both being perceived as forms of a revival of the separatist tendencies, if not Puritanism, of the seventeenth century.[15] In short, in the reaction against

---

[13] For an example. See [Francis Blackburne], *Memoirs of Thomas Hollis* (London, 1780), I, p. 227. See also L.P. Curtis, *Anglican moods of the Eighteenth Century* (Hamden, CT, 1966), p. 5.

[14] On the Hutchinsonians, see Robert Spearman, *The life of John Hutchinson prefixed to a supplement to the works of John Hutchinson Esq.* (Oxford, 1765), pp. i-xiv; George Horne, *An Apology for certain gentlemen in the University of Oxford, aspersed in a late anonymous pamphlet* (Oxford, 1756); [J.A. Park], *Memoirs of William Stevens Esq* (London, 1812), pp. 22-7; Edward Churton, *A Memoir of Joshua Watson*, 2 vols. (London, 1861), pp. 39-42. See also, C.B. Wilde, 'Hutchinsonianism, Natural Philosophy and Religious Controversy in Eighteenth-Century Britain', *History of Science* 18:1 (March 1980), pp. 1-24; John C. English, 'John Hutchinson's critique of Newtonian Heterodoxy', *Church History*, 68:3 (September 1999), pp. 581-97; C.D.A. Leighton, 'Hutchinsonianism: a Counter-Enlightenment reform movement', *Journal of Religious History* 23:2 (June 1999), pp. 168-84. See also note 30.

[15] See [J. Douglas], *An Apology for the clergy, with a view to expose the groundless assertions of a late commentator on the 107th Psalm, and to undeceive the admirers of*

latitudinarianism and rationalism, it was not always clear that high churchmen and Evangelicals would emerge on opposite sides of a doctrinal divide. That great bone of doctrinal tension between Calvinists and Arminians was more of a source of division within Evangelicalism and Methodism—notably between the followers of John Wesley on the one hand and George Whitefield on the other—than at least until the last decade of the century it was between Evangelicals and high churchmen. On key questions of soteriology, 'orthodox' divines such as Archbishop Secker and high churchmen such as George Horne and Samuel Horsley steered the path of moderation and toleration and refused to let anti-Calvinism become a litmus-test of sound 'Anglicanism'.[16] Orthodox divines like Secker shared Anglican Evangelical complaints about the apparent neglect of the central dogmas of the Christian faith as a consequence of the latitudinarian emphasis on the practical and non-mysterious.[17] Moreover, it is instructive to contrast Secker's negative reputation as almost a crypto-papist in the eyes of ultra-latitudinarians such as Blackburne and Hollis, with his favourable reputation among Calvinist Evangelicals such as John Overton.[18] Horne and Horsley also remained favourites with Anglican Evangelicals in a way which sharply contrasted with Daubeny's reputation as 'high church bigot' among many members of that school as well as with Protestant Dissenters.[19]

The source of the unravelling of an Anglican Evangelical/high church *rapprochement* in the latter part of the century lay not so much in conflicting attitudes towards Protestant Dissent and notions of church communion (though these were evident) but in the gradual emergence of doctrinal divisions, especially relating to the Gospel plan of salvation. If the shadow of seventeenth-century religious conflict had helped foster the spirit of Anglican moderation and a conciliation of Dissent in one direction, it also helped keep alive high church Anglican hostility towards Protestant Dissent fuelled by fears of a revival of the spectre of Puritanism, in another. In particular, the prevailing consensus of moderation was blamed for an apparent reluctance among churchmen to insist upon the Church's distinctive doctrines and liturgical treasures and for acquiescence in the government's refusal to support repeated attempts by Bishops Berkeley and Sherlock, and Archbishops Potter and Secker, to establish colonial bishoprics in North America. One high church Anglican controversialist complained in 1750 that Protestant Dissenters, notably the lecturers of

---

    certain popular declaimers, by showing the dangerous consequences of their manner of preaching (London, 1755), p. 3.
[16] Mather, *High church prophet*, p. 13.
[17] Walsh and Taylor, 'The Church and Anglicanism', pp. 42-3.
[18] Young, *Religion and Enlightenment in Eighteenth-Century England*, p. 62. On Secker's clash with Blackburne, see Ingram, 'Thomas Secker', pp. 228-31.
[19] John Overton, *The True Churchmen Ascertained: or, an Apology for those of the regular clergy of the establishment, who are sometimes called Evangelical ministers* (York, 1802; 2nd edn.), p. vii, pp. 76-7; J.W. Middleton, *An Ecclesiastical Memoir of the first four decades of the reign of George III* (London, 1822), pp. 323-4, 329.

Salters-Hall in the 1720s and 1730s, did not always reciprocate the pacific spirit of Anglican moderation but, on the contrary, used their diatribes against 'Popery' to deliver glancing blows at the Church of England. In short, the perception grew that Anglican divines were exposed by the pressure of government to be 'cautious of meddling with controversial points'. The consequence, it was argued, was that 'members of our Church in general were perhaps never, at any time since the reformation, less able to give an answer to the objections, made to our liturgy, than they are at present'.[20] The writer's main target, a blueprint for Anglican 'moderation' advocated by the latitudinarian author of *Free and Candid Disquisitions relating to the Church of England* (1749), was condemned primarily as providing a cloak for Puritanical excess. The chilling spectre was raised of the downfall of the Church of England during the Great Rebellion of the middle of the previous century:

> Our governors need only look back to the dreadful scene of misery, which we suffered in the last century, and, I fancy, resemblance between the present attempt (tho varnished over with a glaring show of candour) and the methods taken to bring about that horrid scene of confusion, will be too visible to escape the observation of judicious and thinking men.[21]

Such alarmist rhetoric was never far from the surface among a certain type or style of Anglican high churchman in our period.

Charles Daubeny, born in 1745, emanated from a West Country mercantile family, being the second son of George Daubeny, a wealthy Bristol merchant. After being privately educated at Norton St Philip's, Somerset, and at Winchester College, he went up to Oriel College, Oxford, in December 1762, and gained an exhibition at New College, Oxford, in the following year. After taking holy orders, in 1774 he obtained a New College Fellowship which, on being offered the college living of North Bradley, Wiltshire, he vacated in 1776. Owing to dilapidations, the living yielded him an average annual income of a mere £50. In July 1778, Daubeny married Elizabeth Barnston, 'a lady, whose religious feelings and taste for retirement, were in unison with his own professional duties'. They lived in Clifton, Bristol, with Elizabeth's unmarried sister Catherine, until the vicarage of North Bradley was rendered inhabitable.[22]

Daubeny's domestic life was marked by legal and financial disputes. He became involved in a bitter family feud with his brother-in-law, Thomas Meade (1753-1845), who after the death of his first wife, Mary, Daubeny's sister, claimed that Daubeny had prevented him from marrying

---

[20] *Remarks upon a treatise, entitled 'Free and Candid Disquisitions relating to the Church of England', etc. in some letters to a worthy dignitary of the cathedral church of Wells. Part the first. By a presbyter of the Church of England* [Rev. Boswell of Taunton] (London, 1750), p. 6.
[21] Ibid., pp. 75-6.
[22] *A Guide to the Church...to which is prefixed, some account of the author's life and writings* (London, 1830; 3rd edn.), p. viii.

Catherine Barnston, Daubeny's sister-in-law. Daubeny was accused of 'absurd jealousy', and of plotting to get back a share of family money from Meade. A lengthy trial ensued, in which Daubeny even called on the aid of the bishop of Lincoln, George Tomline. Meade was eventually awarded costs against Daubeny. Intemperate pamphlets were written on both sides, especially by Daubeny, and the opposing parties became irreconcilable after Catherine Barnston married Meade in 1792. It was later reported by Meade that Daubeny even ignored 'his dear friend William Stevens in the street because he had taken my part in the lawsuit'.[23] There was a suggestion that Daubeny's family and legal disputes impaired his ministerial work for a time. Daubeny also never recovered from his wife's death in 1823.

Daubeny's emergence as a staunchly high Anglican churchman with a well-developed sense of not only the episcopal order and constitution of the hierarchical church, owed much to the formative early experience of his continental travels over a period of two decades—he was in Versailles during the first outbreak of the French Revolution in 1789. Daubeny's high churchmanship was also shaped by his long parochial career in an area where he was exposed to the challenge of Protestant Nonconformity. Daubeny's travels were made possible by the fortune which he inherited on the death of his father in 1770, and were partly dictated by the need to restore his always precarious health. It was for the latter reason that in 1770 he travelled not only to Paris and Lausanne, but on the recommendation of a physician, M. Tissot, he went to Germany in order to benefit from German mineral springs at spa resorts, a rest cure which he repeated in the winter of 1788/89. Travelling in the company of his brother the Rev. James Daubeny of Stratton, he visited the courts of Dresden and Berlin. In 1771, Daubeny went further afield and visited St. Petersburg, whereby through the influence of Princess Dashkow whom he had met in Paris, he was introduced at court and made a study of Russian Orthodoxy which, he concluded, was less corrupt than Roman Catholicism.[24]

Daubeny's travels encouraged in him a jaundiced view of continental Protestantism. Brian Young, W.R. Ward, and others have argued that a distinctively theological sense of 'Anglicanism' as a national church weakened in the eighteenth century due to the growth of a pan-Protestant impulse and an awakened sense of a Protestant internationalism.[25] The example of the somewhat negative response of the Anglican hierarchy to the overtures of the Moravians in the 1740s and 1750s hardly supports this

---

[23] *Thomas had two wives. By John A. Meade. Tales from the diaries of John A. Meade* (Victoria, B.C., 1956), p. 72. Stevens chided Daubeny for his behaviour, lamenting that he should be part of a 'long divided and distracted family'. William Stevens to Charles Daubeny, 21 January 1803, cited in Thomas Meade, *A reply to a paper circulated under the name of the Lord Bishop of Lincoln: the object of which is to counteract a verdict in an action brought by Thomas Meade esq. against the Rev. Charles Daubeny* (n. pl, priv. printed, 1806), p. 219.
[24] *Guide to the Church...account of the author's life and writings*, p. xiv.
[25] Young, 'History of variations', p. 107.

supposed 'pan-Protestant' trend. If it was a trend, however, Daubeny bucked or reversed it. In fact, there was an alternative 'catholic' or Anglican/Gallican model exemplified by Bishop Horsley in his dealings with the English Catholic Bishop Milner, to which Nigel Aston and the late F.C. Mather have drawn attention.[26] Daubeny's refusal to define Anglican identity in terms of a 'Protestant international', partly as we shall see, the result of his rigid 'branch theory' ecclesiology, was part of a wider trend evident by the later decades of the century. Daubeny's travels in France and his later stay in Switzerland in the summer of 1789 induced favourable comments on the state of Roman Catholicism and some severe strictures on Calvinism and the state of Protestant religion not only on the continent but in England. During his stay in Provence, Daubeny observed:

> We could not but observe that notwithstanding all the absurdities and corruptions by which the religion of Popery is disfigured, there is a greater appearance of religion amongst the lower orders in a Papal, than amongst the same classes in a Protestant country; a strong proof of the firm hold which the Roman Priesthood retains over the minds of the lower orders, compared with the influence which the Priests of the Church of England have over their congregations.[27]

One can find here the seeds of Daubeny's later attempts, exemplified in his *Guide to the Church*, to reassert the power of the Anglican priesthood and the apostolical claims of the Church of England. Daubeny's sojourn in Switzerland even led him to condemn the apparent excesses of the continental Reformation (a point that was to become a familiar trope in his published writings) and to the ecclesiastical irregularity of contemporary continental Protestantism. After condemning what he had seen of Calvinist worship in Geneva, he lamented:

> Such is Reformation, when carried into effect by those who have more zeal than judgement; who, in their anxiety to steer wide of the superstition of Popery, are content to plunge themselves into the depths of absurdity...The primitive Christians were kneeling Christians—but those to whom we are now alluding, may properly be called peripatetic Christians.[28]

Daubeny was clearly acquiring ammunition for his later published assault on contemporary Calvinist Evangelicals in the Church of England such as Toplady, Hervey, and Hill. Moreover, even when criticizing continental Catholicism as it presented itself in Naples, Daubeny cautioned Protestants against adopting a superior attitude to their Roman Catholic co-religionists. Thus, he insisted that 'the substitution of the form of religion for the substance and vital spirit of it', was 'not confined to Popish countries'. On the contrary, 'Protestants, we lament to say, have so much to lay to their

---

[26] Nigel Aston, *Christianity and Revolutionary Europe, c. 1750-1830* (Cambridge, 2003), p. 202; Mather, *High church prophet*, esp. pp. 94-106.
[27] *Guide to the Church...account of the author's life and writings*, p. xvi.
[28] Ibid., p. xviii.

own charge, that they ought not to be too insistent upon this general subject of complaint'.[29]

Daubeny's European travels gave him a sense of a wider Catholic Christendom of which the Church of England was a part and which distinguished him from contemporaries who either extolled a pan-Protestant ecumenical vision or else retreated into mere Anglican insularity. Domestic circumstances also shaped his churchmanship. While residing at Clifton in 1778-79, Daubeny came under the influence of Alexander Catcott (1725-79), Hutchinsonian divine, natural philosopher and geologist, and the vicar of Temple Church, Bristol. Catcott, who had been a Hebraist scholar at Oxford where he first met the high churchman William Jones of Nayland, was described as 'a man of primitive manners, great piety, and a divine of the old school—to whom the Archdeacon always expressed himself much indebted for the correct notions, which in the early days of his ministry, he had imbibed on the fundamental principles of his sacred office'.[30]

Moreover, Daubeny's experience of Protestant Dissent in his North Bradley parish gave a cutting edge to his antipathy towards and strictures on Protestant irregularity and separatism. Most Anglican churchmen had regarded Protestant Dissent as in apparent terminal decline by 1750. Therefore, its remarkable revival by the 1790s, fuelled by the growth and quasi-separation of Methodism, was certainly enough to sow alarm even amongst the complacent.

Daubeny's parochial exertions which made him something of a model of pre-Tractarian pastoral practice, were encouraged by his acute consciousness of the challenge which the growth of Protestant Dissent represented to the Church of England and its national identity and status as the established church. He was anxious to remove from his parishioners any excuse on grounds of lack of parochial oversight for attending Dissenting services. Thus, he responded positively by introducing a Sunday evening service, weekday services, and the monthly celebration of the eucharist at North Bradley. He was assiduous in rebuilding not only the vicarage and in raising the income of the living to above £180 per year, but in restoring the dilapidated church which he inherited and in founding and financially supporting a Sunday school. In 1790, while wintering in Bath, he began to promote the erection of a free church (with space for 1,300 sittings) for the local poor. His sermon in aid of the first free and open church in the country raised over £1,200. The first stone of the new church, Christ Church, Walcot, was laid in 1795, and it was consecrated by Charles

---

[29] Ibid., p. xx.
[30] Ibid., p. x. I have benefited from discussions with Dr. Derya Gurses of the University of Bilkent, Ankara, Turkey, who is currently working on Hutchinsonianism and Catcott's significance as a Hutchinsonian divine. On Catcott, see Derya Gurses, 'The Hutchinsonian defence of the Old Testament Trinitarian Christianity: the controversy over Elahim, 1735-1773', *History of European Ideas* 29 (2003), pp. 393-409, especially pp. 395-400.

Moss, bishop of Bath and Wells in 1798.[31] Meanwhile, Daubeny did not neglect North Bradley. In 1808 Daubeny endowed an almshouse for four poor inhabitants of his parish and built a school at his own expense. In 1817 he built a poorhouse in the parish. In 1822 he commenced plans for a new church at Rode in his parish.[32] On 25 June 1823 the foundation stone was laid; the church was completed in the autumn of 1824 and consecrated by John Fisher, bishop of Salisbury. The cost, with the endowment and parsonage, exceeded £13,000, of which Daubeny contributed nearly £4,000.[33]

The challenge posed by Protestant Dissent was also the making of Daubeny the high church controversialist and polemicist. In spite of his generous benefactions and the publication of *A Friendly and Affectionate Address to his Parishioners* (1785), Daubeny initially made himself very unpopular in his parish, especially amongst Protestant Dissenters towards whom he adopted an uncompromising and combative approach. Such was the intensity of Dissenting antagonism towards him that in 1785-86, in correspondence with Shute Barrington, bishop of Salisbury, he even contemplated an exchange of livings. His rigid high churchmanship first found published expression in his *Lectures on the Church Catechism* (1788), originally delivered to the children of his Sunday school. However, it was the publication of Daubeny's *Guide to the Church* (1798), based on discourses on the themes of church of unity and the sin of schism which he had delivered in his parish church in preceding years,[34] followed by an *Appendix to the Guide* (1799) and *Vindiciae Ecclesiae Anglicanae* (1803), which established his credentials and national and international fame as an uncompromising high church controversialist. These works won Daubeny numerous Anglican admirers in the episcopal churches of Scotland (where they proved particularly serviceable)[35] and the United States of America

---

[31] Ibid., pp. xxiv-xxv.
[32] Ibid., p. xxxix.
[33] Ibid., p. xliv.
[34] The discourses were 'originally designed for private circulation in a particular parish'. Charles Daubeny, *A Guide to the Church in several discourses; to which are added two postscripts; the first, to those members of the Church who occasionally frequent other places of public worship; the second, to the clergy. Addressed to William Wilberforce Esq. M.P.* (London, 1798), p. xi.
[35] With Daubeny's blessing, the bishop of Edinburgh, William Abernethy Drummond, applied the arguments of his *Guide* to the Scottish Episcopalian context in order to undermine the ecclesial status of the Presbyterian Kirk and of the so-called 'English chapels' in Scotland. See, *An Abridgement of the Reverend Charles Daubeny's 'Guide to the Church', by a worthy Scots Episcopalian clergyman...the Rt. Rev. William Abernethy Drummond* (Edinburgh, 1799). As Daubeny informed his friend Jonathan Boucher: 'The Bishop has done me the honour to think that the *Guide* will do good in Scotland, and has therefore requested permission that it may be abridged there'. The College of William and Mary, Swem Library, Williamsburg, Virginia, Jonathan Boucher Papers [hereafter: Boucher Papers], B/5/2: Charles Daubeny to Jonathan Boucher, 20 June 1798. Daubeny's friend and ally, the high church layman, John Bowdler,

(the Episcopal Church of America passed a unanimous vote of approbation of the *Guide*),[36] as well as in the Church of England.

Daubeny's *Guide* lies squarely in the tradition of Laudian and early eighteenth-century 'high church' and Nonjuring apologetic such as George Hickes's *Christian Priesthood* (1702) and William Law's *Three Letters to the Bishop of Bangor* (1717), and represented a return to a defence of the foundations and claims of the established church on *jure divino* principles of apostolic truth and order rather than political expedience or utility. It represented not only a full-blown assault on the very *raison d'etre* of Protestant Dissent but on its apparent allies or protectors within the established church itself. One of the *Guide's* main targets were the ultra-latitudinarian and anti-sacerdotal principles of the notorious Benjamin Hoadly, which Daubeny roundly condemned as subversive of ecclesiastical authority and as partially responsible for the low esteem in which the Church of England and its clergy had come to be regarded in his own day. William Warburton, the celebrated author of *Alliance between Church and State* (1736), and the writings of Daubeny's contemporary, William Paley were also censured. Daubeny's polemic against recent and contemporary latitudinarian notions was evident in his bold assertion:

> It is not, indeed, to be wondered at, that the opinions of the modern clergy should become less settled upon church matters, than they have been; since the authority of a Hooker, a Hickes, and a Lesley, is by many considered to be in a manner superseded by that of a Hoadly, a Warburton, and a Paley.[37]

Significantly, Daubeny criticized the way in which latitudinarian Protestant divines had used 'arguments drawn against the usurped tyranny of Rome' to discredit the very principle of submission to ecclesiastical authority. In order to refute this apparent misapplication of a legitimate trope of anti-Roman Catholicism, Daubeny insisted on the conservative and orderly principle of the English Reformation as enshrined in the writings and mode of proceedings of the Reformers themselves. Hoadly and Warburton had posited the principle of the Reformation as one of Christian liberty giving the right of every man to worship according to his conscience. Protestant Dissenters, Daubeny complained, had misused this supposed right to justify their own separation from the established church as a mere following out of the example of the Church of England's breach with Rome at the Reformation.[38] Against this, Daubeny disclaimed any precedent of the one for the other. On the contrary, for Daubeny, the two cases of separation were totally distinct in principle. Thus, Daubeny argued in reference to Warburton's argument in the *Alliance*: 'The

---

first suggested an abridgement of the *Guide*, 'in order to procure for it a more general perusal'. [Thomas Bowdler], *Memoir of the life of John Bowdler, Esq* (London, 1824), p. 165.
[36] *Guide to the Church...account of the author's life and writings*, pp. xxix-xxx.
[37] Daubeny, *Guide to the Church* (1798), pp. 399-400.
[38] Ibid., pp. 390-2.

corruption of the Church of Rome...was the ground upon which our separation from it was built, not that right of Christian liberty, for which Bishop Warburton is here pleading; a right which Bishop Jewel never admitted'.[39]

Another aspect of Daubeny's apologetic and repudiation of the views of Hoadly, Warburton, and Paley, lay in his uncompromising anti-erastianism and consequent identification with the principles of the nonjurors, if not the particular political cause on which they had made their stand. At a time when Anglican churchmen were rallying in defence of 'the establishment' as a focus of both religious and national identity in the face of the spectre of Jacobinism, Daubeny reminded his readers in almost proto-Tractarian fashion:

> The connection of the church with the state appears to be an accidental circumstance, which may, or may not exist; and which consequently did not constitute a part of the plan upon which it was originally established. The state may come into the church as in the days of Constantine; but the church is not to accommodate itself to the state, to produce this effect; or the state may be in opposition to the church, as in the days of the Apostles.[40]

Daubeny was dismissive of Paley's defence of an ecclesiastical constitution so framed as to be 'adapted to real life, and to the actual state of religion in the country'. For Daubeny, obviously mindful of the implications of this utilitarian argument for the ascendancy of the established church in Ireland, Paley's view amounted to resting the establishment of a Christian church upon a human rather than divine foundation, and a 'placing of the subject in that political point of view, in which it was never designed to stand'.[41] The obvious implications of Daubeny's anti-erastianism and *jure divino* high churchmanship as the basis of his vigorous later anti-Roman Catholicism, which only to a later generation of post-Tractarian high churchmen might have seemed a contradiction, will be explored below.

Daubeny's concern to defend the status and respect for the clerical order was by no means a purely high church trope. As has recently been well shown, anti-clericalism took many forms and provoked varying strands of defence and defenders. For example, Beilby Porteus, then bishop of Chester, in 1782 had sought to vindicate both the clerical and episcopal order from a variety of anti-clerical aspersions, complaining about unfounded contemporary suspicions of 'the prelatical dignity'.[42] Anglican Evangelicals notoriously had a high concept of the clerical vocation, even if their view of episcopacy was deficient by high church standards. Daubeny's critique, however, was but part of a much wider treatise in

---

[39] Ibid., p. 406.
[40] Ibid., pp. 420-1.
[41] Ibid., pp. 421-2.
[42] [Beilby Porteus], *A Vindication of the observations on the decline of the clerical credit and character* (London, 1782), p. 50.

which he reasserted the high church principles of the constitution, authority, and order of the church, redolent of the Caroline era of Anglican apologetic.

Where Daubeny's *Guide* became especially controversial was the way in which it touched critically on not only Protestant Dissenters and their latitudinarian Anglican allies, but on Evangelicals within as well as without the established church with whom high churchmen had hitherto had not been in overt conflict and indeed sometimes in uneasy alliance. Although high churchmen and Anglican Evangelicals could unite on a platform of anti-latitudinarianism and anti-heterodoxy, the issue of Evangelical 'irregularity', highlighted by the itinerancy and separatist tendencies within the Methodist movement, from the 1740s onwards, had long been an object of concern among high churchmen. In the political climate fostered by the reaction to the French Revolution in the 1790s, Evangelicals of all description, but especially the 'irregular', were vulnerable to high church charges of being agents of 'subversion'.

The familiar Evangelical complaint that the clergy of the established church were not 'preaching the Gospel', might have earned some sympathy from the likes of a Horne or Horsley. In fact, John Overton sought to embarrass Daubeny by pointing out that appeals to the clergy for a restoration of 'evangelical preaching' had been made by many 'unimpeachable witnesses', including high churchmen and notably 'such great prelates as Secker, Porteus, Horne, Horsley, and Barrington'.[43] It was Daubeny who had broken ranks with even high churchmen such as Horsley by acknowledging in the *Guide* his disagreement with Horsley's argument that if the clergy 'preached the Gospel' then the parish churches would be full.[44] In his *The True Churchmen Ascertained* (1801), Overton actually cited Secker in the frontispiece: 'We have in fact lost many of our people to sectaries, by not preaching in a manner sufficiently Evangelical'.[45] Overton lost no opportunities in identifying the Evangelical tenets which he espoused under Secker's name, claiming that

> few men, it may be presumed, have worn the Mitre with more lustre than Archbishop Secker. And there is, perhaps, no writer whose works are more generally recommended to the perusal of the clergy, by the present bishops, and other dignitaries of our Church.[46]

Of course for Daubeny and like-minded high churchmen, Overton's assertions and selective citation of Secker and Horsley, begged the question: what was 'Gospel' or 'Evangelical' preaching? Daubeny made clear that he regarded complaints over the lack of it to be a spurious justification for irregularity or semi-separation. Johnson Grant, a high

---

[43] Overton, *The True Churchmen Ascertained*, p. 390.
[44] Nockles, 'Church parties', pp. 344-5.
[45] Overton, *True Churchmen Ascertained*, 'Preface'.
[46] Ibid., p. 36.

church chronicler of the religious history of the period, later was explicit on this point. In his *Summary History*, he complained of the Evangelical party:

> In the assumption of the term Evangelical, they sheltered their body under the sanction of Archbishop Secker, who had complained, in his day, of the want of Evangelical preaching. But widely different from their understanding of the phrase, was what that prelate meant. Secker assailed the moral-philosophy preaching, and wished for a basis of doctrinal matter. They aimed at a solifidian system.[47]

There was, however, a well-attested trend within Anglican Evangelicalism towards 'regularity' and a respect for church order which was partly fostered by the anti-Jacobin conservative climate of the 1790s onwards. Post-Tractarian equations of Evangelicalism with 'low churchmanship' are anachronistic for this period; there was a historical distinction between the two.[48] Even Overton was anxious to satisfy Daubeny on the issue of Evangelical 'irregularity', denying that Thomas Haweis was, 'a fair specimen of the general opinions of the clergy of the Church of England who are called Evangelical. The general body of these divines, as sincerely lament the schism of Dr. Haweis, as the heterodoxy of some other doctors'.[49] He readily conceded that,

> the whole external structure of the Church of England is either founded on express injunctions of Scripture, or on the undoubted practice of the Apostles and early Christians. This has been satisfactorily shown by Hooker and Milner; and, except where they attempt too much, by Jones and Daubeny.

Overton insisted that he took no issue with these writers on these grounds, and 'that the present work solicitously disclaims all intention of apologising for any species of irregularity in any matters of the Establishment'.[50] A reviewer in the *British Critic*, a mouthpiece of the orthodox church party, commended Overton for censuring 'directly the loose notions of Dr. Haweis'.[51] Similarly, Sir Richard Hill insisted to Daubeny: 'As to the excellency and antiquity of episcopal government, there is no dispute at all between us; and for my own part I should be happy to see it as universal as I think it preferable to any other'.[52]

---

[47] Johnson Grant, *A Summary of the History of the English Church, and of the Sects which have separated from its communion, with answers to each Dissenting body relative to its pretended grounds of separation* (London, 1811-25), IV, pp. 585-6.
[48] Nockles, *The Oxford Movement in Context*, pp. 31-2.
[49] Overton, *True Churchmen Ascertained*, p. 399.
[50] Ibid., p. 384.
[51] *British Critic* 22 (October 1803), p. 43.
[52] Sir Richard Hill, *Reformation-Truth Restored: being a reply to the Rev. Charles Daubeny's 'Appendix' to his 'Guide to the Church'. Demonstrating his own inconsistency with himself, and his great misrepresentation of some historic facts. With a more particular vindication of the pure, reformed, episcopal Church of England, from the charges of Mr Daubeny, and other doctrinal dissenters of that gentleman's sect,*

Moderate elements within the Anglican Evangelical party were even prepared to give favourable attention to large parts of Daubeny's *Guide*. The Anglican Evangelical chronicler, John White Middelton, later conceded that Daubeny's *Guide* 'contained much excellent matter'.[53] A reviewer in the moderate Evangelical *Christian Observer* agreed with 'many of the arguments contained in the work now before us', and joined with Daubeny in lamenting the prevailing 'laxity of sentiment' in regard to ecclesiastical matters.[54] The same reviewer even commended Daubeny's historical arguments for episcopacy and the constitution of the Church. As the reviewer commented glowingly:

> In the tenth discourse, on the advantages of a conscientious communion with the church, and the disadvantages of wilful separation from her, are many arguments and particular passages which it would give us pleasure to meet with in any author.[55]

Wherein then lay the point of the emerging quarrel? Of course, the antipathy of Protestant Dissenters, especially the heterodox, could hardly be surprising. They resented the strictures which Daubeny heaped upon them in the *Guide* and responded with indignation and sarcasm. One reviewer in the *Protestant Dissenters' Magazine* derided Daubeny's method of trying to win back separatists:

> We cannot help pitying a man of such a narrow mind; we may say a weak mind, if he thinks that such a system as his will frighten back Dissenters into the bosom of his mother, or restrain those who are disposed to leave her.[56]

Why did Daubeny's strictures provoke another class of opposition—that of leading Anglican Calvinist Evangelicals such as Overton and Hill—into such a series of lengthy polemical responses? Moreover, why did such a fierce controversy break out between orthodox and Evangelical clergy in 1801/2, disturbing a long period of previous, albeit sometimes uneasy, cooperation and relative harmony? Was Daubeny's *Guide* and the apparent intemperance and combative tone of his rhetoric to blame for the sudden outbreak of hostilities?

Firstly, Daubeny cast doubt on the loyalty of Evangelicals towards the establishment, arguing that they consciously or unconsciously aided and abetted the forces of Protestant Dissent by placing 'the purity of religion',

---

who are fomenting schisms and divisions, and disseminating errors, in the very bosom of the establishment. In a series of letters to Mr Daubeny (London, 1800), p. 20.

[53] Middelton, *An Ecclesiastical Memoir of the first four decades of the reign of George III*, p. 301.
[54] *Christian Observer* 4:39 (March 1805), p. 159.
[55] Ibid., p. 161.
[56] *Protestant Dissenter's Magazine*, V (1798), pp. 316-18. I owe this reference to Dr. Grayson Ditchfield.

defined in their own narrow terms, 'against the establishment of it'.[57] Such were Daubeny's sensitivities on the point that he even criticized the celebrated Anglican Evangelical lay woman Hannah More for her foundation of Sunday schools in the Somerset village of Blagdon for being 'schismatical in tendency', though he himself had previously been prominent in promoting Sunday schools.[58] For Daubeny, the example of the separation of Methodism after John Wesley's death from the established church was the natural end-product of the Evangelical emphasis on the doctrine of the invisible church, 'the favourite child of Puritanism'.[59] Daubeny was but one of several high church voices in making the charge that Anglican Evangelicals were semi-detached members of the established church. Johnson Grant later defended Daubeny's *Guide* for 'exposing' the 'low views respecting church government' of what he called 'the Evangelical body'. Johnson Grant conceded that Evangelicals were prepared to extol episcopacy but complained that this was only on grounds of expediency and rarely on grounds of apostolic institution:

> When they speak favourably of their Church, and signify their attachment to it, it is still and always with a reservation,—they mean their own party. They pretend, that it is only by an extension of their principles and deportment, that the Church can be saved. Doctrine is everything with them; and 'the Gospel', as they call it, is the test of the Church (though they cannot satisfactorily explain what Gospel preaching means). The commission to teach is nothing. Their biases lead them to shake hands with the dissenters, and this they term liberality, moderation, charity.[60]

Some Evangelicals could not resist rising to the bait, in response to Daubeny's representation of Evangelicalism as potentially subversive.

Secondly, Daubeny was not content to confine his arguments to matters of ecclesiastical discipline and order, but opened up a 'second front' of attack on Evangelical doctrine and preaching, notably Calvinism which he regarded as synonymous. For Daubeny, 'Evangelical preaching' involved a revival of doctrinal Puritanism, and not only semi-separatism.

---

[57] Charles Daubeny, *Eight discourses on the connection between the Old and New Testament...containing some remarks on the late Professor Campbell's 'Ecclesiastical History'* (London, 1802), p. 141.

[58] Daubeny had argued that the establishment of Sunday schools held out 'to us some prospect of the reformation of manners among the lower ranks of the country'. Charles Daubeny, *Twelve lectures on the Church Catechism, designed to promote the object of Sunday schools addressed to the parishioners of North Bradley, in the county of Wiltshire* (Bath, 1788), p. 8. For Hannah More's Sunday school ventures and their significance, see Anne Stott, *Hannah More: the first Victorian* (Oxford, 2003), pp. 232-57; Anne Stott, 'Hannah More and the Blagdon controversy, 1799-1802', *Journal of Ecclesiastical History* 51:2 (April 2000), pp. 319-46.

[59] Charles Daubeny, *On the nature, progress, and consequences of schism. With immediate reference to the present state of religious affairs in this country* (London, 1818), p. 91.

[60] Grant, *Summary History*, IV, p. 104.

Thirdly, Daubeny did not confine his anti-Evangelical critique to notorious 'irregulars' such as Thomas Haweis, disowned by more regular Anglican Evangelicals such as Isaac Milner,[61] or to castigating the supposedly subversive principles of the *Gospel Magazine*. Even moderate Evangelicals, such as William Wilberforce, to whom Daubeny addressed his *Guide*, and Hannah More, both of whom had initially been inclined to be conciliatory towards Daubeny and some of his apologetic, were drawn into the net of his opprobrium.

Daubeny's questioning of the basis of Evangelical allegiance to the establishment was touched on in a 'postscript to occasional separatists' in the *Guide*. It was here that Daubeny included, albeit qualified, criticisms of passages in that manifesto of the 'Clapham Sect', Wilberforce's influential *A Practical View of the Prevailing Religious System of Professed Christians* (1797). The criticisms were deemed patronizing but were provoked by fears over the likely impact of Wilberforce's denunciations of the failure of the clergy to 'preach the Gospel' and live up to their sacred calling. Daubeny might have been expected to share at least the latter concern, but his almost apocalyptic spectre of a subversion of the Church in the era of the French Revolution which mirrored that of the Great Rebellion of the 1640s, made him acutely sensitive to such public admissions. The recent examples of the American colonial rebellion, blamed by Daubeny's friend Jonathan Boucher (in *A View of the Causes and Consequences of the American Revolution*) on the machinations of Dissenters and the failure to establish a colonial episcopate in North America,[62] were also invoked. Thus, Daubeny warned,

> Our author [Wilberforce] would be a professed friend to our happy establishment. No one can feel more disposed to see him in that light than myself. At the same time, I trust, it will not be regarded as any intentional impeachment, either of his knowledge or judgment, to remind him, that railing against the clergy of the establishment, has been that preparatory step to its subversion, which has been twice adopted with success by the subjects of Great Britain. It may be unnecessary to add, that the Revolution of the last century in this kingdom, and that lately effected in our colonies, are the instances which I have in view.[63]

Johnson Grant was later even more critical about what he regarded as Wilberforce's ambivalent loyalty to the church establishment, complaining that:

---

[61] See, *Animadversions on Dr. Haweis's 'Impartial and Succinct History of the Church of Christ. By the Rev. Isaac Milner, D.D. being the preface to the second edition of Volume one of the late Rev. Joseph Milner's 'History of the Church of Christ'* (Cambridge, 1800).

[62] See, Jonathan Boucher, *A view of the causes and consequences of the American Revolution in thirteen discourses, preached in North America between the years 1763 and 1775* (London, 1797).

[63] Daubeny, *Guide to the Church* (1798), p. 379.

he [Wilberforce] introduced that equivocal attachment to the church, which means attachment to peculiar doctrines; and while it denies the Church of England to be the church of Christ independently of those peculiarities, clings to any sect professing to teach them, regardless of its deficiencies in Apostolical government.[64]

Daubeny's dispute with Wilberforce went to the heart of a revived soul searching as to what constituted Anglican religious identity in terms of doctrine as well as polity and discipline.

The key to Anglican Evangelical disquiet over Daubeny's uncompromising restatement of high church principles was firstly that it appeared to be directed as much against themselves as against latitudinarian Anglicans or heterodox Dissenters; secondly, for them as much as for Daubeny, doctrine was involved (and in their own eyes, false doctrine) and not merely ecclesiastical order and discipline. Thus, the moderate reviewer of the *Guide* in the Anglican Evangelical *Christian Observer* offset his initial qualified agreement with the author on matters of the authority and constitution of the church, with criticism of Daubeny for neglecting 'purity of doctrine':

> The leading error in the ecclesiastical theory of Mr Daubeny seems to be his exclusion of pure doctrine as an essential ingredient in the composition of the visible church. In this representation it is not our intention to do the smallest injustice to Mr Daubeny...This exclusion he has plainly professed and endeavoured to vindicate...We, on this subject, continue to take the affirmative side, and assert, that purity of doctrine is at least as essential to the very being of the church as her external government. In this opinion we follow the venerable authorities of that article of our church which professedly treats of the subject; of her homilies; of her brightest ornaments, Jewel, Hooker, Hall, and others.[65]

The reviewer conceded the importance of treating the nature and constitution of the visible or external church as Daubeny had done, but with the somewhat amorphous definition of the church as enshrined in Article 19 to fall back upon, resisted 'the assertion, that this is the whole church, as men are concerned with it in the world, or as it is exhibited in Scripture'.[66] Sir Richard Hill was more dismissive of the rigid nature of Daubeny's ecclesiology, showing, as Middelton put it, 'both the absurdity and impolicy of pushing the point of episcopacy too far, and tracing the descent of a bishop with the same accuracy as is usually applied to the genealogy of a racehorse'.[67]

Clearly, to have accepted Daubeny's position *in toto* would have been to allow Protestant Dissenters to be 'unchurched'. Thus, in his *Apology for Brotherly Love*, Hill 'claimed for a servant of God in a conventicle of the

---

[64] Grant, *Summary History*, IV, pp. 93-4.
[65] *Christian Observer* 4:39 (March 1805), p. 161.
[66] Ibid., p. 162.
[67] Middelton, *Ecclesiastical Memoir*, p. 302.

eighteenth century the right to be esteemed as a brother by the worshipper in the parish church'.[68] Given that many Evangelicals would have distanced themselves from Hill's relatively latitudinarian ecclesiology, what mattered about Daubeny's teaching for all Anglican Evangelicals was that it seemed to jeopardize the paramountcy of Evangelical doctrine in the schema of salvation. There was no way of bridging this gap. Ecclesiology might be negotiable, but not the central canons and shibboleths of Evangelical doctrine and preaching.

High churchmen such as Daubeny felt challenged by Evangelicalism, not merely on grounds of irregularities in parochial and church order (moderate Evangelicals of the *Christian Observer* might go some way to meeting their position on this question), but because of a perception that the Evangelical agenda involved a remodelling of the doctrinal basis, history, and identity of the Church of England which undercut their own position. Resentment at the exclusive appropriation of the title 'Evangelical' for themselves, was grounded in these fears of doctrinal divisiveness. In Overton's hands, Evangelicalism, if not Calvinism, was being made the doctrinal test of true churchmanship (the very title of his work was faulted as divisive and unwarranted,[69] though this only mirrored Anglican Evangelical complaints about the exclusive appropriation of the term 'orthodox' by their opponents). The apparent Evangelical preoccupation with a certain set of distinctive doctrines in itself had the effect of rendering unimportant the differences (if based on doctrine) between Anglican Evangelicals and Protestant Dissenters. Athough as Grayson Carter has shown, Anglican Evangelicals by the end of the century had gone out of their way to distance themselves from disorderly Methodism and Dissent,[70] their differences with Dissent could still be presented as only relating to discipline and therefore of secondary significance.

Daubeny's *Guide* was initially answered by the Calvinist Sir Richard Hill's *An Apology for Brotherly Love* (1799), followed up by his provokingly entitled works *Daubenism Confuted and Martin Luther Vindicated* (1800) and *Reformation-Truth Restored* (1800); works that were designed to display and vindicate Anglican Evangelical claims to moderation and charitable forbearance, especially in regard to Dissenters, and to turn the tables on Daubeny and his school, portraying him as a 'doctrinal dissenter'. Hill,

---

[68] Ibid., pp. 302-3. In praising the latitudinarian Bishop Hoadly, Hill was untypical of Anglican Evangelicals. Sir Richard Hill, *An Apology for Brotherly Love and for the doctrines of the Church of England, in a series of letters to the Rev. Charles Daubeny, with a vindication of such parts of Mr Wilberforce's 'Practical View', as have been objected to by Mr Daubeny, in his late publication, entitled 'A Guide to the Church'* (London, 1798), pp. 164-5.

[69] Grant, *Summary History*, IV, p. 564; Edward Pearson, *Remarks on the controversy subsisting, or supposed to subsist, between the Arminian and Calvinistic ministers of the Church of England: in a letter to the Rev. John Overton, A.B. author of 'The True Churchmen ascertained'* (London, 1802), p. 6.

[70] Grayson Carter, *Anglican Evangelicals: Protestant secessions from the via media, c. 1800-1850* (Oxford, 2001), p. 13.

whose *Apology for Brotherly Love* was suggestively subtitled an *Apology for the doctrines of the Church of England*, also maintained that the dissenter 'in doctrine' was more culpably in error than the dissenter 'in discipline' such as the old nonconformists who had had little or no dispute with the Church of England in points of doctrine. On the other hand, according to Hill, Daubeny rejected several doctrines of the Church of England.[71] A reviewer of the work in the extremist evangelical *Gospel Magazine*, characterized Hill's *Apology for Brotherly Love* as designed,

> to check the daring progress of error and false doctrines in general, especially as propagated by too many of our clergy in particular, contrary to the sound doctrines of the reformation, contained in the liturgy, articles and homilies of our Church, which they have solemnly subscribed...He establishes the doctrine of grace, by the united testimony of confessors and martyrs, especially of our own reformers in the aforesaid homilies, liturgy and articles of the Church of England.[72]

If this description was meant to be confined to latitudinarian and Arian 'false' subscribers to the Thirty-nine Articles, then high churchmen could heartily concur and the 'orthodox' might act in concert with Anglican Evangelicals as they did in 1772-33 in defence of subscription to the Articles against the latitudinarian 'Feathers Tavern' petition campaign. However, the description also prompted many questions: what constituted 'false doctrine' and 'sound doctrine'? What was the sense in which the 'liturgy, articles and homilies' of our church were being interpreted? In fact, the reviewer's inclusion of 'the doctrine of grace', explicitly identified with the apparent teaching of the Reformers, in his description of 'sound doctrine' seemed to point to a wider Calvinist agenda and a radically different soteriology.

It was the bugbear of Calvinism and solifidianism, with its theological implications as well as apparently subversive political associations, as much as differences over ecclesiology, that underscored the major controversy which broke out between Daubeny and Overton. For even a moderate Evangelical, the doctrinal position of Daubeny and like-minded high churchmen was defective. As Middelton argued, 'in stating the plan of salvation, they were not always sufficiently clear in representing repentance and faith as the conditions of the Christian covenant, and obedience as the fruit or evidence of justifying faith'.[73]

Overton infuriated high churchmen not only by trying to make Daubeny out to be a mere 'formalist' but for lumping him and his school in with avowed latitudinarians and even 'near Socinians' such as Richard Fellowes and Thomas Ludlam, though Overton conceded that these

---

[71] Hill, *Reformation-Truth restored*, pp. xvii-xviii.
[72] *Gospel Magazine* 3:30 (June 1798), p. 236. Daubeny referred to the *Gospel Magazine*, as 'that schismatic courier'. Boucher Papers, B/5/8: Daubeny to Boucher, 10 April 1799.
[73] Middelton, *Ecclesiastical Memoir*, pp. 32-3.

divines were 'still more heterodox than himself'.[74] Even the moderate Anglican Evangelical Middelton was criticized by Johnson Grant for classing 'among the latitudinarians, all who reject the tenet of justification by faith alone', as interpreted in a narrowly 'Evangelical' sense.[75]

Doctrinal and soteriological differences soured Daubeny's dealings with even the Arminian Wilberforce and Hannah More, and allowed an opening for Calvinist Anglican critics such as Hill and Overton to enter the controversy. Daubeny provoked great offence in moderate Anglican Evangelical circles for his criticisms of Hannah More whom he, albeit privately, described to Boucher as 'the great idol of half informed divines', and as 'a true child of Enthusiasm'.[76] More's high church friend, the Irish lay divine Alexander Knox, sided with her, referring to Daubeny, as 'a strange kind of clergyman at Bath', who had 'attacked Mrs More most unjustly, for something which he (I almost think wilfully) misconceived, in her book'.[77] However, Daubeny and Wilberforce privately remained on good terms. Even the Evangelical Middelton later commented that Daubeny's 'language was dignified, his tone chastened, and his treatment of Mr Wilberforce respectful'.[78] In fact, Daubeny's tone was almost obsequious in his personal dealings with Wilberforce. Prior to the publication of the *Guide* and soon after the appearance of *A Practical View*, Daubeny privately wrote to Wilberforce to assure him that he had read his book with 'increasing satisfaction from the first to the 123rd page'. He emphasized the 'respect I entertain of your character added to the opinion I have formed of your abilities as a writer, and expressed his conviction 'that our Faith is the same', even if 'our manner of defining it would in certain points be somewhat different'.[79] Daubeny hoped that Wilberforce could, 'become the blessed instrument in God's hand of raising the dead to life, by bringing back the soul of Christianity to that body from which it has long departed; any minister of Christ who feels as he ought must congratulate himself that the declining cause of his Master has found so able an advocate'.[80]

Wilberforce's renowned reputation as a moral crusader, however, did not prevent Daubeny taking issue with him for supposedly overemphasizing Justification by Faith at the expense of Good Works and for seeming 'to depreciate the moral precepts of the gospel'. Daubeny felt that Wilberforce failed to distinguish sufficiently between 'Works of the Law under the Judaic dispensation, and those under the Christian

---

[74] Grant, *Summary History*, IV, pp. 63-4.
[75] Ibid., p. 33.
[76] Boucher Papers, B/5/16: Daubeny to Boucher, 7 November 1800; B/5/10: Daubeny to Boucher, 24 September 1799.
[77] Alexander Knox to Miss Ferguson, 28 October 1800, *Remains of Alexander Knox*, edited by J.J. Hornby, (London, 1834-37), IV, p. 80.
[78] Middelton, *Ecclesiastical Memoir*, p. 302.
[79] Bodleian Library, Wilberforce Papers, MS Wilberforce d. 13, f. 112: Daubeny to William Wilberforce, n.d, 1797; Daubeny, *Guide to the Church*, (1798), p. v.
[80] Daubeny, *Guide to the Church* (1798), pp. v-vi.

dispensation'.[81] He rejected Wilberforce's apparent dictum that the duties of Christianity were a natural and necessary product of its doctrines. Daubeny argued that when Faith was unaccompanied by Works, then it was unprofitable. Faith could not truly exist, he maintained, without producing the evangelical fruits of holiness.[82] Similarly, against Hannah More's contention that religious practice constituted no substitute for the merits of Christ, Daubeny argued that 'Faith' could become 'no substitute for the performance of Christian duties'.[83] Privately, Daubeny decried what he chose to describe as Hannah More's 'doctrine that Faith is necessarily productive of Works' as 'a most dangerous error',[84] but far from acknowledging, when it was suggested even by friends, that he might have overstepped the mark in publicly criticizing her or Wilberforce, he insisted that he had treated them gently. As he told his friend Boucher,

> Mrs Hannah More you do not appear to see quite in the same light that I do. I read her as well meaning, but neither well informed, or well judging. Inflated with adulation, and encircled with not the wisest men. What I have written, I have written tenderly, because the ground was tender. But if weighed in the balance of the sanctuary, however right she may be in some things, and however strong she may be on some subjects, she would doubtless...be found wanting. Her faith, like that of Mr Wilberforce is Calvinism in disguise; her practice, like his, is schismatical; her attachment to the Church of England, like his, of a very doubtful kind...Faith according to her idea, is necessarily productive of the fruits of Christianity. Neither St Paul, Peter, James, or John, ever preached this faith.[85]

In another letter to Boucher in 1800, Daubeny was even more critical, accusing Hannah More of keeping

> a sort of school for the younger clergy, in which they gain as much knowledge in a few lectures, as old divines have been able to draw from a whole row of bulky folios...This hop, step & jump Divinity, as I call it, never fails to be accompanied with much confidence & self importance and consequent contempt of all who do not study in the same school with themselves...A spurious system of Calvinistic Divinity is poisoning the minds of the rising

---

[81] Bodleian Library, Wilberforce Papers, Ms. Wilberforce d. 13, f. 114: Daubeny to Wilberforce, n.d., 1797.
[82] Charles Daubeny, *A letter to Mrs Hannah More, on some parts of her late publication, entitled 'Strictures on Female Instruction'* (London, 1799), pp. 39-41.
[83] Ibid., p. 36.
[84] Boucher Papers, B/5/14: Daubeny to Boucher, 27 February 1800.
[85] Ibid., B/5/10: Daubeny to Boucher, 24 September 1799. In another letter, Daubeny rebutted Boucher's attempt to argue for her attachment to the Church of England: 'With respect to Mrs More's being firmly attached to the Church of England, I must confess I have much reason to doubt and shall continue to doubt it as I understand she frequents places of worship separated from the establishment.—This has been notoriously the case'. Ibid., B/5/14: Daubeny to Boucher, 27 February 1800.

clergy'.[86]

Against Overton and Hill, Daubeny was still more strident in deprecating what he regarded as an unbalanced doctrine of Justification. Daubeny did not repudiate the basic Reformation doctrine itself, but argued that Calvinists such as Overton overlooked the crucial distinction between 'the first and final justification of Christians'. The first could be lost after baptism by those who failed to maintain good works, because good works 'springing from faith' were 'necessarily a condition of our final justification on the last day'.[87] Moreover, like most high churchmen, Daubeny was alarmed by the apparent Evangelical emphasis, especially among Methodists, of sensible religious impulses and even convulsions being interpreted as signs of Faith, if not inspiration. As Daubeny put it in his sermon, *The Trial of the Spirits* (1804), directed against what he called 'the enthusiastic reveries of Methodism',

> When we talk of sudden impulses, violent emotions, and sensible experiences as demonstrations of immediate inspiration, we are justified in concluding that some strange and unhappy delusion prevails in their case; because we know from scripture and the history of the church, that the work of the Spirit has been generally carried out in a very different manner.[88]

He rejected 'all those extravagant and supposed supernatural effects, to which Enthusiasm, that spiritual intoxication of the brain, has had such frequent recourse' because, in his view, they undermined proper use of ordinary channels of grace through the spiritual services of the Church.[89]

Daubeny's concerns about Evangelical 'enthusiasm' and the Calvinist doctrine of election linked directly to what he regarded as the Evangelical undermining of the Church of England's doctrine of Baptismal Regeneration as apparently enshrined in the Liturgy. The baptismal controversy between orthodox and Anglican Evangelical churchmen flared up in the 1810s and notoriously involved Richard Mant on the one side and

---

[86] Ibid., B/5/15: Daubeny to Boucher, 16 April 1800. Daubeny, however, in an earlier letter to Boucher, had struck a more conciliatory, if patronizing, note: 'Of some parts of Mrs H. More's work [on Female education] you cannot think higher than I do. And it is from the grand idea I have formed of that lady and her writings that I wish her to be compleat on every subject she undertakes. Because, thinking it in her power to do much good, I wish her to be wholly with us'. Ibid., B/5/11: Daubeny to Boucher, 23 October 1799. In contrast to Daubeny's critical response, most of the Anglican bishops, Bishop Tomline included, liked More's *Strictures*, in spite of its 'explicit avowal of Evangelical theology in its final chapters'. Stott, *Hannah More*, pp. 226-7.

[87] *British Critic* 24 (1804), p. 28.

[88] Charles Daubeny, *The Trial of the Spirits, a seasonable caution against spiritual delusion, in three discourses, addressed to the congregation assembled in Christ's church, Bath* (London, 1804), p. 66.

[89] Charles Daubeny, *A sermon preached in the cathedral church of St Paul's, London, on Thursday, 1 June 1809* (London, 1809), p. 29.

John Scott on the other. Daubeny was one of several protagonists. He accused Scott of setting aside Baptismal Regeneration 'by representing Baptism to be merely the form of admission into the visible church', and by arguing that the 'sanctification of fallen man may either proceed, or follow after baptism, but that it is at all times independent of it'.[90] For Daubeny, there was no room for compromise:

> Regeneration by the sacrament of Baptism either is the doctrine of the Church of England, or it is not. If it be not, the sooner the language of her Formularies is altered, the better. In the contrary case, all her ministers, as honest men, stand committed by the Formularies to which they have subscribed.[91]

In this debate, the appeal to and use of the earlier religious history of the Church of England, especially the century following the Reformation, was a crucial element. Daubeny took issue with Wilberforce for classing the nonconformist Richard Baxter along with acknowledged seventeenth-century Anglican divines such as Hooker, and bishops Andrewes, Hall, and Beveridge, as 'among the brightest ornaments and pillars of the Church of England', rather than recognizing him, as Hooker and Andrewes would have done, as a 'schismatic'.[92] However, it was the doctrinal history of the earlier Church of England that proved the main source of dispute. Daubeny's sensitivities to what he perceived as the dangers of solifidianism were only increased by Overton's and Hill's doctrinal and historical interpretations of the meaning or sense of the Thirty-Nine Articles as the overriding test of 'true' Anglican churchmanship at the expense of an Arminianism which was identified with Socinianism.

Overton and Hill drew on an historical tradition of anti-Arminianism, stretching at least as far back as William Prynne's *The Church of England's Old Antithesis to New Armianisme* (1629).[93] The tendency to elevate a Calvinist reading of the Articles and Homilies as the litmus-test of a Protestant orthodoxy which encompassed Trinitarian Dissenters also had been evident early in the Evangelical Revival. For example, Jonathan Warne in his *Downfall of Arminianism* (1742) had attempted to promote accord between the Church of England and Dissenters, 'by setting down

---

[90] Charles Daubeny, *Considerations on the doctrine of Regeneration, in the sense in which that term is used by the Church of England, in her public formularies, respectfully addressed to the clergy* (London, 1816), pp. 51-2; R. Laurence, *The doctrine of the Church of England upon the efficacy of baptism vindicated from misrepresentation* (Oxford, 1816), pp. 163-4. Against Mant, Scott had argued against an *ex opere operato* understanding of sacramental grace in baptism, citing Cranmer and Jewel in his favour. John Scott, *An Inquiry into the effects of Baptism, according to the sense of Holy Scripture, and of the Church of England: in answer to the Reverend Dr. Mant's two tracts on Regeneration and Communion* (London, 1817).

[91] Ibid., p. 101.

[92] Daubeny, *Guide to the Church* (1798), pp. 337-8.

[93] See Nicholas Tyacke, *Aspects of English Protestantism, c. 1530-1700* (Manchester, 2001), p. 222.

the Thirty-nine Articles in one column and the Articles of those Dissenters in another'.[94] The high church Anglican contribution to the vast anti-Methodist pamphlet literature from the late 1730s had represented a response to this challenge. However, the main focus tended to be over breaches of church order, discipline, and polity. There were frequent attacks on 'enthusiasm' in general and on the doctrine of the 'New Birth' as espoused by George Whitefield and other Evangelicals as subversive of the doctrine of baptismal regeneration and the Church's sacramental system, but doctrinal considerations were otherwise peripheral. The controversy over the supposed Calvinism or Arminianism of the Articles in the early 1770s had been a largely intra-Evangelical dispute, involving Toplady and Sir Richard Hill on the Calvinist side and John Fletcher of Madeley and John Wesley on the Arminian side. When the dispute began to divide the Church more widely, it was the Calvinist Evangelicals who were the conservative 'neo-confessionalists' who opposed any amendment to the Articles, because they did not wish to be 'reformed out of the Reformation'. On the other hand, while orthodox and high churchmen defended the Articles against Arian equivocators, they privately contemplated in 1772-73 their own reform of Article 17 on predestination, so that it might be less liable to be wrested by their adversaries in a Calvinistic sense.[95]

A key element in the Calvinist dimension of the Evangelical revival had been a call for the recovery of what were presented as key Reformation doctrines of grace and election, doctrines reputedly cast aside from pulpits from the Laudian era onwards. As Warne put it,

> We are to remember, that...God's eternal decrees, Justification by Faith alone etc. were the great barriers against Popery at the Reformation...therefore now they are being thrown away by so many of our eminent divines, it is to be feared it will be difficult to preserve ourselves from coming too close.[96]

Thomas Haweis made a similar historical point, complaining in 1801 that, 'That which, for the first hundred years after the Reformation, had been received as the undisputed doctrine, is now become so little short of heresy, and treated as a ground of marked reproach and opposition'.[97]

---

[94] [Jonathan Warne], *The downfall of Arminianism; or, Arminius (who falsely calls himself a son of the Church of England) tried and lost* (London, 1742), p. iii.

[95] See [Thomas Winchester], *A dissertation on the XVIIth Article of the Church of England, wherein the sentiments of the compilers and other contemporary Reformers, on the subject of the Divine decrees, are fully deduced from their own writings. To which is subjoined, a short tract, ascertaining the reign and time in which the Royal Declaration before the XXXIX Articles was first published* (Oxford, 1773). I have benefited here from discussions with Dr. John Walsh. See John Walsh, 'The Thirty Nine Articles and Anglican identity in the eighteenth century', in Christiane d'Haussy (ed.), *Culture et Religion dans les Pays Anglophones* (Paris, 1998), pp. 61-70.

[96] [Warne], *Downfall of Arminianism*, p. iv.

[97] [Thomas Haweis], *The Church of England vindicated from misrepresentation, showing her genuine doctrines as contained in her Articles, liturgy, and homilies. With*

Overton and Hill, following Toplady and Haweis, insisted that the Calvinist doctrines of election and predestination were part of the teaching of the English Reformers and Elizabethan divines and enshrined in the Church's formularies which they helped to frame, notably the seventeenth of the Thirty-Nine Articles. It was argued that the first separatists from the reformed Church of England were the so-called 'free-willers' and not Calvinist predestinarians, as Daubeny and others alleged.[98] Overton triumphantly cited the evidence of an apparently Calvinistic confession of faith drawn up by the future Protestant martyrs in the first year of Queen Mary's reign, and concluded that it deserved

> the more attention, because it is common to insinuate that the interpretation of the Articles now termed Methodistic or Calvinistic, was only introduced by the return of the Exiles, on the accession of Elizabeth, and was not in the primary intention of our Church.[99]

Of course, much depends on the type of Calvinism (high, hyper, or moderate) for which Hill and Overton were claiming historical legitimacy. Daubeny, however, rejected their claim that even the moderate of Calvinism which they espoused was unsupported by the Church's formularies.

Bishop Horsley refused to ally or identify high churchmanship exclusively with Arminianism, thereby earning the plaudits of moderate Anglican Evangelicals who highlighted the difference of his approach from that of Daubeny, Bishop Tomline, and others.[100] Horsley's view that it was enough to fault any narrowly Calvinist reading of the Articles merely on the ground that the Articles had always been intended to be only articles of religion and not articles of faith, had a long high church pedigree.[101] By this reading, Arminians and Calvinists could be equally good churchmen; it was enough to demonstrate that the Calvinistic doctrine of election was not an essential article of faith. Daubeny, like Tomline and Dean Kipling, went much further: claiming that a Calvinistic interpretation of the Articles and Liturgy was untenable.[102] This involved an alternative Arminian reading of the earlier doctrinal history of the reformed Church of England. Just as

---

a particular reference to the 'Elements of Christian Theology' by the Bishop of Lincoln. By a presbyter of the Church of England (London, 1801), p. 32.

[98] Overton, *True Churchmen Ascertained*, p. 53.
[99] Ibid., p. 59.
[100] John Overton, *Four letters to the editor of the 'Christian Observer'*, pp. 76-7; Edward Sheppard, *A letter to the Rev. Arch-Deacon Daubeny, occasioned by his late Charge to the clergy of his Arch-Deaconry in Wiltshire, delivered in July 1805, wherein some strictures are made on the said Charge* (Bath, 1805), pp. 16-17.
[101] See [Winchester], *Dissertation on the XVIIth Article*.
[102] See Thomas Kipling, *The Articles of the Church of England Proved Not to be Calvinistic* (Cambridge, 1802); Charles Daubeny, *Vindiciae Ecclesiae Anglicanae, in which some of the false reasonings, incoherent statements, and palpable misrepresentations in a publication entitled 'The True Churchmen ascertained', by John Overton A.B., are pointed out* (London, 1803), p. 89.

Daubeny had insisted against latitudinarians of the school of Hoadly that the English Reformation was not grounded on any unqualified right of private judgement, so he also insisted against Calvinist apologists that 'our first' English reformers and the Reformation formularies themselves were not Calvinistic or solifidian. Like Tomline in his *Refutation of Calvinism* (1811), Daubeny blamed Protestant exiles under Queen Mary for introducing 'a portion of the Calvinistic leaven into this country; which, though not indigenous to the soil, took, notwithstanding, deep root in it, and has never since been completely eradicated'. He blamed the 'poison' for sowing 'the first seeds of that civil and religious discord' which was to lead to the downfall of the Church of England in the 1640s.[103]

In expounding this historiography, Daubeny relied heavily on the testimonies of Peter Heylin and Jeremy Collier, Laudian and nonjuring historians respectively, while rejecting 'the foolish testimony of Bishop Burnet'.[104] Daubeny's anti-Calvinist priorities even led him to seek some strange allies such as the leading follower of John Wesley, John Fletcher of Madeley, on account of his reputed Arminianism. Daubeny's Calvinist critic, Sir Richard Hill, was quick to seize on this anomaly:

> Your partiality to Mr Fletcher both is, and is not to be wondered at. You justly extol him as a very able, pious, learned, acute divine...But supposing you had not found in him a decided ally against the Calvinistic doctrines of grace, what would you have said of his schismatical origin and baptism at the lake of Geneva; and what of his frequent preaching in barns, fields, conventicles, and Methodist meeting houses, as well as of his inviting similar preachers, and laymen into his own parish? Had he been a Calvinist, fire and faggot, some might have thought, would have been too good for him.[105]

Daubeny's efforts to downplay the role of Calvin and Calvinists in the proceedings of the English Reformation were not entirely successful. A reviewer in the *Christian Observer* of Daubeny's *Vindiciae* denied Daubeny's charge that (the reviewer) had represented Bishop Jewel as a Calvinist but poured scorn on Daubeny's claim that Jewel was an anti-Calvinist merely because he had omitted Calvin's name in his *Apology* (1562), the reviewer triumphantly concluding:

---

[103] Charles Daubeny, *A vindication of the character of the pious and learned Bishop Bull, from the unqualified accusations brought against it, by the Archdeacon of Ely, in his Charge delivered in the year 1826* (London, 1827), p. 21.

[104] Cited in *Christian Observer*, iv, no. 45 (September, 1805), p. 569. On the anti-Calvinist use of the Reformation and post-Reformation historiography of Peter Heylin, see Peter B. Nockles, 'A disputed legacy: Anglican historiographies of the Reformation from the era of the Caroline Divines to that of the Oxford Movement', *Bulletin of the John Rylands University Library of Manchester*, 83:1 (Spring 2001), pp. 159-60.

[105] Sir Richard Hill, *Daubenism confuted and Martin Luther vindicated...in a letter to Mr Daubeny* (London, 1800), p. 14-15.

In order to show the futility and inconclusiveness of this remark, we stated that Bishop Jewel, in another of his publications, had represented Calvin as a revered father and worthy ornament of the church of God. And we left it to our readers to infer, what was sufficiently obvious, that the impression which Mr Daubeny meant to convey of Jewel's dislike of Calvin was unfounded.[106]

One of the main elements in Overton's and Hill's charge that Daubeny was a 'doctrinal Dissenter', was not only that he had denied the letter of the Articles, had argued that the Reformers were Calvinists, and had denigrated Luther, but that he had subverted the consensus Anglican teaching on Justification of post-Reformation Elizabethan and Jacobean divines: a consensus exemplified not only in Jewel's *Apology*, but in the early Caroline divine Bishop Joseph Hall's *Old Religion* (1628). Hill was confident that he had earlier Anglican history on his side, likening his own churchmanship in terms of doctrine and discipline to the moderate Calvinist Jacobean Bishop Carleton. He taunted Daubeny: 'you have not found one divine of any note for learning and piety, from the time of the Reformation, till towards the end of Charles the First's reign, who maintained your notions on the points controverted between Calvinists and Arminians'.[107]

Similarly, the Calvinist John Newton had earlier maintained: 'my divinity is unfashionable enough at present, but it was not always so; you will find few books written from the era of the Reformation, till a little before Laud's time, that set forth any other. There were few pulpits until after the Restoration from which any other was heard'.[108] For Calvinist Evangelical historiographers, it was the Arminianism or 'free-will' heresy of the Laudian era onwards which had triggered a causal chain leading on to latitudinarianism and outright infidelity.[109] Hill even claimed that Daubeny was more Arminian than Arminius himself: 'As he far outstrips the original founder of his sect, I might have been more correct if I had all along distinguished his tenets by the name of Daubenism instead of Arminianism'.[110]

Conscious perhaps that his opponents had a strong case for the Calvinism of a consensus of Elizabethan and Jacobean divines, Daubeny, like most orthodox churchmen, confined his historical argument to the sense of the earlier English Reformers and compilers of the Church's formularies, arguing that the Calvinist teaching of many Elizabethan and Jacobean divines represented 'corruptions' of 'the originally established doctrines of our Church'.[111]

---

[106] *Christian Observer* 4:45 (September 1805), p. 567.
[107] Hill, *Reformation-Truth restored*, p. 73.
[108] Cited in Bruce Hindmarsh, *John Newton and the English Evangelical tradition between the conversions of Wesley and Wilberforce* (Oxford, 1996), p. 79.
[109] See Thomas Haweis, *An impartial and succinct history of the rise, declension and revival of the Church of Christ from the birth of Our Lord Saviour to the present time* (London, 1800).
[110] Hill, *Reformation-Truth restored*, p. 64.
[111] Daubeny, *Vindiciae Ecclesiae Anglicanae*, pp. 82, 125.

It is important to keep the Daubeny/Overton controversy of the early 1800s in perspective, however. Daubeny on the hand and Overton and Hill on the other, might be regarded as not entirely representative figures among orthodox and Anglican Evangelicals respectively. There is evidence that Hill (a veteran of the Calvinist/Arminian controversies of the 1770s) was regarded by *Christian Observer* circles as an *outré* figure by 1800, and that Overton was deemed to be too combative by moderate Evangelicals. Moreover, in the short term there were both theological factors (the check given to religious heterodoxy by the reaction to events in Revolutionary France) and European political and military factors (the Peace of Amiens), which helped explain the timing of the opening up of an orthodox/Anglican Evangelical rift and the rise and subsequent decline of the controversy in question. As Johnson Grant later explained by use of a telling analogy:

> It happened that these controversies became the more noticed, by reason of the tranquil state of Europe. As Pharisees and Sadducees would forget their mutual hostility, that they might entangle Christ in his talk, but at other times made an uproar touching points in dispute between them; so in a better cause, all religious parties united in England, to repel the common enemy, infidelity,—and when that object was effected, resumed their suspended differences. With the cessation of military warfare, internal factions revived...the dwellers upon doctrine, and the perceptive moralists, retook their stations aloof from each other; and such a juncture was favourable to that apple of discord, which Overton threw into the Church.[112]

Daubeny himself, however, kept up his critique of Anglican Evangelical doctrine as well as practice after the particular controversy with Overton had died down by 1805, notably in his opposition to Evangelical support for the non-denominational British and Foreign Bible Society, especially in the period 1810-16. Significantly, Daubeny represented the issue at stake as one of 'Anglican identity' versus a merely 'generalized Protestantism', not only in terms of breaches of apostolic order but of the theological implications flowing from an unfettered right of private judgement. Daubeny employed not only legal and constitutional arguments but also the more explicitly high church view of apostolic Tradition being necessary as an aid or subordinate court of appeal for the interpretation of Scripture; an argument which would be developed by the Tractarians in the next generation. Thus, he condemned what he regarded as the Bible Society's espousal of a 'levelling principle' between the Church and Dissent which, he maintained, promoted the aims of Dissenters 'at the expense of the

---

[112] Grant, *Summary History*, IV, pp. 99-100. Hannah More's recent biographer, Anne Stott, argues that the juxtaposition of the Blagdon controversy and the Peace of Amiens (1802) 'says much about the conspiratorial agenda of More's more implacable opponents'. Stott, *Hannah More*, p. 252.

establishment'.[113] Daubeny's more theological high church point was that the Bible needed to be rightly interpreted in order to guard against 'an almost continued state of agitation from every wind that blows'.[114] Daubeny went so far as to claim that had the Reformers been alive at this time, then they would have advocated the general circulation of the Prayer Book to accompany bible distribution.[115] In taking this stand, Daubeny was allied with Bishop Marsh and other orthodox churchmen, but opposition to the Bible Society was by no means unanimous among orthodox or high churchmen. Nor was support for the Society by any means a mark of Anglican Evangelical allegiance. One of the staunchest supporters of the Bible Society was the orthodox churchman, Bishop Thomas Burgess, who criticized Marsh's contention that the Bible should only be distributed with the Prayer Book, as, 'in its principle of so anti-protestant in complexion, that the Roman Catholics claim the chief supporter of it [Bishop Marsh], as their friend, and have congratulated him on renouncing the great principle of the Reformation'.[116]

Burgess's comment as applied to his fellow bishop Herbert Marsh could have been applied much more fittingly to Daubeny. Daubeny actually went further than Marsh in apparently opposing the very principle of the 'Bible alone' as the rule of faith; Marsh, perhaps shaken by the advantage taken by Roman Catholic controversialists, such as Bishop John Milner and Peter Gandolphy, of his admissions,[117] felt the need to clarify his position by maintaining that the rejection of Tradition constituted 'the vital principle of Protestantism'.[118] Daubeny even took issue with the way in

---

[113] Charles Daubeny, *The substance of a discourse, delivered at the Abby church in Bath, on Thursday 31 March 1814...giving a churchman's reasons for declining a connection with the Bible Society* (London, 1814), p. 23.

[114] Ibid., p. 4.

[115] Charles Daubeny, *Reasons for supporting the S.P.C.K. in preference to the new Bible society, partly given in a Charge to the clergy of his archdeaconry at his Visitation in 1812* (London, 1812), p. 73.

[116] See Thomas Burgess, *A Charge delivered to the clergy of the Diocese of St. David's in the month of September 1813* (London, 1813), pp. 26-8.

[117] Gandolphy discomfited Marsh by ironical compliments: 'You may easily conceive then, with what real delight and satisfaction I observed, that, in these writings, you contend for this principle, "true religion cannot be found by the Bible alone". The soundness of this doctrine was originally contested by Luther...Allow me then to congratulate... you...on the bold and manly manner, in which you have given up this vital principle of Protestantism'. Peter Gandolphy, *A congratulatory letter to the Rev. Herbert Marsh...on his judicious 'Inquiry into the consequences of neglecting to give the Prayer-Book with the Bible'* (London, 1812), p.6. See also idem, *A second letter to the Rev. Herbert Marsh, D.D. F.R.S. Margaret Professor of Divinity in the University of Cambridge; confirming the opinion that the vital principle of the Reformation has been lately conceded by him to the Church of Rome* (London, 1813), especially p. 7.

[118] See Herbert Marsh *A Comparative View of the churches of England and Rome*, (London, 1814), pp. 1-41, 60-75. For fuller discussion of differences over the role of Tradition between the orthodox churchmen Marsh, Burgess, and Daubeny, see Nockles, *Oxford Movement in context*, pp. 107-9; E.A. Varley, *The last of the*

which supporters of the Bible Society sheltered behind the celebrated maxim of the seventeenth-century Anglican divine William Chillingworth—'the bible only is the religion of protestants'. Although some high churchmen were to claim that Chillingworth's religious views were misrepresented by his later low church and latitudinarian apologists, Daubeny was convinced that he was not a sound authority, complaining that he was,

> in himself but a sort of loose Protestant. His Protestantism, according to his statement of it, not being the defined Protestantism of the Church of England; but a Protestantism abstracted from the Creeds and Confessions of particular churches; and appealing to the Bible as its general standard; in which respect it bore a striking resemblance to that general Protestantism, which the plan of the new Society is calculated to promote.[119]

Daubeny's distinction between a 'loose' or 'general Protestant' and a 'defined Protestant' was symptomatic of his anxiety to promote an 'Anglican' as distinct from merely 'Protestant' identity, and in this sense he was a true forerunner of Tractarian polemicists who coined the term 'ultra-Protestant' as a term of opprobrium.

Daubeny's religious identity as an Anglican high churchman was shaped and represented as much by his position in relation to Roman Catholicism as it was towards Protestant Dissent and Anglican Evangelicalism. Recent studies have emphasized anti-Catholicism as the essential ingredient of, if not the glue or cement for, an emerging British Protestant national identity. As such, it could provide a point of union for Anglican and Dissenters against a common Catholic enemy.[120] However, as Grayson Ditchfield has perceptively observed, even anti-Catholicism fell short of providing a Protestant consensus.[121] Anti-Catholicism certainly played a crucial role in the construction of an 'Anglican' national identity, but it is important to distinguish the distinctively high church strand of anti-Catholicism, exemplified by Daubeny's writings, from its other variants, Anglican Evangelical, Anglican latitudinarian, and Protestant Dissenting. Daubeny's distinctive brand of anti-Catholicism bears out Ditchfield's argument that a common sense of Protestant identity was something of a myth after mid-century.

Sir Richard Hill's comment that Daubeny inhabited 'the meridian of Rome'[122] was characteristic of the attitude of Daubeny's Anglican Evangelical as well as Protestant Dissenting theological opponents.

Prince Bishops: William Van Mildert and the high church movement of the early nineteenth century (Cambridge, 1992), pp. 58-9.

[119] Daubeny, *Reasons for supporting the S.P.C.K*, p. 19.

[120] See Haydon, *Anti-Catholicism*, pp. 137-8; Gibson, *Church of England, 1688-1832*, pp. 217-18.

[121] G.M. Ditchfield, 'Church, Parliament and national identity, c. 1770-c. 1830', in Julian Hoppit (ed.), *Parliaments, nations and identities in Britain and Ireland, 1660-1850* (Manchester, 2002), p. 70.

[122] Middelton, *Ecclesiastical Memoir*, p. 302.

Daubeny was criticized for his 'popish performances', and likened to Laud.[123] In Puritan and later Protestant Dissenting polemic, firstly Laudian and then high church principles, notably those of Daubeny himself, were often portrayed as savouring of 'Popery' (a perception encouraged by Daubeny's writings, and later by the Oxford Movement). As Andrew Thompson and Grayson Ditchfield have demonstrated, for eighteenth-century Protestant Dissenters, 'Popery' was often viewed as residing in the Church of England itself and its high church exponents, the term symbolizing not merely papal tyranny but any tyrannical imposition of clerical or episcopal authority in matters of religion which could be perceived as curtailing or denying the right of private judgement.[124] Daubeny's frequent strictures on an unreserved right of private judgement laid him open to the charge of 'Popery' from a rational Dissenting and anti-clerical quarter. Typical of this genre of invective was that of a critic who in 1808, after complaining that reading his *Guide to the Church* had lulled him 'to peaceful slumber', then rather inconsistently accused Daubeny of 'combining the vindictive spirit of Bonner, the pompous ostentation of Laud, the pride of Lucifer, and the bigotry of "mother church"'.[125] Another Protestant Dissenter concluded his attack on Daubeny with a standard anti-Catholic rhetorical flourish: 'if his principle be carried to its length, tis easy to see that it terminates in Smithfield, the final resort of his elder brethren'.[126] Daubeny's opposition to the distribution of Bibles without note or comment was also a gift to this type of critic. Joseph Lancaster, a proponent of non-denominational schemes of popular education, poured scorn on Daubeny's opposition as worthy of 'the days of fire and faggots, when it was thought dangerous that the Bible should be in the vulgar tongue'.[127]

Daubeny's position in relation to Catholicism, however, was more complex and ambivalent than that suggested by his Dissenting and more extreme Anglican Evangelical critics. In high church Anglican theological discourse Rome and Geneva were usually perceived as twin enemies,

---

[123] Hill, *Reformation-Truth restored*, pp. v-vi.
[124] Andrew Thompson, 'Popery, Politics, and Private Judgement in early Hanoverian Britain', *Historical Journal* 45:2 (June 2002), pp. 333-56, especially pp. 342-3; Ditchfield, 'Church, Parliament and national identity', pp. 64-82.
[125] *High Church Claims exposed, and the Protestant Dissenters and Methodists vindicated; or free remarks on a pamphlet entitled 'Strictures on subjects chiefly relating to the established church and the clergy, in two letters to his patron, from a country clergyman. In a letter to the author. By a layman* (Harlow, 1808), p. 3.
[126] *The Rights of Protestants asserted; and clerical encroachment detected. In allusion to several recent publications, in defence of an exclusive priesthood, establishments and tithes, by Daubeny, Church, and others, but more particularly in reply to a pamphlet lately published by George Markham entitled 'More truth for the Seekers'* (London, 1798), p. 41.
[127] Joseph Lancaster, *An Appeal for justice, in the cause of ten thousand poor and orphan children, and for the honour of the holy scriptures; being a reply, exposing the misrepresentations in the Charge delivered at the Visitation of Charles Daubeny, Archdeacon of Sarum, in June 1806* (London, 1806), p. 14.

sometimes being portrayed as reverse sides of the same coin. They both provided an object for vilification of 'the other'. Eirenical attitudes towards the Church of Rome were never normative in high church rhetoric. Alongside the supposed eirenicism towards Rome in the 1630s of some ultra-Laudians such as Richard Montagu and John Pocklington (though even Montagu's *Appello Caesarem*, censured by the parliamentary Puritan faction in the 1620s was ostensibly anti-Catholic in origin),[128] there was always a strong strain of anti-Catholicism within the high church tradition, notably in the 1680s. However, James Sack, F.C. Mather, and others, have traced a moderation or dilution of anti-Catholicism within high church Anglicanism in the second half of the eighteenth century, corresponding to a perceived heightened sense of danger from an opposite quarter—notably that of Socinianism and Voltairean infidelity.[129]

Anti-Jacobinism and a new form of anti-Revolutionary Francophobia helped replace or modify traditional anti-Catholicism during the 1790s. In the face of the dual and apparently interrelated challenge to the established church from revolutionary politics and heterodoxy or infidelity, Catholics could be welcomed as useful recruits to the cause of British loyalism and allies in the tide of political and ecclesiastical reaction unleashed by the French Revolution. Counter-revolution encouraged a trend towards religious inclusiveness, with both 'Anglican' and 'Protestant' identity becoming somewhat diluted out of the necessity of building a consensus in favour of a conservative British national reaction. High churchmen such as Bishop Horsley, by developing cordial relations with the leading English Catholic Bishop John Milner, exemplified this trend. At a time of unusual danger to the constitutional order of church and state posed by events in France, it shows that a high church Anglican and 'Ultramontane' Catholic could find political, if not theological common ground; Horsley even siding with Milner against the 'Cisalpine' faction within the English Catholic community in negotiations over Catholic relief. Milner certainly sought to ingratiate himself with the high church party in the Church of England with his assault on 'Hoadlyism', Socinianism, and political radicalism, and with a respectful notice of Laudian divines, in his *Letters to a Prebendary* (1800).[130] Daubeny's position also well represented the shifting sands of high church Anglican attitudes to Roman Catholicism.

---

[128] Anthony Milton, *Catholic and reformed: the Roman and Protestant churches in English Protestant thought, 1600-1640* (Cambridge, 1995), Pt. 1.

[129] James J. Sack, *From Jacobite to Conservative: reaction and orthodoxy in Britain, c. 1760-1832* (Cambridge, 1993), ch. 9; Mather, *High church prophet*, pp. 94-5. As Nigel Aston argues, 'the Gallican church had long represented to High Church Anglicans the tolerable side of popery'. Nigel Aston, 'Burke, Christianity, and the British State', idem (ed.), *Religious change in Europe 1650-1914: essays for John McManners* (Oxford, 1997), pp. 200-1.

[130] Peter B. Nockles, 'The difficulties of Protestantism: Bishop Milner, John Fletcher and Catholic apologetic against the Church of England in the era from the first Relief Act to Emancipation, 1778-1830', *Recusant History* 24:2 (October 1998), especially pp. 206-9. On Horsley's role in securing Catholic Relief in 1791

Aidan Bellenger has demonstrated the extent and significance of Anglican clerical support for the beleaguered exiled French émigré clergy in England in the 1790s,[131] many of whom were accommodated in the King's House at Winchester. The consciences of several high churchmen were shocked by accounts of Revolutionary violence inflicted on the exiled clergy before their flight. Thomas Rennell, later Dean of Winchester, referred to instances of barbarity which had 'been related to the author by various members of that venerable college of French ecclesiastics now inhabiting the King's House at Winchester'.[132] However, the charitable impulse on behalf of the French clergy was by no means confined to the high church wing of the Church of England, but also encompassed latitudinarians and even Anglican Evangelicals; Richard Cecil maintained that 'the exiled French priest raises the pity and indignation of all Christians'.[133] Daubeny played his part in providing generous practical support as well as expressions of sympathy for the exiled emigrant clergy of the downtrodden Gallican church. Significantly, in the *Guide* he explicitly used his parochial experience of raising relief for the French clergy in order to embarrass Protestant Dissenters and score points against an example of apparent Calvinist bigotry. Daubeny related:

> Upon collecting through my parish, some time since, for the relief of the emigrant French priests, I found an almost universal disinclination among the dissenters from the Church to contribute. At length one, more open than the rest, furnished the following reason for it; by telling me that 'Christ never died for those priests and therefore he had no feeling for them, or concern about them'. Another who had learnt his Christianity in the same school, upon my application to him on the same occasion, immediately exclaimed, 'what, Sir, to a Romanist! Give to a Roman! One that lives in such error? If I had ten thousand guineas I would not bestow a single mite upon him!'.

Daubeny, confident that he had made his point, concluded rhetorically: 'What think you would this Saviour say to those professors of His religion,

---

and his relations with Bishop Milner, see Mather, *High church prophet*, pp. 95-100, 102-3. The abrasive controversialist Milner, praised Horsley as 'that great ornament of the Episcopal bench'. John Milner, *The End of Religious Controversy* (London, 1819), p. 13.

[131] Dominic Aidan Bellenger, 'The émigré clergy and the English church, 1789-1815', *Journal of Ecclesiastical History* 34 (1983), especially pp. 392-400; idem, *The French exiled clergy in the British Isles after 1789* (Bath, 1986), pp. 28-46.

[132] Thomas Rennell, *Principles of French Republicanism essentially founded on violence and blood-guiltiness. A sermon preached on Sunday, 26 October, 1793, in the cathedral church of Winchester. Occasioned by the murder of Her Most Christian Majesty* [Winchester, 1793], p. 23.

[133] Josiah Pratt, *The Works of the Rev. Richard Cecil, M.A....with a Memoir of his life, arranged and revised, with a view of the author's character* (London, 1816; 2nd edn.), III, p. 417.

who would suffer a fellow creature to starve at their doors, because he lived in error?'[134]

There was also a deeper theological as well as charitable or philanthropic short-term basis as to why Daubeny could be restrained, if not eirenical, in his attitude towards Roman Catholicism at this time when compared to his attitude towards Protestant Dissent. In the *Guide* and its *Appendix*, Daubeny gave a classic exposition of the high church 'branch theory', which accorded the Church of Rome a respectable status as a true, if corrupt, branch of the universal church. According to the same theory, Protestant Dissenters were left outside its pale (as the phrase went, 'to the uncovenanted mercies of God') and even continental non-episcopal Protestant churches were put in a problematic position (though in so far as they could plead 'necessity' for their loss of an episcopal regimen, they were in a better position than native Dissenters). Catholicity implied a federation of separate territorial entities that each upheld certain notes or 'fundamentals' of Trinitarian catholic faith and apostolic order. The Church of England was not itself the Catholic or universal church, as the Church of Rome claimed to be, but rather, a branch of that universal church; a claim that rested primarily on its preservation of apostolic order through an episcopal succession. The claim of other branches to true catholicity rested on the same basis. As Daubeny put it:

> Every Christian society, possessing the characteristic marks of the Church of Christ, I consider to be a separate branch of the Catholic or Universal visible Church upon earth. The Church of England, the Church of Ireland, and the episcopal church of Scotland and America possess these marks. In the same light, the churches of Denmark, Sweden and Rome, are to be considered, not to mention the great remains of the once-famous Greek church, now to be found in the empire of Russia and in the East.[135]

Daubeny justified the Reformation within the terms of the 'branch theory', arguing that, 'the Protestantism, therefore, of the Church of England, consists in the right which one independent branch of the church of Christ claims of protesting against another branch of it'.[136] Protestant Dissenters continued to deride this view as undermining Daubeny's argument that to separate from the one body of the church of Christ was schism. As one such critic put it: 'what do the Papists call his reformation, and who gives him a

---

[134] Daubeny, *Guide to the Church*, pp. 86-7. The object of Daubeny's scorn is likely to have been an extreme Calvinist with a doctrine of limited Atonement. Daubeny's closest friend, Jonathan Boucher, had particularly friendly relations with French refugee clergy and laity who settled in his parish in Epsom, Surrey, in the 1790s, and whom he advised and assisted. A.Y. Zimmer, *Jonathan Boucher: Loyalist in exile* (Detroit, 1978), p. 246; *Memoirs of William Stevens Esq. Treasurer of Queen Anne's Bounty* (London, 1814; 2nd edn.), pp. 171-8.

[135] Charles Daubeny, *An Appendix to the 'Guide to the Church' in several letters in which the principles advanced in that work are more fully maintained in answer to objections* (London, 1804), pp. 106-7.

[136] Daubeny, *Guide to the Church* (1798), p. 149.

better right to call Dissenters schismatics, than the Papists have to call Protestants heretics'.[137] Moreover, such a rigid ecclesiological framework seemed to leave little room for a shared Protestant identity encompassing non-episcopal continental Lutheran or Calvinist bodies, let alone native Protestant Dissenters.[138] In contrast, for the orthodox and virulently anti-Calvinist Tomline, the claim to recognition of non-episcopal Protestant churches rested on the 'grand fundamentals' of Christianity as enshrined in their state-authorized confessions of faith, so that the 'Church of Holland' and 'Church of Geneva were as much parts of the visible Church of Christ as were the apostolic churches of Jerusalem, Antioch, or Alexandria';[139] a view which closely mirrored that of his Anglican Evangelical opponents on questions of soteriology. Daubeny was aware of the differences in ecclesiology between him and the bishop of Lincoln. In 1799, he told Boucher that he hoped that

> the bishop is what he is represented to be, and what, it should appear he wishes to be considered, orthodox & apostolical, both with respect to doctrine & discipline. But I must own I have my doubts whether he is 'totus teres'. If he was, I think a Bishop, who directs his clergy...to defend our discipline on the high ground of Apostolical institution, & to state the authority transmitted to us from the Apostles etc, would have felt himself called upon to have said thank you, for the letter, which accompanied the presentation of books expressly written on that subject...From want of precision in the Bishop's language, I conceive his ideas on certain subjects have not long been made up, if they are at present.[140]

It would be misleading, however, to accept the 'Popery' charges against Daubeny by Protestant Dissenting and Anglican Evangelical critics at face value. Daubeny's attitude towards Rome, like that of most high churchmen, notably hardened from about 1801 onwards, for both domestic and European reasons. These included a resurgent Papacy under Pope Pius VII and Cardinal Consalvi, a resurgent and more self-confident English Catholicism under Bishop Milner's leadership, the fall-out from the Irish Rebellion of 1798 (with anti-Irish and anti-Catholic prejudice fuelled by the lurid published accounts of Sir Richard Musgrave), and the threat posed by the issue of Catholic emancipation gaining a high profile on the domestic political and parliamentary agenda.[141] Anti-Catholicism had, anyway, only been submerged rather than eradicated by the anti-Jacobinism and rallying

---

[137] *Rights of Protestants asserted*, p. 42.
[138] Charles Daubeny, *A word in season on the nature of the Christian church, and the ground on which the Church of England as a branch of that church stands; the probable danger attendant on a wilful unnecessary separation from the Church of England considered* (Bath, 1817), p. 12.
[139] George Pretyman-Tomline, *Elements of Christian Theology* (London, 1799), II, pp. 396-7.
[140] Boucher Papers, B/5/16: Daubeny to Boucher, 7 November 1800.
[141] On the rise of anti-Catholicism on the religious 'Right' after 1801, see Sack, *From Jacobite to Conservative*, pp. 30-51.

of sympathy to the cause of the exiled French clergy in the 1790s. It did not take much of a change in the domestic and international political climate to reignite it, though theological principles as much as ecclesiastical politics underpinned and shaped its revival.

Support for the French émigré clergy among the Anglican clergy had always been conditional and based on the assumption that there would be no proselytizing. Like many high churchmen, Daubeny became alarmed by the apparent advantage which 'emissaries of Catholicism' seemed to have gained by establishing a foothold in England during the exile of the émigré clergy, many of whom were perceived to have outstayed their welcome by the 1800s. He always had a keen sense of the proselytizing zeal of the Catholic priesthood. On his early continental travels, he had been impressed by examples of this which he encountered, contrasting it with sluggishness on the part of Protestant clergy. However, when faced with examples of Catholic proselytism at home from the 1800s, he became less detached. His new-found anti-Catholicism constituted something of a back-handed compliment to the spiritual influence and attraction of Catholicism. As he put it late in life:

> For when we consider the genius of the Romish religion, and the character of the Romish priesthood, of which proselytism has ever constituted a principal feature, and place it in contrast with the too general supineness of our own clergy in this respect, it must follow as an unavoidable consequence, that Popery, if encouraged, will increase among us.[142]

Clearly, it was one thing to rally in support of persecuted members of a fallen branch of the Catholic Church when at the receiving end of apparently diabolical forces that might threaten to engulf 'Throne and Altar' in Britain as they had in France, but quite another to acquiesce in the face of the dramatic turnaround in European and English Catholic fortunes after 1800. The result was a new nervousness among Anglican high churchmen and a consequent furious back-pedalling on earlier expressions of sympathy and welcome for what had once been considered persecuted co-religionists, especially noticeable in the later vitriolic anti-Catholicism of Thomas Rennell, but also to a lesser extent in other high churchmen such as William Jones of Nayland and above all, in Daubeny himself.[143]

Implicit always in Anglican high churchmanship was a consciousness that, given the closeness in terms of apostolical foundation between the Church of England and Rome, it was necessary to demonstrate and justify the causes of the separation at the Reformation by dwelling on Rome's supposed 'corruptions' in doctrine and practice. It was also necessary in order to refute the analogy claimed by Protestant Dissenters as a precedent

---

[142] Charles Daubeny, *A letter to the Right Honorable George Canning...in the character of one of the old Reformers* (London, 1827), p. 30. On limited evidence for proselytizing, see Bellenger, *French exiled clergy*, pp. 38-40.

[143] Nockles, *Oxford Movement in context*, pp. 168-9; Sack, *From Jacobite to Conservative*, pp. 233-4.

for their own separation from the established church.[144] This meant arguing that there were no fundamental doctrinal grounds (only differences over 'external forms and non-essential ceremonies') for the separation of Dissenters from the Church of England to compare with the doctrinal reasons for the separation of the Church of England from Rome.[145] In the *Guide*, Daubeny had given the impression that the Church of England was closer to Rome than to Protestant Dissent, with Sir Richard Hill expressing his amazement at Daubeny's statement that, 'in the most essential articles of the Christian Faith, the Church of England and the Church of Rome are agreed'.[146] The admiration for Daubeny's *Guide* expressed by English Catholic divines such as John Fletcher was also a potential source of embarrassment.[147] As a consequence, Daubeny's emphasis was modified in his later anti-Catholic writings, wherein it was argued that such was the extent of her doctrinal corruption, that the Church of England was 'compelled to separate from the Church of Rome'.[148] The same need to remove excuses for Protestant Dissent, prompted charges of 'idolatry', common amongst Anglican Evangelicals, to be made by high churchmen against the Church of Rome, Daubeny later asserting that 'the idolatry of the Church of Rome is neither more nor less than the idolatry of heathenism Christianised'.[149] Among the increasing instances of idolatry that he now chose to attack were the invocation of saints, the 'worship' of images, relics, and the Host. It was in this context that the traditional Protestant prophecies of Antichrist applying to Rome were revived by high churchmen.[150]

Daubeny's published sermon on *The Fall of Papal Rome* (1798), published in the same year as his *Guide*, illustrated the way in which the apocalyptic strain in reactions to events in Europe of Anglican churchmen, high church or orthodox as well as Evangelical, could take a traditionally anti-Catholic turn. Protestant writers such as Joseph Mede and Thomas

---

[144] Nockles, *Oxford Movement in context*, pp. 164-7.
[145] Charles Daubeny, *A Charge delivered at the Primary Visitation of the Archdeacon of Sarum, on the 9th, 10th, 11th, and 12th July 1805* (London, 1805), pp. 20-1.
[146] Hill, *Reformation-Truth restored*, p. xv.
[147] As Fletcher put it, 'the principle, the reasoning, the conclusion' of Daubeny's Guide to the Church, 'are precisely the same with mine'. Nockles, 'Difficulties of Protestantism', p. 213. This Roman Catholic priest John Fletcher is not to be confused with Wesley's ally, the Evangelical John Fletcher of Madeley.
[148] Charles Daubeny, *A Supplement to the Protestant's Companion; containing, among other subjects in discussion, a particular analysis of Bishop Baines's novel doctrine of Transubstantiation, at decided variance from the doctrine of the Church of Rome, as established by the Council of Trent* (London, 1825), p. 223.
[149] Charles Daubeny, *Protestant's Companion, or a seasonable preservative against the errors, corruptions, and unfounded claims of a superstitious and idolatrous church; with a chapter respectfully addressed to civil governors, and another to the clergy* (London, 1824), pp. 64, 115.
[150] For an example of the genre, see Ralph Churton, *Antichrist, or the Man of Sin. A sermon preached before the University of Oxford, at St Mary's, on Sunday, May 23, 1802* (Oxford, 1804).

Newton had kept alive the strongly eschatological and prophetical basis of the anti-Catholicism that characterized the first century of the reformed Church of England.[151] In this tradition of prophetical writing, the Papacy was commonly identified with the Antichrist, the Pope being labelled 'the Man of Sin'. The convulsions in Europe in the 1790s were conducive to a sense of apocalyptic fulfilment, but the trend at least among high churchmen such as Samuel Horsley and Jones of Nayland had been to transfer the image of Antichrist to the spirit of the French Revolution.[152] In portraying the Revolution as Antichrist, Horsley seemed to reject the eschatological basis of anti-Roman Catholicism, condemning Mede's 'unwarrantable, monstrous supposition, that Christian Rome is Antichrist'.[153] Daubeny's *Fall of Papal Rome* sermon signified a reversal of this trend and marked an early shift to what was to become a resurgence of anti-Catholicism within Anglican high churchmanship.

The context of Daubeny's sermon was the exile of Pope Pius VI and the fall of Rome. As Nigel Aston comments, 'Protestant apologists felt thoroughly vindicated and found it impossible to resist a note of triumphalism that the historic enemy had been overthrown'.[154] Daubeny shared in what was to be a temporary triumph, adding his voice to those of numerous Evangelical preachers on the apparent prophetic fulfilment. In the sermon, whether or not for merely rhetorical effect, Daubeny enthusiastically identified with the classic Protestant doctrine concerning Antichrist and readily proclaimed it as a leading principle of the Reformation in a way which even his normally sternest Evangelical critics could warmly commend. A reviewer in the Calvinist *Gospel Magazine*, between Daubeny and whom there was mutual hostility on all other issues, described Daubeny's sermon as having unfolded and displayed the doctrine Antichrist 'with such ingenuity and brightness of illustration that we would recommend it to the public perusal at this period with more than common earnestness'.[155] The reviewer must have particularly appreciated Daubeny's following frank avowal:

> That Papal Rome was the Babylon of the Revelations, out of the communion of whose church Christians are commanded to come forth, was the principle

---

[151] Bishop Thomas Newton was the author of the influential *Dissertation on the Prophecies* (1754-58).

[152] W.H. Olliver, *Prophets and Millennialists: the use of biblical prophecy in England from the 1790s to the 1840s* (Auckland, 1978), pp. 50-1; J.A. Oddy, 'Eschatological prophecy in the English theological tradition, c. 1790-c. 1840' (University of London, Ph.D. dissertation, 1982), ch. 3; Robert Hole, *Pulpits, politics, and public order in England 1760-1832* (Cambridge, 1989), pp. 170-72.

[153] Mather, *High church prophet*, pp. 260-68. See Samuel Horsley, *Critical Disquisitions on the Eighteenth chapter of Isaiah* (1799). On the significance of Horsley's position, see A. Robinson, 'Identifying the Beast: Samuel Horsley and the problem of the Papal Antichrist', *Journal of Ecclesiastical History* 43:3 (October 1992), pp. 592-607.

[154] Aston, *Christianity and Revolutionary Europe*, p. 235.

[155] *Gospel Magazine* 3:30 (May 1798), p. 199.

upon which the Reformation in this country proceeded. And the more this important subject has been investigated, the more strongly has that principle been confirmed in the minds of every impartial reader.[156]

Like several contemporary Evangelical commentators, Daubeny saw the hand of Providence at work in the apparently progressive weakening of the power of the Papacy, which seemed to lie prostrate before Buonaparte and Revolutionary France and to be about to become extinct. Thus, Daubeny confidently, if prematurely, proclaimed:

> The Papal power has long been upon the decline. It received an irrevocable wound at the period of the Protestant Reformation; since which it has been gradually sinking into insignificance preparatory to its final extinction. That event has now taken place; an event in which all nations are more or less concerned.[157]

Daubeny remained as alive as Horsley to the reign of infidelity which had been unleashed by events in France, but no longer shared that prelate's confidence (if he ever did) that the danger from Rome had abated. On the contrary, like Bishop Barrington, Daubeny not only blamed the 'corruptions' of Rome for the rise of French Revolutionary atheism, but even shared the Protestant prophetical view that popish tyranny had to be broken in pieces by a temporary prevalence of infidelity in order that 'the reign of primitive Christianity' could be re-established.[158] In short, 'Anglican' and not merely 'Protestant' identity could only be fully restored once the power of 'Popery' had been destroyed. Thus, he concluded: 'The gross corruption of genuine Christianity generated by degrees that infidelity, which, in the wisdom of Him, who bringeth good out of evil, has been employed as the instrument of destruction to the parent which gave it birth'.[159]

Daubeny's hopes, however, were to be dashed. Daubeny now turned to a conspiracy theory to explain away the fact that Roman Catholicism, far from being overthrown or weakened, was actually greatly strengthened, especially in England, by the French Revolution. Thus, in his last publication, *A Letter to the Right Honorable George Canning* (1827), he cited letters apparently written by a Spanish observer in England, Dom Manuel Alfonso Espiella:

> The French Revolution materially assisted the true religion. The English clergy trembling on their benefices, welcomed the emigrant priests as brethren, and forgetting all their former railings about Antichrist, Babylon, and the Scarlet Whore, lamented the downfall of religion in France. An outcry was raised against the most daring heretics at home, and the tide of popular fury let loose

---

[156] Charles Daubeny, *The fall of Papal Rome: recommended to the consideration of England, in a discourse on Isaiah xlvi, 9, 10* (London, 1798), pp. 25.
[157] Ibid., p. 26.
[158] Ibid., p. 33.
[159] Ibid., p. 34.

upon them. Whilst this dread of Atheism prevailed, the Catholic priests obtained access every where...These noble confessors did not let the happy opportunity pass by unimproved; they sowed the seeds abundantly, and saw the first fruits of the harvest.[160]

Prophetical interpretation, however, was just one element in the anti-Catholic armoury which Daubeny increasingly marshalled. Far from being a contradiction to his anti-Protestant Dissenting and anti-Evangelical polemic, Daubeny's anti-Catholic writing complemented it. There was the high church ecclesiological imperative—the need to justify the Reformation and refute Dissenting jibes about the Church of England's separation and therefore 'schism' at that time, jibes which mirrored those raised by Catholic controversialists such as Bishop Milner from an opposite quarter. Thus, Daubeny's earlier emphasis on the shared apostolical foundations of both churches, evident in the *Guide*, was replaced in his later anti-Catholic polemic by a concern to highlight theological differences. The need to rebut the threat of imminent Catholic emancipation prompted his *Letter to...Canning*, in which he argued that

> Protestantism and Popery are powers at such irreconcilable variance, that they cannot possibly for any length of time travel on in harmony together, since one or the other will be continually struggling for the ascendancy; an though Protestantism, in the true spirit of Christianity, grants toleration, yet Popery, in the known spirit of bigotry, cannot.[161]

Another factor shapingDaubeny's later more strident anti-Catholicism, was the need to challenge the increasing political alliance of Whig latitudinarians and even some heterodox Dissenters with Catholics in support of a toleration which encompassed English and Irish Catholics. This realignment represented an important ideological shift within the Anglican latitudinarian and pro-Dissenting camp, following the passing of the anti-Catholic latitudinarian generation of Archdeacon Blackburne and Thomas Hollis; it was a realignment which meant that Daubeny's long-standing anti-latitudinarian rhetoric could find an anti-Catholic outlet. Daubeny's anti-Catholicism, no less than his antipathy to Protestant Dissent, was a reflection of his anti-latitudinarianism and disdain for 'laxity in religion'. It was an adjunct of, and actually buttressed by his rigid high church ecclesiology. He made clear that it was the latitudinarian principles of Warburton's *Alliance between Church and State* which were proving potentially destructive of the Protestant establishment by assuming that the religion established by the civil power had 'no connection whatever with the truth of religion', but only to its civil utility.[162] This was an argument which he had employed in the *Guide*, but in the context of the 1820s it had come to take on a more explicitly anti-Catholic application.

---

[160] Daubeny, *Letter to the Right Honorable George Canning*, pp. 40-1.
[161] Ibid., p. 17.
[162] Ibid., p. 29.

'Anglican' identity for high churchmen traditionally assumed not only theological, but national, constitutional, and territorial dimensions. Daubeny's anti-Catholicism became increasingly infused by the constitutional element—the defence of the Protestant constitution in church and state. The dominance of the issue of the 'Catholic claims' for full civil liberties from the 1800s onwards, posed a direct constitutional and legislative challenge to the 'Anglican' national hegemony in church and state. In short, Protestant constitutionalism became almost synonymous with Anglican high churchmanship, and Daubeny was in the forefront of this development. For him, the two strands were never in conflict. A *jure divino* high church defence of the Protestant establishment on grounds of religious truth and conformity to the primitive church, and not utility or expedience (as Daubeny complained of Warburton and Paley) was the safest bulwark against the encroachments of Roman Catholicism. Although always disdainful of erastianism, the 'establishmentarian' element in Daubeny's rhetoric undoubtedly became more pronounced in his later anti-Catholic polemic, perhaps as a defence mechanism.

The last years of Daubeny's life witnessed the apogee of his anti-Catholic polemic, in a bitter controversy with the Benedictine Peter Augustus Baines. According to his biographer son-in-law, of all Daubeny's writings, 'no production obtained more general approbation', than his suggestively entitled treatise *The Protestant's Companion, or A Seasonable Preservative against the errors, corruptions, and unfounded claims of a superstitious and idolatrous church* (1824),[163] followed up by *A Supplement* (1825). Although Daubeny insisted that he had refrained 'from speaking disrespectfully of the Church of Rome, as a Church, considering her foundation is right',[164] Catholic critics of the work gained a different impression. Baines responded to Daubeny's onslaught on Catholicism, commenting that he regarded

> this aged churchman as a man of former days, who has survived his companions in antiquated zeal, whose prejudices are in his bones, and whose abuse consequently ought to make no more impression on my mind than if it came from Luther, Jewel, or his own grandmother.[165]

Baines also contrasted Daubeny's anti-Catholic hostility with the humane and tolerationist attitudes towards Catholics displayed by the Whig latitudinarian bishop of Norwich, Henry Bathurst.[166] He concluded that Daubeny's frenzied zeal betrayed weakness, 'an acknowledgment that the Church of England is not the church of Christ', for the logic of Daubeny's

---

[163] *Guide to the Church...some account of the author's life and writings*, p.xlii.
[164] Daubeny, *Protestant's Companion*, p. vii.
[165] Peter Augustine Baines, *An Inquiry into the nature object, and obligations of the religion of Christ; with a comparison of the ancient and modern Christianity of England; in reply to the Archdeacon of Sarum's 'Protestant Companion', in a fourth letter to the Archdeacon of Bath* (Bath, [1824]), p. 12.
[166] Ibid., p. 1.

position was that 'the Church of England must assuredly fall the moment it ceases to persecute'.[167]

In conclusion, while the Protestant constitution acted as something of a ballast and guarantor of a certain internal consensus and cohesion within the established church prior to 1829, this was only in relative terms compared to the greater divisions notoriously evident in the era of the Oxford Movement from the 1830s onwards.[168] Although the actual term 'Anglicanism' would only gain currency in the 1830s,[169] a distinctive 'Anglican' identity re-emerged over the preceding fifty years, overlapping with but separate from, a common 'Protestant' or 'establishment' identity. Pre-Tractarian high churchmanship may have defined itself primarily in constitutional terms, but it became imbued once again with greater theological coherence long before the era of the Oxford Movement. This was reflected in a much harder line against Protestant Dissenters and a cooler attitude towards foreign Protestant churches when compared even to orthodox churchmen of a previous generation, such as Archbishop Secker.[170] Daubeny symbolised this trend, a trend which was encouraged by the vacuum which opened up as old-fashioned latitudinarianism lost much of its former constituency. By espousing an increasingly confrontational anti-Dissenting posture, Daubeny in turn contributed to a longer term shift in the attitude of Protestant Dissent itself towards the Church of England. Hitherto, Dissenters (and some Anglican Evangelicals) disapproved of the Church of England's structures and regarded its near monopoly of public life to be tyrannical but at the same time believed its doctrines to be more or less soundly Protestant. Daubeny helped the beginning of the transition that was to be completed by the impact of the Oxford Movement, when Dissenters came to doubt the Church of England's Protestantism at the very time when its monopoly of public life was being dismantled.[171]

As latitudinarianism waned, the prospect of a clash between a rival and mutually resurgent high churchism and Evangelicalism increased.[172] Daubeny's often bitter controversy with John Overton and Sir Richard Hill in the period 1798-1805, marked the reopening of a deep-seated split within the established church not over discipline or the principle of subscription to the Thirty-Nine Articles but doctrine (the relationship between Faith and Works, Justification and Sanctification, and Baptism), as expressed especially in the Thirty-Nine Articles themselves; a doctrinal division

---

[167] Ibid.
[168] Nockles, 'Church parties', especially pp. 357-9.
[169] Nockles, *Oxford Movement in context*, pp. 39-41.
[170] For an example of Secker's more tolerant attitude to non-episcopal churches, see [Thomas Secker], *An Answer to Dr. Mayhew's 'Observations on the character and conduct for the Society for the Propagation of the Gospel in foreign parts'* (London, 1764), p. 68.
[171] I am indebted here to discussions with Dr. Grayson Ditchfield.
[172] Martin Fitzpatrick, 'Latitudinarianism at the parting of the ways: a suggestion', in Walsh, Haydon, and Taylor (eds.), *From Toleration to Tractarianism*, pp. 226-7.

which had existed in the seventeenth century but which had become blurred in the closing of ranks against latitudinarian opponents of clerical subscription. For Daubeny, doctrinal Evangelicalism could not be accommodated in the exclusivist image of Anglican religious identity which he expounded. On the other hand, for Overton and Hill, 'Daubenism' itself was the problem, as they defined Evangelical churchmanship on their own Calvinist terms. The proponents of each set of competing identities constructed an image which was supported by historical evidence—hence the battleground of the Reformation and Elizabethan epochs. Of course, each side was selective in its historiography, with Daubeny frequently criticized for his reliance upon Heylin and the nonjuror Jeremy Collier's *Ecclesiastical History*.[173] Neither side was a clear 'winner'. For as Nancy Murray has observed, 'if the experience of the French Revolution could be mobilized against rational religion', it could not, as high churchmen gradually discovered, 'be so effectively used against "enthusiasm"'.[174] The problem for Daubeny, was akin to that later experienced by the Tractarians in their attempt to give a definitive 'catholic' doctrinal identity to the Church of England: for, as Judith Pinnington has observed, the eighteenth-century Church of England had for so long operated under an umbrella theory of 'national religion' defined in loose and non-doctrinal terms, 'that it was not so easy now to present a credible image of what was the truth as "the Church" saw it'.[175] In short, neither high churchmen nor Evangelicals were able to enforce their own doctrinally specific content onto the wider religious identity of the Church of England in either the pre-Tractarian or later eras.

Even in his later virulently anti-Catholic writings, Daubeny did not revert to promoting a merely 'common Protestant' identity for the Church of England. For example, far from denying Roman Catholic charges about the divisions among Protestants resulting from a private interpretation of the Scriptures, Daubeny acknowledged them but blamed the Church of Rome for causing them.[176] Moreover, in one of his last works, *A Vindication of the character of the pious and learned Bishop Bull* (1827), he returned to an assault on what he called that 'mutilated sketch of the Gospel system' which went 'under the imposing title of Evangelical preaching'.[177] Any admiration which some Anglican Evangelicals of the Calvinist type felt for Daubeny's anti-Catholic stand was not allowed to take root and did not result in any long-term burying of differences.

Daubeny's construction of an 'Anglican' religious identity was characterized by vigorous polemical assaults on the 'other', whether

---

[173] Hill, *Reformation-truth restored*, pp. 175-8.
[174] Nancy U. Murray, 'The influence of the French Revolution on the Church of England and its rivals, 1789-1802', (Oxford DPhil dissertation, 1975), p. 71.
[175] John E. Pinnington, 'Anglican reactions to the challenge of a multiconfessional society, with special reference to British North America, 1760-1850' (University of Oxford D.Phil. dissertation, 1971), p. 155.
[176] Daubeny, *Supplement to the 'Protestant's Companion'*, p. 182.
[177] Daubeny, *Vindication of the character of...Bishop Bull*, p. 2.

represented by Geneva or Rome; rigid Calvinists were 'the spawn of the Scotch Covenanters'[178] and Papists were 'idolators'. In the conspiratorial climate created by the reaction to the French Revolution, the term 'Calvinism' was no longer used with theological precision; rendered synonymous with 'Puritanism' and 'Methodism', it meant political subversion as well as unsound doctrine. It was not always clear what Daubeny meant by 'Calvinist'. Calvinism was a *portmanteau* term, seldom satisfactorily unpacked. High church writers such as Daubeny often attributed doctrines found in Calvin's *Institutes* on to Anglican Evangelicals, though many of them had never read Calvin and were not predestinarians.[179] For Daubeny, if 'Calvinism' could not be found on the surface, then even moderate Anglican Evangelicals like More and Wilberforce were guilty of 'Calvinism in disguise'.

Of course, Daubeny was not representative of all orthodox churchmen. Many orthodox and staunchly Arminian churchmen, such as Bishops Porteus, Burgess and Barrington, and notably Alexander Knox and Bishop John Jebb, acted in close consort with Anglican Evangelicals (either in patronage of Hannah More, in support of the Bible Society, and most notably in moral reformation societies) even while maintaining some doctrinal differences. More was a friend with one of the highest churchmen on the bench, William Cleaver, bishop of Chester, and even cultivated Bishop Tomline and his wife.[180] Moreover, anti-Calvinism and an outspoken Arminianism could coexist or even encourage a latitudinarian theology. Daubeny found fault in terms of defective churchmanship with even allies such as bishops Tomline and Marsh on the anti-Calvinist and anti-Catholic fronts, Daubeny privately casting doubts on 'the Bishop of Lincoln's...orthodox and apostolical' views to his friend Boucher after the publication of Tomline's *Elements of Christian Theology* (1799).[181] Daubeny and Tomline also differed in their sacramental and liturgical views, with the former expressing a preference for the first Edwardian Prayer Book of 1549,[182] while the bishop of Lincoln welcomed the changes made in a Protestant direction in the second Edwardine rite of 1552.[183] Nor did Tomline appear to share Daubeny's degree of anti-erastian concern for the support of the non-established Scottish Episcopal church.[184]

---

[178] Boucher Papers, B/5/11: Daubeny to Boucher, 23 October 1799.
[179] I have benefited here from discussions with Dr. John Walsh.
[180] Stott, *Hannah More*, pp. 177, 247-8.
[181] Boucher Papers, B/5/14: Daubeny to Boucher, 7 November 1800. For the high churchman Johnson Grant's strictures on Tomline's *Refutation of Calvinism* (1811), see Grant, *Summary of the History of the English Church*, IV, p. 77.
[182] Daubeny, *Appendix to the Guide to the Church*, pp. 195-6.
[183] George Pretyman-Tomline, *Elements of Christian Theology* (London, 1799), II, pp. 22-3.
[184] Daubeny intervened on behalf of the Scottish episcopal hierarchy in the so-called 'English chapels schism' in the 1800s. In a public letter to the Scottish episcopalian noble, Lord Kinnoul, he insisted: 'English Bishops have no authority in Scotland so the claim of the clergy of the Anglican communion in Scotland to be attached to the Church of England is without foundation; they

Daubeny differed also from even distinctively high churchmen such as Horne and Horsley (who favoured the 1549 rite and did much to negotiate the relief of the Scottish Episcopal church).[185] Horsley himself could be confrontational and regarded unlicensed Evangelical preachers and Sunday schools that were not under parochial management as potential sources of subversion.[186] Yet, like Horne, he displayed a striking eirenicism towards Anglican Evangelicals, even of the 'Calvinist' type, and reserved the full force of his controversial genius and polemical strictures to the forces of heterodox Dissent and infidelity (represented by Joseph Priestley and Tom Paine respectively).[187] Unlike Daubeny, Horsley might have been capable of restoring that essentially pre-Laudian alliance of 'high church' episcopal claims and moderate sacramental theology with a doctrinal 'Evangelicalism' and even moderate Calvinism; a synthesis which could have appealed even to an Overton or a Hill. Anglican Evangelicals such as Overton, preferred to look back not so much to Calvin but to the Anglican episcopal 'Calvinists' of the early seventeenth century. On the other hand, Daubeny's approach was more combative and divisive. Ultimately, the difference in religious 'identity' was as much to do with personality and temperament as with any deep-seated theological divergence.

It was sometimes orthodox churchmen of the more 'high and dry' type such as Tomline, notorious for the vigour of their anti-Calvinism (though befriended by More) but with an almost latitudinarian Protestant leaning in ecclesiological and sacramental matters, who were the most confrontational. Daubeny combined his intolerance with an extreme high churchmanship that made him in this sense a worthy heir of a less eirenical strand of the Laudian tradition. A biographer of Sir Richard Hill looking back from the vantage point of 1839 compared Daubeny's attack on Hill with contemporary assaults on 'evangelical truth' (especially the Reformed doctrine of Justification) by the Tractarians, concluding: 'The same spirit which caused a Tomline and a Daubeny to oppose reformation principles yet remains, though the shape it assumes is framed to meet the changes of the times'.[188] Significantly, however, Hill's biographer compared Daubeny and Tomline very unfavourably with the Tractarians of his own day: 'The former added persecution to error; the latter conduct themselves with mildness and write like gentlemen. The one class excited indignation; the other calls forth pity and regret, but demands an honest exposure'.[189]

None the less, Daubeny differed markedly from the Tractarians in his view of the English Reformers. Whereas the Tractarians came to abandon,

---

owe canonical obedience to the Scottish Bishops and any resistance is resistance to the Ordinance of God'. Boucher Papers, B/5/19: Daubeny to Lord Kinnoul, November 1800 (copy).

[185] On Horsley's efforts on behalf of the Scottish Episcopal church, see Mather, *High Church Prophet*, pp. 123-34.
[186] Mather, *High Church Prophet*, pp. 278-83.
[187] Ibid., pp. 55-60.
[188] Edwin Sidney, *The life of Sir Richard Hill, Bart* (London, 1839), p. 484.
[189] Ibid., p. 130.

if not denigrate, the Reformers, Daubeny claimed in his battle with Anglican Evangelicals to be their latter-day mouthpiece and champion. The only *caveat* was that what mattered for Daubeny was 'not the sentiments of our Reformers individually, but what was their judgement collectively'.[190]

Several factors probably restricted Daubeny's wider influence, given his prodigious publishing output. Daubeny was not blessed with a pleasing or gracious manner, and in one of his last controversial pamphlet jousts, with the Benedictine and future Catholic bishop, Peter Augustus Baines, he almost conceded as much.[191] Regarded by critics as a 'haughty dignitary' and 'high priest', he was socially handicapped by extreme nervousness, rigidity of manner', and 'constitutional shyness'.[192] Even his son-in-law conceded that 'there may be some truth in the remark' that he did 'not possess the knack of talking', and was too rigid and upright 'to associate generally with the world'.[193]

His private self-effacement was accompanied by an apparently warm spirituality, nourished on the devotional writings of the Caroline and nonjuring divines.[194] It also coexisted with a warm temper and reputation as an acerbic controversialist, happy in his last publication to write 'in the character of the old Reformers'. His private verdict on those with whom he disagreed could be severe: he described the mild-mannered bishop of London, Beilby Porteus, as 'neither sound nor honest', and criticized him for his support of Hannah More.[195] Even Daubeny's strictly private criticisms of the views of Bishop Tomline seemed to have been prompted by a sense of personal slight and lack of gratitude to him on the bishop's part.[196] Although high church friends regarded Daubeny as the ablest champion of their cause in his time, his controversial temper sometimes got the better of his judgement, as in his unfortunate dispute with Hannah More in the so-called 'Blagdon controversy'.[197] He was charged with misquoting or garbling More's views on the relationship between doctrine and moral duties in the plan of salvation by the transposition of a comma; as More's defender put it, 'was there ever a more perverse, or unreasonable misconstruction'.[198] It is not surprising that Hannah More herself should

---

[190] Daubeny, *Vindiciae Ecclesiae Anglicanae*, p. 71.
[191] 'Bishop Baines, I understand to be a man of most insinuating manners and complimentary address. I profess not to meet Bishop Baines on this his advantage ground'. Daubeny, *Protestant's Companion*, p. 332.
[192] *Guide to the Church...some account of the author's life and writings*, p. xlvii.
[193] Ibid., p. lii.
[194] Ibid., p. xvi. Daubeny transcribed Lancelot Andrewes's *Morning Prayer* for daily use.
[195] Boucher Papers, B/5/14: Daubeny to Boucher, 27 February 1800.
[196] Ibid.
[197] Hannah More's recent biographer has also found evidence of Daubeny's duplicitous conduct in the Blagdon controversy. See, Stott, *Hannah More*, pp. 249-50.
[198] *A brief confutation of the Rev. Mr Daubeny's strictures on Mr Richard Baxter in the 'Appendix' to his 'Guide to the Church'; and also of his animadversions on Mrs*

have privately referred to Daubeny as 'the High Church Dragon'.[199] More's defender commented on Daubeny's unerring habit of picking a quarrel: 'Mr Daubeny was predestined, like the Wolf in Aesop, to pick a quarrel at all events, and afterwards to find a pretext, the best way he could'. He conceded that 'in Baxter there are some circumstances to warrant the animadversions of high church zeal', but asked rhetorically, 'what is in the labours of Hannah More to call forth the acrimony even of an HEYLIN or an HICKES?'. He concluded his criticism of Daubeny's scatter-gun attacks, with a telling observation: 'For never was there a more absurd, or more self-defeating attempt to find in a sun-beam that darkness, which existed only in the eye of the beholder'.[200]

Daubeny's circle of private friends was small, though he was close to a group of like-minded high churchmen which included the layman John Bowdler, the American Loyalist, Jonathan Boucher, vicar of Epsom and William Van Mildert, later bishop of Llandaff and Durham. Based in Bath and Salisbury, Daubeny only had the loosest of links with the dominant London high church coterie of the 1810s and 1820s, the 'Hackney Phalanx' (the leader of the 'Phalanx', Joshua Watson, married Daubeny's niece).[201] Stevens, Boucher, and Bowdler acted as candid advisers, sometimes restraining Daubeny's pugnacity and toning down his more intemperate polemic, while recommending his voluminous works to a wider audience; Daubeny conceding that his writings were 'much improved' by Boucher's revisions.[202] Bowdler also planned (but never completed) a work in support of Daubeny's *Guide* and against Sir Richard Hill's anti-Daubnean *Apology for Brotherly Love*.

It is significant that Daubeny never attained the highest offices in the Church, but this does not appear to have reflected any ministerial displeasure over his theological principles. Other orthodox churchmen flourished in the scales of preferment, and Daubeny himself noted in 1818, 'that there was a time, now long since past, when sound church principles did not constitute the high road to ecclesiastical preferment' as they by implication then did.[203] Daubeny, who was appointed Archdeacon of Sarum in 1804, might have been expected to reach the episcopal bench. George III favoured his preferment and Queen Charlotte approved of his

---

Hannah More. In a letter to the editor of *Sir James Stonhouse's letters. By a layman of the established church* (Shrewsbury, 1801), p. 19.

[199] Hannah More to Alexander Knox, 6 January 1805, cited in Stott, *Hannah More*, p. 262.
[200] *Brief confutation of the Rev. Mr Daubeny's strictures on Mr Richard Baxter*, p. 13.
[201] On the 'Hackney Phalanx', see Edward Churton, *Memoir of Joshua Watson* (London, 1861); Alan B. Webster, *Joshua Watson. The story of a layman* (London, 1954); Clive Dewey, *The passing of Barchester: a real life version of Trollope* (London, 1991).
[202] Boucher Papers, B/5/25: Daubeny to Boucher, 19 November 1801.
[203] Charles Daubeny, *On the nature, progress, and consequences of schism; with immediate reference to the present state of religious affairs in this country* (London, 1818), p. 153.

sermons. According to his son-in-law, 'Dr. Daubeny was, on royal suggestion, under three successive administrations, destined for a seat on the Episcopal bench, but that intervening circumstances prevented his promotion'.[204]

These 'intervening circumstances' seem to have been entirely self-induced. It was Daubeny's retiring personality and precarious health (in 1816 he suffered a paralytic stroke which affected his left side and impaired his speech)[205] that led him repeatedly to turn down offers of a bishopric.

Daubeny's polemic is important as an influential voice attempting to foster an 'Anglican identity' in more explicitly 'high church' terms that would come to characterize the Oxford Movement. Consideration of the theological issues thrown up in Daubeny's controversial career helps illustrate a trend away from Protestant cohesion and unity within the later Georgian Church (still paramount in constitutional terms) towards fragmentation and disunion in doctrinal terms. This division, over not merely free will/predestination, but the wider issue of *sola fide*, conversion and baptismal regeneration, was serious because it involved conflicting interpretations of the Church's theological title-deeds—her official formularies, especially the Thirty-Nine Articles. Yet it remains debatable as to whether these divisions were so fundamental as to prove a lack of a secure base for a wider sense of Anglican identity. The high churchman William Palmer of Worcester College later argued that such disputes were not of a different or more basic order than those between Jesuit and Jansenist within the Roman Catholic church.[206] Moderate Anglican Evangelicals of the *Christian Observer* school regarded such disputes as those between Overton and Daubeny as a 'borderer's' war within the same country, not a war to the death between rival theological systems. As John Walsh has wisely concluded, beyond the internecine warfare among extreme elements, a wider Anglican theological consensus survived on core doctrines such as Justification by Faith and the paramountcy of Scripture. The moderate Anglican Evangelical J.W. Middelton repeatedly commended orthodox churchmen, for example referring to their standing 'in the gap' in the 1720s and 1730s—'in that season of latitudinarianism and heterodoxy'.[207] As Anne Stott has observed, the loose spectrum represented by the pre-Tractarian high church party, meant that reasons for supporting or opposing Evangelicals such as Hannah More tended to be personal.[208] This helped isolate Daubeny and other hard-line anti-Evangelicals such as the *Anti-Jacobin Review*. An indication of the degree of loyalty to the notion of an 'Anglican' identity, however disputed, perhaps lay in the relative

---

[204] *Guide to the Church...some account of the author's life and writings*, pp. xlviii-xlix.
[205] Ibid., p. xxxviii.
[206] William Palmer, *A treatise on the Church of Christ* (London, 1842; 3rd edn.), I, p. 195, 244.
[207] Middelton, *Ecclesiastical memoir*, pp. 31-2.
[208] Stott, *Hannah More*, p. 247.

paucity of seceders from the Church of England in this period.[209] Anglican Evangelicals agreed with Daubeny in repudiating 'the latitudinarian sentiments of Archdeacon Paley',[210] and that the separation of the Church of England from Rome did not justify the secession of Dissenters: their language about 'schism' could sometimes be almost as fierce as his own.[211] Hannah More tried to tone down Wilberforce's *Practical View* while in the press, on account of what she called its 'unmitigated High Church-ness'.[212] None the less, the first seeds had been sown of that later more pronounced internal doctrinal division within the established church which would characterize the era of the Oxford Movement.

Daubeny's distinctive and sometimes quirky personality and character, ultimately suggests the limitations of drawing wider implications from a biographical study of one individual. 'Daubenism', however caricatured by opponents who coined the term, in so far as it encapsulated an inherited set of theological and political beliefs and values, was part of a wider religious tradition and lived on to be reinvigorated by the Oxford Movement. Daubeny himself, of course, was unique.

---

[209] A point made to me by Dr. John Walsh. On the establishmentarian majority among Evangelicals, see Carter, *Anglican Evangelicals*, ch. 1.
[210] Hill, *Apology for Brotherly Love*, p. 165.
[211] Anglican Evangelicals, rather than high churchmen, were the chief critics of the so-called 'Western Schism' in 1815. Carter, *Anglican Evangelicals*, p. 106.
[212] Hannah More to William Wilberforce [1797], cited in Scott, *Hannah More*, p. 204.

Chapter 11

Richard Price on Reason and Revolution

H.T. Dickinson

Richard Price (1723-91) gained fame and attracted notoriety because of the range of his intellectual accomplishments and the depth of his commitment to religious and civil liberty. He was well known in Britain, America, and France for his contributions in many fields: as a Dissenting minister, an educationist, a theologian, a moral philosopher, a mathematician, a financial expert, and a best-selling political propagandist commenting upon the American and French revolutions.[1] These activities led him to mix with leading British politicians (particularly Lord Shelburne), to be beloved in Dissenting circles (even by such a noted controversialist as Joseph Priestley), and to correspondence with leading men in France and America (such as Turgot, Condorcet, Mirabeau, Jefferson, Franklin, Rush, John Adams, and Winthrop).[2] While he lived he was offered the citizenship of the United States and of France, and when he died, in 1791, he was mourned by reformers across the Atlantic world as 'the apostle of liberty'. None the less, despite his formidable achievements, he was bitterly attacked for both his religious and his political views. He was criticized for the shallowness and inconsistency of his moral philosophy and his religious opinions, and he was accused of being a political fanatic who inflamed the passions of the multitude and disturbed the public peace. To this day, he is best remembered as the principal British target for Edmund Burke's invective in his *Reflections on the Revolution in France* (1790).

This essay will recognize and pay tribute to only some of Price's many talents, and it will concentrate on his writings on religious and civil liberty.

---

[1] The best study of Price's numerous intellectual accomplishments is D.O. Thomas, *The Honest Mind: The Thought and Work of Richard Price* (Oxford, 1977). The same author has also produced two useful shorter works: *Richard Price 1723-1791* (Cardiff, 1976); *Richard Price and America* (Aberystwyth, 1975). Also of value are Roland Thomas, *Richard Price: Philosopher and Apostle of Liberty* (Oxford, 1924); Carl B. Cone, *Torchbearer of Freedom: The Influence of Richard Price on Eighteenth Century Thought* (Lexington, KY, 1952). There are many useful articles on Price in The *Price-Priestley Newsletter* (1977-80) and its successor journal, *Enlightenment and Dissent* (1982-). See also D.O. Thomas, John Stephens, and P.A.L. Jones (eds.), *A Bibliography of the Works of Richard Price* (Aldershot, 1993).

[2] For Price's extensive and valuable correspondence, see *The Correspondence of Richard Price*, D.O. Thomas and W. Bernard Peach (eds.), 3 vols. (Durham, NC and Cardiff, 1983-94) [hereafter: *CRP*].

In doing so it will endeavour to combat the two main grounds on which Price has been attacked. It will seek to show that, while there were some inconsistencies in his thinking, Price's views were surprisingly coherent. It will also maintain that Price was a reforming Whig and a child of the rational Enlightenment, rather than being an advocate for revolutionary republicanism. Throughout all his many writings, on a wide range of subjects, Price was always inspired by the same ideals: reason, virtue, liberty, self-determination, and self-mastery.

I

Richard Price's moral philosophy has been largely neglected and his achievements have been undervalued. Leslie Stephen's low opinion (and neglect) of his work was a typical nineteenth-century response:

> His philosophical speculations are curious, though they hardly possess high intrinsic merit. His book on morality is the fullest exposition of the theory which it advocates; but the theory was already antiquated; and Price, though he makes a great parade of logical systematization, is a very indistinct writer. It is often difficult to discover his precise drift, and the discovery does not always reward the labour which it exacts.[3]

Since Stephen penned these words only a few scholars have attempted to take Price's philosophical views seriously. In doing so, however, they have shown that Price's opinions were more significant and more coherent than has generally been recognized.[4]

These scholars have shown that Price's moral philosophy was influenced by his reading of Plato, Cudworth, Clarke, and Butler in particular, and by his desire to combat the views of Shaftesbury, Hutcheson, and Hume. He rejected empiricism, scepticism, and utilitarianism (though he was influenced to some extent by all of these).

---

[3] Leslie Stephen, *History of English Thought in the Eighteenth Century*, 2 vols. (London, 1962; Harbinger edn.), II, p. 3.

[4] Richard Price's most important work of moral philosophy, *A Review of the Principal Questions in Morals*, first appeared in 1758. The third, revised edition of 1787 was edited by D.D. Raphael for Oxford University Press in 1948 (reprinted in 1974) and is the edition referred to throughout this chapter. In addition to the major study by D.O. Thomas noted above, the best studies of price as a moral philosopher are Henri Laboucheix, *Richard Price as moral philosopher and political theorist*, translated from the French by Sylvia and David Raphael (Oxford, 1982); W.D. Hudson, *Reason and Right: A Critical Examination of Richard Price's Moral Philosophy* (London, 1970); A.S. Cua, *Reason and Virtue: A Study in the Ethics of Richard Price* (Athens, OH, 1966); Lennart Aqvist, *The Moral Philosophy of Richard Price* (Uppsala, 1960); and Winston H.F. Barnes, 'Richard Price: A Neglected Eighteenth-Century Moralist', *Philosophy* 17 (1942), pp. 159-73.

Above all, he was a rationalist, who believed that knowledge of reality is provided by reason, not by feeling or sensation. He wanted to erect a universal moral system resting primarily on truth and reason, rather than on experience. He believed in the order of creation and in an ultimate cause of all things, and he regarded these as proof of the existence of God. This God is an omnipotent, omniscient, and benevolent being; an infinite and eternal being who constitutes pure reason, infinite truth, and eternal justice: 'He is therefore, wisdom, rather than wise; and reason rather than reasonable...eternity, rather than eternal; immensity rather than immense; and power, rather than powerful.'[5] Since God is eternal truth and justice, good and evil are not merely His will or the judgement of human beings, but exist in the very nature of things. An act is right not because it conforms to the will of mankind, or even to the will of God, but because it is right in itself according to the nature of things, according to the very intelligibility of the moral world, and according to the necessary, eternal and immutable laws which underpin this moral world. Morality is based on truth and reason, it is intelligible to human beings through reason and intuition, and the necessary truths of morality are the axioms of moral society. The nature of God, the nature of eternal truth and the nature of things are one and the same. Moral good is therefore a fundamental obligation in the nature of things. It is a universal, unalterable and necessary law which men ought always to strive to obey.

Price believed that the moral law existed independent of man, but it can be apprehended at once by reason and understanding, by what he called intuition: 'our ideas of *right* and *wrong* are simple ideas, and must therefore be ascribed to some power of immediate perception in the human mind.'[6] Moral good is grasped as a self-evident truth by the immediate power of intuition, as a true perception of the mind—without making use of any process of reasoning. All rational beings, by thought alone, can perceive certain actions to be right or wrong and can discover universally valid rules of action. Human beings have an immediate perception of right and wrong. They know right and wrong, not by revelation, ecclesiastical authority, or social customs, but by rational understanding and they cannot define right and wrong by any other means. Moral distinctions are absolute, immutable, and eternal. There is one standard of right and wrong, which applies to all, and hence the moral law is obligatory. A morally good person does what he or she believes to be right and does it because it is the right thing to do.

Price rejected the utilitarian view that the whole of virtue was to be found in benevolence, in the duty to promote the happiness of others. He claimed that there are five other moral obligations besides benevolence: a duty to God, a duty to oneself as a matter of prudence, a duty of gratitude, a duty to tell the truth, and a duty to pursue justice (particularly in matters

---

[5] Price, *A Review*, p. 290.
[6] Ibid., p. 41.

of property).[7] These duties he regarded as compelling, even when human beings ignore all thought of the effects that such duties might have on society. Indeed, Price insisted that, when considering human actions in the light of these duties, human beings do not take into account distant consequences, but approve or disapprove of such actions immediately. Although a rationalist in principle, Price was quite prudent and pragmatic in the application of his rational principles. He acknowledged that these different moral obligations could come into conflict with one another and hence human beings were often faced with the difficult task of determining which moral obligation should take precedence.[8] He recognized that human beings were often in the dark as to how best to act morally in a complicated situation. Price was a prudent, cautious empiricist in the way he advised human beings to act in such situations. In order to judge how best to act, when different moral obligations were in conflict with one another, Price advised human beings to examine and weigh the respective influences, demands, and consequences of these different moral duties before coming to a decision.

In Price's opinion, human beings will achieve true happiness and universal liberty only by discovering the laws of the moral world and by seeking to apply them. He rejected the utilitarian effort to measure virtue by the consequences of actions and focused instead on the agent's conscience and intentions. He drew a distinction between abstract or absolute virtue, which really applies to an action, and practical or relative virtue, which applies to the agent performing that action.[9] The former term applies to an action which is objectively right. It is what a human agent would perform if he or she sought to act morally while possessed of a complete and accurate knowledge of all the circumstances. Price acknowledged that, while human beings can try to discover what is absolute virtue, their actions cannot be judged by this absolute standard. Only God could ever be in possession of universal and unerring knowledge. Only God could act with infallible judgement in such situations, because only God was omniscient and could know all aspects of a complex situation and could know in advance all the consequences of any possible action. The latter term—practical virtue—Price applied to actions which human beings actually perform, having done their best to understand the situation and having sincerely endeavoured to do what is morally best in the circumstances. If their intentions have been morally good and they have made a sincere effort to understand all the moral obligations required by the situation, then they have acted virtuously, regardless of whether their actions would be wrong when judged by the standards of absolute virtue. Human beings can be praised or blamed only when they achieve or fail to achieve practical virtue. Price, however, was insistent that human beings have a moral duty to seek the truth and to act

---

[7] Ibid., pp. 138-64.
[8] Ibid., pp. 166-70.
[9] Ibid., pp. 177-8.

upon it when it is found. He always had an optimistic view of the inherent ability of the rational faculty to direct human action along the right moral lines, though he did recognize human weakness and limitations. He believed that the general principles of morality can be perceived with perfect clearness if sufficient effort is made. In difficult circumstances and complex situations human beings have to use their rational judgement to weigh the conflicting moral principles involved. This act of moral judgement is still the function of intuitive knowledge, not the result of feeling or sense perception.

Once human beings perceive a moral rule and a moral obligation by the exercise of reason and understanding, then, Price argued, they are absolutely and strictly obliged to follow that rule. They are morally bound to act in conformity with it. If they do not, they are doing violence to their reason, to their nature, and to their dignity as rational human beings. No rational agent was devoid of all moral judgement or ever acted without applying reason. To Price, it was self-evident that reasonable beings would choose to do what is right and would try to abstain from what they knew to be wrong. Reason should govern their conduct and should seek to direct their passions. But, since no one is infallible or omniscient, he or she is not always able to judge correctly what is the right course of action to take in a complex situation. This does not mean, however, that anyone can then decide to renounce the moral responsibility God has imposed. Everyone must do his or her honest best to understand a situation and to choose the most moral course of action to take. In doing so, he or she must not rely uncritically on accepted custom or received opinion. No political or ecclesiastical authority should dictate how anyone should act, and so everyone must be prepared to question authority, prejudice, partiality, and selfishness. Their judgement must rest on their own free choice, reached following every effort to understand the complexity of the situation and to recognize the various moral issues involved. Fallible human beings can act only to the best of their knowledge, and in accordance with sincere good intentions to act in a moral fashion. They must exercise their reason, liberty, and free will. Intellectual gestation must then be followed by action. Every person must always strive to do 'what, according to his best judgement, he is persuaded to be the will of God'.[10] Moral principles can be weakened by the passions, but it is a moral obligation to seek to be morally strong. Human beings are prone to error, but they are also capable of limitless discovery and infinite improvement. As speculative knowledge expands, so does human understanding of moral good. Human beings are infinitely perfectible, though they could never reach absolute perfection.

Price believed that human beings were accountable for their moral actions only when these originate from within and not from without: 'Our own determinations alone are, most properly, our actions. These alone we have absolute power over, and are responsible for.'[11] If human beings are compelled by external forces or superior authorities to act in a certain way,

---

[10] Ibid., p. 180.
[11] Ibid., pp. 184-5.

then, Price claimed, they are not free agents able to choose how to act. Hence their actions are not moral actions for which they can be held responsible: 'it is hard to say what virtue and vice, commendation and blame mean, if they do not suppose *agency*, free choice, and an absolute dominion over our resolutions'.[12] Price therefore believed that liberty—both religious and civil liberty—were essential if human beings were to perform moral actions and to live as the free agents God had created. He also claimed that intelligence was an essential requirement of moral action because there could be no moral action where the agent of that action had no perception of good and evil. Those with a low level of rationality—such as idiots and very young children—cannot be regarded as moral agents and cannot be held fully responsible for their actions. They deserve neither praise nor blame.

II

Richard Price belonged to a small religious minority that strove in vain throughout his life to secure a greater measure of religious toleration than the established church and its supporters were prepared to concede. Despite Price's best efforts, the Church of England clung to its many privileges. Even within the Rational Dissenting minority Price held views that were not widely shared. Indeed, one of his closest acquaintances, Joseph Priestley, who was a fellow Unitarian, but a Socinian rather than an Arian, waged a prolonged controversy in print, seeking to refute Price's religious opinions. After years of controversy, Priestley was confident that he had had the better of the dispute and he thought that Price's views were not shared by any other Dissenting minister.[13] A scrutiny of Price's religious views, however, suggests that they were based on his moral philosophy, were expressed with charity and candour, and are fully deserving of respect.

Price's religious views were consistent with his moral philosophy and his emphasis on reason. He believed that human beings should believe only what was acceptable to their own understanding and that they are not helpless creatures, but have the ability to command events. They possess free will and can shape their own destiny, but this freedom carries with it an awesome responsibility. They have been given a commission by God, which they can refuse or can endeavour to fulfil. There may be different kinds of happiness that they can pursue, but the only true happiness, the 'rightest happiness', is that of the commission fulfilled. True virtue is possible only because human beings are free to choose evil. What commends human beings to God is not the correctness of their beliefs so much as the honesty with which they hold them. Sincere and diligent

---

[12] Ibid., p. 182.
[13] *CRP*, III, p. 158.

enquirers, who try but fail to free themselves from error, are much more likely to win God's approval than those whose laziness has not prevented them from holding true beliefs. Much in religion, as in scientific and speculative knowledge generally, is obscure. The best that human beings can do is to inform their conscience and act accordingly. No one is sufficiently virtuous to merit eternal life because of his or her own good works: 'perfection is above human capacity, and cannot be the condition of our acceptance [i.e., salvation]. All that is necessary is, not *innocence*, but *integrity* of character; not *sinless*, but *true* virtue'.[14] While it is God's grace that ultimately saves human beings, each and every rational being should act in the belief that he or she can help to achieve salvation by living a virtuous life: 'We have before us the prospect of a *blessed immortality* which we cannot lose, but through our own fault'.[15] Price never claimed that the joyous prospects of a future state were guaranteed, but he generally maintained that God can be relied upon to redress the injustices of life on earth by securing justice for the virtuous in another world. In any future state, present inequalities and injustices will be set right and a suitable distinction made between the virtuous and the sinful. Price thought it probable that the latter would be annihilated, not condemned to everlasting torment and misery, but 'all the useful and virtuous shall meet in a better country, beyond the grave'.[16]

Price was a strong believer in both general and particular Providence, accepting that God created human beings for a purpose, used them as His instruments and constantly sustained and supervised His creation.[17] Human beings should be conscious of these facts and should act to achieve God's purposes. Human beings had a moral obligation to create the earthly conditions that would serve God's purposes and to pave the way for the millennium. At times he intimated that Providence was at work in both the American and the French revolutions. Unlike his friend and fellow Dissenter, Joseph Priestley, however, he was not a millenarian who expected the fairly imminent Second Coming of Christ. Rather he was a millennialist of the kind who believed that the millennium would precede Christ's Second Coming and would inaugurate a lengthy time of gradual improvement prior to the rule of Christ.[18]

Price described his personal religious beliefs as 'not a sour or enthusiastical religion but a rational and catholic religion, a religion free from bigotry, superstition, and uncharitableness, and that shows itself in all good works and amiable qualities as well as in the discharge of the duties

---

[14] Ibid., I, p. 48.
[15] Richard Price, *Four Dissertations* (reprint of 1768 edition, Bristol, 1990), p. 122 [hereafter: *Four Dissertations*].
[16] *CRP*, III, p. 304.
[17] *Four Dissertations*, pp. 5, 71.
[18] *Richard Price: Political Writings*, edited by D.O. Thomas (Cambridge, 1991), pp. xi-xii [hereafter: *Political Writings*]. See also Jack Fruchtman, Jr., *The Apocalyptic Politics of Richard Price and Joseph Priestley: A Study in Late Eighteenth-Century English Republican Millennialism* (Philadelphia, PA, 1983).

of devotion'.[19] He was a Unitarian and an Arian: 'I am not [to be] understood to hold that he [Christ] is *almost equal to the supreme God*, a sentiment at which I shudder, and which probably no *Arian* now holds'.[20] God alone is the one supreme being and the only object worthy of religious worship. Price regarded Christ as an exceptional human being, of pre-existent dignity, but not as divine and not as God. Christ was the son of God in the sense that all men are the sons of God. He was a being with superior powers and more excellent virtues, but he was not the saviour of the whole universe and his moral reign did not extend to all the many worlds that Price believed existed throughout creation. Christ was a guide and master, but man could grow continually nearer to him as his own reason, knowledge and virtues improved.

In Price's view God is ultimately unknowable and unfathomable. Human beings have limited faculties and human civilization in this world is still young and man has so far made only limited progress in knowledge of the material world and of God. Price was profoundly sceptical about mankind's present ability to discover the true purposes of God or the absolute truth about religious doctrines, creeds, and dogma. Since human beings cannot totally eliminate error and ignorance, they should be compassionate and charitable about different religious views. Moreover, the progress of knowledge in morality, religion, and science can advance only if human beings are free to exercise their reason. They must be free to pursue, without fear, what they think is true and just. No state therefore can have a legitimate right to interfere in the realm of ideas or religion. Civil government exists to protect property and to preserve the peace of society, not to support a particular version of the truth or to care for human souls. The state cannot legitimately prescribe or proscribe particular religious beliefs and practices, or give privileges to one sect and impose penalties on another. Price was therefore profoundly opposed to all religious establishments.[21] No one—not secular rulers, bishops nor ordinary clergy—could exercise dominion over the religious beliefs of others. He regularly supported the campaigns of the Protestant Dissenters to extend the bounds of religious toleration and to repeal the Test and Corporation Acts. Indeed, he believed that all human beings should be free to worship God as they saw fit, and he was ready to extend toleration to Catholics, Jews, and Muslims. Indeed, he wanted more than just toleration for all. He advocated a complete separation of church and state—in Britain, America, and France—and the removal of all privileges and penalties imposed on particular religious groups by the state. No human being and no church or sect possessed the monopoly of truth and therefore if the state intervened in religion it would just impose error or superstition. Religious tests would limit the rights of honest people and encourage

---

[19] Quoted in D.O. Thomas, *Richard Price*, p. 159.
[20] *CRP*, III, p. 177.
[21] *Political Writings*, pp. 4-5.

others to be hypocrites. Christianity, in particular, did not need state support. It would prevail because it was true.

While Price maintained that no civil government should require subjects to comply with a particular form of worship or raise one religious group above another, he did believe that all human beings had a clear duty to worship God and he did recognize the usefulness of religion in making subjects into good citizens:

> When a people become generally irreligious and impious, they become ungovernable, untractable, ready for every evil work, and ripe for misery and destruction. Religion, to say the least of it, is a most useful engine of state, and one of the best supports of public order.[22]

In Price's opinion religious freedom in particular and freedom of enquiry in general would bring human enlightenment and progress, and would increase and improve the very dignity of man. He admitted that man was ignorant, but he was very optimistic about his ability to improve his knowledge. A wise and gradual education would render the mind free and unfettered, and would teach men to be deliberate and prudent: 'Ignorance is the parent of bigotry, intolerance, persecution and slavery. Inform and instruct mankind, and these evils will be excluded'.[23] Human beings, Price believed, have been on earth but a short time and they have already made great advances from the savage state. Allowed the free exercise of their reason, they would make continuous, steady, and indefinite progress. Human beings 'are capable of existing in a higher state. They are capable of an *endless* future improvement in knowledge and happiness'.[24] Price himself spent much of his life educating himself and promoting the education of many young men. He helped found a Dissenting Academy, promoted the welfare of other educational establishments, and took a great interest in the education of the young. The best education would avoid the vile dogmatism that was so prevalent in the world and would seek to inculcate the love of virtue and to encourage ardent benevolence, while making all students conscious of the fallibility of the human understanding.[25] Price always maintained that students should not be told what to believe, but advised on how to learn for themselves:

> The end of education is to direct the powers of the mind in unfolding themselves and to assist them in gaining their just bent and force. And, in order to do this, its business should be to teach how to think, rather than what to think, or to lead into the best way of searching for truth, rather than to instruct in truth itself.[26]

---

[22] *Four Dissertations*, pp. 266-7.
[23] *Political Writings*, p. 182.
[24] *Four Dissertations*, pp. 151-2 note.
[25] *Political Writings*, p. 169.
[26] Ibid., p. 137.

III

Price's moral philosophy, his emphasis on reason, and his commitment to religious liberty, all greatly influenced his political opinions and his views on liberty. If a person has a duty to worship God according to his conscience, he must possess the freedom to do so. It was part of the dignity of man (Price never discussed the political rights of women) that he was not under the will or direction of another. If a man has a moral responsibility for the state of the society in which he lives, he must have the right to participate in the processes of government. There are, in Price's opinion, four kinds of liberty. These are: physical liberty (which allowed man to be the author of his own actions), moral liberty (which allowed man to follow his own conscience), religious liberty (which allowed man to follow God's will), and civil liberty (which allowed civil society to decide its own political institutions).[27] He believed that by careful thought every man can determine for himself the principles that should govern the distribution of civil liberty and political rights. God does not require man to establish a particular form of government, but delegates to him the responsibility for creating civil society and establishing a particular form of civil government suited to his circumstances. No legitimate form of civil government can be based on absolute or arbitrary authority or be created by force or conquest. Only free governments are consistent with the natural equality of mankind.[28] Civil government is an institution erected for the benefit of the people and hence should seek to promote the liberties of the community.[29] The aim of civil government is to obtain security for civil society—to preserve the life, liberty, and property of all—and to assure the physical, moral, and religious liberties of all members of the community.[30] These political ends could be achieved only if civil society is self-governing and the largest number of responsible individuals participated in its government. The ultimate aim is justice for the members of civil society and this can be obtained only if there is a political power sufficiently strong and sufficiently enlightened to curb the powerful and to protect the weak.

Price undoubtedly took many of his political ideas from John Locke. He rejected absolute and arbitrary government and the principles of non-resistance and passive obedience. He believed that all men possessed natural rights to their life, liberty, and property and that civil governments were erected to preserve these natural rights. The only legitimate form of government is based on consent and is established by contract:

> Mankind came with this right [of equality or independence] from the hands of their maker. But all governments which are not free are totally inconsistent with it. They imply that there are some of mankind who are born with an

---

[27] Ibid., pp. 21-3.
[28] Ibid., p. 85.
[29] Ibid., p. 64.
[30] Ibid., p. 109.

inherent right of dominion, and the rest are born under an obligation to subjection...[31]

The people are the ultimate source of sovereignty and all magistrates and legislators are but trustees acting on behalf of the sovereign people. The legitimate role of the state is limited: it exists primarily to protect the individual's right to life, liberty, and property. Those in positions of authority must govern by the rule of law and must apply the same laws equally to all members of society. The people only delegate authority to those in power and they can recover their sovereign authority if governors betray their trust: 'without all doubt, it is the choice of the people that makes civil governors. The people are the spring of all civil power and they have a right to modify it as they please'.[32] Even resistance by force is justified when governors seriously abuse the power entrusted to them. Like John Locke, however, Price maintained that only gross oppression was likely to provoke the people to take up arms against their governors:

> Mankind are naturally disposed to continue in subjection to that mode of government, be it what it will, under which they have been born and educated. Nothing rouses them into resistance but gross abuse or some particular oppression out of the road to which they have been used.[33]

This conviction did not lead Price, however, to believe that the people should take an interest in politics only when there was a serious abuse of power by their governors. Governors had always to be scrutinized in their exercise of power: 'There is nothing that requires more to be watched than power'.[34] The people therefore could only defend their natural rights and preserve their civil liberties by remaining vigilant: 'The safety of a free people depends entirely on their maintaining a constant and suspicious vigilance, and as soon as they cease to be quick at taking alarms, they are undone'.[35]

Price regularly insisted that he was an old-style Whig who supported the Glorious Revolution and the Hanoverian succession. In his opinion, the Glorious Revolution of 1688-89 enshrined the principles of liberty in the British constitution. The Revolution Settlement ensured:

> First, the right of liberty of conscience in religious matters. Secondly, the right to resist power when abused. And, Thirdly, the right to chuse our own governors, to cashier them for misconduct, and to frame a government for ourselves.[36]

---

[31] Ibid., p. 86.
[32] Ibid., p. 88.
[33] Ibid., p. 50. See also p. 92.
[34] Ibid., p. 30.
[35] Ibid., p. 109.
[36] Ibid., pp. 189-90.

It was this apparently radical interpretation of the Glorious Revolution—particularly as Price went on to insist that the Glorious Revolution had not restored a fair and equal system of representation—that alarmed Edmund Burke. It provoked Burke to write both his *Reflections on the Revolution in France* and *An Appeal from the New to the Old Whigs* in order to rebut this interpretation of the Glorious Revolution. It also led to the charge that Price was a democrat, a republican, and even a revolutionary. A close reading of his political writings, however, does not justify this claim.[37] Price always expressed his respect for the spirit and principles of Britain's mixed government and balanced constitution: 'so far am I from preferring a government purely republican, that I look upon our constitution of government as better adapted than any other to this country, and in theory excellent'.[38] He went on to deny that the Dissenters in general wished to exchange Britain's present mixed government—combining monarchical, aristocratic, and democratic elements through the institutions of King, House of Lords, and House of Commons — for a pure democracy:

> I know not *one* individual among them, who would not tremble at the thought of changing into a Democracy, our mixed form of government, or who has any other wish with regard to it, than to restore it to purity and vigour, by removing the defects in our representation, and establishing that independence of the three states on one another, in which its essence consists.[39]

Price regularly stressed that he preferred incremental change made by wise and prudent citizens in a rational and deliberate manner. For him revolution was an act of last resort by a people driven by oppression to take desperate measures. He was never a radical in the mould of Thomas Paine or a political partisan or organizer like John Cartwright. He was a reformer who sought change by evolutionary means wherever this was possible. His reforming zeal was almost always tempered by caution and prudence, though he did have a higher regard than most Whigs for the principle of self-government and the liberties of the subject. He did believe passionately that the enjoyment of liberty was part of the dignity of man, but this did not encourage him to ignore the need for loyalty or to advocate drastic alterations to the British constitution. He advised virtuous subjects not to despise their government or to speak ill of their rulers, but to assist them where possible.[40] He believed that the British constitution would be admirable if only crown influence over Parliament was reduced and the system of representation was reformed: 'I have repeatedly declared my

---

[37] See, in particular, D.O. Thomas, 'Neither republican nor democrat', *The Price-Priestley Newsletter* 1 (1977), pp. 49-60, and idem, 'Was Richard Price a Radical?' in Chris Williams (ed.), *Richard Price and the Atlantic Revolution* (Bridgend, 1991), pp. 58-72.
[38] *Political Writings*, pp. 164-5.
[39] Ibid., p. 165, note 19.
[40] Ibid., p. 187.

admiration of such a constitution as our own would be, were the House of Commons a fair representation of the kingdom and under no undue influence.'[41] Price was certainly an advocate of abstract natural rights, but, in practice, he placed limits on the practical exercise of these inalienable natural rights. In his moral philosophy Price recognized that different moral obligations could conflict in practice and in his political writings he also revealed that different duties might conflict with one another and he concluded that something might be desirable in theory, but might not be practicable. Price made a distinction between a free government and the best form of government. The first was more easily obtained.[42] Moreover, while he laid great stress on individual liberty, he did not regard liberty as the sole requirement for creating a stable and effective government. The principle of liberty did not always outweigh the principle of order and stability:

> Liberty, though the most essential requisite in government, is not the only one. Wisdom, union, dispatch, secrecy, and vigour are likewise requisite, and that is the best form of government which best unites all these qualities or which, to an equal and perfect liberty adds the greatest wisdom in deliberating and resolving, and the greatest union, force and expedition in executing.[43]

Price admired the American Revolution in part because it abolished monarchy and aristocracy, but this does not mean he supported the idea of establishing republican government in all countries. He believed that republicanism suited America because there was no established aristocracy, there were few poor men, and there were large numbers of freeholders and yeoman farmers in the middle ranks of society.[44] He acknowledged that this was not the case in France.[45] He died before republicanism was even thought about in France, and there is no indication that he thought it was impossible to establish a free government under the Bourbon monarchy. At home, he regarded Britain's mixed government and balanced constitution as the form of government best suited to the British people and to British traditions. He never advocated the abolition of monarchy or aristocracy, but rather accepted that both were inevitable given the social and economic distinctions that had long existed. A republican government would not suit Britain, because 'Britain, in particular, consists too much of the high and the low, (*of scum* and *dregs*) to admit of it'.[46] The monarch, however, he regarded as the servant of the people, not their master, and he regularly argued that the monarch's authority was limited by law, custom, and tradition: 'A king, in particular, is only the first executive officer, the creature of the law, and as much

---

[41] Ibid., p. 16.
[42] Ibid., pp. 105-6, 109.
[43] Ibid., pp. 79-80.
[44] Ibid., pp. 56, 144-5.
[45] *CRP*, III, p. 218.
[46] *Political Writings*, p.146, note. 16.

accountable to the law as the meanest peasant'.[47] What Price consistently feared, however, was that, while the monarch's prerogative powers had been limited by the Glorious Revolution, his powers of patronage had been steadily increasing ever since. The size of the executive, the scale of the National Debt, the strength of the standing army, and the pursuit of luxury had all significantly increased during the eighteenth century. These developments placed enormous patronage in the hands of the executive and enabled the crown and its agents to distribute honours, places, and contracts that could influence the composition of, and the decisions reached by, both houses of Parliament. He rightly feared that crown influence was endangering the independence of Parliament and the liberties of the people: 'it became the policy of men in power, impatient of its [i.e., Parliament's] control, to destroy its efficiency in the constitution by subjecting it to undue influence.'[48] If this development were not halted, then Price feared that Britain's cherished constitution would soon become a hollow sham:

> The time may come...[w]hen the influence of the crown, strengthened by luxury and an universal profligacy of manners, will have tainted every heart, broken down every fence of liberty, and rendered us a nation of tame and contented vassals: when a general election will be nothing but a general auction of boroughs; and, when the Parliament...will be degenerated into a body of sycophants, dependent and venal, always ready to confirm any measures, and little more than a public court for registering royal edicts.[49]

Price was a firm believer in personal liberty and he believed that civil government should be accountable to the people at large. He also believed that all social and economic distinctions among men were artificial and temporary, and he wanted them to be measured by their personal abilities, merits, and worth, not according to their birth or inheritance. He welcomed the rejection of aristocracy in newly independent America, and he approved of the union of the three estates of the French States General into a single body in order to achieve a measure of reform in France in 1789. These views, however, did not lead him to urge the abolition of aristocracy or the House of Lords in Britain. Price did not have a visceral hostility to aristocracy in the way that Paine did; he accepted their social superiority, he admired the Earl of Chatham, for example, and he was on excellent personal terms with Lord Shelburne over many years. He also shared with John Adams[50] a fear that a unicameral legislature might give too much power to the popular will and might not give due weight to powerful social and economic interests in the state:

> In order to form the most perfect constitution of government, there may be the best reasons for joining to such a body of representatives [as the House of

---

[47] Ibid., p. 88.
[48] Manuscript source quoted in Thomas, *The Honest Mind*, p. 200.
[49] *Political Writings*, pp. 42-3.
[50] *CRP*, III, p. 272.

Commons] an hereditary council consisting of men of the first rank in the state...This will form useful checks in a legislature and contribute to give it vigour, union, and dispatch, without infringing liberty...[51]

None the less, there is abundant evidence in Price's political writings and in his correspondence that he believed that Britain's free constitution required the House of Commons to be representative of the people at large and to act as the essential bulwark of their civil and religious liberties. What deeply concerned him were two related fears: that the House of Commons was losing its political independence as more of its members succumbed to crown influence and that the system of representation was so inadequate that it did not represent the true interests of the people. It was the former fear that led Price to be concerned with the growth of crown patronage and the corrupting effects of luxury, a huge and insupportable National Debt, and a mercenary standing army. He was always deeply concerned about the size of the National Debt and he was fearful of its ability to corrupt the individual and to undermine the independence of Parliament. He feared that Britain's enormous National Debt would lead not only to national bankruptcy, but would allow power to accumulate in too few hands.[52] He was not content to see the National Debt remain as a perpetual burden, but devised various schemes, such as his famous Sinking Fund, as the means of eventually paying off this vast public debt.[53] Price also condemned stockjobbing practices, feared the spread of luxury in a commercial society, regarded large towns as a threat to civilization, and praised the lifestyle of the hardworking farmer. On several occasions he warned against the danger of a nation relying upon a standing army for the defence of its liberties: 'They are everywhere the grand supports of arbitrary power, and the chief causes of the depression of mankind.'[54] He believed that liberty was best defended by a citizen militia: 'No wise people will trust their defence out of their own hands, or consent to hold their rights at the mercy of armed *slaves*'.[55]

Price was even more insistent, however, that the liberties of the people required a reform of the system of representation to ensure that the House of Commons was accountable to the people. In his opinion, there were too few voters in total and too many of these were ready to sell their votes to the government or to aristocratic patrons. Liberty could not be defended while the system of representation remained so inadequate:

---

[51] *Political Writings*, pp. 26-7.
[52] See, for example, *CRP*, I, p. 166; II, pp. 35, 38; and *Political Writings*, pp. 60-63, 98.
[53] *Political Writings*, pp. 120-1; *CRP*, II, pp. 330-33, 334-7; Price, *Observations on Reversionary Payments* (London, 1771); and idem, *An Appeal to the Public on the Subject of the National Debt* (London, 1772).
[54] *Political Writings*, p. 123.
[55] Ibid.

if a state is so sunk that the majority of its representatives are elected by a handful of the meanest persons in it, whose votes are always paid for...it will be an abuse of language to say that the state possesses liberty.[56]

On another occasion, Price lamented that, while there were nearly six million people in Britain, a mere '5723 persons, most of them the lowest of the people elect one half of the *House of Commons*; and 364 votes chuse a ninth part.'[57] When he compared the British political situation with that of America and France, Price certainly did become increasingly concerned about the need to widen the system of representation in Britain:

> ...the most important instance of the imperfect state in which the [Glorious] Revolution left our constitution, is the inequality of our representation. I think, indeed, this defect in our constitution so gross and so palpable, as to make it excellent chiefly in form and theory...When the representation is fair and equal,...a kingdom may be said to govern itself, and consequently to possess true liberty.[58]

When Christopher Wyvill led a campaign in the early 1780s to create a hundred new county seats, Price insisted that this reform did not go far enough. In his view, the most important change needed in the distribution of seats was the abolition of the numerous rotten boroughs whose tiny electorates were under the control of the Treasury and the Admiralty: 'till this can be procured, we deceive ourselves when we think ourselves free; the first requisite to Constitutional Liberty being a fair and equal representation.'[59]

Some British reformers had begun from the later 1770s to advocate a range of radical reforms of Parliament, including the extension of the franchise to all adult males. Price believed in natural rights and advocated some of the measures proposed by these reformers— such as more frequent general elections, the abolition of the small rotten boroughs with few electors, and the right of the voters to instruct their MPs about how to cast their votes.[60] But he did not conclude that all men had a right to vote in parliamentary elections. He was conscious that many men were too poor, too ignorant, and too dependent to be trusted with the franchise. He believed that the vote needed to be exercised responsibly and he was convinced that this therefore required voters to have a level of education and a measure of economic security in order to be independent of those who might seek to persuade or bribe them. Despite the fears of his critics, Price balanced the claims of liberty with those of prudence. Like Burke, he was aware that forms of government ought to conform to the realities of a particular society. He feared anarchy and mob rule, and he readily conceded that, since men have different levels of knowledge, wealth, and

---

[56] Ibid., pp. 25-6.
[57] Ibid., pp. 25-6, note 2.
[58] Ibid., p. 23.
[59] CRP, II, p. 158.
[60] Ibid., II, pp. 190-91; *Political Writings*, pp. 25, 79, 123.

social status, they cannot all expect to play an equal role in public affairs. He was therefore willing to restrict the franchise to all rational men who were capable of exercising independent judgement. Any man desirous of participating in public affairs must be well-informed about morality and about the circumstances of affairs. He must be responsible for himself and for his society, and he must uphold the dignity of human nature and devote himself to the welfare of his fellow men. Political rights were only a first step to discharging moral duties and assuming philanthropic responsibilities.[61]

Price, while regularly stressing the need for a more equal representation, was never very precise about which British citizens should actually possess the vote. He wrote mostly about the human qualities necessary to exercise the franchise responsibly, rather than the precise property qualifications that should be required of an elector able to vote in the counties or the boroughs. He does appear to have accepted that the franchise could not—at least at present—be exercised responsibly by the very poor and he obviously opposed it being in the hands of a few rich men. The vast majority of the House of Commons, he lamented, was chosen 'not by the people...[but] by a few Grandees and Beggars'.[62] Who he regarded as 'the people', however, is by no means clear. He certainly seems to have put great faith in the abilities of the middling sort, particularly the freeholders and the yeoman farmers of the rural areas and the thoughtful men of education in the boroughs. Wisdom and goodness, he claimed, are 'found chiefly in middle ranks of life and among the contemplative and philosophical who decline public employments and look down with pity on the scramble for power among mankind and the restlessness and misery of ambition'.[63] When asked for advice about what reforms should be instituted in Ireland, he commented on the situation with regard to the franchise at home:

> In England I have wished, that the friends of reformation had confined their views at present to the extension of the right of voting to Copyholders, and Leaseholders; and the substitution of a hundred knights for counties in the room of a hundred members for boroughs. This, though in theory unspeakably too little, would have been a very important reform; and less than this, I have not thought much contending for.[64]

IV

Price wrote three of his major works directly on the American Revolution: *Observations on the Nature of Civil Liberty* (1776), *Additional Observations on*

---

[61] CRP, II, p. 188.
[62] Ibid., II, p. 192.
[63] Political Writings, p. 87.
[64] CRP, II, p. 189.

the *Nature and Value of Civil Liberty, and the War with America* (1777), and *Observations on the Importance of the American Revolution and the Means of making it a Benefit to the World* (1784). These thoroughly condemned the policies of successive British governments and fully sympathized with the American cause. They earned him the gratitude of the Americans, who invited him to come to America to advise the new republic on how best to cope with its National Debt, but they also brought him much criticism from conservative writers within Britain. Price, however, did not welcome the separation of the American colonies from Britain and he did not approve of all aspects of the new state created across the Atlantic.

Price rejected the principal constitutional claim made by British governments and parliaments during the American crisis:

> Nothing...can be more absurd than the doctrine which some have taught with respect to the omnipotence of parliaments. They possess no power beyond the limits of the trust for the execution of which they were formed...All delegated power must be subordinate and limited. If omnipotence can, with any sense, be ascribed to a legislature, it must be lodged where all legislative authority originates; that is, in the people. For their sakes government is instituted, and theirs is the only real omnipotence.[65]

Price attacked the Stamp Act of 1765, the Declaratory Act of 1766, the Townshend Duties of 1768, and the Coercive or Intolerable Acts of 1774, including the Quebec Act.[66] It was these policies which he believed had eventually driven the colonies into armed resistance. He supported the charter rights of the colonists[67] and accepted the colonists' claim of 'no taxation without representation':

> ...no one community can have any power over the property or legislation of another community which is not incorporated with it by a just and adequate representation...a country that is subject to the legislature of another country in which it has no voice, and over which it has no controul, cannot be said to be governed by its own will. Such a country, therefore, is in a state of slavery.[68]

Price, however, was not opposed to an empire under the authority of a supreme executive power, provided it was united by bonds of interest and affection. What he opposed was an empire in which one part could exercise arbitrary authority over another part. He believed that all nations or distinct communities, like all individuals, had the natural, God-given right to liberty and self-determination: 'all the nations now in the world who...are subject to arbitrary power, have a right to emancipate themselves as soon as they can'.[69] But he hoped that the British empire might be so well constructed that the American colonies would not regard

---

[65] *Political Writings*, pp. 28-9.
[66] Ibid., pp. 37, 43, 51-3.
[67] Ibid., p. 40.
[68] Ibid., p. 30.
[69] Ibid., p. 33.

themselves as subject to an arbitrary power and would therefore not seek complete separation from Britain. In an interesting aside, when he was writing principally about the American crisis, Price suggested that all the states in Europe should be independent so far as their internal affairs were concerned. In order to avoid conflict with each other, however, each might elect representatives to a Senate which would manage to act as an arbiter or umpire in all disputes between these different states. There seems little doubt that Price hoped this suggestion might provide a model for a federal British empire, with the American colonies being in control of their internal affairs but with a Senate elected by Britain and the colonies to arbitrate between them in any dispute.[70] Price never explained in detail how this Senate would be elected, how many representatives each state (or part of the empire) would choose or how its authority would be exercised and implemented. In the event, of course, the British government refused to abandon its claim to the sovereign authority of the Westminster Parliament over the whole British empire, while the colonists refused to acknowledge this authority and resisted it by force of arms. Given this situation, Price undoubtedly sided with the rebellious colonies and urged Britain to concede American independence without recourse to war. He was convinced that war should be avoided at all costs.

Price undoubtedly regarded the American crisis as a tragedy that could have been avoided if the British government had shown greater wisdom and moderation. Price condemned government policy as an unjust desire to extend British power and he regarded war with the American colonies as an unmitigated disaster: 'this is a contest from which no advantages can possibly be derived'.[71] He believed that the Americans would prove to be a more formidable adversary than the British government expected, because the Americans were brave, virtuous, and growing fast both numerically and economically; but he was still concerned that they might suffer heavily in a protracted conflict.[72] For the colonies the war was an enormous risk and defeat could bring utter disaster and the loss of liberty. As early as 1776, however, Price feared that France would join the war against Britain and defeat would follow.[73] The British would not be able to find sufficient troops or enough money to afford a prolonged contest that would ruin the nation's credit, increase taxation and undermine her own civil liberties. War would enormously increase Britain's National Debt, victory would prove elusive and even impossible, and British liberties would be endangered whether British arms prevailed or not.

Price was a staunch defender of American rights and liberties, but he had no wish to see a permanent breach between Britain and the American colonies. Once he accepted that the stark choice was between American independence and an American surrender to parliamentary sovereignty, however, he chose the former. As early as March 1778 he was advising his

---

[70] Ibid., pp. 24-5.
[71] Ibid., p. 47.
[72] Ibid., pp. 47-9, 68; CRP, I, pp. 166, 187, 207.
[73] Ibid., I, pp. 249-50.

friend and patron, Lord Shelburne, that Parliament should recognize the independence of the rebellious colonies, even though he knew that Shelburne opposed such a concession.[74] He welcomed American independence once it was conceded in 1783 and he regularly protested thereafter at the failure of the British to restore good relations with these former colonies. He was convinced that what really mattered was good commercial and human relations between Britain and the United States of America and he often expressed disappointment that British resentment hindered efforts to restore these commercial links to their former strength.[75] There was no question but that in his mind the Americans remained brethren to be warmly embraced.

Before the War of American Independence even began, Price declared: 'I consider America as an asylum for the friends of liberty here, which it would be a calamity to lose.'[76] He frequently made the same point in the years to follow.[77] After the Americans had gained their independence, Price wrote optimistically:

> I see the revolution in favour of universal liberty which has taken place in America, a revolution which opens a new prospect in human affairs and begins a new aera in the history of mankind...next to the introduction of Christianity among mankind, the American Revolution may prove the most important step in the progressive course of improvement.[78]

He praised America as the most liberal society that the world had yet known and he was delighted that the new republic had neither an aristocracy nor a state church. He was particularly pleased that America had rejected religious bigotry, abolished religious tests for civil offices, extended religious liberty and defended the right of free discussion and speculative enquiry.[79] None the less, he was concerned about several problems that the new republic had still to face. He warned about the dangers of a large National Debt, about the growth of luxury, venality, and corruption, and about the prospect of an increasingly unequal distribution of wealth if America became a successful commercial economy. He urged the Americans to strive to retain their rural hardiness and to avoid concentrating too much wealth in too few hands.[80] He also advised the Americans to reject a standing army and to rely for their defence on a citizen militia.[81] Recognizing the expansionist energy in American society, he wished to see it channelled into a moral philosophy of action, but action in defence of civil and religious liberty.

---

[74] Ibid., I, pp. 274-5.
[75] Ibid., II, pp. 233, 291-2.
[76] Ibid., I, p. 189.
[77] Ibid., I, pp. 164, 189; II, pp. 35, 36, 38, 185; III, pp. 151; and *Political Writings*, p. 117.
[78] *Political Writings*, pp. 117-19.
[79] Ibid., pp. 124-36.
[80] Ibid., pp. 120-21, 143-9.
[81] Ibid., p. 123.

Price was also concerned that the various American states might not long remain united and that one of the stronger states might impose its authority on the smaller states by force of arms. As early as 1784 he suggested that the powers of Congress should be extended,[82] and he was most interested to note the discussions in America that led to the creation of the new Federal Constitution. He was pleased to see a stronger federal union and the powers of Congress extended and he welcomed the adoption of a bi-cameral legislature.[83] The one aspect of the new republic that he found reprehensible, however, was the retention of slavery. He advised the new republic to emancipate the slaves: 'The negro trade cannot be censured in language too severe. It is a traffic which…is shocking to humanity, cruel, wicked and diabolical'.[84] Until slavery was abolished the Americans 'will not appear they deserve the liberty for which they have been contending'.[85] He did however acknowledge that this would not be easy and it might take time to change men's minds:

> I am sensible, however, that this is a work which they cannot accomplish at once. The emancipation of the negroes must, I suppose, be left in some measure to be the effect of time and manners.[86]

While stressing how much the Americans had done for the cause of liberty, however, he could not refrain from pointing out to the Americans: 'I rejoice that on this occasion I can recommend to them the example of my own country. In Britain, a negro becomes a freeman the moment he sets his foot on British ground.'[87]

V

Price in his early career as a writer had been very critical of France: 'that cruel and faithless nation, which has so long been the plague of Europe, and in whose weakness our whole security lies'.[88] By 1789, however, he was one of the most committed British supporters of the French Revolution and he was hoping for an alliance of peace and brotherhood with France.[89] As early as March 1789 he was expressing the hope that the

---

[82] Ibid., pp. 122-4.
[83] CRP, II, p. 162; III, pp. 57, 115, 271-2.
[84] Political Writings, p. 150.
[85] Ibid.
[86] Ibid.
[87] Ibid. Not surprisingly, one of his correspondents, Henry Laurens, touched to the quick no doubt by Price's observations on the survival of slavery in America, retorted that slavery had not been completely eliminated in Britain either and that it was Britain that had brought the slaves to America in the first place. CRP, II, pp. 263-4.
[88] Political Writings, p. 11.
[89] Ibid., p. 181.

spirit of liberty would produce a free constitution in France and that liberty might then extend throughout Europe.[90] He gained his greatest notoriety with his speech to the Revolution Society in London on 4 November 1789, which was subsequently published as *A Discourse on the Love of our Country*.[91] Twice translated into French in 1790, it led to Price being made an honorary citizen of Paris and to his being elected to the National Assembly of France. When he died in 1791 the National Assembly of France went into mourning for six days and many reform societies across France wrote to express their condolences. While Price's name was honoured throughout France and he was dubbed by the French as 'the apostle of liberty',[92] Edmund Burke singled him out as the most dangerous British radical in his *Reflections on the Revolution in France* (1790). Many other conservative propagandists also attacked Price as a most dangerous republican, though Christopher Wyvill did recognize in print that Price was in fact a moderate reformer within the English tradition of radicalism, and that he was very different from Thomas Paine and the French revolutionaries.[93]

Price wrote his *Discourse* just a few months after the fall of the Bastille, an event which he celebrated but also one that was widely seen in Britain as a welcome defeat for arbitrary and absolute monarchy and not as a harbinger of either the revolutionary 'Terror' or the military dictatorship that occurred years afterwards. Price appears to have thought that the French reformers were endeavouring to create a constitutional or parliamentary monarchy, on the lines of the Glorious Revolution of 1688-89, and he had no idea that events in France would eventually lead to a radical republic or a military dictatorship. His contacts in France were with reformers such as Mirabeau and la Rochefoucauld, men who cannot be regarded as republicans or violent revolutionaries, and with Thomas Jefferson who hoped that the French would follow the example of the United States. When celebrating Bastille Day in 1790 Price expressed the hope that Britain and France might combine together to promote truth, virtue and liberty. He proposed a toast: 'An alliance between France and Great Britain, for perpetuating peace, and making the world happy'.[94] Price may have been naïve in his interpretation of events in France and he may have been too optimistic about the chances of creating a liberal constitutional monarchy there, but these failings were shared at this time

---

[90] *CRP*, III, p. 208.

[91] On Price's views relations with the revolution Society at this time, see Martin Fitzpatrick, 'Richard Price and the London Revolution Society', *Enlightenment and Dissent* 10 (1991), pp. 35-50; and idem, 'Patriots and patriotisms: Richard Price and the early reception of the French Revolution in England' in Michael O'Dea and Kevin Whelan (eds.), *Nations and Nationalisms: France, Britain, Ireland and the eighteenth-century context* (Oxford, 1995), pp. 211-29.

[92] D.O. Thomas, *Richard Price*, pp. 141-6.

[93] Christopher Wyvill, *A Defence of Dr. Price and the Reformers of England* (London, 1792), pp. 64-5.

[94] Fitzpatrick, 'Patriots and patriotisms', p. 219.

by many in Britain who could not be called republicans or revolutionaries. There is not the slightest suggestion that Price wished to encourage the French to remove their monarch by force and to set up a radical democratic republic.

A perusal of Price's *Discourse* shows that very little of it was taken up with events in France or with observations on these events. Several pages of it are taken up with promoting religious and civil liberty within Britain. A substantial section of it was also taken up with celebrating and justifying the Glorious Revolution of 1688-89—the Revolution Society, after all, was not a new society set up to welcome the French Revolution, but was an old society dedicated to 'commemorating' Britain's own Glorious Revolution of a century before. While Price maintained that the Glorious Revolution was a major achievement, he denied that it was a perfect work because it had not repealed the Test and Corporation Acts and it had left the system of parliamentary representation unreformed. Admittedly, Price offered in his *Discourse* a radical interpretation of the principles underlying the Glorious Revolution—claiming that the people had the right to remove their governors and to create a new system of government whenever it suited them. It was this claim that Burke soon condemned, but it was an interpretation widely accepted in British reforming circles in the 1790s. In looking briefly at France, Price advanced the enlightened view that the British should not be so patriotic that they descend into xenophobia and come to hate other nations. They should learn to love their French neighbours like themselves. He expressed the hope that the French might soon come to enjoy greater religious and political liberty than they possessed so far. Price did publish a translation of the French 'Declaration of Rights' as an appendix to his *Discourse*, but he pointed out that Articles 10 and 11 did not do enough to defend religious liberty or the right of free enquiry in all speculative matters.[95] In the fourth edition of his *Discourse* he tried to ward off some of the criticisms he had attracted. He insisted that it should not be seen as a defence of the violent attack on the royal family in October 1789. He also explained that, in expressing the hope that the British Parliament might become a National Assembly, he was not trying to undermine the British constitution, but was simply advocating that Britain should adopt the broader system of representation adopted in France.[96] The French after all had not created a genuinely democratic franchise.

Price's *Discourse* appeared much more radical than it was largely because of the millennial tone and ecstatic enthusiasm adopted at the conclusion of what after all had been a lecture to fellow-reformers who were in celebratory mood. He had concluded with an optimistic prophecy that played into the hands of those easily alarmed by the prospect of radical change:

---

[95] D.O. Thomas, *Response to Revolution* (Cardiff, 1989), p. 39.
[96] Fitzpatrick, 'Patriots and patriotisms', p. 223.

And now, methinks, I see the ardor for liberty catching and spreading; a general amendment beginning in human affairs; the dominion of kings changed for the dominion of laws, and the dominion of priests giving way to the dominion of reason and conscience....Tremble all ye oppressors of the world! Take warning all ye supporters of slavish governments, and slavish hierarchies!...You cannot hold the world in darkness. Struggle no longer against increasing light and liberality. Restore to mankind their rights; and consent to the correction of abuses before they and you are destroyed together.[97]

This looks much more radical than a careful perusal of the corpus of Price's works would justify. Price often concluded his works with exhortations which seem to be appeals to emotion rather than to reason, but, in fact, they come at the conclusion of deliberate arguments influenced by reason.[98] Even when praising the French, however, Price clearly indicated that he wished to restore the purity of Britain's mixed government and balanced constitution by peaceful means. Henri Laboucheix is right to claim that 'Price's philosophy is a call to vigilance, to action, to reform, to evolution, and if necessary, but as a last resort, to revolution'.[99] The enlightened, tolerant, and prudent Price—with his strong belief in truth, virtue, and liberty, and with his recognition that practical considerations might prevent the establishment of a perfect system of government—had much more in common with Burke than the violent attack made on him in the latter's *Reflections* might lead us to believe.

---

[97] *Political Writings*, pp. 195-6.
[98] *Richard Price and the Ethical Foundations of the American Revolution*, Bernard Peach (ed.), (Durham, NC, 1979), pp. 30-31.
[99] Laboucheix, *Richard Price as moral philosopher and political theorist*, p. 146.

Chapter 12

The 'most horrid and unnatural state of man': John Henry Williams and the French Wars, 1793-1802[*]

Colin Haydon

Hymns Ancient and Modern currently advises that the National Anthem's second verse—'O Lord our God, arise,/Scatter our enemies...' —may be omitted. In the eighteenth century, the Church of England rarely displayed such reserve or doubts about invoking God's aid. The Church taught that God intervened directly in the world: He not only shaped the lives of individuals but also raised and pulled down nations at His pleasure. During the period, Britain waged a series of costly and protracted wars, and her army crushed three major uprisings—the Jacobite rebellions of 1715 and 1745, and the Irish rising of 1798. In times of conflict, England was often portrayed as a state specially favoured by God, a latter-day Israel. But as war was simultaneously viewed as one of Providence's scourges, special wartime services were held so that clergy and congregations could implore God's mercy and assistance. From their pulpits, parsons delivered Jeremiads, fast sermons, and, following victories or peace treaties, thanksgiving sermons. David Napthine and W.A. Speck have delineated the themes of such preaching. Jeremiads exhorted the people to renounce vice and embrace virtue, to repent of past sins, and to seek God's forgiveness. In fast sermons, preachers also emphasized the nation's sinfulness and the possibility that continuing disobedience to God's will might forfeit His protection—the fate of Israel. But, additionally, they often stressed God's special care of Britain, instanced His many blessings, and sought to justify the state's engagement in war. Thanksgiving sermons proclaimed victories, or a war's conclusion, as God's work, and the preachers again implored congregations to renounce sin and lead godly lives.[1]

---

[*] I am very grateful to Susan Campbell, Dr. Sylvia Pinches, Dr. Mike Rogers, and Dr. John Walsh for their help with this essay's preparation.
[1] D. Napthine and W.A. Speck, 'Clergymen and Conflict 1660-1763', in W.J. Sheils (ed.), *The Church and War*, Studies in Church History XX (Oxford, 1983), pp. 231-51.

The War of the French Revolution saw the renewal of such services and sermons. Following the conflict's outbreak in February 1793, the government determined to institute fast days on which the clergy and their congregations would implore God's 'Blessing and Assistance on the Arms of His Majesty by Sea and Land'.[2] Appropriate psalms, lessons, and sentences of Scripture were selected and special prayers composed; the resulting forms of service for morning prayer, the Communion, and evening prayer were sent to the parish clergy. Parts of the services were uncontroversial. There were exhortations to national and personal repentance in the hope of 'obtaining Pardon of our Sins, and for averting those heavy Judgements which our manifold Provocations have most justly deserved'.[3] There were comfortable words: 'Thou, O Lord God, art full of compassion and mercy, long suffering, plenteous in goodness and truth' (Psalm 86:15);[4] 'A thousand shall fall at thy side, and ten thousand at thy right hand; but it shall not come nigh thee' (Psalm 91:7).[5] There were, too, prayers for the restoration of peace. However, much of the services seemed calculated to excite both a bellicose patriotism and xenophobia. The revolutionaries in France, one prayer declared, had 'cast off their faith in Thee, the Living God, and...plunged themselves into those horrible iniquities, and cruelties, which astonish the Christian World'.[6] A collect, in 1793, described the adversary as 'an enemy to all Christian Kings, Princes, and States; who...trusteth in Violence, and delighteth in Blood'.[7] The following year, the denunciation was still stronger. The French were 'the declared Enemies to all Christian Kings, Princes, and States, the impious and avowed Blasphemers of Thy Holy Name and Word'.[8] They 'threaten[ed] destruction to Christianity, and desolation to every Country where they...[could] erect their bloody Standard'.[9] Parsons conducting the services were expected to evince their wholehearted support for such sentiments. They were to read the sentences of Scripture 'with a loud Voice'.[10] Moreover, the form of service for the Communion stipulated that, after the Nicene Creed, a sermon would be preached:[11] the clergy could not evade composing or delivering this *pièce d'occasion*. The government and the Church hierarchy

---

[2] *A Form of Prayer, to be Used in All Churches and Chapels...upon Friday the Nineteenth of April Next [1793], being the Day Appointed by Proclamation for a General Fast and Humiliation before Almighty God* (1793), title page.
[3] Ibid.
[4] Ibid., p. 4.
[5] Ibid., p. 5.
[6] Ibid., pp. 13, 21.
[7] Ibid., pp. 6, 17.
[8] *A Form of Prayer, to be Used...upon Friday the Twenty-eighth of February Next [1794]* (1794), pp. 6, 17.
[9] Ibid.
[10] *Form of Prayer, to be Used...upon Nineteenth of April [1793]*, p. 3.
[11] Ibid., p. 12.

naturally wanted the sermons to conform to the services' general tenor. Parsons were to justify the war and the government's actions in their own words, and denounce the French and the politics of the Revolution. If they had reservations—and it was largely presumed that this was improbable—compliance was still required. Indeed, the fasts were to be observed, royal proclamations warned, 'upon Pain of such Punishment as We may justly inflict on all such as contemn and neglect the Performance of so religious and necessary a Duty'.[12]

I

John Henry Williams was the vicar of Wellesbourne in south Warwickshire—five miles east of Stratford-upon-Avon—from 1778 to 1829, and also served the nearby chapel of Walton Deyville.[13] In addition, he was the rector of Fleet Marston in Buckinghamshire.[14] From a genteel family who lived in Gloucester, he matriculated at Pembroke College, Oxford, in 1763.[15] Little is known of his life at university, but, in 1766 and 1767, one can glimpse his theological reading—he borrowed from the College library Samuel Clarke's *An Exposition of the Church-Catechism* (1729), Humphrey Prideaux's *The Old and New Testament Connected in the History of the Jews and Neighbouring Nations* (1716-18), and the first volume of Daniel Whitby's *A Paraphrase and Commentary on the New Testament* (1703).[16] Williams took an LLB and was ordained; he became rector of Fleet Marston in 1776.[17] When he sought the living at Wellesbourne, three Warwickshire clerics testified to Bishop North of Worcester that they had known him for the previous three years and that 'during that time [he has] lived Piously soberly and honestly'.[18] His picture shows a man with a high brow, dark, searching, thoughtful eyes, a long nose, and short chin; the expression is earnest and slightly

---

[12] *London Gazette*, 13-17 January 1795; ibid., 10-13 January 1801.
[13] Mary Ransome (ed.), *The State of the Bishopric of Worcester 1782-1808*, Worcestershire Historical Society, New Series, VI (Leeds, 1968), pp. 184, 185; *Gentleman's Magazine* XCIX, Part II (1829), p. 90.
[14] Lincolnshire Archives Office, PD 132/26 [hereafter: LAO]; ibid., PD 185/36.
[15] Joseph Foster, *Alumni Oxonienses: The Members of the University of Oxford 1715-1886* (Oxford, 1888), IV, p. 1,567. Foster noted that the family was armigerous.
[16] Pembroke College, Oxford, Archive 45/2/1, ff. 33v-4r. I am grateful to Miss Ellena Pike for permitting me to consult the Library Register.
[17] Ransome (ed.), *Bishopric of Worcester*, p. 185; LAO, PD 132/26.
[18] Worcestershire Record Office, BA 2337, Ref. 732.4, Parcel 47, No. 1,005a [hereafter: Worcestershire RO].

anxious.[19] Williams seems cultured: judging by his publications, he was well read; and he apparently liked music.[20] He could be humorous.[21] He was also modest: when he made his will, he unpretentiously described his study—often a cleric's pride—as just 'my own little Room'.[22] Regarding politics, he was a convinced Whig. A conscientious parson, he saw himself as his congregation's 'teacher and...neighbour';[23] for him, 'the whole and sole business of a parish-priest...[was], by the influence of his example, and the frequency and soundness of his instruction, to promote the general cause of virtue and religion, and to increase the number of real christians and good men'.[24] In 1782, at Wellesbourne (whose population exceeded a thousand by the turn of the century),[25] he conducted two services each Sunday, and dutifully said prayers on all holy days and on Wednesdays and Fridays in Lent.[26] Weekday services were unlikely to attract many parishioners: Williams once described how he read the Ash Wednesday office to 'empty seats, and irresponsive pews'.[27] But it is significant that a respectable proportion of Wellesbourne's laity were communicants: in 1782, the figure was 100 out of '813 souls'.[28]

Williams' life at Wellesbourne appears ordered and tranquil before the French wars. But the outbreak of the conflict, and the resulting institution of the fast days, produced a crisis for the Vicar.

For Williams doubted whether Anglican clergymen should justify war from the pulpit.[29] Should a parson, he wondered, promote 'the thirst of bloodshed' in his sermons, or 'by the sullenness of his doubts...[incur] the imputation of disloyalty'?[30] His mind writhed 'under the torture of this galling alternative'.[31] But his decision was courageous, grounded on 'upwards of thirty years increased conviction of the Truth, and mature consideration of the real nature, of that holy religion which...[he] was

---

[19] The picture is in the vestry of St Peter's Church, Wellesbourne. I am grateful to the vicar, Canon Norman Howes, for kindly showing it to me.
[20] Warwickshire County Record Office, MI 142, Entry, 10 November 1797 [herafter: Warwickshire CRO].
[21] See J.H. Williams, *War the Stumbling-block of a Christian; or, the Absurdity of Defending Religion by the Sword* (1795), pp. 30-31.
[22] Public Record Office, Kew, Prob. 11/1759, f. 115r [hereafter: PRO].
[23] Williams, *War the Stumbling-block*, p. 10.
[24] J.H. Williams, *Two Sermons Preached on the Public Fasts of April 1793, and February 1794* (1794), pp. vi-vii.
[25] *Parliamentary Papers [348] XVIII: Comparative Account of the Population of Great Britain in the Years 1801, 1811, 1821, and 1831* (1831), p. 290.
[26] Ransome(ed.), *Bishopric of Worcester*, p. 185.
[27] Williams, *Two Sermons*, p. 34; cf. ibid., pp. 10-11.
[28] Ransome (ed.), *Bishopric of Worcester*, p. 185.
[29] Before this time, he stated, he had preached only about 'righteousness, temperance, and judgment to come': Williams, *Two Sermons*, p. viii.
[30] Ibid.
[31] Ibid.

called to teach'.³² He refused to follow the line expected and, in contravention of it, preached four 'disloyal' sermons in 1793, 1794, 1795, and 1802.

Nor was the sermons' message intended merely for a country congregation: Williams wanted to reach a wider audience. He therefore arranged for the publication of the first sermon, *Piety, Charity, & Loyalty*, by a printer in Birmingham, John Thompson. It is clear why Williams chose him. Thompson published radical political writings and Dissenters' works—notably many by Joseph Priestley.³³ In 1793, he was accused of publishing a seditious libel and held in solitary confinement, though he was subsequently acquitted at the Warwickshire sessions.³⁴ But Thompson was only a provincial printer, and it was subsequently decided that *Piety* should be reprinted by George Robinson, the great London publisher and bookseller, and issued with the sermon of 1794. Robinson had a huge wholesale trade, and supplied bookshops across the kingdom. Intelligent, enterprising, and well-connected, he published radical works, notably William Godwin's *Political Justice*, and, in 1793, was fined for selling Thomas Paine's *The Rights of Man*.³⁵ Admiring principle, and enjoying controversy, Robinson was presumably very pleased to publish Williams' first two sermons, and his firm also published those of 1795 and 1802. For his part, the Vicar of Wellesbourne was doubtless confident that Robinson's company would successfully market the pieces.

II

What, briefly, were the arguments and character of Williams' sermons?

At the outset, one must emphasize, as Martin Ceadel does,³⁶ that Williams was not a pacifist, always opposed to war. Although this was perhaps not entirely clear from the first sermon,³⁷ he later stated explicitly that a Christian had a right to self-defence. In 1794, he spoke of 'the sober collected firmness of christian self-defence' and, the

---

[32] J.H. Williams, *A Thanksgiving Sermon for the Peace, Preached June 1, 1802* (1802), pp. 9-10.
[33] Nesta Jenkins, 'Printing in Birmingham in the Eighteenth Century. A Bibliography with Biographical Notes on Printers' (Library Association Fellowship thesis, 1972), pp. 230-45.
[34] Clive Emsley, 'An Aspect of Pitt's "Terror": Prosecutions for Sedition during the 1790s' *Social History* 6:2 (May 1981), pp. 173, 183.
[35] *Gentleman's Magazine* LXXI, Part I (1801), pp. 578-80; Derek Roper, *Reviewing before the Edinburgh 1788-1802* (1978), pp. 32, 292, n. 18.
[36] Martin Ceadel, *The Origins of War Prevention* (Oxford, 1996), pp. 159-60.
[37] 'Such a state as this [i.e. war] can only be justified in a moral light by the law of self-defence, but in a religious view it is ever a state to be deplored...': Williams, *Two Sermons*, pp. 20-21. Cf. ibid., p. 27.

following year, maintained that 'we can perceive no grounds for the assertion that a Christian must not fight'.[38] By extension, a war undertaken by the state for self-defence was just. None the less, Williams maintained that self-protection was the sole Christian justification for armed conflict. In his thanksgiving sermon for the Peace of Amiens, he declared: 'One general principle...I shall content myself with asserting once more, before the subject is banished, I hope, from this place for ever; which is, that A Christian may not fight, either individually or collectively, except in the unavoidable and unequivocal necessity of self-defence'.[39] This stance was perhaps more problematical for Williams than might initially appear. He could not judge, he said in 1793, if the struggle with France was 'both just and necessary' (a mildly evasive remark, given that it was the French who had declared war): he knew little of foreign and domestic politics.[40] But, in any case, even when war was justifiable, many of its attributes were loathsome to true Christians.

War, stated Williams, was 'the most horrid and unnatural state of man'.[41] The physical horrors of conflict were appalling: battles, sieges, conflagrations, plunder, confiscations, 'the cries of the orphans, and the lamentations of the widows'.[42] But, in addition, war was 'the moral scourge of nations', which spawned 'hatred, ambition, profaneness, blasphemy, [and] cruelty'.[43] It was 'pregnant with moral anarchy...[and] religious corruption'.[44] Its outbreak was a tragedy in the eyes of right-thinking people. At home, the effects of war were anti-social. It bred malice which, in turn, encouraged suspicion and intolerance among individuals. Discussion, and differences of opinion, were stifled. Against the introduction of such 'intolerance into the community', Williams objected 'as a citizen...because it is unsocial; [and] as a minister of the Gospel of Peace and Charity...because it is unchristian'.[45] In short, malice altered or destroyed 'every form and circumstance of social life'.[46] Williams also feared the corruption of the soldiers. 'You read, indeed, in the Acts of the Apostles, of one devout soldier', he noted in 1794, but 'this was after a continuance of long and profound peace, and in established quarters among fellow-citizens and friends.'[47] In wartime, 'By converting man into a hireling man-killer, you unavoidably introduce...into his mind' 'blasphemy, vain swearing, a total neglect of public and private

---

[38] Ibid., p. 63; Williams, *War the Stumbling-block*, p. 23.
[39] Williams, *Thanksgiving Sermon*, p. 9.
[40] Williams, *Two Sermons*, pp. 21-2.
[41] Ibid., p. 19.
[42] Ibid., p. 41.
[43] Williams, *Thanksgiving Sermon*, pp. 8, 9.
[44] Ibid., p. 9.
[45] Williams, *Two Sermons*, pp. 18-19.
[46] Ibid., pp. 17-18.
[47] Ibid., p. 45.

prayer,...[and] frequent and almost necessary drunkenness and dissipation'.[48]

Williams scorned the notion that the defence of religion was one of the conflict's chief objects. Wars stifled Christianity's growth:

> The cross of Christ would have been preached unheard on the plains of Pharsalia, or amidst the opposed legions at Philippi; but when the Temple of Janus was shut, it was preached with boldness and with effect in the forums of the people, in the streets of cities, and in the palaces of Emperors.[49]

'The Sword of Christianity', Williams stated unequivocally, 'is the Word of God, and it will not admit of carnal warfare, either for its propagation or its defence'.[50] He cited Christ's command, at his arrest, to Peter to sheathe his sword—though the disciple sought to defend 'not problematically the doctrine of our blessed Lord, but positively and immediately his person and his life'.[51] There was no purpose in fighting for 'Virtue and Religion' since they were 'the only things, "which no man can take from us"'.[52] Williams recalled with disgust the Crusades and Europe's 'holy and unanimous desire of deluging Asia with blood'.[53] He ridiculed 'the tumultuous clamours of enthusiasm' at the Council of Clermont,[54] and observed that 'the shedders of...blood [in the church's history]...might be Popes, Monks, Princes, or Demagogues, but they were not Christians'.[55] Moreover, modern wars for religion gave sceptics and atheists dangerous ammunition against Christianity: 'supporters of the peaceful Gospel' appeared hypocritical when defending violence.[56] This was certainly a clever parry of the common justification of the war on the ground that France was now an atheistical state (though Williams evasively said little about French atheism, despite his dismay at growing infidelity at home).[57] In short, he insisted that 'there is no sense in which it can be affirmed that a Christian is fighting for his religion, and that there is no instance to be produced, in which he ever did'.[58]

Williams was, of course, principally concerned for men's souls. He reminded his congregation of 'those Terrors of the Lord which await the impenitent',[59] and in 1794 envisaged, if the war continued, 'a whole generation of mortals...arraigned together at the bar of Heaven, as

---

[48] Ibid.
[49] Ibid., pp. 62-3.
[50] Williams, *War the Stumbling-block*, p. 6.
[51] Ibid., p. 15.
[52] Ibid., p. 32.
[53] Williams, *Two Sermons*, p. 23.
[54] Ibid., p. 24.
[55] Williams, *Thanksgiving Sermon*, p. 4.
[56] Williams, *War the Stumbling-block*, p. 26.
[57] Williams, *Two Sermons*, pp. 3-4, 8.
[58] Williams, *War the Stumbling-block*, p. 23.
[59] Williams, *Thanksgiving Sermon*, p. 30.

conspirators against its holy law'.[60] If war spawned vice, peace nurtured virtue. 'Without the dew of peace', Williams maintained, 'the seeds of the Gospel will neither spring nor grow'.[61] In 1802, delighted at the Treaty of Amiens, he declared: 'Peace is as necessary to virtue, as air is to sound, or space to motion. With Peace dwell piety, charity, science, literature, industry, security and liberty.'[62] The time was ripe for 'all true Patriots...to serve their country...by enlarging the Fold of Christ'.[63] He concluded:

> The minds of the truly virtuous will ever be wishing for...something that will have a fixed influence on the sentiments and hearts of men, and attract them to one centre of justice, liberty, and peace...[M]ay God incline their hearts to seek it, where alone it can be found, in the simple Faith, the pure Morals, and the eternal Sanctions of the Gospel.[64]

Of course, Williams recognized that 'the Parchment of Peace is soon transferred to the Drum of War'.[65] Less than a year after he preached the 1802 sermon, the Napoleonic wars began. Williams published no more sermons. Perhaps he was too mortified to do so. But perhaps Bonaparte's massive camp at Boulogne, and the invasion alarm which swept England,[66] convinced him that the new conflict was indeed one of legitimate self-defence.[67] Despite his general principles, Williams was sensitive to the mutations of war. In 1793, he hoped that the struggle would end quickly—'The French are at this time retreating on all quarters'—but, by 1795, he was dejected at the slaughter.[68]

Williams chose his texts with care: 'Behold! Ye fast for strife and debate' (Isaiah 58:4); 'Blessed are the peace-makers; for they shall be called the children of God' (Matthew 5:9); 'Let no man put a stumbling-block in his brother's way' (Romans 14:13); 'Let us, therefore, follow after the things which make for peace' (Romans 14:19). The Old Testament was usually the clergy's quarry for bellicose watchwords.[69] But Williams cleverly extracted the first text from the very chapter in Isaiah prescribed for morning prayer by the 1793 form of service.[70] Williams also

---

[60] Williams, *Two Sermons*, p. 40.
[61] Ibid., p. 62.
[62] Williams, *Thanksgiving Sermon*, p. 8.
[63] Ibid., p. 27.
[64] Ibid., pp. 35-6.
[65] Ibid., p. 12.
[66] For a description of the panic in a Midland village, see J.W. and Anne Tibble, (eds.), *The Prose of John Clare* (1951), pp. 46-7.
[67] Cf. Emma Vincent Macleod, *A War of Ideas: British Attitudes to the Wars against Revolutionary France 1792-1802* (Aldershot, 1998), p. 149, n. 45 on the comparable change of thinking of Bishop Watson of Llandaff in 1798.
[68] Williams, *Two Sermons*, p. 29, note; Williams, *War the Stumbling-block*, p. 27.
[69] Williams, *Two Sermons*, p. 9.
[70] *Form of Prayer, to be Used upon Nineteenth of April* [1793], p. 5.

included numerous biblical quotations in the sermons. They provided, in his view, irrefutable arguments—unless 'Handle[d]...partially or deceitfully'.[71] When discussing John 18:36 ('My kingdom is not of this world: if my kingdom were of this world, then would my servants fight'), he observed caustically, 'An host of commentators cannot destroy the simplicity of this declaration'.[72] Thus, in 1793, he emphasized 'God's sacred commandment, Thou shalt not kill'.[73] The following year, when he considered wartime propaganda, he reminded his hearers that '"He that hateth his brother...is a murderer"'; 'the standing orders of Heaven' were, he stressed, '"Glory to God on high, on earth Peace, Goodwill to Men"'.[74] In his 1802 sermon, he discussed '"Blessed are the Meek"', and their promised reward, that '"They shall inherit the earth"'.[75] God would help the nation if it trusted properly in His protection and fully submitted to His will.[76]

Williams' churchmanship was conventional—he decried heresy and infidelity, 'Roman pomp' and 'Genevan fervency', the 'deformity of superstition' and the 'insanity of fanaticism'[77]—but the government's arrogance alarmed him. He deplored its presumption in expecting the clergy to propagate 'a pious assent to the justice and necessity' of the conflict.[78] The secular arm, now enjoying 'a complete ascendancy', had converted, the church 'into a mere engine of the state'.[79] The church's 'ministers [were] considered as so many tenants in vassalage to their feudal lord, who must be ready at all times to...crowd to the standard regardless of the cause'.[80] The issue of church-state relations was, of course, topical, given the Dissenters' attempts to repeal the Test and Corporation Acts between 1787 and 1790. Williams naturally emphasized his loyalty to George III, and praised 'the piety and the known humanity of our beloved Sovereign'.[81] But he was suspicious of government propaganda concerning the danger from radicals—'of whom one hears so much, and sees so little'[82]—and thought the French 'nation intended well:—for it intended to be free' (a calculatedly naïve comment?).[83] As for

---

[71] Williams, *Thanksgiving Sermon*, p. 28.
[72] Williams, *War the Stumbling-block*, p. 18.
[73] Williams, *Two Sermons*, p. 20.
[74] Ibid., pp. 49, 58.
[75] Williams, *Thanksgiving Sermon*, p. 20.
[76] Ibid., pp. 19-20.
[77] Ibid., pp. 28, 29.
[78] Williams, *Two Sermons*, p. vii.
[79] Ibid., pp. v-vi.
[80] Ibid., p. vi.
[81] Ibid., p. 27.
[82] Ibid., p. 3.
[83] Ibid., p. 46. 'But it was corrupted to its centre by generations of iniquity, and it sought freedom without a due regard to piety and virtue...which is one principal reason why they have hitherto sought in vain.'

fellow clergymen, he despised those who meekly submitted to the government's commands, condemning 'the bitter aloes of rancour and intemperance,...[and] the politico-theological harangues of those who are now ransacking the Jewish armoury for weapons to use in their christian warfare, employing fanciful adaptations of the Old Testament'.[84] He strongly criticized the clergy's practice of 'assuming a fanatical discernment of...Almighty Providence',[85] because nearly all pro-war sermons, as Emma Vincent Macleod notes, interpreted the struggle in providentialist terms:[86] rather, one could not uncover the purposes of God, 'whose way is in the sea, whose paths are in the great waters, and whose footsteps are not known'.[87] When the conflict ended, Williams rejoiced at clergymen's release from 'the vain task of ransacking the pages of the peaceful Gospel after excuses for bloodshed'.[88]

Williams' language is interesting too. He plainly crafted his sermons very carefully (though it is, of course, impossible to know how far he polished them before publication); sometimes, interestingly, they echo the cadences of Gibbon. He vividly described the horrors of war, and employed graphic imagery—of contagion and ocean storms, for instance.[89] Some of the images are memorable—'the standard of the holy Lamb amidst the ramping lion and the ravening eagle in the fields of blood'[90]—and one neatly satirizes the absurdity of his opponents' stance—'the pure ethereal form of Christianity leaning familiarly on the fleshly arm of Policy, or sculking for protection behind the Warrior's shield'.[91] Williams was also concerned to discredit his opponents' association of martial service, civic virtue, and patriotism. He linked the teaching of the Gospel with the social conduct extolled by the Enlightenment. 'Christianity, when...duly practiced [sic]', he stated, '[is] the greatest of all social blessings, or rather...the consummation of all social bliss.'[92] Christianity could salve international relations; patriotism was not a crazed zeal for bloodshed.[93] And sometimes the language is simply caustic—as, in 1793, when he ridiculed those lay

> bosoms [that] are now burning with vengeance at the recital of foreign enormities, which never felt a single spark of indignation at the review of their own sins...[and the] many eyes...now streaming for the fate of a

---

[84] Ibid., p. 9.
[85] Ibid.
[86] Macleod, *War of Ideas*, p. 143.
[87] Williams, *Two Sermons*, p. 9.
[88] Williams, *Thanksgiving Sermon*, p. 32.
[89] Williams, *Two Sermons*, pp. 26, 28.
[90] Williams, *War the Stumbling-block*, pp. 26-7.
[91] Ibid., p. 20.
[92] Williams, *Thanksgiving Sermon*, p. 26.
[93] Ibid., pp. 14-20, 24.

slaughtered king, which never let fall one single drop for the agonies of a crucified Saviour.[94]

III

Williams had sought a wide readership and courted controversy. When criticized, he defended his opinions in the newspaper press.[95] So how were Williams' sermons received by reviewers?

Reviews of the sermons naturally reflected a periodical's political and ecclesiastical stance.

The Anglican, Tory *British Critic* reviewed the first two sermons cursorily, in a frosty and headmasterly tone. 'The writer of these sermons', it began, 'is a man of talents, which, in our judgment, he might have employed in a manner more to the advantage of his hearers and the public'.[96] We shall not, it continued loftily, 'go out of our way to animadvert upon the partiality of his reasonings, or the insidiousness of his inferences'.[97] Williams' statement that he was 'a Non-associate, and a Servant of the gentle Jesus' prompted a barbed retort: 'We pretend not to affirm that these characters can not co-exist; but we must be allowed to lament, at least, that the temper of the latter is in so few instances improved by a union with the former'.[98] Another Anglican periodical, started in 1801, *The Orthodox Churchman's Magazine*, pointedly chose to advertise, but not to review, the 1802 sermon.[99]

The responses of *The Critical Review* and *The Monthly Review* were very different. Both periodicals espoused Whig and Dissenting principles.[100] Moreover, George Robinson was a part-owner of *The Critical*.[101] Williams, *The Critical* pronounced, was a writer of 'more than common ability and energy' and 'a friend to peace upon the most enlarged principles'.[102] In 1796, the reviewer—strongly opposed to the war's prolongation—noted that the periodical had earlier described 'the talents of Mr. Williams in terms of high commendation',[103] and now found

---

[94] Williams, *Two Sermons*, pp. 9-10.
[95] Nancy Uhlar Murray, 'The Influence of the French Revolution on the Church of England and its Rivals 1789-1802' (University of Oxford D.Phil. thesis, 1975), p. 99, n. 1.
[96] *The British Critic* III (1794), p. 578.
[97] Ibid.
[98] Ibid.
[99] *The Orthodox Churchman's Magazine* II (1802), p. 337.
[100] Stuart Andrews, *The British Periodical Press and the French Revolution 1789-99* (Basingstoke, 2000), p. 139.
[101] Roper, *Reviewing before the Edinburgh*, pp. 22, 31, 177.
[102] *The Critical Review; or, Annals of Literature*, 2nd Series, XII (1794), p. 112.
[103] Ibid., XVI (1796), p. 223.

his arguments entirely convincing: 'He exposes in very strong terms the absurdity of pretending to fight for religion, to fight for God!'[104] The comments of *The Monthly Review* were still more laudatory. It extolled the sermons of 1793 and 1794: 'Most excellent!...truly manly and Christian...'[105] '[M]ore full of thought and Christian sentiment, more spirited, and of a better tendency' than other fast sermons, they merited a lengthy review.[106] Williams' mind was, it declared, 'independent and liberal', his depiction of war, and its effects, 'true and affecting'.[107] The comments on the 1795 sermon were similar.

> Mr. W. writes with animation and force; and we must acknowledge that his reasoning, aided by the resistless weight of the sacred writings, has made a greater impression on our minds, than has always been the case when we have risen from the perusal of discourses of the same kind.[108]

IV

The Analytical Review praised Williams' courage, his 'manly and independent spirit'.[109] The Vicar of Wellesbourne needed courage, for, in his locality, hostile, conservative sentiment was marked. The Earl of Warwick was a convinced Tory: 'There was a French party in this country,' he told the Lords in 1797, 'and it was possible that there might be a French party in parliament'.[110] On 20 November 1792, John Reeves founded his Association for the Preservation of Liberty and Property against Republicans and Levellers. And on 11 December, an association was established for Warwick and its vicinity (Wellesbourne was only seven miles from Warwick); the Earl headed its committee.[111] Among other resolutions, the associators agreed 'to disclose and make known any Treasonable or seditious Expressions, which may come to our knowledge; in order that the guilty persons may receive due Punishment'.[112] Sermons criticizing the government might well alarm loyalists: as one of Reeves' correspondents observed, 'sedition from the pulpit may have more effect upon the vulgar than common conversation'.[113] Other associations were

---

[104] Ibid., p. 224.
[105] *The Monthly Review*, New Series, XIV (1794), p. 355.
[106] Ibid., p. 357.
[107] Ibid., pp. 356, 357.
[108] Ibid., XVI (1795), p. 475.
[109] *The Analytical Review, or History of Literature, Domestic and Foreign* XVII (1793), p. 56.
[110] William Cobbett, (ed.) *The Parliamentary History of England, from the Earliest Period to the Year 1803* XXXIII (1818), col. 188.
[111] British Library, Add. MS 16931, f. 156r [hereafter: BL].
[112] Ibid.
[113] BL, Add. MS 16921, f. 131v.

soon established at Banbury, Blockley (Worcestershire), Henley-in-Arden, and Woodstock—all near enough for accounts of their proceedings to reach Wellesbourne.[114] Williams naturally declined to become an associator, and, consequently, was 'continually assailed' with 'calumnious misrepresentations'.[115] Perhaps he also feared physical attack. In 1791, the Priestley rioters threatened to march from Birmingham to the village of Hatton, near Warwick, in order to destroy the parsonage, the home of the celebrated Whig clergyman Dr. Samuel Parr.[116] Hatton was but eight miles from Wellesbourne, and Williams and Parr sometimes dined together.[117] Given their shared political outlook,[118] they doubtless discussed the war on these occasions.

Certain clergymen living near Williams paraded their loyalist convictions. In the diocese of Worcester, such clerics followed the lead of their bishop, Richard Hurd. Hurd was George III's favourite bishop; his cast of mind, politically, was cautious and conservative. Dr. Hole notes that, in a fast sermon of 1776, he anticipated Burke's *Reflections* in maintaining the folly of applying abstract theories 'directly to the correction of established governments'.[119] When writing to the King in 1797, 1798, and 1800, Hurd discerned the workings of Providence in Britain's victories or contemporary politics;[120] he thought republican France 'the most malignant enemy that has appeared in the world'.[121] His episcopal charge of 1800 praised his clergy for doing the 'utmost to infuse into others...A ready obedience to the authority of Government, and...A zeal for the support and maintenance of our invaluable Constitution'.[122] The charge also described the war as 'just and unavoidable', 'against an enemy the most outrageous that has ever alarmed Christendom'.[123] If Hurd were informed about, or read, Williams' sermons, he presumably deplored them.[124] So, presumably, did the local loyalist parsons. At

---

[114] BL, Add. MS 16923, ff. 31r-v; Add. MS 16931, ff. 5v-6r, 23r, 70r.
[115] Williams, *Two Sermons*, p. viii.
[116] Warren Derry, *Dr. Parr: A Portrait of the Whig Dr. Johnson* (Oxford, 1966), p. 137. Cf. Samuel Parr, *A Sequel to the Printed Paper Lately Circulated in Warwickshire by the Rev. Charles Curtis*, 2nd edn. (1792), p. 45.
[117] Warwickshire CRO, MI 142, Entries, 5 December 1797, 29 March 1798.
[118] On Parr's politics, see Derry, *Parr*, esp. pp. 128-68, 191-250.
[119] Robert Hole, *Pulpits, Politics, and Public Order in England 1760-1832* (Cambridge, 1989), p. 49, n.46.
[120] A. Aspinall (ed.), *The Later Correspondence of George III*, II (Cambridge, 1963; reprinted 1968), p. 633; III (Cambridge, 1967), pp. 158, 310.
[121] Ibid., III, p. 158.
[122] *The Works of Richard Hurd, D.D.* (London, 1811), VIII, p. 132.
[123] Ibid., pp. 131-2.
[124] However, his surviving correspondence does not mention them. I am grateful to Marion Symonds, Honorary Librarian of the Hurd Library, Hartlebury Castle, for this information.
When Vicesimus Knox preached a controversial anti-war sermon (on which see below, pp. 271-2, 275), one newspaper expressed the hope that his diocesan '"would make...[him] an example to other pulpit politicians"': Vicesimus Knox,

Banbury and Warwick, the loyalist associations' committees included clerics;[125] at Blockley and Henley-in-Arden, the associations' meetings were chaired, respectively, by the Reverend Charles Jasper Selwyn and the Reverend Daniel Gaches.[126] From Woodstock, the Reverend William Mavor corresponded enthusiastically with Reeves.[127] For such men, Williams' defiance of the rightful authorities—in both Church and state—was shocking and inexcusable. How precisely, in 1793-94, did Williams view the radicals at home and the regicidal, bloody, and anti-Christian régime in France?

Some Whigs detested the stridently loyalist parsons: the young Walter Savage Landor published a brutal attack on one Tory clergyman, whom he depicted as an odious sycophant of the Earl of Warwick.[128] And political differences might also poison relations between clerics (Williams loathed 'party zeal' and the 'overbearing tide of political enthusiasm').[129] Compromise could prove difficult since politics and religion proved inextricably tangled, and the issues were fundamental; tempers might be lost, but consciences racked too. John Morley was the vicar of Wasperton, curate of Hampton Lucy, and master of its school.[130] He was a committed Whig and enjoyed the friendship of Williams, whom he often mentioned in his diary and with whom he sometimes dined.[131] Morley was also a friend of Dr. Parr;[132] and, in June 1797, he entertained William Godwin, who described him as 'a clever and amiable man'.[133] When Morley heard Bishop Hurd's charge of 1800, he was outraged:

A Narrative of Transactions Relative to a Sermon, Preached in the Parish Church of Brighton, August 18, 1793, 3rd edn. (1794), p. vii.

[125] BL, Add. MS 16931, ff. 5v-6r, 156r.

[126] Ibid., ff. 23r, 70r.

[127] BL, Add. MS 16922, ff. 17r-18v; Add. MS 16923, ff. 32r, 99r; Add. MS 16924, ff. 148r-v; Add. MS 16925, ff. 7r-v. From 1790 to 1795, Mavor was vicar of Tysoe—not ten miles from Wellesbourne: Ransome (ed.), *Bishopric of Worcester*, p. 183. For his outlook, see William Mavor, *The Duty of Thanksgiving, for National Blessings* (Oxford, 1798) and David Eastwood, *Governing Rural England: Tradition and Transformation in Local Government 1780-1840* (Oxford, 1994), pp. 16, 19, 20. Mavor wrote a sonnet 'To Rational Liberty', 'Written on Reading the Horrid Acts of the Paris Mob': William Mavor, *Miscellanies* (Oxford, [1829]), p. 483.

[128] Walter Savage Landor, *To the Burgesses of Warwick*, R.H. Super (ed.), Luttrell Society Reprints VIII (Oxford, 1949), pp. 1-2.

[129] Williams, *Two Sermons*, p. 29; Williams, *War the Stumbling-block*, p. 5.

[130] Ransome (ed.), *Bishopric of Worcester*, pp. 171, 184. I am currently preparing an article on Morley. For a hostile picture of him, see Alice Fairfax-Lucy, *Charlecote and the Lucys* (1958), pp. 247, 248.

[131] Warwickshire CRO, MI 142, Entries, 5 December 1797, 29 March 1798.

[132] Ibid., *passim*; Warwickshire CRO, CR 2486, *passim*.

[133] C. Kegan Paul, *William Godwin: His Friends and Contemporaries* (1876), I, pp. 247, 248-9.

The Bishops Charge has been usually theological, & never yet, since I have been in Orders, debased by unnecessary Reference to the political Contests of the Times. To Day, the Exordium contained some very acrimonious Language concerning the present state of Government & Religion in France, which have been of late daily improving...Indeed had not this Charge been delivered by so great an Authority as Bishop Hurd...I shd. have thought it altogether a very contemptible Performance.[134]

Politics produced a furious attack on Morley by the Reverend John Lucy, the rector of Hampton Lucy, patron of the Wasperton living, and squire of Charlecote, a belligerent (and sometimes physically violent) Tory.[135] When, after a dinner in June 1797, 'Mr. Lucy had taken more than his usual Quantity of Wine,' Morley recorded in his diary,

he began to tell me that if...I...spent more Time with my Family, & busied myself less with the Affairs of the Nation, it might have been as well for me...He... as if to shew the immense Difference between Rector and Curate, and to give a Specimen of the Arguments he could employ to most Advantage, said that he had made a Determination to dispossess me of the Curacy and School at Hampton Lucy, but that Compassion for my Family had restrained him.[136]

Despite other trouble at the school, Morley did not lose his curacy and schoolmastership.[137] Moreover, his politics did not necessarily mar his relations with conservative-minded clerics. In May 1801, he dined with Daniel Gaches (they shared a love of the classics).[138]

Given the stance of the Church's establishment, and the pressures from local society, Williams no doubt considered abandoning his public calls for peace. He was certainly riled by the loyalist bodies, which he described at the end of his 1793 sermon as 'self-constituted dictatorial and inquisitorial associations'.[139] His little chapel of Walton Deyville stood beside the mansion of the powerful Mordaunt family. The Mordaunts had rebuilt the chapel and worshipped there;[140] and, in 1794, Sir John, the Tory MP for Warwickshire, supported the Earl of Warwick's scheme to create loyalist volunteer companies for the county, subscribing £100 towards it.[141] Moreover, since Williams published no sermons between 1795 and 1802, one might well presume that, during that period, he prudently kept silent. Those years afforded many opportunities for new

---

[134] Warwickshire CRO, MI 142, Entry, 17 June 1800.
[135] Ransome (ed.), *Bishopric of Worcester*, pp. 171, 184; Fairfax-Lucy, *Charlecote*, p. 249.
[136] Warwickshire CRO, MI 142, Entry, 19 June 1797.
[137] Fairfax-Lucy, *Charlecote*, p. 248; Ransome (ed.), *Bishopric of Worcester*, p. 171.
[138] Warwickshire CRO, CR 2486, Entry, 1 May 1801; Ransome (ed.), *Bishopric of Worcester*, p. 8; Kegan Paul, *Godwin*, I, p. 249.
[139] Williams, *Two Sermons*, p. 30.
[140] *The Victoria History of the County of Warwick* (1949), V, p. 197.
[141] BL, Add. MS 38480, ff. 139r-v, 140r; Charles J. Hart, *The History of the 1st Volunteer Battalion the Royal Warwickshire Regiment and its Predecessors* (Birmingham, 1906), p. 17.

publications. Further fast days were held annually, in February or March. In December 1797, a service commemorated the navy's 'many signal and important Victories' during the struggle.[142] And, in November 1798, a thanksgiving service was appointed following the Battle of the Nile and other 'Interpositions of...[God's] Providence'.[143] The forms of service directed that sermons were to be preached on these occasions.[144] But, although Williams resolved not to publish any sermons between 1795 and 1802, it is likely that, when preaching in his church, he continued to decry the conflict (though in 1798, probably not until later in the year—before May, a French invasion was an alarming possibility).[145] In the sermon celebrating the Peace of Amiens, he recalled that he had '*often* asserted [his opinions about war] in this place'.[146] Furthermore, John Morley's diary and *Aris's Birmingham Gazette* record other work which Williams undertook in the cause of peace. In 1797, the Whigs co-ordinated the production of petitions asking George III to dismiss Pitt's ministry and to stop the war.[147] To this end, in Warwickshire, Dr. Parr drew up a requisition for a county meeting at the start of May, and Williams signed it, as did Morley, who obtained further signatures and arranged the printing and distribution of handbills.[148] The meeting was held at the race ground at Warwick on 31 May, and, despite the endeavours of the Pittites, it was resolved to petition the King to remove the government, the essential 'requisite, to the Attainment of a speedy, proper, and lasting Peace'.[149] Although two great landowners, Bertie Greatheed of Guys Cliffe and Sir John Throckmorton of Coughton, proposed and seconded the address, and Sir Francis Burdett and Lord Dormer supported it and attended the meeting, it was Williams who read the petition.[150] That a mere vicar, and not an aristocrat, did so was the clearest testimony to Williams' standing as a champion of peace—though, with characteristic modesty, he apparently did not attend the celebratory dinner which followed the meeting.[151]

---

[142] *A Form of Prayer and Thanksgiving...to be Used...on Tuesday the Nineteenth Day of December 1797* (1797), title page.
[143] *A Form of Prayer and Thanksgiving...to be Used...on Thursday the Twenty-ninth Day of November 1798* (1798), title page.
[144] *Form of Prayer to be Used on Nineteenth of December 1797*, p. 11; *Form of Prayer to be Used on Twenty-ninth of November 1798*, p. 11.
[145] J.E. Cookson, *The Friends of Peace: Anti-war Liberalism in England 1793-1815* (Cambridge, 1982), p. 163; Ceadel, *Origins of War Prevention*, p. 176.
[146] Williams, *Thanksgiving Sermon*, p. 9. My italics.
[147] Cookson, *Friends of Peace*, pp. 157-62.
[148] Warwickshire CRO, MI 142, Entries, 1, 2, 26, 27, 29, 30 May 1797; *Aris's Birmingham Gazette*, 29 May 1797.
[149] Cookson, *Friends of Peace*, p. 161; *Aris's Birmingham Gazette*, 5 June 1797.
[150] Warwickshire CRO, MI 142, Entries, 31 May, 19 June 1797; *Aris's Birmingham Gazette*, 5 June 1797.
[151] Warwickshire CRO, MI 142, Entry, 31 May 1797.

Or was it just modesty? One wonders if the petition's wording disappointed Williams. Whilst the address mentioned the vileness of war, it stressed political and economic, not religious and ethical, arguments for peace. Bungling diplomacy, undue interference in other states' internal concerns, Pitt's 'System of Terror' to curb radicalism, the crisis in Ireland, poverty and high taxation resulting from the conflict: 'Such are the Errors, and such the Crimes, which we impute to your Ministers'.[152] Williams' sermons imputed much more to them.

V

Unsurprisingly, the Reverend John Lucy was appalled at Williams' conduct. The address, he spluttered, was 'one of the "most vilest & most foolishest Things as...[he] ever heard"'.[153] Lucy's political outlook was, of course, shared by most Anglican clerics. Paul Langford describes their politics as 'conformist, conservative, [and] conventional' during the years of the American Revolution;[154] and the French Revolution stiffened that conservatism. Moreover, specifically regarding attitudes to the French wars, Dr. Macleod produces a clear conclusion from her survey of clerical publications treating the subject: that most Anglican parsons supported the government's war-effort and preached accordingly.[155] None the less, as Macleod notes, a small minority of parsons, along with some Dissenting ministers, openly opposed the conflict.[156] It is, therefore, worth examining briefly the degree to which the views of such men resembled, or diverged from, those of John Henry Williams.

One well-known opponent of the conflict was the master of Tonbridge School, the Reverend Vicesimus Knox, not only because of his publications but also because an anti-war sermon, which he preached at Brighton in August 1793, occasioned a demonstration by soldiers.[157] His opinions closely resembled Williams'. Knox accepted the legitimacy of defensive war, which, he maintained, 'is certainly exempt from all the censure which falls on war wantonly and cruelly undertaken from pride and

---

[152] *Aris's Birmingham Gazette*, 5 June 1797.
[153] Warwickshire CRO, MI 142, Entry, 19 June 1797. Lucy had signed the requisition for the county meeting but claimed that Morley had duped him about the matter: ibid.; *Aris's Birmingham Gazette*, 29 May 1797. Cf. Warwickshire CRO, MI 142, Entry, 1 May 1797.
[154] Paul Langford, 'The English Clergy and the American Revolution', in Eckhart Hellmuth (ed.), *The Transformation of Political Culture: England and Germany in the Late Eighteenth Century* (Oxford, 1990), p. 307.
[155] Macleod, *War of Ideas*, p. 137.
[156] Ibid., pp. 148-9, 153-6.
[157] Hole, *Pulpits, Politics, and Public Order*, p. 222.

ambition'.[158] He used biblical texts effectively: '"Love your enemies,"—"Blessed are the peace-makers,"—"Do unto others as you wish they should do unto you"';[159] he chose as the text for his Brighton sermon Williams' 'standing orders of Heaven', 'Glory to God in the highest, on earth peace, good-will towards men'.[160] The thinking of Peter Peckard, master of Magdalene College, Cambridge, and dean of Peterborough, was also like Williams'. On 25 February 1795, Peckard delivered the fast-day sermon in his cathedral. '[T]he duty of the day', he felt, 'seem'd to lead him' to give 'his opinion on the subject of War'; and in his preface to the published text, he crisply summarized that opinion: 'nothing can equal the absurdity of War, but its wickedness'.[161] He emphasized, too, God's judgement on those that 'delight in War, [who] will certainly receive their Full Pay according to their deserts'.[162]

Although Peckard, like Williams, thought defensive war was justified, he nevertheless considered self-defence a complex notion—indeed, one so ill-defined that it was sometimes impossible to know 'how far it may be legitimately extended'.[163] Other clerics went further, and, unlike Williams, espoused pacifism. One Anglican clergyman anonymously produced a unyielding pacifist publication in 1798, *The Lawfulness of Defensive War upon Christian Principles Impartially Considered*.[164] '[A]re we to rush into murder,' the author asked, 'and in determined opposition to the will of the Supreme Being, to hazard our eternal welfare...?'[165] A man, he continued, has

> a soul to guard from every taint of guilt and disobedience to his Creator's will...[and] to preserve this...he should give up all, even the natural life itself, rather than suffer it to contract a pollution which might accompany him beyond the grave, and incapacitate him for future happiness.[166]

Duty to God took precedence over duty to one's relations, friends, and country.[167] For the writer, and other pacifists, the key text was Christ's command to Peter in the garden of Gethsemane: 'Put up thy sword' (John 18:11).[168] Disobedience to injunctions to peace, stated *The Lawfulness of*

---

[158] Knox, *Narrative*, p. xvii.
[159] Ibid., p. 86.
[160] Ibid., p. 11.
[161] Peter Peckard, *National Crimes the Cause of National Punishments* (Peterborough, n.d.), pp. iii, iv.
[162] Ibid., p. v.
[163] Ibid., p. 11.
[164] On its possible authorship, see Ceadel, *Origins of War Prevention*, pp. 176-7.
[165] *The Lawfulness of Defensive War upon Christian Principles Impartially Considered. By a Clergyman of the Church of England* (1798), p. 14.
[166] Ibid., p. 30.
[167] Ibid., p. 32.
[168] Ibid., p. 8. Opponents countered this, and Matthew 26:52, by citing Luke 22:36—'he that hath no sword, let him sell his garment, and buy one'.

Defensive War...Considered, was as sinful as disobedience to any other biblical prohibition.[169] The prominent Baptist minister Joseph Hughes so loathed bloodshed that he argued that conflict should be avoided at any cost, and although other Baptists, like Robert Hall and John Rippon, rejected such pacifism, they endorsed Williams' belief that war was socially pernicious, corroding morality and religion.[170] After war with France resumed in 1803, the Reverend Richard Warner, curate of St. James's church, Bath, stridently advocated pacifism. The New Testament, he maintained, drew no distinction between 'offensive and defensive hostilities, between warfare of aggression and repulsion'.[171]

Williams' concerns about the souls of the military were echoed in other publications during the 1790s. Such concerns were, of course, not new. In 1780, the Naval and Military Bible Society was instituted. An account of the body, published in 1806, explained its purpose:

> At every period, and in every state, life is uncertain; but the lives of our valiant defenders are in peculiar danger, and, if it becomes one man to be more immediately prepared for death than another, it is surely that man whose death may happen suddenly, in a moment. How much then is it our duty to endeavour to prepare them![172]

The Society therefore issued Bibles to the navy and army. Nearly forty thousand were distributed between 1780 and 1806.[173] The Society wanted the sailors and soldiers to embrace Christian virtues wholeheartedly: it hoped that they would, for instance, pray for their enemies and show kindness and compassion to captives and the vanquished.[174] Thus, 'the Sailor will steer his course...to the haven of eternal peace...[and] the Soldier will...pursue victory till he is more than a conqueror'.[175] Williams' anxiety about the souls of soldiers clearly paralleled this. But there was a crucial difference between Williams' perceptions and the Society's. To Williams 'the incompatibility of piety with military rage' was evident;[176] he was convinced that military service bred manifold vices. By contrast, the Society lauded 'the valour...of...[the forces'] brave

---

[169] *Lawfulness of Defensive War Considered*, pp. 18-19.
[170] Deryck Lovegrove, 'English Evangelical Dissent and the European Conflict 1789-1815', in Sheils (ed.), *Church and War*, pp. 272-3.
[171] Richard Warner, *War Inconsistent with Christianity*, 5th edn. (Bath, 1805), p. xiv.
[172] *An Account of the Naval and Military Bible Society, Instituted in 1780* (1806), p. 5.
[173] Ibid., p. 3.
[174] Ibid., p. 8.
[175] Ibid., pp. 5-6.
[176] Williams, *Two Sermons*, p. 45.

and generous men'.[177] Even the pacifist author of *The Lawfulness of Defensive War...Considered* described the military as 'brave, but mistaken men';[178] though in a postscript, addressed largely to them, he made a suggestion at which Williams never hinted. He wanted them to lay down their weapons, and, 'by ceasing from contentions for a perishable chaplet and an uncertain reward from men, become candidates for an unfading immortal crown, the sure recompense of the just'.[179] Given the unprecedented mobilization for service abroad and the massive recruitment to volunteer companies, it was natural for clerics to consider the spiritual well-being of the soldiery in general and, more particularly, the souls of men enlisting from the parishes entrusted to their care and nearby. In Warwickshire, 1,245 volunteers had enlisted by 1798.[180] By 1803, there was a volunteer corps (encouraged, one supposes, by John Lucy) at Hampton Lucy, one of the parishes for which John Morley had responsibility.[181] In 1799, there were over one hundred men in the Loyal Warwick volunteers and, by 1803, Stratford-upon-Avon boasted three volunteer companies, totalling 250 officers and men; the Vicar of Stratford was the first company's chaplain.[182] The Warwickshire Regiment went to Ireland, and was there during the appalling suppression of the 1798 rising; Charles Mordaunt, Sir John's elder son, was an officer.[183] Williams had had responsibility for the Walton Deyville chapel since Charles was a boy; presumably the two knew each other well. All this doubtless caused Williams considerable distress.

Lastly, for many clerics—including supporters of the wars—there was much to ponder in the thesis that the Church had become, by the late eighteenth century, 'a mere engine' of government. The radical, Dissenting *Analytical Review* naturally gloated about Williams' contentions concerning this:

> Whatever degree of splendour or stability the church may be supposed to derive from it's [sic] alliance with the state, it is certain, that the clerical body is never so thoroughly degraded as when it condescends to become the tool of a crafty statesman—the obedient instrument, to be managed at pleasure, for the purpose of exciting and leading the public mind.[184]

---

[177] *Account of the Naval and Military Bible Society*, p. 5. After the resumption of war in 1803, some preachers praised aspects of military life such as 'habits of self command and obedience': Ceadel, *Origins of War Prevention*, p. 185.
[178] *Lawfulness of Defensive War Considered*, p. 34.
[179] Ibid., pp. 34-5.
[180] Linda Colley, *Britons: Forging the Nation 1707-1837* (New Haven and London, 1992), p. 383.
[181] PRO, WO 13/4573.
[182] PRO, WO 13/4571; ibid., 13/4,573; Ransome (ed.), *Bishopric of Worcester*, p. 180.
[183] Elizabeth Hamilton, *The Mordaunts* (1965), pp. 238-51.
[184] *Analytical Review* XVII, p. 56.

None the less, Anglican clergymen had long seen the risk to the Church's sacerdotal authority from an overweening state. This was true not only of High Church Tories: 'Walpole's Pope', Bishop Edmund Gibson, had likewise recognized the threat.[185] In the 1790s and 1800s, overmuch support for the government's policies, could, in the eyes of Knox, Peckard, and Warner, as well as Williams, compromise the Church's integrity. When Peckard preached his 1795 sermon, he pointedly observed that 'I fear it frequently happens [with justifications of war] that Moral Rectitude...is not so much considered as Political convenience'.[186] Like Williams, too, he knew that his opinions on the conflict would 'not be well relish'd by worldly Politicians'.[187] 'The preachers of the Gospel', said Warner, 'have no authority to become the heralds of senates, and the interpreters of cabinet intrigues'.[188] 'To write and speak freely is the duty of every clergyman', Knox declared. 'His office demands and justifies it.'[189] And he satirized loyalists' expectations of the clergy: 'Remember the Pulpit ought to be a State Engine'.[190] Williams' dismay about Church-government relations—the Church's 'situation of absolute dependence, and menial degradation', 'the supernal pressure of...[secular] arbitrary interference'[191]—was the understandable, and not unreasoning, antithesis of the total, anti-Jacobin Church-state alliance advocated by Samuel Horsley and like-minded men.[192]

VI

John Henry Williams died on 12 May 1829 at Leamington and was buried at Wellesbourne six days later.[193] When one visits Wellesbourne church today, although there are tablets to members of his family, the monument to Williams himself has vanished. And when he died, his sermons on the war were, of course, ancient history. Indeed, Williams' funeral service was performed by the Reverend John Watson, who had been born after the

---

[185] John Walsh and Stephen Taylor, 'Introduction: The Church and Anglicanism in the "Long" Eighteenth Century', in John Walsh, Colin Haydon, and Stephen Taylor (eds.), *The Church of England c.1689-c.1833: From Toleration to Tractarianism* (Cambridge, 1993), p. 35.
[186] Peckard, *National Crimes*, p. 12.
[187] Ibid., p. iii.
[188] Warner, *War Inconsistent with Christianity*, p. 25.
[189] Knox, *Narrative*, p. xii.
[190] Ibid., p. 171.
[191] Williams, *Two Sermons*, pp. v, vi.
[192] F.C. Mather, *High Church Prophet: Bishop Samuel Horsley (1733-1806) and the Caroline Tradition in the Later Georgian Church* (Oxford, 1992), pp. 250-68.
[193] Worcestershire RO, BA 2245/24, Ref. S132-8, p. 41, No. 326.

conflict which Williams had decried.[194] The *Gentleman's Magazine* baldly recorded, under 'Clergy Deceased', 'Aged 82, the Rev. John Henry Williams, Vicar of Wellsbourne, Warw.' and erroneously noted his Oxford college as Merton.[195] It was sad that his principled, courageous stand was forgotten. None the less, in old age, Williams probably valued a decent obscurity. At Oxford, he had possibly entertained ambitions for significant preferment in the Church. But sixty years later, thinking on death, he perhaps recalled a comment in *The Monthly Review*, which had doubtless pleased and reassured him when under attack for his sermons: 'The author may not be rewarded with a bishoprick, but he may obtain what is of still greater value'.[196]

---

[194] Ibid.; J.A. Venn, *Alumni Cantabrigienses...Part II. From 1752 to 1900* (Cambridge, 1954), VI, p. 372.
[195] *Gentleman's Magazine* XCIX, Part II, p. 90.
[196] *Monthly Review*, New Series, XVI, p. 475.

Chapter 13

Sir George Pretyman-Tomline: Ecclesiastical Politician and Theological Polemicist[*]

G.M. Ditchfield

Inasmuch as Sir George Pretyman-Tomline (1750-1827)[1] has received any kind of press at all, it has been a generally unfavourable one. He has never attracted a biographer, and was not even the subject of the sort of two- or three-volume life, stitched together from relatively innocuous passages of correspondence and designed to give a general impression of worthiness, that was characteristic of the Victorian period. No member of his family and no beneficiary of his extensive patronage (categories which frequently overlapped) produced a literary monument of devotional loyalty. Nor was a complete edition of his works, which could have offered a flattering prefatory memoir, ever undertaken. For his career it is necessary to turn instead to the important but necessarily brief entries in the obvious works of reference, and to general accounts of the bishops of the two dioceses which he served. Recourse must also be had to biographies of William Pitt the Younger, to whom Tomline acted as tutor, secretary, adviser, and memorialist, and under whose shadow he remains.[2]

---

[*] I am grateful to Mrs. M. Bence-Jones and the East Suffolk Record Office, Ipswich, for permission to consult and quote from the Pretyman papers, and to Dr. Nigel Aston and Dr. Bill Gibson for valuable advice in the preparation of the chapter.

[1] The subject of this chapter was known by his family name of George Pretyman until 1803, when he adopted the name Tomline on succeeding to the property of a distant relative, Marmaduke Tomline. He was frequently known thereafter as Pretyman-Tomline and often features under that name in academic studies. In 1824, three years before his death, he established a claim to a baronetcy and was known as Sir George Pretyman-Tomline. For purposes of convenience he is referred to in this essay simply as Tomline.

[2] See the article by William Carr in the *Dictionary of National Biography* and the entry by G.M. Ditchfield in *The Oxford Dictionary of National Biography*, (forthcoming, 2004); J.A.Venn, *Alumni Cantabrigienses, Part II 1752-1900* (Cambridge, 1940-54), V, p. 190; G.G. Perry and J.H. Overton, *Biographical Notes of the Bishops of Lincoln, from Remigius to Wordsworth* (Lincoln, 1900), pp. 346-54; S.H. Cassan, *The Lives of the Bishops of Winchester* (London, 1827), II, pp. 281-8; John Ehrman, *The Younger Pitt* (New York, 1969-96), especially I, pp. 13-18, 221-3, 264-6, 576-8; III, pp. 90-91, 516-19, 750-52, 822ff.

The deficiency is not explained by a lack of source material. In addition to the extensive Pretyman family archive at the East Suffolk Record Office, Ipswich, there are letters from Tomline among the papers of most of the leading churchmen and politicians, especially Pitt and Grenville, of his time. No doubt a major factor behind the relative neglect was the nineteenth century's disdain for the later Georgian church. As early as the 1830s Tomline appeared to evangelicals and to Tractarians alike as a relic of a past and rather inglorious age, an obstacle both to institutional reform and to spiritual renewal. Even the cautious rehabilitation of the eighteenth-century clergy that owed its primary inspiration to the work of Norman Sykes did little for any possible reappraisal of his reputation.[3] In the list of Georgian prelates who have attracted distinguished academic biographers—William Wake, Francis Atterbury, White Kennett, Samuel Horsley—or have received other forms of scholarly attention—Thomas Secker, Beilby Porteus, Richard Hurd, Richard Watson, and George Horne—Tomline's name does not feature. The lack of a biography or similar treatment of Tomline reinforces the purpose of the present volume in its reassertion of the value of biographical studies for the ecclesiastical history of eighteenth- and nineteenth-century Britain.

That same biographical dearth has meant that contemporary opinions of Tomline, including obituaries, have exerted considerable authority. On his death in November 1827 the *Gentleman's Magazine* implied that with his undoubted stateliness and dignity went also an impersonal aloofness. The *Christian Reformer; or New Evangelical Miscellany*, pointed wryly to his wealth, observed that 'it is supposed from his habits of getting and saving money, that he has died very rich', and described him as 'one of the most successful of our church adventurers'.[4] He was not known for personal asceticism. His pluralism was no secret; in addition to the sinecure livings which he enjoyed before his elevation to the bench, he held the deanery of St. Paul's *in commendam* during the entire length of his tenure (1787-1820) of the see of Lincoln. He conferred important appointments upon close relatives; his brother John became archdeacon of Lincoln, his second son George became chancellor of that diocese and a prebendary of Winchester, while his third son Richard became precentor of Lincoln. As David Thompson has pointed out, between 1793 and 1866 at least one member of his family was a residentiary canon of Lincoln.[5] Although not so extreme a nepotist as Bishop Philpotts of Exeter, Tomline was held up as a leading example of pluralism and as a symbol of 'Old Corruption' in John Wade's

---

[3] See the brief comment on Tomline's nepotism in Norman Sykes, *Church and State in England in the XVIIIth Century* (Cambridge, 1934), pp. 163, 403.

[4] *Gentleman's Magazine* 98 (1822), p. 204; *Christian Reformer; or New Evangelical Magazine* XIII (January-December 1827), p. 521.

[5] D.M. Thompson, 'Historical Survey, 1750-1949', in Dorothy Owen (ed.), *A History of Lincoln Minster* (Cambridge, 1994), p. 213. Dr. Thompson's balanced survey offers the mitigating factor (p. 225) that Tomline's nepotism was partly motivated by an anxiety to avoid any repetition of the financial misfortunes of his own family as tradesmen in Bury St Edmunds.

Black Book (1820). That vehement and highly prejudiced work also repeated the allegation that Tomline had misapplied the funds of the Mere and Spital Hospitals in Lincolnshire, of which he was patron, by appointing one of his sons as Master of the Spital and another as Warden of the Mere.[6] The artist Joseph Farington recorded in 1821 that his friend Mrs. Girdlestone, the wife of the Chancery barrister Samuel Girdlestone, said of Tomline 'that it was a question whether he had done more good by his writings or harm by his selfishness'.[7] Such opinions were both widespread and of long duration. In 1893 Archbishop Benson wrote that 'Our Tomlines and Moores' were 'really commercial adventurers', seeking preferments and perquisites without corresponding obligations.[8] The author of the relevant section of the *Victoria County History of Lincolnshire* implicitly accused him of pastoral neglect with the comment 'he was more occupied with public events than with the details of his diocese'.[9]

The purpose of this chapter is neither to bury nor to praise Tomline, but to re-examine his ecclesiastical and political importance and to suggest a modification of some aspects of that conventional understanding of his churchmanship that have become accepted orthodoxy. For his image is not only that of a representative of a corrupt order, but also of a high churchman and of a political Tory. Each is in need of considerable qualification and that process of qualification should also lead to a revision of verdicts upon Tomline's career which have tended to diminish his importance.[10] Through his connection with Pitt he was for some fifteen years close to the centre of ecclesiastical and political power. It is necessary to ask what use he made of opportunities thus presented to him. This chapter will do so in three stages, by examining Tomline's career as churchman, as theological controversialist, and as politician.

---

[6] John Wade, *The Black Book; or, Corruption Unmasked!* (London, 1820), pp. 83-4, and the same author's *Supplement to the Black Book* (London, 1823), pp. 225, 301. There is an entertaining account of the Pretyman family's domination of these charities in G.F.A. Best, 'The Road to Hiram's Hospital: A Byway of Early Victorian History', *Victorian Studies* 5:2 (December 1961-62), pp. 141-3. See also Gregory Claeys (ed.), *Political Writings of the 1790s* (London, 1995), II, p. 72 n.1, where Brooke Boothby's *Letter to the Right Honourable Edmund Burke* (1791) draws unfavourable attention to the wealth of the dean of Lincoln and where the editor wrongly identifies the Dean of Lincoln as Tomline. In fact, neither Tomline nor any member of his family ever held this office; the dean of Lincoln in 1791 was Richard Kaye, the future bishop of the diocese.

[7] Kenneth Garlick and Angus Macintyre (eds.), *The Diary of Joseph Farington* (New Haven, CT and London, 1978-98), XVI, p. 5670.

[8] A.C. Benson, *The Life of Edward White Benson* (London, 1900), I, p. 534.

[9] W. Page (ed.), *The Victoria History of the County of Lincolnshire* (London, 1906), II, p. 75; the author was Miss S. Melhuish.

[10] It is notable, for instance, how little Pitt's nineteenth-century biographer Earl Stanhope, in his *Life of the Right Honourable William Pitt*, says about Tomline. I have used the second edition of this work (London, 1862). Moreover, Tomline hardly features in the six articles on various aspects of Pitt's career in *History* 83: 270 (April 1998).

I

As Bishop of Lincoln, Tomline exercised responsibility for one of the largest dioceses in the country. Before its division in 1836, its 1,380 parishes sprawled over the counties of Lincolnshire, Leicestershire, Huntingdon, Bedfordshire, most of Buckinghamshire, and Hertfordshire, together with parts of Oxfordshire and Rutland, and a few parishes in Northamptonshire and Warwickshire.[11] His appointment in 1787 at the age of 36 owed nothing to theological distinction and everything to his close friendship with Pitt, with whom he had worked at Downing Street in a secretarial and advisory capacity almost from the beginning of Pitt's administration in 1783. George III, fearing that he was a political nominee rather than a devoted churchman, had been most reluctant to consent to his elevation and did so only on Pitt's insistence.[12] Yet Tomline proved to be a conscientious diocesan. He conducted regular triennial visitations of his large diocese, amounting in total to eleven over the thirty-three years of his Lincoln episcopate. Like many in his position he sometimes found the routines of visitation to be tiresome. After one such occasion he confided to his wife that 'these public dinners and suppers are dreadful things'.[13] One suspects that many of his clergy would have agreed. At other times he found genuine reward in the exercise of his duty. At Spilsby in 1797 he recorded that he confirmed 678 persons and was pleased to observe 'the spinning schools in this part of the County', promoted by the Rev. J.K. Bowker, and their beneficial effects in creating employment and reducing the financial burden of the poor rate.[14] In his *Charge* of 1800 he commented favourably upon 'the additional number of persons brought to me for Confirmation, notwithstanding that I have regularly confirmed throughout my Diocese every third year' and praised the diligence of his clergy which had led to this happy outcome.[15] During his 1809 visitation he wrote, 'We were five hours at Newport Pagnel Church, 1102 confirmed, the greatest number I remember there'.[16] His *Charges* virtuously extolled the advantages of

---

[11] William White, *Gazetteer and Directory of Lincolnshire and the City and Diocese of Lincoln* (1856; reprint, Newton Abbot, 1969), p. 74.

[12] For the well-known story of the King's reluctance to appoint Tomline, see *Gentleman's Magazine* 98 (March 1828), p. 201. George III was equally reluctant to appoint him to the deanery of St Paul's *in commendam*; Public Record Office, Kew, 30/8/103/2, ff. 209-21 (Chatham Papers): George III to Pitt, 22 January 1787 [hereafter: PRO]. However, this was by no means the only instance in which a leading politician conferred a bishopric upon a former tutor; for other examples from this period see William Gibson, *Church, State and Society, 1760-1850* (Basingstoke, 1994), p. 53.

[13] Suffolk Record Office, HA119 (T108/45/1): Tomline to Elizabeth Tomline, (n.d.). Internal evidence suggests the letter was written in 1797 [hereafter: SRO].

[14] SRO, HA119 (T108/45/1): Tomline to Elizabeth Tomline, c. 1797.

[15] Tomline, *A Charge delivered to the Clergy of the Diocese of Lincoln...* (London, 1800), p. 5.

[16] SRO, HA119 (T108/4/45/1): Tomline to Elizabeth Tomline, 24 May 1809.

residence and catechizing. He shared with the Evangelically-minded Bishop Porteus an admiration for the Sunday School movement. In 1794 he thanked 'the providence of God' for the 'seasonable institution of Sunday-Schools, which seem mercifully designed as an antidote against the prevailing temper of the times'.[17] From 1786 he was a member of the Society for the Propagation of the Gospel and preached its Anniversary Sermon on 17 February 1792, applauding the efforts of the newly-appointed Bishop Seabury in the independent American colonies and expressing modest hopes for converting 'the Indian Nations' to Christianity.[18]

As a bishop, however, Tomline was efficient and conscientious rather than inspirational. One senses that he was anxious to avoid any possible accusation of negligence. Accordingly, he attended diligently to his correspondence and was assiduous in promoting the interests of his diocese when occasion demanded in the House of Lords.[19] He took care to note the value of livings in his dioceses. Writing from Brigg in 1807 he noted approvingly that 'My Lincolnshire Clergy really make a most respectable figure, even in this district, where there are many livings of 20 & 30 £ a Year'.[20] It was concern over the educational levels of many of his ordinands which led him to produce his two-volume *Elements of Christian Theology* (1799). A detailed exposition of the Old and New Testaments as well as of the Thirty-Nine Articles of the Church of England, it achieved a wide readership and passed through many editions.[21] The burdens of Lincoln over so long a period should not be underestimated in any assessment of his career. It is perhaps not surprising that he declined a translation, at the age of 63, to the even more onerous see of London on the death of John Randolph in 1813. He seems to have regarded the diocese of Winchester, to which he was nominated in July 1820, as somewhat less demanding. But at his primary visitation two years later he made a careful summary of the state of his new diocese, commenting that the forty-six benefices without a resident clergyman amounted to 'a far greater proportion than I could have wished'. He spoke in conventional terms about the disadvantages of non-residency and urged that funds be

---

[17] Tomline, *A Charge delivered to the Clergy of the Diocese of Lincoln...1794* (London, 1794), p. 18.

[18] Tomline, *A Sermon preached before the Incorporated Society for the Propagation of the Gospel...February 17, 1792* (London, 1792), pp. 23, 24-25.

[19] For specific examples see *Journals of the House of Lords*, XLVII, pp. 59, 83, 267-8, 285, 292 (Holland Fen Chapel Bill, 1809); XLVIII, pp. 645, 833, 894, 986, 989, 1006 (Shadwill Bill, 1812); XLIX, pp. 490, 568, 603, 606, 623, 709, 750 (Rev. Egerton Robert Neve's exchange bill, 1816).

[20] SRO, HA119 (T108/45/1): Tomline to Elizabeth Tomline, n.d. Internal evidence suggests this letter was written in 1807.

[21] The *Elements of Christian Theology* reached a 16th edition in 1826; there were also numerous abridged editions.

borrowed from Queen Anne's Bounty for the construction of houses for the clergy to encourage residence.[22]

Tomline had ample opportunity to familiarize himself with the particular problems in the diocese of Lincoln. During the later 1790s he became increasingly concerned by evidence from his visitation returns that the church was rapidly losing ground to popular Methodism. Hence in 1799 he commissioned an inquiry into the state of religious worship in 100 parishes of his diocese. It revealed that the church could command the formal allegiance of barely one-third of the population and that the registration of Methodist meeting houses had risen in a manner which he found to be alarming; the figure had risen from twenty-nine between 1785 and 1789 to 103 between 1795-9.[23] In his *Charge* of 1800 he complained that the report showed

> That besides those who really and openly dissent from our Church, the numbers who profess to believe all its doctrines, and yet renounce its authority, and revile its ministers, are very greatly encreased...The effect of this miscalled Evangelical Preaching, too often appears in the despondence of religious melancholy, or in the licentiousness of shameless profligacy, and in principles and conduct, which the precepts of the Gospel, and the whole history of mankind, declare to be absolutely inconsistent with true Religion and the well-being of Society.[24]

It was 'the well-being of Society' which mattered most to Tomline. He understood the social conditions which had encouraged the success of Methodist itinerancy. They included a large number of parishes which lacked the paternalistic domination of an Anglican squire and where Dissent was consequently strong, together with a high incidence of clerical non-residence and a disturbing separation between the clergy and the labouring population. Tomline played some part in alerting ministers to the problem posed to the church by evangelical Dissent in the countryside as well as in the rapidly expanding towns. Lord Grenville conveyed the Lincoln report to Pitt with the warning, 'the facts are truly alarming, especially as relating to a part of England where one might least expect to find such a state of things'.[25]

---

[22] Tomline, *A Charge delivered to the Clergy of the Diocese of Winchester...1822* (London, 1822), pp. 6-7.

[23] See David Hempton, *The Religion of the People: Methodism and Popular Religion, 1750-1900* (London and New York, 1996), p. 161; W.R. Ward, *Religion and Society in England 1790-1850* (London, 1972), pp. 47-8; Alan Everitt, *The Pattern of Rural Dissent: the Nineteenth Century* (Leicester, 1972), pp. 48-9. The findings of the 1799 investigation were published in *Report from the Clergy of the Diocese of Lincoln* (London, 1800).

[24] Tomline, *A Charge delivered to the Clergy of the Diocese of Lincoln...1800* (London, 1800), pp. 17, 19.

[25] Historical Manuscript Commission, 13th report, Appendix, Part 3, *Report on the Manuscripts of J.B. Fortescue, Esq., preserved at Dropmore* (London, 1892-1927), VI, p. 6.

However, Grenville did not entirely agree with Tomline's proposed remedies. He believed that the solution was the enforcement of clerical residence and he urged this measure upon Tomline.[26] The latter, however, had too much respect for clerical autonomy to take the step of requiring, rather than recommending, clerical residence. Indeed, he favoured parliamentary moves to suspend the prosecution of non-resident clergymen under the Henrician statute of 1529 and did not share Horsley's enthusiasm for the Act to enforce clerical residence (43 Geo. III, c. 84), promoted by Sir William Scott in 1803.[27] In 1830, ten years after his long episcopate, no fewer than 61% of the parishes of South Lindsey were served either by a non-resident incumbent or a non-resident curate.[28] Tomline's antidote to the growth of evangelical Dissent was governed by fear of subversion associated with the French Revolution and he responded to the report of 1799 in a more negative way by demanding legislation to curb the licensing of itinerant preachers. He was far from alone. William Cleaver, bishop of Chester, who, like Tomline, was responsible for a large, unwieldy diocese, took a similar view, and Samuel Horsley, bishop of Rochester, complained that political radicals were evading the provisions of the Seditious Meetings and Treasonable Practices Acts of 1795 by posing as religious teachers.[29] Pressure from these quarters lay behind the bill proposed, unsuccessfully, by Michael Angelo Taylor in 1800 to restrict such itinerant preaching. But in a more positive sense, Tomline was the inspiration for Pitt's 'ecclesiastical plan' of 1800. A device for the augmentation of poor livings to be charged upon the Consolidated Fund, it would have been accompanied by an enhanced degree of episcopal oversight. But it had to be abandoned when Pitt's ministry fell early in 1801.[30]

Tomline's financial expertise, reinforced by the mathematical acumen which had been recognized at Cambridge by his status as a Wrangler, led Pitt to consult him on financial issues which concerned the church. His ability as a statistician rivalled that of his contemporary Richard Price. In 1796 he persuaded George Rose, the Secretary to the Treasury to secure the repeal of the tax on births and burials.[31] He played an integral part in the redemption of the Land Tax in 1798-99, which involved a removal of previous restrictions on the sale of ecclesiastical land, together with the

---

[26] Ibid., pp. 6-7.
[27] For the background, see F.C. Mather, *High Church Prophet: Bishop Samuel Horsley (1733-1806) and the Caroline Tradition in the Later Georgian Church* (Oxford, 1992), pp. 153-5.
[28] James Obelkevich, *Religion and Rural Society: South Lindsey 1825-1875* (Oxford, 1976), p. 116.
[29] *Fortescue MSS*, VI, pp. 20-21: Cleaver to Grenville, 13 November 1799; Michael Watts, *The Dissenters. Volume II: The Expansion of Evangelical Nonconformity* (Oxford, 1995), p. 368.
[30] SRO, HA119 (T108/42): Pitt to Tomline, 2 January, 10 February, 20 February 1799; see also G.M. Ditchfield, 'Ecclesiastical Legislation during the Ministry of the Younger Pitt, 1783-1801', *Parliamentary History* 19:1 (March 2000), pp. 69-71.
[31] SRO, HA119 (T108/44/1): Rose to Tomline, 3 November 1796.

establishment of the church and Corporate Land Tax Office to supervise such sales.[32] Though a staunch defender of the church's economic interests, there were occasions on which Tomline, in alliance with Pitt, was prepared to go further than his fellow-bishops. Recognizing the nature of the grievance, he encouraged Pitt to pursue the controversial question of reform of the tithe laws. In 1786 and again in 1795-96 he encouraged Pitt to prepare legislation for the commutation of tithes into a cash payment based upon corn rents. There was considerable episcopal opposition, led by Archbishop Moore and supported by such clerical economists as Morgan Cove, to corn rents, and the proposals did not reach the statute book. When, during the 1820s Tomline, in old age denied that Pitt had ever contemplated such a scheme,[33] he was attempting to present Pitt in a more conservative light than was really the case, but he also obscured the reforming attitudes which he had himself entertained earlier in his career. In fact, throughout Pitt's first ministry and indeed thereafter, Tomline was no blind opponent of internal church reform, although after the Catholic emancipation crisis of 1801 he tended to regard proposals of that nature with greater scepticism. But as late as 1821 Liverpool had to dissuade him from raising the possibility of an inquiry into episcopal incomes and palaces; such an inquiry, the prime minister told Tomline, would simply be exploited 'by those, whose only Object is to destroy'.[34]

In terms of ecclesiastical patronage, Tomline was Pitt's closest adviser. Pitt repeatedly wrote to 'My dear bishop' for advice on episcopal vacancies. It was through Tomline's influence that his friend and examining chaplain in the diocese of Lincoln, Jacob Mountain, was appointed as the first Anglican bishop of Quebec in 1793.[35] Mountain had become a prebendary of Lincoln immediately after Tomline's elevation in 1787 and from 1790 was Rector of Buckden, Huntingdonshire, the location of the bishop's palace. In 1794 Tomline used his influence with Pitt and Henry Dundas to secure Mountain's nomination to the province's Executive Council.[36] On the death of Robert Lowth, bishop of London, in 1787, Pitt turned to Tomline for advice as to the suitability of Porteus to succeed him, and sought Tomline's confirmation for Cleaver's appointment to the consequent vacancy at Chester.[37] In 1791 Tomline's influence reassured Pitt about the appointment of Shute Barrington to Durham and of John Douglas to replace him at Salisbury. Pitt's doubts about the qualifications of Lord Stafford's client Edward Venables Vernon

---

[32] For a summary of the consequent financial benefits to the church, see Mather, *High Church Prophet*, p. 148.

[33] Jennifer Mori, *William Pitt and the French Revolution 1785-1795* (Edinburgh, 1997), pp. 3-4.

[34] British Library, Add. MS 38289, ff. 45-8: Liverpool to Tomline, 24 January 1821 [hereafter: BL].

[35] PRO, Colonial Office 42/97, ff. 210, 216; Peter M. Doll, *Revolution, Religion, and National Identity: Imperial Anglicanism in British North America, 1745-1795* (Madison and London, 2000), pp. 252-3.

[36] Doll, *Revolution, Religion, and National Identity*, p. 256.

[37] SRO, HA119 (T108/42): Pitt to Tomline, 4 November 1787.

as Douglas's successor at Carlisle – 'I doubt whether Dr. Vernon is of Consideration enough in the Church, to make his Promotion generally satisfactory' – were eased by Tomline.[38] Nor did Tomline hesitate in using his influence with Pitt to advance the interests of his own family in the church.[39] But he did not impose a reactionary bench upon Pitt; his principal role was to advise and reassure Pitt rather than to advance a 'school' of protégés. What emerges from his correspondence is a fidelity to Pitt's own need to balance Cambridge and Oxford 'turns' for the bench, and an inclination to seek to strengthen the 'Protestant' presence among the episcopate.

After Pitt's death, Tomline's influence over episcopal appointments and his authority in ministerial circles sharply declined. But his opinions were still treated with respect. Indeed, the offer of a translation to London, and Lord Liverpool's positive response to his solicitation for the bishopric of Winchester in 1820,[40] suggest that he still carried considerable political weight. But Lord Liverpool's chief advisers on ecclesiastical appointments were William Howley of London and, later, Charles Blomfield of Chester. The cautious reformism of Liverpool's policy of episcopal appointments owed little to Tomline and it was hardly due to him that the number of commendams fell from thirty-five in 1812 to ten in 1827.[41] Indeed, during the 1820s Lord Liverpool exerted more influence than Tomline over appointments to prebendal stalls at Winchester.[42]

A commonly received opinion about Tomline is that he was a high churchman.[43] Professor Mather, more judiciously, sees him as a 'moderate' high churchman.[44] The term does indeed require heavy qualification if it is to be applied to Tomline. Mather, for instance, identifies four key features of high churchmanship as evinced by Samuel Horsley. They were the 'divine origin of the ministerial commission' and the belief that episcopacy was ordained and sanctioned by the Apostles; a 'leaning to the Catholic view of the Eucharist'; an emphasis on the mysterious elements of Christianity; and the elevated authority accorded to the early Fathers of the church.[45] To these qualities may be added a belief in 'the divine rather than popular basis of political allegiance and obligation'.[46] Tomline shared some,

---

[38] SRO, HA119 (T108/42): Pitt to Tomline, 27 May, 15 June 1791.
[39] See, for instance, SRO, HA119 (T108/42): Tomline to Pitt, 19 September 1797.
[40] BL, Add. MS 38284, f. 6: Liverpool to Tomline, 1 April 1820.
[41] See William Gibson, 'The Tories and Church Patronage: 1812-30', *JEH* 41:2 (April 1990), pp. 266-74.
[42] See for instance BL, Add. MS 38300, f. 68: Tomline to Lord Liverpool, 13 May 1825; Ibid., f. 71: Lord Liverpool to Tomline, 14 May 1825.
[43] See, among many examples, Elizabeth Elbourne, 'The foundation of the Church Missionary Society: the Anglican missionary impulse', in John Walsh, Colin Haydon, and Stephen Taylor (eds.), *The Church of England c.1689-c.1833: From Toleration to Tractarianism* (Cambridge, 1993), p. 252.
[44] Mather, *High Church Prophet*, p. 217.
[45] Ibid., pp. 201-9.
[46] I am indebted here to Peter B. Nockles, *The Oxford Movement in Context: Anglican High Churchmanship, 1760-1857* (Cambridge, 1994), pp. 25-6.

but by no means all, of these characteristics. As Mather pointed out, Tomline derived his sacramental doctrine from Daniel Waterland. In his exposition of Article 29, Tomline wrote:

> The Sacrament of the Lord's Supper is a foederal act, and if men neglect to perform the conditions required of them by due preparation and suitable disposition of mind, they will derive no benefit from eating and drinking the bread and wine, they will in no wise be partakers of Christ, that is, they will have no share whatever in those blessings which Christ purchased by his death.[47]

However, he showed not the slightest sympathy with the Catholic doctrine of the Eucharist and inclined more towards the commemorative rite, although falling well short of explicitly endorsing the teaching of Zwingli.[48] His exposition of Article 23, while defending the apostolical sanction for episcopacy and for the church's order more generally, shared the careful measure of acceptance of non-episcopal Protestant religions entertained by many high churchmen. Indeed he justified a diversity of ecclesiastical arrangements by citing the existence of a wide variety of types of civil government:

> I readily acknowledge that there is no precept in the New Testament which commands that every church should be governed by bishops. No church can exist without some government...yet it does not follow that all these things must be precisely the same in every Christian country; they may vary with the other varying circumstances of human society, with the extent of a country, the manners of its inhabitants, the nature of its civil government, and many other peculiarities which might be specified.[49]

No doubt this perception was informed, at least indirectly, by Tomline's anti-Catholicism, which is discussed below. In his analysis of Article 31, he emphasized his Protestant interpretation of the Church of England's doctrines with an excoriation of the practice of prayers for the dead.[50] 'The whole doctrine of purgatory has been shown to be unfounded', he wrote, adding, 'The sacrifices of masses may, therefore, justly be called fables, since they have no authority in Scripture; and they are blasphemous, inasmuch as they derogate from the sufficiency of the death and passion of Christ, as an expiation for the sins of mankind'.[51]

However, the most decisive reason for placing a qualification upon Tomline's status as a high churchman is his rejection of the high church cult of Charles I as a martyr. In his 30 January sermon before the House of Lords in 1789 Tomline strongly reasserted the Reformation principle 'that it

---

[47] Tomline, *Elements of Christian Theology*, 2 vols. (London, 16th. ed. of Vol. I; 12th. ed. of Vol. II, 1826), II, p. 496.
[48] Ibid., II, pp. 483-90.
[49] Ibid., II, p. 400. See also Nockles, *Oxford Movement in Context*, pp. 156-7.
[50] *Elements of Christian Theology*, II, pp. 507-15.
[51] Ibid., II, pp. 514-15.

is the unalienable privilege of every Christian to form his own religious opinions, and to worship God in the manner which appears to him the most agreeable to the Scriptures'. He then delivered a verdict on Charles I which was at variance with the high church perception:

> The unfortunate and misguided Prince, whose fate we now lament, had in his early youth imbibed notions of civil government totally inconsistent with the spirit of a limited monarchy. Not satisfied with that degree of power which the laws allowed him, or to govern the nation by the established mode of a free Parliament, he vainly endeavoured to render himself independent and absolute. In his speeches from the Throne he avowed the most unconstitutional principles, and arrogated to himself an authority which had been claimed by no former Sovereign. In his proclamations, and in his whole plan of executive government, he shewed a determined contempt for the dearest rights and most valuable privileges of the People. He repeatedly violated his promise respecting the discouragement of Popery, and continued to employ many declared Papists in situations of trust and importance, and in offices of honour about his own person.[52]

The timing of the sermon is significant, coming as it did immediately after the Regency Crisis of 1788-89. Tomline had loyally supported the administration, by his presence and votes in the House of Lords, and Pitt had defended the right of Parliament to determine the person and powers of the Regent during George III's incapacity. Ironically it had been the Whig Charles James Fox who in December 1788 had rashly asserted the Prince of Wales's automatic right to the regency. In his sermon, Tomline in effect justified Pitt's handling of the crisis by praising the British constitution as a *via media* between 'the licentious spirit of Republicanism and the degrading principles of despotism' and by presenting political obedience, while desirable and sanctioned by Christian teaching, as not unconditional.[53] He attributed the fanaticism of Charles I's opponents at least in part to the King's own despotic ambitions. Indeed, in his *Charge* to the clergy of Lincoln in 1794 he laid greater stress upon the utility of religion as a means of securing public order than he did upon the importance of divine sanction as the legitimization for institutions of government.[54]

Tomline had very little in common with the circles of old high churchmen. He had virtually no personal association, for instance, with the Hutchinsonians George Horne (briefly his episcopal colleague as bishop of Norwich from 1790 to 1792), William Jones of Nayland and the Society for the Reformation of Principles, or the Hackney Phalanx, whose ethos has been analyzed by Dr. Nockles. Tomline shared neither their 'emphasis

---

[52] Tomline, *A Sermon preached before the Lords Spiritual and Temporal...30 January 1789* (London, 1789), p. 13.

[53] Ibid., pp. 14-18 (quotation on p. 18). See also Robert Hole, *Pulpits, Politics and Public Order in England 1760-1832* (Cambridge, 1989), pp. 102, 110.

[54] Tomline, *A Charge delivered to the Clergy of the Diocese of Lincoln at the Triennial Visitation...1794* (London, 1794), especially pp. 8-13.

upon the mysterious quality of the Christian religion' nor their aspirations towards personal asceticism.[55] Indeed, there were high churchmen, such as Jonathan Boucher, who disliked Tomline's hero Pitt as an erastian secularizer, whose only virtue was his resistance to the wider ramifications of the French Revolution.[56] Tomline's presence as dean of St. Paul's on state occasions, moreover, identified him as a key figure in the association between the church and the closest interests of the state and of Pitt's administration, rather than as one who stood for the church's spiritual independence. He enjoyed public triumphs as master of ceremonies, notably on 23 April 1789 at the thanksgiving service for the recovery of George III and on 19 December 1797 at the thanksgiving for the naval victories of St. Vincent and Camperdown.[57] George III, indeed, suspected that he was too close to Pitt's ministry to serve as an ecclesiastically independent archbishop of Canterbury. When he refused Pitt's earnest wish to appoint him to that office in 1805 the King told Pitt that the archbishop should be 'the Person on the Bench on whom he must most depend & of whose Dignity of Behaviour, good Temper as well as talents & Learning He feels best satisfied'.[58] Clearly he did not believe that Tomline would prove a disinterested servant of king or church.[59]

One of the most perceptive verdicts upon Tomline's churchmanship was provided by someone who had occasion to know him well in his capacity as dean of St. Paul's Cathedral. In 1814 Thomas Hughes, a resident canon of St. Paul's from 1807 to 1833, told Joseph Farington 'I do not consider the Bishop to be what is called a pious man, but He is a man of principle. In writing and publishing on Religious topics He appears to me to do it because it becomes Him in his situation to do what He can to maintain those Doctrines which He professes to support'.[60] It was an observation which encapsulated both Tomline's undoubted conscientiousness and his avoidance of the most profound forms of high church commitment.

---

[55] Mather, *High Church Prophet*, p. 205.
[56] See Ditchfield, 'Ecclesiastical Legislation', p. 80.
[57] See Nigel Aston, '"Come up now to the Great House of God in our Metropolis": St Paul's Cathedral and the public culture of eighteenth-century Britain', in Arthur Burns, Derek Keene, and Andrew Saint (eds.), *The History of St Paul's Cathedral, 604-2004* (New Haven, CT, forthcoming, 2004). I am grateful to Dr. Aston for allowing me to consult this chapter before publication.
[58] SRO, HA119 (T108/42D): George III to Pitt, 23 January 1805 (copy); see also G.M. Ditchfield, *George III: An Essay in Monarchy* (London, 2002), pp. 94-5.
[59] George III had resisted Tomline's appointment to Lincoln in 1787 for the same reason, although it is worth observing that the previous bishop of Lincoln, Thomas Thurlow, was also a political appointment and owed his elevation in 1779 to his brother, the Lord Chancellor.
[60] *Farington Diary*, XIII, pp. 4552 (capitals as in the original).

II

The extent of Tomline's distance from traditional high churchmanship is evident in one of the two most important features of his controversial writing. He was and remained a vehement critic of Roman Catholicism both in theological and political terms. Just as he blamed the policies of Charles I for the excesses of the Puritans, so he attributed the violence of the French Revolution to the Popish superstition and tyranny of the *ancien régime*, which had provoked the growth of deism and irreligion. In his Lincoln *Charge* of 1794 he equated Catholicism with Socinianism as the worst of evils and provided his own explanation for events in France:

> It is among the maxims of Popery, by forbidding the reading of the Scriptures, and by performing the religious services in an unknown language, to keep the lower ranks of mankind in extreme ignorance: hence, their minds, enslaved by a blind superstition, are peculiarly liable to receive any evil impressions, and they become, in the hands of ill-designing men, fit instruments for the worst of purposes.[61]

In his thanksgiving sermon of 19 December 1797, Tomline came close to exulting over the downfall of the Gallican church. He invoked 'the study of prophecy' in apocalyptic terms when he declared that 'the conclusion of the present century should be the commencement of a period…of great calamity and distress among the nations professing the doctrines, and involved in the consequent vices, of Anti-Christian Rome'.[62] At a time of war with revolutionary France and serious internal unrest, he still perceived the principal danger as emanating from Catholicism:

> From obvious causes, the cruelty, the tyranny, and the impiety of the Church of Rome have almost faded from our memory; but we must bring them back to our recollection, if we would understand 'the judgments of God which are abroad in the earth'. She is now persecuted in her turn…[W]e have now more abundant reason than ever to rejoice in our reformed religion. Our fathers obeyed the warning voice, and left her corrupt communion when she had risen to the zenith of her glory; and we have hitherto escaped the plagues by which she is now tormented.[63]

He accepted an obligation of Christian charity towards the émigré French clergy in the early 1790s, but insisted that 'As a national church we can have neither part nor lot in this matter', since 'Our causes are distinct, and must ever remain so'.[64] He was not prominent in the campaign to raise funds for their relief.

---

[61] Tomline, *Charge…1794*, p. 17.
[62] Tomline, *A Sermon preached at the Cathedral Church of St Paul…December 19th 1797* (London, 1798), p. 10.
[63] Ibid., p. 13.
[64] Ibid.

Tomline was pleased with his performance in 19 December 1797 and told his wife that Pitt and others had praised him: 'My Sermon was 37 minutes long—no complaints on that head'. He considered it 'a very glorious day for Mr Pitt just at this moment of heavy Taxation'.[65] Grenville, on the other hand, disapproved of the sermon and thought it 'ill judged—against Catholics—instead of following subject before him', while Pitt thought that the anti-Catholic polemic went too far.[66] Here lay the seeds of his serious disagreement with Pitt over Catholic emancipation in 1801. Pitt viewed the Catholic issue in a pragmatic, Tomline in a dogmatic, light. When Pitt was on the verge of resignation over George III's refusal to countenance emancipation in February 1801, Tomline remonstrated with him, urging him to drop the matter and to return to office. As he informed his wife, he told Pitt:

> That in thinking of the Cath. of Ireland he was not to forget the Protestants of England—that there was still, & ought to be, a great Prejudice in this Country against Popery—& that the state of things might become such as to leave only the alternative of his taking office without proposing that Measure or of abandoning the Country to be ruined by a Jacobin government...I begged him, whenever he had an opportunity, that he would state publicly the restraints & qualifications which he intended to put both upon Papists & Prot. Diss. For that at present people supposed that they were all to be put upon the same footing as those of the Church of England.[67]

Although the question involved no personal breach with Pitt, Tomline became a powerful opponent not only of emancipation, but also of any further concessions to the Catholics of Britain and Ireland in addition to those granted during the 1790s. In July 1801 he expressed the opinion that 'Mr Pitt was deceived with respect to the state of the Irish Catholics'.[68] While he espoused the Protestant constitutionalism which became a feature of 'the royalist and political dimensions of High Churchmanship',[69] Tomline went much further than the 'anti-Romanism' which characterized such anti-Catholic sentiment as was held by high churchmen. In his *Charge* of 1812, he declared, with some understatement:

> I have never regarded the Roman Catholic Question solely in a political light, because in my judgement it involves in it the safety of the Protestant Interest in these Kingdoms; and I am persuaded that the severing this question from all religious considerations has greatly increased the number of Friends to what is called Catholic Emancipation...Can it be safe to place men in authority under the King, who are thus attached to a foreign Power, and that foreign Power at

---

[65] SRO, HA119 (T108/45/1): Tomline to Elizabeth Tomline, 20 December 1797.
[66] Ibid.; *Farington Diary*, III, p. 964.
[67] SRO, HA119 (T108/45/1): Tomline to Elizabeth Tomline, 25 February 1801.
[68] BL, Add. MS 42773, f. 1: Tomline to Rose, 24 July 1801.
[69] Nockles, *Oxford Movement in Context*, p. 60.

this moment under absolute subjection to the most inveterate Enemy of this Country?[70]

It is difficult to establish a clear distinction in Tomline's controversial writing between disapproval of Catholic doctrine and hostility to the centralized authority, temporal claims and allegedly tyrannical tendencies of the Papacy.[71] He had devoted much of his *Elements of Christian Theology* to the former; much of his *Charge* of 1812 focused upon the latter. One detects elements of each in his reiteration of the familiar arguments that Catholicism was not 'genuine Christianity', that Catholics already enjoyed full toleration and that it was a delusion to suppose that 'the Papists of the present day are different from the Papists of former times'.[72] He immediately incurred the strictures of the Unitarian John Disney, whose rational Dissenting principle of universal toleration insisted that a Protestant state, by its libertarian nature, was bound in principle to move from toleration to full civil equality for all religions.[73] Tomline remained unmoved. Indeed, in October 1812, Lord Liverpool had some difficulty in dissuading him from initiating in the House of Lords a motion to reassert the rights of the established church against the Catholic claims. Tomline cited a petition from the clergy of Leicestershire to this effect, adding that 'the Clergy of every County in England would almost unanimously present similar Petitions'.[74] The prime minister feared that such a move would raise fears that the newly-formed administration had actually determined upon emancipation, whereas its internal unity depended upon the maintenance of the issue as an open question.[75] Tomline was in part responsible for the long postponement of Catholic emancipation. As he explained to his wife, he had warned Pitt in 1801 of the political obstacles which would confront any attempt to introduce emancipation:

> I mentioned to him my Opinion that if he had proposed the measure, he could not have carried it in the House of Lords—that I believed all the Bishops would have been against it, & that their number was considerable—besides, that in a question of religion where Religion was concerned I thought that the unanimous opinion of the Bishops ought to have weight, & that it probably would influence many persons in the house of Lords.[76]

---

[70] Tomline, *A Charge delivered to the Clergy of the Diocese of Lincoln...1812* (Dublin, 1812), pp. 7, 19.
[71] For this distinction, see Colin Haydon, *Anti-Catholicism in Eighteenth-Century England: A Political and Social Study* (Manchester, 1993), pp. 11ff.
[72] Ibid., pp. 7-10, 19.
[73] John Disney, *Remarks on the Bishop of Lincoln's Charge...* (Bath and London, 1812), especially pp. 7-8.
[74] BL, Add. MS 38249, f. 348: Tomline to Liverpool, 19 October 1812.
[75] SRO, HA119 (T108/45/11): Liverpool to Tomline, 21 October 1812.
[76] SRO, HA119 (T108/45/1): Tomline to Elizabeth Tomline, 25 February 1801.

He was influential in persuading Pitt to return to office in 1804 with a pledge to George III that he would not revive the issue.[77] His prediction that the Lords would in future prove a solid obstacle to emancipation proved to be accurate.

Second only to Tomline's anti-Catholicism was the energy which he committed from the late 1790s to a campaign against popular evangelical preaching, especially in its Calvinist forms. Anxious about the success of such preaching in the diocese of Lincoln, he began to construct his triennial *Charges* around admonitions to his clergy to guard against what he saw as an immediate danger. In his *Charge* of 1800 he complained of 'Fanatics' who, by 'pretending to an extraordinary degree of sanctity, to a species of faith not to be found in the Gospel', seduced the people from the church and spread 'the most dangerous opinions, with the most active enthusiasm'.[78] His target, clearly, was the threat that he believed the antinomianism associated with predestinarian teaching posed to moral obligation, social duty and civil order, particularly when preached to the unlettered. Already in the *Elements*, he had sought to deny the Calvinistic implications of Article 17, strongly reasserting the doctrine of human free-will and reinforcing it with a lengthy quotation from Bishop Burnet's exposition of the Thirty-Nine Articles.[79] In his *Charge* of 1803 he required from his clergy a 'full and immediate notice' of, and response to, those who 'maintained that the doctrines of Calvinism are founded in Scripture'. One of Tomline's gravest allegations against such preachers was that they insisted 'that they only, who hold these doctrines, have any claim to be considered as true members of the Church of England'.[80] Accordingly, the central question for him was the familiar but highly topical one as to whether or not the Church of England's doctrines leaned in a Calvinist direction, and whether or not that was the intention of the early Reformers. In 1811 he drew upon his earlier *Charges* in *A Refutation of Calvinism*, a work of much depth and ingenuity which went through five editions in 1811 alone and reached an eighth edition in 1823.

His principal difficulty was with Article 17, 'Of Predestination and Election', where he laboured to deny its Calvinistic meaning. Although avoiding the 'double decree', Article 17 sets out the doctrine of predestination to life with some clarity ('Predestination to Life is the everlasting purpose of God'). Tomline's main counterargument was to draw upon scripture to assert the inconsistency between predestination and an all-merciful God, and upon the Fathers of the church to insist that 'they maintained doctrines in direct opposition to the peculiar tenets of

---

[77] See SRO, HA119 (T108/45/1): Tomline's letters to Elizabeth Tomline, 1804 and 1805. See also Julian R. McQuiston, 'Canning and Rose in Opposition', *Historical Journal* 14:3 (September 1971), pp. 503-27.

[78] Tomline, *A Charge delivered to the Clergy of the Diocese of Lincoln at the Triennial Visitation...1800* (London, 1800), pp. 18, 19.

[79] Tomline, *Elements*, II, pp. 311-14.

[80] Tomline, *A Charge delivered to the Clergy of the Diocese of Lincoln at the Triennial Visitation...1803* (London, 1803), p. 6.

Calvinism'. His assemblage of authoritative texts from the Fathers was an impressive piece of scholarship, and he cited patristic teaching with particular effect to reassert the doctrine of baptismal regeneration. He was more than willing, in common with many high churchmen, to draw upon the work of leading divines of the Caroline period, notably Peter Heylin's *Cyprianus Anglicanus*, for anti-predestinarian arguments.[81] In his exegesis of Article 12 he relied heavily upon the *Defension Fidei Nicaenae* (1685) of the high church Bishop George Bull, in order to support the teaching that good works are an appointed condition of salvation as well as a mark of faith ('Good works are never represented as unnecessary to salvation').[82] One of his more powerful arguments was his appeal to the authority of the Anglican liturgy and homilies to deny the Calvinist intentions of the reformers. 'Not one of the peculiar doctrines of Calvinism is mentioned in either of the two Books of Homilies', he wrote.[83] More tendentious was his repetition of the familiar attempt to explain away the predestinarian intent of Article 17 by claiming that it meant merely that God 'by his prescience, foresaw who would accept and who would reject' the offer of salvation which was made to all.[84] Tomline concluded:

> I reject the Calvinistic doctrine of Predestination, not because it is incomprehensible but because I think it irreconcilable with the justice and goodness of God. I do not reject the doctrine of the prescience of God, though I profess myself incapable of comprehending how it consists with the other attributes of the Deity, and with the free-agency of Man.[85]

He denied also that the Articles were Arminian ('they were drawn up in their present form in 1562, and Arminius was born in 1560').[86]

The *Refutation of Calvinism* provoked a spirited debate, in which the most effective defence of the Calvinistic interpretation of the Articles was published in 1811 by Thomas Scott, rector of Aston Sandford, Buckinghamshire, in his *Remarks on the 'Refutation of Calvinism' by G. Tomline*. To Scott and others, Tomline appeared to be denying the Protestant heritage of the Church of England. It was an unjust allegation. He cited Foxe's *Book of Martyrs* to support his claim that the early reformers who suffered under Queen Mary were far more influenced by Luther and Zwingli than by Calvin.[87] Disturbed by the undeferential ethos and implicit

---

[81] For the background to this theme, see Peter Nockles, 'A disputed legacy: Anglican historiographies of the Reformation from the era of the Caroline divines to that of the Oxford Movement', *Bulletin of the John Rylands University Library of Manchester* 83:1 (Spring 2001), pp. 121-67. I am grateful to Dr. Nockles for allowing me to consult this article before publication.
[82] Tomline, *Refutation of Calvinism* (3rd ed., London, 1811), p. 585.
[83] Ibid., p. 587.
[84] Tomline, *A Scriptural Exposition of the Seventeenth Article...* (Binghampton, 1822), p. 14.
[85] Tomline, *Refutation*, p. 252.
[86] Ibid., p. 585, note h.
[87] Ibid., p. 589, note k.

radical agenda of Calvinistic Methodism in particular, he was anxious not only to counteract its political effects but to deny any claim that the church's Reformation heritage was a predestinarian one. Such an attitude does not necessarily identify Tomline as a high churchman. His distaste for popular Calvinistic preaching was shared by many Anglican Latitudinarians, whose 'Protestant' credentials could hardly be impeached. Moreover the bill to outlaw unlicensed preaching in 1800 was the work of the Foxite Whig Michael Angelo Taylor.[88] A most infrequent speaker in the House of Lords, moreover, Tomline took no part in the debates on Lord Sidmouth's unsuccessful bill of 1810 to curb popular evangelical preaching.

Nor was Tomline so prejudiced an opponent of Evangelicals as some of his critics supposed. He made a clear distinction in his first Winchester *Charge* of 1822 between 'insidious and mischievous publications' and 'the excellent Tracts' published by the S.P.C.K., 'that correct expounder of evangelical truth, that firm supporter of the Established Church'.[89] He was a referee for the annotated S.P.C.K. Bible prepared by Richard Mant and George D'Oyly in 1814. He shared to the full, moreover, the Evangelical loathing for Socinianism; Thomas Scott was one of the strongest exponents of that loathing.[90] In 1789 John Thornton was surprised at Tomline's civility to the Evangelical John Berridge of Everton. He added:

> It seems Dr. Prettyman in his first zeal refused Orders to a Person from the University of Cambridge for being deemed a Methodist & he being a Man of learning the College had it under consideration to attack the Bishop this made him for a time not a little Uneasy in his Mind & he determined not to do the same again. Berridge was struck with his Civility to him & remarked prayer opened Bishop [sic] Hearts as well as prison Doors for Peter.[91]

Similarly, Isaac Milner was a strong critic of Tomline's *Refutation of Calvinism*, confiding in a letter that 'The Bishop's notions are Pelagian, or semi-Pelagian at best'. Yet it had been through Tomline's influence that Milner was appointed dean of Carlisle in 1791, as indeed the latter gratefully acknowledged.[92] Evangelicals who sought personal and moral, rather than constitutional or organic reform were not to be seen as a menace. Tomline sympathized with the evangelical assault upon the slave trade and voted for measures to regulate the trade in the 1790s. In May

---

[88] See Nancy U. Murray, 'The Influence of the French Revolution on the Church of England and its Rivals, 1789-1802' (University of Oxford D.Phil. thesis, 1975).

[89] Tomline, *A Charge delivered to the Clergy of the Diocese of Winchester...1822* (London, 1822), pp. 12, 12-3.

[90] Thomas Scott, *The Force of Truth; an Authentic Narrative* (3rd edn., London, 1790), especially pp. 5ff.

[91] Cambridge University Library, Add. 7674/1/C/19 (Thornton Papers): John Thornton to William Richardson, 6 October 1789. I owe this reference to the kindness of Dr. John Walsh.

[92] See Mary Milner, *The Life of Isaac Milner* (London and Cambridge, 1842), p. 71; for Milner's opinion of the *Refutation of Calvinism*, see pp. 445-8.

1799 Pitt, aware of his abolitionist sympathies, urgently summoned him to London to vote for the Sierra Leone Bill, declaring, 'I am anxious not merely for the sake of your personal Attendance, but for the means of Communication with your Bench'.[93] Tomline voted for the Slave Trade Limitation Bill on 5 July 1799 and for the second reading of the successful abolition bill in February 1807.[94] His real objections were to evangelical proselytizing at a popular level which threatened social subordination. Just as the early Methodism of the 1740s was widely perceived as politically subversive, so was the new generation of Primitive Methodists, Kilhamites, and other groups at the turn of the century.

III

Tomline's most important contribution to nineteenth-century Toryism was his depiction of the Younger Pitt as a devout, indeed pious, member of the Church of England. In his much-criticized biography of his patron, of which the first (and only) two volumes were published in 1821, Tomline eulogized Pitt as one who 'manifested his zeal in defence of the national faith'. He implied that the reason why Pitt had resisted moves for relief from the penal laws for Unitarians was a personal commitment to the doctrine of the Trinity.[95] He used his status as Pitt's confidant to convey the story that Pitt had received the sacrament on his deathbed.[96] His *Elements of Christian Theology* had been prefaced by a panegyric of Pitt, while his eldest son William Edward Pretyman-Tomline delivered a laudatory sermon to Pitt's memory in the chapel of Trinity College, Cambridge, on 17 December 1806.[97] Tomline (and his family) were not alone in this endeavour. George Rose gave a general imprimatur to Tomline's biography, of which he read a draft, while Lord Malmesbury recorded that Pitt had 'discoursed on the beauties of our Liturgy'.[98] In 1809 John Gifford's biography of Pitt, to which Tomline was a subscriber, rehearsed the deathbed account, although the author carefully noted that Tomline had offered the sacrament to Pitt, but

---

[93] SRO, HA119 (T108/42): Pitt to Tomline, 26 May 1799.
[94] Lambeth Palace Library, MS 2104, f. 86 (Diary of Bishop Beilby Porteus); *The Times*, 10 February 1807.
[95] Tomline, *Memoirs of the Life of the Right Honorable William Pitt* (London, 1821), II, p. 615; see also II, pp. 377-85, 451-4.
[96] See James J. Sack, *From Jacobite to Conservative: Reaction and Orthodoxy in Britain, c.1760-1832* (Cambridge, 1993), pp. 83-90.
[97] W.E. Pretyman-Tomline, *A Speech on the Character of the Right Hon. William Pitt...Being Commemoration Day* (Cambridge, 1806), especially p. 20, where the speaker claimed that 'throughout life, Religion was in him an habitual principle, influencing and governing every feeling of his mind, and every part of his conduct, public and private'.
[98] SRO, HA119 (T108/44/7): Rose to Tomline, 3 October 1816; *Diaries and Correspondence of James Harris, First Earl of Malmesbury, edited by his Grandson* (London, 1844), IV, p. 347, n*.

omitted to say whether or not it had been accepted.[99] But because of his long personal acquaintance with Pitt, few could match Tomline's authority. His purpose was to confer the sanction of Pitt's name upon the defence of the early nineteenth-century Anglican constitution, and in particular its Protestant exclusivity. Aware of the power of Pitt's reputation, and observing the struggle for his mantle among his pro-Catholic former colleagues, notably Castlereagh and Canning, Tomline sought to deploy Pitt's name to further his opposition to Catholic emancipation. In this he achieved success, despite the literary failure of the biography, which was dismissed by critics as little more than a scissors-and-paste compilation of Pitt's parliamentary speeches.[100]

In adopting such an imaginative approach, Tomline helped to fashion an image of himself, as well as of Pitt, as a Tory. It was strengthened by the perception of radical Dissenters who objected strongly to his criticism of their allegedly subversive doctrines. The Unitarian minister Theophilus Lindsey denounced Tomline's *Charge* at his 1791 Lincoln visitation as 'A libel against the dissenters, reprobating in very strong terms their late attempt to procure a repeal of the test laws'. He added that the bishop was 'by no means certainly a messenger of peace, which his divine master would have his disciples to preach'.[101] Such perceptions of Pitt and of Tomline were misleading. Pitt's later biographer, Earl Stanhope, was almost dismissive about Pitt's religion. He wrote that Pitt's religious principles 'were seldom if ever discussed by him in general conversation' and went no further than to quote Lord Wellesley's dictum that Pitt was 'completely armed against all sceptical assaults, as well as against all fanatical illusion; and in truth he was not merely a faithful and dutiful, but a learned member of our Established Church'.[102] Pitt's approach to religious issues was determined by pragmatic considerations; he opposed relief for Unitarians in 1792, for instance, not on theological grounds but for reasons of practical politics. Similarly, he declined to countenance the repeal of the Test and Corporation Acts in 1787-90, despite earlier sympathy with leading Dissenters, because the opposition of the bishops and clergy would have caused him more political difficulty than the wrath of the disappointed Dissenters. Public order mattered far more to him than did

---

[99] John Gifford (pseudonym of John Richard Green), *A History of the Political Life of the Right Honourable William Pitt* (London, 1809), III, pp. 778-9. George Rose gave Gifford's book his general approval, adding only that 'Some of the most important Points on which Posterity will form an Opinion of his Character are slightly touched & in one or two Instances mistaken'; see SRO, HA 119 (T108/44/7): Rose to Tomline, 14 January 1810 and n.d.

[100] Tomline was aware of this criticism and had been warned of it by George Rose, who, on reading a draft, told Tomline that it might be considered as 'a Collection of Mr Pitt's Speeches'; BL, Add. MS 42773, f. 105: Tomline to Rose, 6 August 1816.

[101] John Rylands University Library of Manchester, Lindsey MSS: Lindsey to William Tayleur, 16 July 1791.

[102] Earl Stanhope, *Life of the Right Honourable William Pitt* (2nd edn., London, 1862), IV, pp. 403-4.

doctrine. Hence in 1800-01 he was prepared to advocate Catholic emancipation as a preservative of control in Ireland. Pitt was certainly not a doctrinaire defender of the Anglican constitution and it has recently been suggested that the ecclesiastical policy pursued by his ministry of 1783-1801 was driven more by pragmatism than by an Anglican agenda to defend the confessional state.[103]

It is now increasingly fashionable for historians to describe Pitt as a 'conservative Whig', rather than a Tory.[104] It is a verdict which might be applied with equal validity to Tomline. It was to the 'Whig' Pitt that Tomline gave his devoted support, both in life and in his biography. That loyalty was energetic and durable. Although he hardly ever spoke in the House of Lords,[105] and all the initiatives which he took in that chamber were local in nature, he attended with regularity during Pitt's ministry when important divisions were likely to take place. During the various stages of the Regency Bill of 1788-89, for instance, he was present on twenty-five of a possible 36 days between 20 November and 24 February to help sustain Pitt.[106] Like Pitt he not only favoured abolition of the slave trade but countenanced a mild measure of electoral reform, albeit of a regulatory rather than a democratic kind. Pitt's cousin Lord Stanhope listed him as 'friendly' to his electoral registration bill of 1788.[107] Like Pitt, he proposed moderate ecclesiastical reform and only after the French Revolution came to oppose most if not all political reform. Similarly, it was only after the French Revolution that he became a principled, rather than a tactical, opponent of the repeal of the Test and Corporation Acts. That he denounced the Revolution is unsurprising; the distinguishing feature of his response to it was the continuity of his perception of Catholicism as the principal external enemy.

At Cambridge Tomline had been a member of the Hylson Club of ex-Wranglers, where he associated with the Evangelical Isaac Milner and the future radical Gilbert Wakefield.[108] He maintained cordial friendships with Whig clergymen such as Samuel Parr. With a gentle allusion to the latter's idiosyncrasies as well as his political opinions he responded to Parr's congratulations upon his elevation to the bench in 1787 with the cheerful assurance that 'no episcopal censures shall come from me upon tobacco,

---

[103] Ditchfield, 'Ecclesiastical Legislation', *passim*.

[104] J.W. Derry, 'Governing Temperament under Pitt and Liverpool', in John Cannon (ed.), *The Whig Ascendancy: Colloquies on Hanoverian England* (London, 1981), pp. 126-27; Mori, *William Pitt and the French Revolution*, p. 11.

[105] For a rare example of a speech by Tomline (30 April 1806), see William Cobbett, *Parliamentary History of England* (London, 1806-20), VI, pp. 958-9 (Beckwith's Estate Bill).

[106] *Journals of the House of Lords*, XXXVIII, *passim*.

[107] G.M. Ditchfield, 'The House of Lords and Parliamentary Reform in the seventeen-eighties', *Bulletin of the Institute of Historical Research* 54:130 (November 1981), p. 224.

[108] A.M.C. Waterman, 'A Cambridge "Via Media" in Late Georgian Anglicanism', *Journal of Ecclesiastical History* 42:3 (July 1991), pp. 419-37.

great wigs, Greek learning, or Foxite politics'.[109] His Cambridge Whig friendships counted for much. He helped to advance the career of Edward Maltby (his wife was Maltby's cousin) by making him his domestic chaplain and tutor to his eldest son, and conferring upon him a prebend of Lincoln and several livings in the diocese. Maltby was a Whig and an advocate of Catholic emancipation. Tomline also appointed the latitudinarian William Paley as sub-dean of Lincoln in 1795. Some of his most vehement feelings were reserved not for Whiggism in general but Charles James Fox personally, especially after what Tomline regarded as Fox's unpatriotic conduct during the Ochakov crisis with Russia in 1791. Elizabeth Tomline made it clear that she spoke for her husband as well as herself when she told her eldest son that Fox was 'the Evil Genius and Mr Pitt the Good Genius of this Country'.[110] Fox's crime, in their eyes, was his betrayal of old Whig values.

Tomline was a clear example of a moderate Whig who saw in Pitt a cautious and undogmatic reformer. Later, he came to depict, and perhaps actually to believe in, Pitt and his successors as defenders of a church establishment which was threatened by the opposite extremes of Jacobinism and Catholicism. Such was his fear of Popery as an international force that he could not but regard any extension of political rights for Catholics as a menace to the Protestant Constitution, of which he became a more ardent defender once emancipation became a serious possibility. In this cause he undoubtedly carried considerable influence. At the same time he expended much energy in seeking to deny the Calvinistic nature of the Protestantism which the Church of England represented. In his controversy with Thomas Scott he believed that he was engaged in a struggle for the church's very identity. That identity as he understood it, was neither high church nor evangelical but much more broadly based than either: 'Our Church is not Lutheran—it is not Calvinistic—it is not Arminian—it is Scriptural: it is built upon the Apostles and Prophets, Jesus Christ himself being the chief corner-stone'.[111] He perceived the Articles as 'Articles of peace', just as he placed a heavy stress upon the importance of public order and social obligation. In these respects Tomline illuminates the complexities of high churchmanship, some values of which he shared but from others he remained distant. Furthermore, his career demonstrated that there was no necessary contradiction between the role of a 'political' bishop and that of a conscientious diocesan. Such a mentality necessarily characterized neither a high churchman nor a political Tory. But had Tomline lived for five further years after his death in 1827 he would almost certainly have been linked with 'Ultra' Tory resistance to Catholic emancipation. Only with hindsight could that judgement be made and it is one that does less than full justice to an important ecclesiastical statesman and powerful controversialist.

---

[109] *The Works of Samuel Parr, LL.D.* (London, 1828), VIII, pp. 33-4. Parr was a prebendary of St. Paul's when Tomline was dean.
[110] SRO, HA119 (T108/45/12): Elizabeth Tomline to W.E. Tomline, n.d. [c.1822].
[111] Tomline, *Refutation of Calvinism*, p. 590.

Chapter 14

'Achitophel Firebrand' at St. Asaph: Dean Shipley and the Withering of Whiggism in the Church of England, 1775-1825

Nigel Aston

'Achitophel Firebrand': not quite the epithet normally considered applicable to an eighteenth-century Anglican dean. Its connotations of false counsel and treachery are unmistakable, recalling both the original Achitophel of the Second Book of Samuel and Dryden's allegorical recreation of the Old Testament character to fit the first earl of Shaftesbury, Whig leader during the Exclusion Crisis of 1679-82, in his satirical masterpiece *Absalom and Achitophel*. Achitophel was a traitor, an enemy of legitimate monarchy, and a schemer who would happily destabilize a kingdom and its institutions so long as he thought it would advance his personal ambition. These were precisely the characteristics of the Rev William Davies Shipley (1745-1826), dean of St. Asaph, at least as they were identified by a senior prelate, John Douglas, bishop of Salisbury and dean of Windsor, writing to Shipley's North Wales neighbour, the antiquarian and traveller, Thomas Pennant, in 1798.[1] And though Douglas's view of the Dean as an incendiary was going further than most other local gentry and clergy would have done, they would have been in broad agreement that he was a troublemaker and no friend to the well-being of the establishment.

Shipley's 'sin' lay in uncompromising attachment to Whig principles. His father, Bishop William Shipley (1714-88), was one of the small minority of Anglican prelates openly hostile in the House of Lords to the North government's American policy; his brother-in-law, the great orientalist and lawyer, Sir William Jones (1746-94), was enthusiastic about constitutional reforms of every kind including the abolition of Anglican privileges. Such preferences may have been tolerated in the 1770s; two decades later, when the British state was fighting for its survival against Revolutionary France,

---

[1] Warwickshire Record Office, CR2017/TP/151/11: Bishop Douglas to Pennant, 10 April 1798 [hereafter WRO].

Whig politics within the Church of England were a public embarrassment rather than an eccentric self-indulgence, and consigned their adherents to a life on its margins. The problem for Pittites was that Shipley was not on the margins: he held a deanery, had links to the Grenville clan, and stood at the head of one of the wealthiest families in North Wales. Given that background, he could only be considered 'safe' if he could be confined in his deanery and on his estates, as he was, for his life. If, in personal terms, Shipley was paying a high price for his politics, one might see this as part of a wider trend in the late eighteenth-century Church of England towards the denial of advancement for men whose interest in reform politics—and sometimes heterodoxy—was no longer admissible to the Crown.

There is no evidence to suggest that radical politics were for Shipley the concomitant of religious heterodoxy. He had no appetite or even capacity for theological disputation, and he reserved his strongest feelings for reformist politics. Even those were perhaps sublimated after his trial for seditious libel, and Shipley reserved his energies in maturity for pastoral supervision, administering his estates, and consolidating the social standing of the Shipley family; the steady and respectable careers of his sons partially offset the distrust and disdain their father could never wholly throw off, though living into his eighties. The dean, through political indiscretion and weaknesses of character, was directly and personally responsible for engineering his own lifelong confinement to St. Asaph. However, had the climate of opinion within the established Church in the half century after c.1780 been more propitious for a higher clerical dynast such as Shipley, the chances of him breaking out of his fastness and being awarded a better deanship or even a diocese as his father had been, would have significantly increased. Despite his apparent religious orthodoxy, Shipley's original association with radical politics was enough to make him unacceptable as a candidate for promotion in the era of the French Revolution and its immediate aftermath. His family latitudinarianism was no barrier to his father being awarded the prosperous see of St. Asaph, but it was an insuperable obstacle to his son following in his footsteps. Other clergy were better qualified in the promotion stakes through their churchmanship, their politics, and their connexions and just as Shipley's almost exact contemporary, William Paley, could not advance beyond the archdeaconry of Carlisle, so William Shipley was stuck with the deanery of St. Asaph, both of them, in different ways, victims of the new unfashionability of latitudinarianism and the chronic suspicion of clergy with Whig sympathies.[2]

The contrast between Shipley's fifty-two years as dean of St. Asaph and the mere twenty-nine which he took to obtain that post could scarcely

---

[2] For Paley, see most recently Neil W. Hitchin, 'The Life and Thought of William Paley (1743-1805)' (University of Cambridge Ph.D. dissertation, 2000).

have been starker. William Davies Shipley was born on 5 October 1745 at Midgham in Berkshire, the son of Dr. Jonathan Shipley (1714-88) and his wife Anna Maria, née Mordaunt (d. 1803).[3] It was the very year his father was serving as chaplain-general to the duke of Cumberland in the ill-fated Fontenoy campaign, an appointment that he owed in part to his wife's being the niece of Charles, 3rd Earl of Peterborough (1658-1735), the general, admiral and diplomat, whose chaplain he was. Jonathan Shipley's ascent of the *cursus honorum* appeared steady and untroubled. In 1749 he was appointed to a canon's stall at Christ Church, Oxford (his old college), and in 1760 was advanced to the deanery of Winchester in the very last months of Bishop Hoadly's life.[4] It was conveniently close to a house he had inherited at Twyford moors through his mother, Martha Davies, in which he had been born.[5]

His eldest son was educated at Westminster during William Markham's headmastership and then moved to Winchester College on his father's obtaining the deanery.[6] It was natural, too, that he should proceed thence to the House where he matriculated on 21 December 1763.[7] William Shipley spent just over five years as an undergraduate, not graduating BA until 19 January 1769, and MA in 1771.[8] The reasons are not entirely clear, though it may have been occasioned by a scandal in miniature which curiously anticipated the much more serious allegations which befell his youngest son: he seems to have had a relationship with a servant girl which ended in pregnancy and his having to own the child as his.[9] If the affair actually occurred, then it was an early token of Shipley's indiscretion as well as the passionate side of his nature. Whatever the truth of the case, it did not prevent him from taking holy orders. He was ordained deacon by Bishop Philip Yonge of Norwich on 11 March 1770, and by his father as priest exactly a week later. He was relying principally on his father for patronage. This made much sense. Jonathan Shipley had been advanced by the duke of Grafton's ministry to the diocese of Llandaff in early 1769 and, before the year was out, he had been translated to the more lucrative see of St. Asaph.

---

[3] Bishop Shipley's career is summarized (not always accurately) in Peter Brown, *The Chathamites* (London, 1967), pp. 325-38.
[4] Joyce M. Horn, *Fasti Ecclesiae Anglicanae 1541-1857. VIII. Bristol, Gloucester, Oxford and Peterborough Dioceses* (London, 1996), p. 104; ibid., *III. Canterbury, Rochester and Winchester Dioceses* (London, 1974), p. 85.
[5] For Twyford House and the Shipleys, see Doreen Pearce and Stanley Crooks, *Twyford: Ringing the Changes* (Winchester, 1999), pp. 159-63.
[6] *Records of Old Westminster*, II, pp. 844-5.
[7] Joseph Foster, *Alumni Oxonienses: The Members of the University of Oxford, 1500-1714*, (Oxford and London, 1887-88), p. 1289.
[8] Christ Church, Oxford, archives.
[9] Augustus Hare, *The Years with Mother* (London, 1952), p. 248 recounts the story.

The new prelate wasted no time in advancing his son to valuable livings in his gift as they fell vacant, much as his predecessors had tended to do. Fortuitously for both men, some fine openings coincided with the arrival of the Shipley family in Denbighshire. Bishop Shipley appointed his son rector and vicar of Ysgeifiog on 19 March 1770 even before the latter had taken his MA degree.[10] Other benefices quickly followed, notably the important and prosperous vicarage of Wrexham on 6 February 1771. The family appetite for accumulation was still far from sated. William Shipley took possession of the sinecure rectory of Llangwn on 11 April 1772, which he later exchanged first for Corwen (1774-82), and subsequently for Llanarmon yn Ial (1782-1816).[11] Meanwhile, he had been appointed chancellor of the St. Asaph diocese in 1773 in what must be seen as a classic preferment pattern for episcopal father to make to son in holy orders and then, less commonly, and unbeknowingly, crowning his career at the age of just 28, was named dean of St. Asaph on 27 May 1774.[12] He held all these posts until his death, and they were collectively worth more than £2000 per annum in the early 1780s. William Shipley had shown himself to be an outstandingly successful pluralist at a tender age, the principal beneficiary of his father's largesse, and had thereby established himself as one of the most powerful Anglican figures in Wales. All that was necessary to complete his material standing was a successful marriage and that, too, came the young dean's way. On 28 April 1777 he married Penelope ['Pen'] Yonge, the elder daughter and co-heiress of Ellis (d. 1785) and Penelope Yonge of Bryniorcyn, county Flint, and Acton Hall, Denbighshire, and maternal granddaughter of Sir John Conwy, 2nd and last Bt. (d. 1721).[13] The Conways' land holdings were immense, including Rhuddlan Castle in Denbighshire and a sugar plantation on the West Indian islands of St. Kitts and Nevis, and Dean Shipley thus stood in line to inherit a sizable share of these estates. It also brought him kinship with the Grenville family, for Sir John Conway's second wife had been Penelope, niece of Hester, Viscountess Cobham, and mother of Richard, 1st Earl Temple, Pitt the elder's brother-in-law.[14]

---

[10] It was reported according to his father's recollection by the first archbishop of Wales—admittedly no friend to the eighteenth-century Welsh Anglican establishment—that Shipley let out this vicarage as a public house so that the curate (£20 per annum) was compelled to live in next parish. The living was estimated to give the dean an £800 annual income but the parish church was so dilapidated at his death it was unfit for use. Archbishop of Wales [A.G.K. Edwards], *Memories* (London, 1920), p. 64.

[11] D.R. Thomas, *A History of the Diocese of St. Asaph* (Oswestrym 1911-12; 2nd edn.), II, pp. 84, 149, 213.

[12] Le Neve, *Fasti*, III, p. 83.

[13] *Complete Baronetage*, III, p. 96.

[14] The marriage also brought the dean three formidable surviving aunts-in-law: Catherine Stapleton (d. 1815); Elizabeth (d. 1825), who married Watkin Williams of Penbedw (by Holywell); and Frances (d. 1825), who married in

The match made the Shipleys one of the wealthiest and politically influential families in northeast Wales. In the late 1760s they were unknown in the life of the principality; a decade later they were a force to be reckoned with, interlopers rather than *arrivistes* and determined to shake up the existing pattern of local politics and patronage in both Church and state.[15] As was only to be expected, the bishop and the dean aroused much social resentment among gentry and clergy families unused to having these thrusting clerical dynasts in their midst and, what made the matter worse, were the Shipleys' controversial politics. Bishop Jonathan Shipley was, in company with Bishops John Hinchliffe of Peterborough and Edmund Law of Carlisle, an opponent of the North ministry's American policy and of the war in particular. This befitted a friend of Benjamin Franklin, but it was just part of a wider, reforming, and thoroughly Whiggish stance: he also advocated parliamentary reform and repeal of the Test and Corporation Acts against Protestant dissenters.[16] On every count, these preferences flew in the face of majority opinion among his colleagues on the bench, but the bishop was undeterred. St. Asaph was a comfortable see, he was too old to expect further advancement, and his son had made a good marriage and become a dean at a remarkably tender age. Bishop Shipley could afford to be true to his convictions and his Whiggish politics were, in any case, offset by the intellectual respect in which he was held as a member of Johnson's Club.[17]

Whether his son could hazard such politics was a moot point in the late 1770s, but he did, no doubt cushioned by the wealth of his new wife and the reasonable assumption that, should North's ministry collapse (as appeared increasingly probable in the aftermath of British defeat at Saratoga in 1777), those clergy who had stood out apart from the pro-North mass of the ordained ministry might expect to vault to the front of the queue for preferment at the hands of an administration headed by either the marquess of Rockingham or the earl of Shelburne, especially if his father the bishop was still alive to lobby on his behalf. This turned out to be a staggering miscalculation (Bishop Shipley fell out for a time with Shelburne, Rockingham's successor as premier, soon after the latter's death

---

1767, Sir Robert Salusbury Cotton, Bt., of Combermere Abbey, Cheshire (d.1809). The dean also had a younger sister-in-law, Barbara, who died in 1837. Norman Tucker, 'Bodrhyddan and the families of Conwy, Shipley-Conwy and Rowley-Conwy', *Flintshire Historical Society Journal* 20 (1962), pp. 1-42, at pp. 6-7.

[15] For details of St. Asaph society in the early 1770s see Peter Howell Williams, 'Social Visitations to the Welsh Gentry of Dinbych, 1772', *Denbighshire Historical Society* 51 (2002), pp. 50-60, at p. 57.

[16] His charges of 1774, 1778, and 1782 have been described as 'political dissertations'. Brown, *The Chathamites*, p. 330.

[17] Johnson thought the bishop 'knowing and conversible'. Quoted in ibid., p. 327. See also 'A Georgian Prelate. Jonathan Shipley and his friends', *Times Literary Supplement*, 24 July 1937, pp. 533-5.

on 1 July 1782), one aggravated by the dean's involvement in a national *cause célèbre* after the North government had fallen early in 1782. By that date, North Wales, like other parts of the kingdom, had become caught up in the petitioning movement for economical and political reform and great things were expected from the Shelburne administration of July 1782. Shipley had become chairman of the Flintshire Association and Committee (for Parliamentary Reform) as early as February 1780 and bent his energies to pursuing that cause.[18] In November he informed Christopher Wyvill[19] (another decidedly Whiggish cleric) of his general support for the Association movement and, more specifically, advised consolidating the Welsh boroughs on the model for Scotland at the Union of 1707.[20] Apart from knowing that the campaign met with his father's blessing, Shipley was also impelled in that direction by the arrival in the family circle of the Oxford lawyer and libertarian William Jones, who was courting his sister, Anna Maria.

In August 1782, Jones had published anonymously (under the auspices of the Society for Constitutional Information, founded by the radical reformer, Major John Cartwright in April 1780) a reformist political tract called *The Principles of Government, in a Dialogue between a Scholar and a Peasant*. It attempted to justify the campaign for constitutional change on the basis of Lockean contractualism but its simple dialogue scarcely concealed the eloquence as well as the conviction behind Jones's words. It was not a levelling document but it lent itself to presentation as such and played into the hands of those who wanted to present the supporters of the petitioning movement as crypto-republican malcontents. Dean Shipley now blundered straight into this trap.[21] Having Jones's tract in hand and wanting to give his future brother-in-law (Jones married Anna Maria Shipley in April 1783) some favourable publicity (as he thought), as chairman of the Flintshire Association, he publicly read a copy of *The Principles of Government* at the county meeting of 7 January 1783 without having previously familiarized himself with its contents.[22] This was a

---

[18] David Wager, 'Welsh Politics and Parliamentary Reform, 1780-1832', *Welsh History Review* 7 (1974-75), pp. 427-49, at pp. 430-34. For the Flintshire Committee's disclaimer on 9 March 1780 that it had any 'factious or seditious objects in view', see Herbert Butterfield, *George III Lord North and the People 1779-80* (London, 1949), p. 255.

[19] The Rev. Christopher Wyvill formed the Yorkshire Association and became, in effect, national coordinator of the petitioning movement for economical and parliamentary reform in the early 1780s. Unlike Dean Shipley, he was heterodox in his Christology.

[20] *Wyvill Correspondence*, II, pp. 81-7: Shipley to Wyvill, 28 November 1782.

[21] The most detailed account of the pamphlet and the dean's trial for seditious libel can be found in Emyr Wyn Jones, *Diocesan Discord: St. Asaph 1779-1786: A Family Affair* (typescript, 1982), National Library of Wales [hereafter: NLW], FACS 628.

[22] Ibid., p. 199.

serious miscalculation, but the embarrassment might have been transitory and harmless had not the county meeting carried a resolution that the tract be translated into Welsh. It was a tactical disaster that did enduring harm to the dean's reputation. Opinion well beyond Flintshire suddenly woke up to what was proposed and who had proposed it, and Shipley became the object of some very unfavourable and unflattering language. After a brief interval, he was privately advised (probably by Jones) that the proposal to turn the pamphlet into Welsh might be misinterpreted (a major understatement) and the project was dropped. But the damage was already appreciable and Shipley—with characteristic impetuosity—proceeded to make a bad situation worse.

The Flintshire Committee was already under attack for its initial countenancing of Jones's pamphlet and, as chairman as well as Jones's intended kinsman, Shipley was duty bound to defend it. The means he adopted, however, were decidedly clumsy. On 24 January 1783 he took a copy of the *Dialogue* and with his own hand substituted the words 'Gentleman' and 'Farmer' for 'Scholar' and 'Peasant' throughout the tract. Shipley then asked his curate at Wrexham to have a few copies of the amended tract reprinted by a local bookseller in that town. Quite what he hoped to achieve remains hard to say; all that his stance suggested was a continuing attachment to principle and a willingness to ride out any storm. The situation was hardly defused: Jones's pamphlet still existed, the dialogue was not amended even if the personae had changed, and the dean was associated with what could readily be presented as an inflammatory publication by those who resented his politics at least as much as the sudden rise to local prominence of the Shipley clan.

Shipley's tactics brought down all the wrath of his political opponents on his head. At a county meeting in March 1783, the high sheriff of Flintshire, the Hon. Thomas Fitzmaurice (brother of the recent premier, Lord Shelburne), castigated Shipley as a preacher of sedition, and travelled to London to have the government prosecute him for seditious libel. The Law Officers, however, refused to act, and Fitzmaurice, undeterred, proceeded privately: the dean was indicted by the Grand Jury of Denbighshire at the Wrexham Great Sessions in April 1783 for publishing a seditious libel. The bishop tried to reassure his son as well as pass on inside information:

> Don't let us trouble our heads about Preferment. Thank God we have enough to be independent, & I am determined to keep myself so...Fitzmaurice is full of rage & resentment. Ld Shelburne tells me he has endeavoured to inflame Kenyon to mention it in his charge to ye Grand Jury.[23]

---

[23] NLW, Bodrhyddan Correspondence, Miscellaneous affairs, II, 19: Bishop of St. Asaph to Dean Shipley, 28 March 1783.

While never one to wait on events, Shipley was active in his own defence, particularly after a letter to the *Public Advertiser* abused him unrestrainedly, to the point of repeating the old canard that he had been sent down from Christ Church.[24] He complained to the Society for Constitutional Information on 16 June 1783 that he had been singled out 'for the object of a Prosecution founded on an anonymous letter, supported by anonymous abuse and lying Reports, and carried out under a false name, with the clandestine Malignity of an Informer that feels ashamed of his own malice'. He also insisted that he had only ever 'taught and practised...those duties, which I have always held to be the most important and the most sacred duties even of a Christian'.[25] This letter was subsequently published in the *Public Advertiser* on 30 July in hopes of winning public sympathy and making it harder for Fitzmaurice and his allies to appear plausible. Shipley also won support from his new brother-in-law. Jones had made it known to Lloyd Kenyon (the attorney-general in the Shelburne government) that he was the author of the *Dialogue*, and this intimation had not prevented his nomination as a judge of the Supreme Court of Bengal.[26]

However, the case did come on to court and was heard at Denbighshire Grand Sessions (Wrexham) in September 1783 where Kenyon was again involved, this time as presiding judge (he was a Justice of Chester), with that rising star of the English bar, the Hon. Thomas Erskine as Shipley's counsel, having been retained on the dean's behalf by the Society for Constitutional Information. It was clear that Kenyon considered that the dean had no case to answer when the Wrexham hearing was postponed on legal grounds and the lawyers on both sides spent the winter of 1783-84 wrangling about the next step. Shipley and his family tried to stay as calm as possible, as Philip Yorke reported:

> His Deanship appeared to me in good Spirits; He has certainly political Courage; and the Sense of Injuries, (and surely in some part of his case, he has been injuriously treated) will raise rather than depress the party so injured: But I must not launch into this Great gulph of provincial Politicks, which has suited almost every man's size of abilities, to range-in: I find that Mr Erskine detaches himself from the Coffee-house Legislators, and comes down next Great session to Ruthin, on his own proper grace, and cost, to support Mr Dean: Truly, I shall be sorry...if that Cause is in future to pass through more than common forms: If it is not yet meant to be fully debated, it will be the source I fear, of many unpleasant things yet to come, and will revive every silly Pamphlet, which as it happens, seems to have diffused so much poison, and which, I truly believe the dean republished with no evil will, or intent whatsoever, but from the high and imprudent spirit of the moment, stimulated

---

[24] Wyn Jones, *Diocesan Discord*, pp. 202-3.
[25] See documents in NLW 2598C, Shipley trial.
[26] Jones referred to 'the strange temper, not to say absurdity of Mr Fitzmaurice': *The Letters of Sir William Jones*, Garland Cannon (ed.), (Oxford, 1970), II, pp. 6-7, 10.

by debate, and contradiction: I do now understand, that Mr F. and his Lady, in his name, disclaim the Persecution; But can the world give him credit, so long, as it still proceeds in the name of Jones.[27]

Erskine's expert advice to the Dean was as friendly as it was cautious.

> Give copies of Nothing—Write Nothing—Say Nothing. Keep up as much as possible the spirit of our friends & fear nothing. I will on my part without consulting you or your adversaries put an end to it if I can, for the sake of the peace of the country which it necessarily throws into parties, but it shall be done consistently with the proud condition which your innocence entitles you and in & which my friendship for you would prevent me from surrendering.[28]

But Erskine could only delay the case rather than have it dropped. Eventually, it was removed in April 1784 by a writ of *certiorari* to the king's bench, and from there remitted for trial to the Shrewsbury Assizes where it was finally heard before Mr. Justice Buller on 6 August 1784. The prosecution brief was as follows:

> The Deft. having by some means got himself placed at the Head of a self-appointed Committee of Flint, consisting chiefly of the clergy of his Father's Diocese, and a few Gentlemen whom he had inveigled to enlist under his Banner seemed to vie with his Reverend Brother (Mr. Wyvill) which should make himself the most conspicuous for propagating sedition and making the People dissatisfied with the state and government of this country. The supposed object of this as well as of Committees of Association was to overthrow a bad administration.[29]

Buller directed that the jury was merely to find on the fact of publication and the truth of the innuendoes as laid; whether the words constituted a libel or not was for the court to decide. Erskine resisted this view, and the jury's initial verdict was guilty of publishing only. Buller intervened to ask them to reconsider their verdict and, following his directions, the jury again decided that Shipley was guilty of publishing but did not find on the question of whether the *Dialogue* was a libel or not. Shipley's 'offence' therefore became caught up in a much wider legal debate about the law of libel.[30]

---

[27] WRO, Pennant Papers, C2017/TP151/2: Yorke to Pennant, Dyffrynaled, 4 October 1783.

[28] Beinecke Rare Books and Manuscripts Library, Yale University [hereafter: Beinecke], Osborne files, folder 5052: Erskine to Shipley, 23 December 1783, King's Bench.

[29] Kenyon MS (formerly at Gredington), quoted in Brown, *The Chathamites*, pp. 378-9.

[30] The proceedings commanded national attention and interest. For one anonymous extended legal commentary in letter format on the trial, see Beinecke, Gifford Papers 200104116-n.01.4.7: dated Duffield, 18 August 1784. It noted *inter alia*: '...is it possible there should be any law against the publicly maintaining those Principles on which alone the Revolution can be defended?...It is a pleasant circumstance, that the known author of this

Not that this shift in emphasis much benefited the dean's reputation: the longer the case dragged on (and it was the legal *cause célèbre* of 1784, the greatest of all trials for seditious libel according to Holdsworth)[31] the more Shipley's (mis)judgement was called into question and the deficiencies of his character brought into prominence. However, over time, the original offence was submerged in a host of other details and a groundswell of sympathy for Shipley became evident, although not a great deal among fellow clergy or landowners. On 16 November 1784, before the Court of King's Bench, Erskine argued on grounds of misdirection for a new trial which Lord Chief Justice Mansfield refused.[32] However, the defendant was not committed, and Erskine went on to present a motion to the court in arrest of judgement. Mansfield ruled that as the publication was abstract, no part of the publication was really criminal, and the dean was discharged as a free man. The news was well received in North Wales, and bonfires were lit and houses illuminated as Shipley proceeded in December first on a visit to his father at Twyford, near Winchester, and subsequently through Shrewsbury, his parish of Wrexham (where a balloon ascended in his honour), and Ruthin, to Llanerch Park (his father's other seat, in Denbighshire) to his own residence near St. Asaph. The interest which the protracted proceedings evoked increased pressure from the Portland Whigs in Parliament to transfer the decision of what is libellous from judge to jury, a change eventually embodied in Fox's Libel Act, 1792 (32 Geo. III, c.60).[33]

---

obnoxious Tract has been appointed a Judge in India. It is still a pleasanter circumstance, that the good People of Ireland have actually been doing, for some years past, & with impunity, what the Author of the Tract has said, they have a Right to do. Have not many thousand Copies of the Dialogue been published by the Flintshire Committee & by the Constitutional Society? Is it more criminal to publish it in Welsh than in English?...To the Jury, who may have acted with integrity, but also in Simplicity & Ignorance of the Laws & of their Duty, I wish shame & repentance'.

[31] Sir William Holdsworth, *A History of English Law* (London, 1938), X, pp. 675-80, 686.

[32] The Shipley family had typically Whiggish reservations about Mansfield's politics. Bishop Shipley's views were reported by a minor canon of St. Asaph in July 1780 and they were unflattering. 'Mansfield's doctrines must be received with caution—His powers of misleading his hearers are great'. See Flintshire Record Office [hereafter: FRO], D/DM/115: Clergyman's [Rev. Peter Whitley], diary of 1780. Shipley also attracted the private sympathy of the Whig law lord and member of Pitt's cabinet, writing to his son-in-law Robert Stewart: 'The Dean of St. Asaph's Libel is at an end. The Judgment is awaited, & consequently there can be no writ of error. Thus has M[ansfield] wriggled himself out of this difficulty & by sharing the debt has secured himself from being called to an account in another place for all his false law. As a lazy fellow, I am glad it is so ended, as a Whig, I am sorry for it. If I had leisure & industry, I'd write a Pamphlet upon the subject'. Kent Archives Office, Camden MSS U840/C4/8, n.d. [late 1784].

[33] Details of the various stages of the trial may be found in NLW 2788 D. Misc: 2,598: 'The Proceedings in the cause of the King against the Dean of St. Asaph,

Shipley may have been publicly exonerated, but his notoriety as an ecclesiastical politician had turned him into something of an untouchable.[34] It was very telling that the only gentleman who paid his respects to the dean on his amazing homeward progress was Philip Yorke of Erdigg (and even he privately expressed the half-serious view that '...the whole family was a body of sedition!',[35] the others by their absence suggesting that their sympathies lay firmly with Fitzmaurice whose force in Denbighshire politics was much reduced by the legal expenses he had borne. He gave up residing at Lleweni Hall, northeast of Denbigh, and moved south to his wife's estate at Cliveden, Buckinghamshire. Fitzmaurice may have gone; Dean Shipley would be a fixture in North Wales life for upwards of forty years. Having returned to St. Asaph 'in triumph' he had sense enough to live inconspicuously for the next few years, even going out of his way to emphasise his loyalty to the Crown by having the Bishop, the Chapter, and clergy of St. Asaph send a formal and fulsome address to George III in 1786 on his escaping assassination by the deranged housemaid, Margaret Nicholson.[36] The death of his father the bishop in 1788 was the next event

---

etc.'; Howells, *State Trials*, XXI, pp. 847-1046; Joseph Towers, LL.D., *Observations on the rights and duty of juries, in trials for libel* (London, 1784); Joseph Gurney, *The Whole Proceedings on the trial...against Dean of St. Asaph, for a Libel...at Shrewsbury* (1784); *The Speeches of the Hon. T.E. Erskine*, J. Ridgway (ed.), (London, 1810), I, pp. 137-393.

[34] Shipley's turbulent career to date lent itself to mockery. Thomas Pennant thus venomously lampooned his neighbour in an unsigned paper, c. 1784-5. 'After conviction, it is to be hoped the influence of pity may surely be permitted to take place...Happy for you, yr tryal was not resumed; That greatest of our Lawyers pronounced yr conduct to have been seditious, perhaps treasonable...Heaven forbid that you was not called again to the bar. Had you been convicted of the fact (my ears tingle at my apprehension about yours!) how indecorous wd it have been for a careless dean to have mounted the pulpit...Had treason been the charge & the dignitary been convicted how irreparable would have been the loss to the Church, where could a successor equal in rare merits have been found'. WRO, CR2017/TP151/6. Pennant's view was that 'The dean escaped by a blunder in the indictment, not by an honourable acquittal, and he insisted that five livings had been given out to his supporters at the time of the [Shrewsbury] trial'. NLW, Pennant-[Fielding] MS, Pennant's Literary Life Misc. Letters 12706E/42, 43.

[35] '...the whole family was a body of sedition!'. NLW, 2598C Shipley Trial. There were some expressions of sympathy in the press. *The Morning Herald and Daily Advertiser* noted on 1 November 1784: 'May not the persecuted Dean of St. Asaph, with the strictest propriety, address a certain marked character, in the pointed language of Shakespeare's Clarence?
Are you called forth from out a world of men
To stay the innocent? What's my offence?
Where is the evidence, that doth accuse me?
What lawful 'Quest have given their verdict up
Unto the frowning judge?'
I owe this reference to Dr. G.M. Ditchfield.

[36] Fifty-eight signed in all. The sentence in the address reading 'In offering up these Prayers we depart not from our Character as blameless Ministers of the Gospel...' attracted rueful comment, especially when it was discovered that the

of personal significance. It made Shipley head of his family while depriving him of the one figure on whom he could confidently rely for patronage.[37] Shipley's prospects of leaving the deanery for another one in England, let alone of securing a bishopric, remained poor in the late 1780s and throughout the 1790s. The memories of the trial, with all its significance and its pettiness, were hard to dispel or for the dean, to live down. His father's principled Whiggishness looked increasingly dated in Pittite Britain and was yet another reason—if one was wanted—why Shipley was an unsuitable candidate for promotion. There was no shortage of suitable candidates for promotion to the episcopal bench and the dean had nobody to speak for him when vacancies occurred. He was not known except by reputation—hardly a commendation—to Pretyman (bishop of Lincoln after 1787), Pitt's main adviser on Church patronage; the presence of Kenyon as Attorney-General in the government between 1784 and 1788 was another stumbling block and the possibility that the king might have anything but contempt for the dean in middle age could be dismissed forthwith.

---

printer had apologized for writing 'blameless' as 'shameless'. Another wag parodied the loyal address, ending:
> 'Throw all th'Addresses in the Fire
> Excepting ours, most gracious sire,
> They do but flatter, ours speaks out,
> And must be well received, no doubt.
> Take our advice; and on the Head
> Of S[hipley]——the Arch Mitre spread,
> When M[oore]——that servile fellow dies,
> S[hipley]——will teach you——to be wise.
> Alas! that time is at a distance
> Without Peg Nicholson's assistance,
> Th'Arrangement of their Age is wrong,
> S[hipley]——is old and M[oore]——is young.
> But Peg once more, at large again,
> Then live King G——; the Fourth we mean'.

NLW, Elizabeth Baker MS, 163.
The dean and other St. Asaph clergy and Justices were criticized by *Cambrius Rusticus* (a.k.a. Thomas Pennant) in a long, anonymous doggerel, 'Sunday Amusements. An Historic Riddle' for ignoring the royal proclamation of 1787 and turning a blind eye to the Sunday field sports and boxing they enjoyed themselves. The poem concludes:
> 'Their virtue, yet dormant, can hardly be seen;
> But when its spring cometh, 'twill bud and shew green;
> Till then, they'll watch over game, pastime, and pelf,
> Religion, dame moral, may care for herself!'

Warwickshire County Record Office, Pennant MSS, CR2017/TP584/1.

[37] According to Benjamin Vaughan, Bishop Shipley left over £40,000, chiefly to his widow, and the dean was unhappy with its provisions. He was reported as inclined to contest an unsigned codicil. Dr. Price, however, informed Vaughn that a settlement was likely by way of an amicable suit in the Chancery. *Franklin Correspondence*: Vaughan to Franklin.

The three successive replacements for Bishop Shipley in the see of St. Asaph could hardly have been more different from either the father or the son. All three were intelligent, thoroughly orthodox Anglicans, much less sympathetically disposed to Protestant Dissenters than William Shipley. The first, Samuel Hallifax (1789-90), formerly professor of civil law at Cambridge, only lasted a year before dying quite suddenly; his replacement, Lewis Bagot (1790-1806), was translated from Norwich, and came from an old Staffordshire family which also owned land in Denbighshire. Following on from him was Samuel Horsley (1802-6), perhaps the most famous prelate of his day, an uncompromising opponent of the French Revolution and the most prominent of high churchmen. These were the men who had to work with the dean and he with them. In each case, both parties must have approached the situation with some trepidation, and yet, remarkably, the relationships were harmonious, restraint on display on both sides.[38] It may have initially helped win him episcopal sympathy that the death of the bishop his father was followed a few months later by that of his wife: Mrs. Shipley had died in childbirth aged only 29 at Llanerch on 15 November 1789, leaving five sons and three daughters for the widowed dean to provide for. Shipley might almost have learnt his lesson that discretion was the best policy, certainly in the matter of rising in the Church. Not that the dean could have had any expectation that this succession of Pittite prelates would be inclined to lend him their influence as patrons for all his efforts not to exhibit publicly opinions which might be construed—as many of his enemies were only too eager to do—as evidence of Whiggish condoning of French Revolutionary excesses for the sake of its original, libertarian principles. Privately, he thought the repressive legislation rushed through Parliament in late 1792 an over-reaction. As he told Pennant in a letter about magistrates' meetings in Flintshire:

> That there may be grounds for alarm I will not dispute—But I will say, that the greatest danger to be apprehended is from our own Apprehensions—The Nation runs panic struck, & what is worse, appears proud of it—This is the common Conversation in all Companys & before all ranks—By this alone we can be hurt—Fear itself will often produce the very thing dreaded.[39]

There was also more than a hint of libertarian predilections in the preface he wrote to an edition of his father's works published in 1792 in which he

---

[38] J. Wynne tried to poison the mind of the influential John Lloyd of Wickwar against Horsley by representing the newly translated bishop as both eccentric and violent against Dissenters and likely to quarrel with his dean. That does not appear to have transpired. NLW 12,422.D/48: J. Wynne to Lloyd, 9 December 1802, quoted in F.C. Mather, *High Church Prophet Bishop Samuel Horsley (1733-1806) and the Caroline tradition in the later Georgian church* (Oxford, 1992), pp. 195-6.
[39] WRO, Pennant Papers, C2017/TP584/3: 4 December 1792.

justified the bishop's support of the rebellious American colonists.[40] This was not the only enterprise in which he displayed family pieties. Thus he assisted his widowed sister, Anna Maria, Lady Jones in collecting the letters and other literary remains of Sir William Jones (who had died in India in 1794) for eventual publication in 1799. Otherwise Shipley contented himself with chapter business, managing his own estates, holding respectable entertainments for local society[41] and exhibiting a fashionable commitment to good works: a sermon for Chester Infirmary was published in 1790.

When Britain went to war with revolutionary France in 1793, the dean appeared rock solid in the cause of patriotism and property. He was one of the leaders of county society who signed a handbill on 2 February 1793 offering bounties to seamen and landsmen who entered the king's forces[42] and had no sympathy for the corn riots that rocked Flintshire in 1793 and 1795-96.[43] Bishop Bagot had insisted that JPs and gentry must stand together to maintain order locally and Shipley was behind him, although doubts were not easily dispelled.[44] Just when it seemed as though Shipley was well on the road to recovering respectability he compromised himself by his questionable championing of the Whiggish Mostyn family interest in the 1796 General Election and, more particularly, by supporting the candidature of the under-age baronet Sir Thomas Mostyn in the November by-election which followed the sudden death of his father. It was the opening for which his implacable enemies among the North Wales gentry and freeholders (who seized on any public utterance the dean made that could be used against him) had been waiting. A vague proposal to recommence proceedings against him is mentioned in a letter addressed in the aftermath of the electoral furore to Lord Kenyon (Mansfield's successor

---

[40] Perhaps significantly, this preface does not appear in ordinary copies of the work. Shipley's hereditary Whiggishness was still in place: 'but let them [the clergy] teach the greatest their duty; that they are not only servants of our common master, but, by the very tenure of their office, servants of the people'.

[41] Mrs. Piozzi of Brynbella attended many solid entertainments given by the Bishop of St. Asaph and the dean in the late 1790s. James L. Clifford, *Hester Lynch Piozzi (Mrs Thrale)* (Oxford, 1941), p. 386.

[42] Flintshire Record Office, D/DM/133. The other signatories were Sir Roger Mostyn, Thomas Pennant, Watkin Williams, Hope Wynne Eyton (vicar of Mold), and Bishop Lewis Bagot of St. Asaph.

[43] D.J.V. Jones, 'Corn Riots in Wales, 1793-1801', *Welsh History Review* 2 (1964-65), pp. 323-45, at pp. 329-30.

[44] In a private gloss to the bishop's letter of 26 February 1796 and its phrase 'I have no doubt, provided we are disposed to draw together...success can be accomplished', Pennant had noted sardonically 'With all my heart, my Lord, if you will take one vicious black horse out of the team' (WS). WRO, Pennant Papers, C2017/TP151/7. An anonymous publication referring to the problems faced by magistrates and jurors in securing a conviction: 'But the origin of the evils we labor under may be traced to a time a few years remote from the former. I mean the Dialogue between the farmer & the Gentleman, that prototype of the Rights of Man'. WRO, Pennant Papers, C2017/TP151/5.

as Lord Chief Justice of the King's Bench in 1788) by Thomas Pennant, Kenyon's eldest son, Lloyd, being one of the defeated candidates in the contest. Pennant, who had at one stage entertained serious hopes that his own son, David, might have stood for the county, passed on some spiteful tales of the dean—'that profligate man'—noting the extent to which Bishop Bagot was under his thumb, and concluding bluntly 'the manner he has past his probation from that time [of his trial] to this, convinces everyone of his incorrigibility'. Pennant concluded, menacingly:

> He had fair warning, by his trial. By the manner he has past his probation from that time to this, convinces every one of his incorrigibility. I inclose words attributed to him last year. One man of character would swear to the words; I think two...If there is a possibility of calling up that worthless wretch, for his dialogue, to judgement, as is asserted in Mr William Jones's letter, it would be a happy thing. The tenor of his whole conduct from his trial in 1784, will be a full vindication of the proceedings.[45]

Two months later Pennant was gleefully telling Kenyon about reports of the dean shooting a trespasser on his land after a quarrel about a pig. 'Enraged, he ran after the divine with his spade, but could not overtake him. I am told the affair was made up with a sum of money'.[46]

The tragi-comic incident suggests Shipley's two-fold importance: the second most senior cleric in the St. Asaph diocese and a major landowner in Denbighshire with money to spare, thanks to his wife's inheritance. The combination made him a major force in North Wales society, an uncomfortable presence for the local gentry like Pennant who could neither forget nor forgive his original reformist persuasions. In fact, his failure to gain the kind of advancement in the Church which might remove him from St. Asaph only turned Shipley into playing the role of a squarson more determinedly. At no point was he tempted to remove himself to his father's old residence at Twyford in Hampshire for any length of time. Shipley's secular power base—such as it was—was in north Wales and he had no intention of moving south for long without the lure of a bishopric. Apart from running his estates, the widowed Shipley found compensation and companionship with his widowed sister, Anna Maria, Lady Jones,[47] and in his children as they grew to adulthood. The achievements of his family to some extent over time offset the dean's own damaged reputation

---

[45] 'The Manuscripts of Lord Kenyon', H.M.C., XIV Report, Appendix 4 (1894), 16 November 1796, p. 545.

[46] Ibid., 8 January 1797, p. 546. For full details of the by-election see Thorne, *History of Parliament, 1790-1820*, II, pp. 495-7.

[47] For his visiting her in London, see University College of North Wales [hereafter UCNW], Bodrhyddan Add. MSS 3332: Catherine Stapleton to the Dean, 3 February 1795, Burton Pynsent. He left his sister £100 in his will 'which I trust she will consider as a token of my gratitude of the unvaried kindness she has shewn me in the most trying scenes of my life'. UCNW, Bodrhyddan Add. MSS, 116, p. 5: 19 August 1820.

but it could not be forgotten that he belonged to an extended Whiggish kinship network which included Grenvilles, Spencers, Lyttletons, and Devonshire. Dean Shipley was the cousin of a surprisingly large number of Whig *eminenti*, hardly a recommendation in itself for preferment in the Church of England at the turn of the nineteenth century. When the Whigs were briefly in office during the Ministry of the Talents in 1806-07, Lord Grenville had far more pressing candidates for the episcopal bench than William Davies Shipley. The dean stayed where he had been since 1772.

Politics apart, Shipley had overseas estates as well as those in Britain to supervise. After the death of his father and wife, he was directly concerned with the two Stapleton estates on the West Indian islands of Nevis and St. Kitts, and true to his robust character, soon upset the manager on Nevis with accusations that his pursuit of 'other objects must interfere with the interests of this property' and that problems were not owing to 'general calamity'.[48] Shipley had to contend with crop failure and the destabilising effect of the French Revolutionary war on the Caribbean but the moral dilemma of slave ownership never seems to have been a problem for him. Emancipation would be an economic disaster and retention of the estates was a practical necessity even if profit margins were slim. Another manager on Nevis, Matthew Nisbet, obviously expected the dean to listen sympathetically when he complained in 1791:

> I must sincerely wish, she [Mrs Stapleton] had no concern with the wretched uncertainty of a Westindia property—Not only subject to every misfortune incidental to the climate; but also to the attacks of a set of men, on your side the Water, who, under the cloak of humanity, & without one shilling concern with us, would very humanely have speculated with, and disposed of our all, in the manner that best suited their chimerical, and heated imaginations.[49]

The picture darkened further following the outbreak of slave revolts. From St. Christopher, Robert Thomson reported on 6 April 1795:

> The old English Islands still remain pretty quiet, but God knows how long that may be the case, or how soon the contagion may spread among us. We have been driven to the last & most desperate remedy of arming some of our slaves, which is a dreadful & hazardous experiment....[50]

Despite concerns he and Catherine Stapleton both held about the probity of the managers they employed,[51] Shipley kept his estates, encouraged one

---

[48] UCNW, Bodrhyddan Add. MSS, 3247: George Daniell to Shipley, 21 July 1790. See also, UCNW, Stapleton-Cotton MSS, Bundle 23v: Thomson to Nisbet, St. Christopher's, 23 April 1789.
[49] UCNW, Bodrhyddan Add. MSS, 3248: Mount Pleasant, Nevis, 30 July 1791.
[50] UCNW, Bodrhyddan Add. MSS, 3231.
[51] See UCNW, Bodrhyddan Add. MSS, 3256: 16 May 1795, C. Stapleton to Dean Shipley. Grave doubts expressed as to the probity of their agents on the

of his sons to settle there, enjoyed the rum they produced, and showed a benevolent concern for the slaves. He was keen to encourage the females among them to breed. He authorized to give up work on the plantations while they were pregnant and offered clothes or money to every woman who brought his agents a child in her arms at Christmas.

Shipley's interests as a landowner both in Britain and in the West Indies never diverted him from diligently pursuing his duties in the diocese. In half a century as dean, his status as a diocesan fixture was assured and he was as well-known in Wrexham as he was in St. Asaph itself—and at most points in between. His long chairmanship of the St. Asaph chapter was unremarkable except that he proved himself to be a man of business who managed to work with colleagues as well as any other contemporary dean. He lavished particular care into maintaining and adorning St. Asaph cathedral, still not fully recovered from the damage inflicted on it during the storm of February 1714 when the roof had blown in and sheets of lead smashed the altar as well as many of the stalls and the organ. During Shipley's deanship, the chapter house on the north side of the choir was taken down (1779). Concurrently, Joseph Turner (1723-1807), the leading architect practising in Cheshire and Flintshire,[52] remodelled the choir and faced it with Liverpool stone. The dean gave instructions that no more corpses were to be buried within the choir, a characteristically progressive step. A subscription to insert new tracery into the east window was undertaken in 1800 and a painted window by Francis Eginton was put in. Shipley's concerns were still not exhausted. In 1809 John Turner (d. 1827) was paid for 'completing the Choir with Wainscot, and finishing the plaster to the wood-work'.[53] At about this juncture, a new episcopal throne and pulpit were provided, and a reredos was erected in 1810. The last internal alterations were undertaken just before Shipley's death, Lewis William Wyatt stuccoing the nave and aisles.[54] Externally, the battlemented parapet of the cathedral was renewed in 1806. Shipley, in fact, proved a model of an enlightened cathedral administrator, deploying in one place, two if Wrexham be included, the gifts which might otherwise have been deployed in diocesan government. His initiatives showed what could be done in Church reform at the local level without submitting to legislative changes to the established Church on a national scale. Shipley secured the passing of a local statute, the St. Asaph Cathedral Act of 1814, which paid for the

---

plantations, Nesbit and Daniell. At a loss as to what to do about it and asks the Dean's 'better judgment'.
[52] Howard Colvin, *A Biographical Dictionary of British Architects 1600-1840* (3rd edn., New Haven, 1995), p. 998.
[53] D.R. Thomas, *History of the Diocese of St. Asaph* (1870), p. 207.
[54] Ibid.

repairs and improvements he had commissioned in cooperation with Bishop Cleaver.[55]

Dean Shipley's work in the cathedral and in the diocese at last appeared to have cancelled out the lapse of early middle age. Pennant and Mostyn were both long dead and the Shipley family had become better known for the achievements of the next generation. No fewer than three sons joined the armed forces during the Napoleonic Wars and two of them died in active service. The eldest son, Lt. Col. William Shipley (1778 -1820), was Whig MP for Flint boroughs from 1807 to 1812 and St. Mawes in 1812 to 1813, and did little to draw attention to himself which might reawaken the controversies that had engulfed his father. The two younger sons also predeceased the dean. The second son, Lieutenant Richard Shipley, died of yellow fever in the West Indies in 1812 but it was the third, Conway Shipley (1782-1808) who died as a hero and thereby added incontrovertible patriotic lustre to a tarnished name. He first came to public notice in 1804 when in command of the corvette *HMS Hippomenes*; his capture of the French privateer, *L'Egyptienne*, of much greater tonnage, showed his mettle. It was recognised by rapid promotion to the rank of post-captain and command of the frigate *HMS Nymphe* in the Tagus expedition under Vice-Admiral Sir Charles Cotton. He was killed in a cutting-out expedition against the French sloop *Gaivota* on that river on the night of 22-23 April 1808. A monument was erected on the river bank by his fellow officers.[56] Unfortunately for the Shipley family and the dean in particular, scandal engulfed them again while they were still in mourning for Conway. The only son to follow the dean into holy orders, Charles Shipley, was deprived of his fellowship at All Souls College, Oxford, in 1810, despite a charge of assault with indecency against an Oxford bookseller's boy failing at the Oxford Lent Assizes in 1809. Shipley's determination to appeal to the college visitor, the archbishop of Canterbury, to have his son reinstated at All Souls has been described as 'pig-headed' by the recent historian of the affair.[57] Charles ended what remained of his clerical career as a largely absentee rector in a Dorset country parish (he preferred to spend time with his brother, Col. Shipley, at Twyford) and any possibility that the Shipleys would continue as clerical dynasts was killed off.

The Shipley scandal of 1809 reminded the clerical world that the family were still not beyond reproach, still capable of apparently culpable conduct of the kind that could damage the Church establishment. And if, in his sixties, the dean remained in sound health and no less capable of bearing the burden of a bishopric than many of his contemporaries already

---

[55] Ibid., 1.179.
[56] William James, *The Naval History of Great Britain, 1793-1820* (1837 edn.), V, pp. 38-40; Paul C. Krajeski, *In the shadow of Nelson: The naval leadership of Admiral Sir Charles Cotton, 1753-1812* (Westport, CT, 2000), p. 68.
[57] John McManners, *All Souls and the Shipley Case* (Oxford, 2001), p. 92.

on the bench,[58] the realistic possibility of his being given the chance to exercise his talents thus was constantly receding. After 1807 his political friends were out of government office when the Ministry of the Talents ended. He was still linked to the Whigs through the Grenvilles, Spencers, and Devonshires, and only their presence in government over a sustained period could conceivably have helped him. After 1811-12 that prospect was hard to envisage. The Tories were confirmed in power, and the care put into selecting prelates by Lord Liverpool after 1812 never made him a serious candidate for promotion.[59] Shipley was doomed to spend his remaining years in the deanery of St. Asaph, enjoying the sport on his estates, looking after his tenants and gaining a local reputation for charity. He also enjoyed the hospitality of his Whig cousins, one of his nieces reporting from Althorpe, on 12 November 1809:

> We have an old relation of ours here. the Dean of St. Asaph, Lady Jones's brother, & his son Mr Shipley. Dean Shipley is our cousin. God knows why: a very merry hearted old soul, as ever I saw, and above par, as they say, in conversation, tho' not so agreeable as his sister. I have known clergymen more respectable & reverend, but he is I believe, au fond, a good sort of man. His son is a remarkably quiet pleasant person, & as fond of hunting as is needful to be a very favourite with Althorp.[60]

Shipley accepted his fate with resigned good grace, and relations with the last two bishops of St. Asaph in his lifetime, William Cleaver (1806-15) and John Luxmoore (1815-30), were cordial if not close.[61] There were always those ready to step in and insinuate a bad word against him and, if the dean avoided any unseemly or embarrassing public pronouncements on the great issues of the 1810s, Catholic emancipation for instance,[62] what they were in private could be guessed at by ministers and Liverpool had no wish to have a second Bathurst (bishop of Norwich from 1805 and Shipley's undergraduate contemporary at Christ Church in the 1760s) in the House of Lords. It was his son-in-law, Reginald Heber, who became the bishop, leaving his glittering Oxford career (fellow of All Souls, 1805;

---

[58] Horsley's successor as bishop in 1806, William Cleaver, was, at 64, three years older than Shipley.

[59] William Gibson, 'The Tories and Church Patronage: 1812-30', *Journal of Ecclesiastical History* 41 (1990), pp. 266-74; Norman Gash, *Lord Liverpool* (London, 1984), pp. 202-3.

[60] Letters of Sarah, Lady Lyttleton.

[61] William Cleaver was a follower of Lord Grenville in Parliament, as was Col. Shipley. See James J. Sack, *The Grenvillites 1801-29. Party Politics and Factionalism in the Age of Pitt and Liverpool* (Chicago, IL, 1979). Cleaver resided constantly. He refused to bestow livings where the cure of souls would be in plurality. Luxmoore reversed the trend, and also appointed his son, Charles Scott Luxmoore, to the deanery vacated by Shipley in 1826. Thomas, *St. Asaph*, I, pp. 178-9.

[62] The St. Asaph clergy sent the king a loyal address in 1807 at preventing further measures of Roman Catholic emancipation. NLW, MS12419D.

Bampton Lecturer, 1815) to go out to Calcutta as its second bishop in 1822. Heber's administrative and evangelical gifts, his unstained character, and his Tory politics made him an obvious pattern for a new colonial bishopric, and the contrasts with his father-in-law, the dean, were many and obvious: Heber was a very different model of bishop to anything Shipley would have made, and the connection came much too late in Shipley's life for it to offer him any professional benefits. Heber had married the third Shipley daughter, Amelia, in April 1809 but the dean had taken some persuading. The Heber family, long settled in Shropshire, were obviously the social equals of the Shipleys, but they were suspicious of allying themselves with such notorious Whigs, and the dean was so angry at what he had heard of these rumours that he forced Reginald to defend himself and restate his intentions towards Amelia.[63]

News of Heber's sudden death after only four years in his diocese reached Wales just too late for his father-in-law to hear of it. Shipley had died at Bodrhyddan on 7 May 1826 and was buried at Rhuddlan. Having been ailing for several years previously and wracked by gout, he had put all the preparations in place for his funeral.[64] So ended the chequered career of one of the longest-serving deans in the Church of England. It had, in a sense, both started and terminated prematurely. His beginning was literally his ending. Shipley nursed his thwarted ambitions as best he could by consolidating and managing his family estate holdings, country sports, small-scale politicking, and chapter business. As his integrity endured, so did a reputation for cussedness and ill-temper which recalled the *faux* offence he had never quite succeeded in cancelling out. Such recovery in his standing as there was took place locally rather than nationally, and to a stunted professional life was added the tragedies of his family circle: three of his sons predeceasing him and the fourth unjustly implicated in a homosexual scandal which overthrew his hopes of advancement in the Church of England as surely as the great seditious libel case of 1783-84 had done his father's. It is with some justice that a plaque in Rhuddlan church refers to 'his resignation under heavy afflictions'.

---

[63] In 1817, Heber was appointed by Bishop Dr. Luxmoore to a stall in the cathedral at the request of the Dean. *The Life of Reginald Heber, D.D. Lord Bishop of Calcutta*. By his widow, (London, 1830), I, p. 473.

[64] UCNW, Bodrhyddan Add. MSS, 117: Funeral arrangements dated 14 September 1820. The dean was 'To be carried to Church by 24 laborers in hearse, paying them one guinea in each—then tenants of more than £20 pa. Among followers Sir Thomas Mostyn, Sir Edward Lloyd and Col Hughes. Past vicars, curate of Rhudllan, curate of Dysarth and Henelon and Gresford to be invited & have scarfs on. The curates at Wrexham not to be sent to, but to have scarfs & hatbands. Pulpit, desk & seat at Rhuddlan & Diserth to be put in mourning. Also pulpit, reading desk, communion tables at St. Asaph & wrexham & Yscefiog. Fifteen guineas offering, 12 to the parson, 3 to the clerk of Rhuddlan. The servants who have lived with me above five years, to have a years wages, above what may be due'.

Would Dean Shipley's career have prospered had he not blotted out his copybook so early? It seems unlikely, for he was running against the new tide in the Church which his personal unsuitability compounded. Rumours about his fathering an illegitimate child while still an undergraduate, his father's Hoadlyite predilections and commonwealth politics were also working against him, not to mention his own fiery character. By the 1780s the Church of England was lacking in the kind of patrons and protectors who would do for Shipley *fils* what their counterparts in the mid-century had done for Shipley *père*. The only way in which Shipley would win back any shred of reputation locally or nationally over time was by building up an alternative reputation and profile. But this would have called forth talents of character which he did not possess; neither was he blessed with intellectual gifts, or with ones he sought to display. Shipley was certainly consistent in remaining true to principle. He never reneged on the ancestral Whiggism which he had inherited and, in a sense, been martyred for. As one obituary notice read, throughout life he was known for his 'sincere attachment...to those liberal principles which produced the Revolution [of 1688]'.[65] Such 'liberal principles' were not calculated to attract the positive notice of the powerbrokers in Church and State between the 1780s and the 1820s. Shipley may have steered clear of compromising himself through heterodox theology; that could never offset what were widely considered to be incendiary politics for a senior cleric to hold, and the Whig kinsmen and well-wishers who might have acted for him were never in power long enough to do so. In any case, Shipley lacked the number of clerical well-wishers his father had enjoyed, and the damage done early to his character naturally made ambitious colleagues think twice about association with him. He died just four years before Earl Grey's administration was formed, a faintly embarrassing survivor from a different age. The Whigs of 1830 initiated a major legislative overhaul of the Church establishment with the assistance of moderate Whig clerics. Their interest in that project was in stark contrast to Dean Shipley's practice of making the existing unreformed apparatus work effectively at a local level. It represented a sea change in outlooks and attitudes. In Bishop Shipley's heyday Whiggery had done a man some good in moving up the *cursus honorum*; so it did in the 1830s. In the intervening era it was a handicap few succeeded in overcoming, and the career of Dean William Davies Shipley stands as a cautionary tale of that example.

---

[65] *Gentleman's Magazine* 96 (1826). II, p. 641.

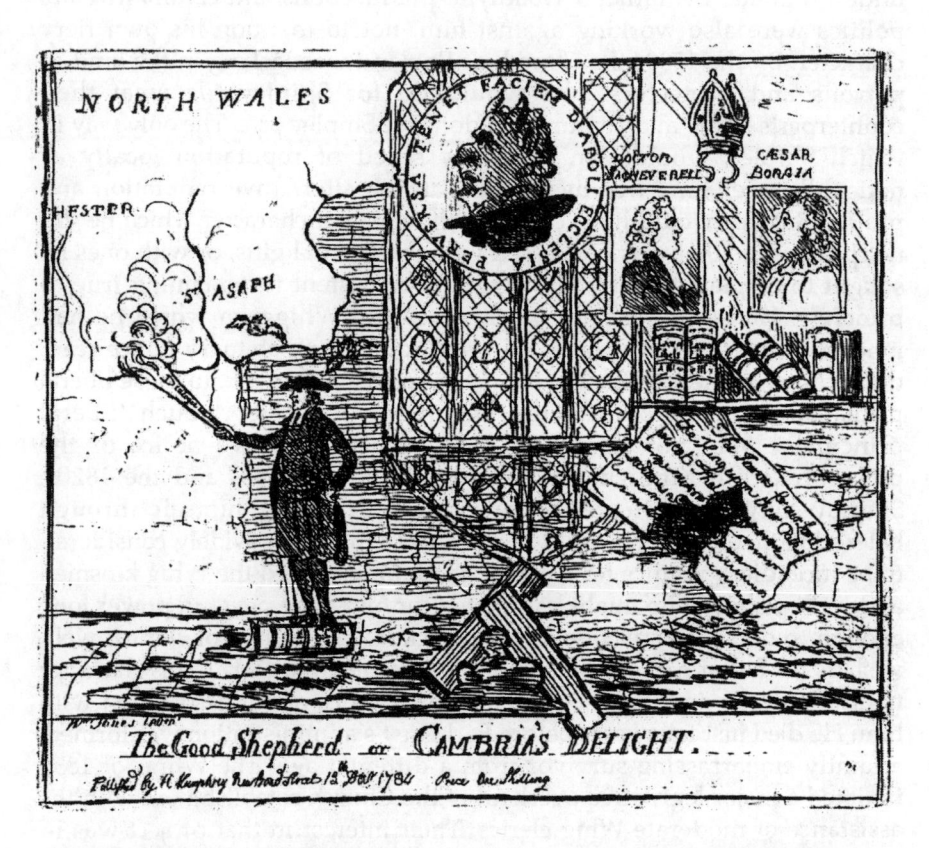

An unpublished pencil sketch (probably by Thomas Pennant) produced at the time of Dean Shipley's 'acquittal' giving him diabolic features and linking him to Cesare Borgia and Dr Sacheverell. Published with the permission of the Warwickshire County Record Office (reference number CR2017/TP584/4) and the Earl of Denbigh.

Index

Abbott, George 21
Abbott, Robert 22
Adam, Thomas 147
Addison, Joseph 124
Aldrich, Charles 46
Aldrich, Henry 44, 47
America 120, 148, 182, 184, 189, 190, 196, 227, 281, 299, 303
American Revolution 29, 33, 180, 231-254, 312
Andrewes, Lancelot 203
Anne, Queen, 38, 45, 52, 136, 179, 182
anti-Catholicism 179-229, 286, 290-298
Arianism 38, 47, 48, 52, 53, 54, 55, 56, 69, 73, 74, 77, 238
Arminianism 20, 22, 23, 70, 176, 184, 200, 203, 204, 207, 208, 224, 293, 298
Arndt, John 168
Ashby de la Zouche 24
Athanasian Creed, 49, 55, 56, 67, 68, 72, 73, 74, 75
atheism 100, 261
Atterbury, Francis 5, 44, 46, 47, 53, 54, 57, 59, 91, 278
Atwell, Joseph 116
Auckinleck 132, 142, 143, 144
Augustine, Saint 148, 150

Babbington plot 82
Bacon, Sir Nicholas 24, 107
Bagot, Lewis 311, 312
Bancroft, Richard 10, 18, 20, 23, 25
Bane, Ralph 14
Bangorian controversy 58, 61-80
Baptists 176, 273
Barchester 13
Barrington, Sir Francis 24
Barrington, Shute 189, 192, 219, 224, 284
Bastwick, William 15

Bath 188, 200, 227, 273
Baxter, Richard 203
Bentley, Richard 44
Berkeley, George 184
Beveridge, William 203
Bingley 177
Birmingham 259
Blackburne, Francis 184, 220
Blackburne, Lancelot 50
Blomfield, Charles James 285
Bolton, Robert 168
Bonaparte, Napoleon 262, 316
Boswell, James 119-145
Bowyer, Thomas, 66
Boyle, Robert 107, 108
Bradford, John, 17
Bramhall, John 64
Brett, Thomas 62
Bristol 152, 185, 188
British and Foreign Bible Society 208, 209
Bromley, Henry 24
Bromley, Margaret 24
Bromley, Thomas 24
Brooke, Henry 164
Bunting, Jabez 155
Bunyan, John 150
Burgess, Thomas 209, 224
Burghley, Lord 18
Burke, Edmund 231, 242, 246, 252, 253
Burnet, Gilbert 31, 35, 37, 38, 40, 41, 42, 57, 58, 67, 206
Bury, Arthur 46
Burton, Henry 15
Butler, Joseph 232

Calamy, Edmund 75
Calvinism 11, 12, 14, 21, 22, 52, 123, 124, 125, 127, 129, 139, 176, 182, 187, 195, 198, 199, 200, 202, 203, 204, 205, 206, 207,

208, 213, 218, 223, 224, 225, 292, 293, 294, 298
Cambridge 17, 18, 22, 47, 69, 104, 272, 283, 285, 295, 297, 298, 311
Campion, Edmund 15
Canning, George 296
Canterbury 177
Carleton, George 21
Caroline, Queen, 46, 53, 56, 68
Cartwright, Thomas 17
Cave, William 68
Castlereagh, Lord 296
Catcott, Alexander 188
Catholic Emancipation 290-298
Catholicism 14, 21, 31, 36, 38, 43, 52, 81-95, 99, 102, 125, 131, 132, 136, 140, 141, 144, 182, 185, 187, 209, 210, 211, 214, 216, 220, 221, 228, 238, 261, 289, 290-298
Cecil, Richard 213
Chapel Royal 136, 137
Charlett, Arthur 44, 56
Charles I 12, 15, 20, 25, 44, 52, 81, 114, 138, 207, 286, 287
Charles II 10, 53
Charles IX 89
Charles Edward, Prince 91, 94
Charlotte, Queen 227
Chillingworth, William 75, 209, 210
Church, Thomas 154, 166, 167, 168
Clapham Sect 196
Clarendon, Earl of, 30, 143
Clarke, Samuel 48, 49, 50, 53, 56, 57, 59, 69, 70, 72, 74, 75, 76, 232, 257
Cleaver, William 224, 283, 284, 317
Clement VII, Pope 89, 93
Cobbett, William 4
Coke, Thomas 155
Collier, Jeremy 206, 223
Collins, Anthony 40
Compton, Henry 57
comprehension 10, 31
'confessional state' 3, 4, 6, 64, 145, 157
Congregationalism 13
Contzen, Adam 17
conversion 154
Convocation 31, 44, 45, 48, 49, 50, 52, 53, 58, 61, 159, 160

Conybeare, John 59
Cope, Sir Anthony 24
Court of High Commission 20, 22
Covenant 21
Coverdale, Miles 17, 20, 129
Cownley Joseph 167
Cranmer, Thomas 17, 18, 19, 64, 143
Cudworth, Ralph 232
Curnock, Nehemiah 153

Dalrymple, Sir David 123, 124, 125, 126
Daubney, Charles 179-229
Dawson, Thomas 67
Defoe, Daniel 29, 32, 39, 40
Deism, 31, 33, 35, 39, 41, 43, 61, 70, 100, 105, 132
Denny, Sir Anthony 14
Deptford 153
Descartes, René 99
Dillon, Arthur 88
Dissent 2, 9-26, 28, 29, 31, 32, 35, 38, 40, 41, 42, 43, 45, 51, 53, 54, 55, 59, 61, 70, 74, 75, 77, 78, 79, 82, 119, 120, 141, 145, 158, 166, 167, 170, 175, 176, 180, 181, 184, 185, 188, 189, 192, 194, 196, 197, 198, 199, 203, 207, 208, 210, 211, 213, 214, 215, 216, 217, 219, 220, 222, 228, 231-254, 259, 282, 296, 311
Divine Right 34
Doddridge, Phillip 6, 102
Dodwell, Henry 32
Downame, George 22
Dun, John 124, 130, 134, 137
Durham 78

earthquakes 111, 112, 116
Ecclesiastical Commission 22
ecumenism 149
Edward VI 14, 17
Elizabeth I 17, 18, 21
English Civil War 1, 11, 14, 23, 25, 26, 31, 38, 185, 196
Enlightenment 92-117, 131, 232, 264
erastianism 31, 34, 57

Eucharist 61-80, 286

Feathers Tavern Petition 183, 199
Fellowes, Richard 199
Field, John 9, 10, 20, 22
Fielding, Henry 57, 58
Filmer, Robert 30, 31, 33
Firmin, Thomas 37
Fish, Simon 20
Fisher, John 189
Fleetwood, William 49
Fletcher, John 175, 204, 206, 217
Foote, Samuel 131
Fox, Charles James 287, 294, 298, 308
Foxe, John 14, 16, 24, 293
France 74, 113, 160, 171, 172, 215, 216, 243, 312
French Revolution and Wars 180, 186, 196, 212, 218, 219, 223, 231-254, 255-276, 288, 289, 299-319

Gardiner, Stephen 18
Gastrell, Francis 54
Gell, Sir Phillip 23
George I 45, 73, 83, 88, 89
George II 77, 78, 79
George III 130, 227, 263, 267, 270, 280, 287, 288, 290, 292, 308, 309
Germany 160, 186
Gibson, Edmund 5, 50, 57, 59, 62, 143, 275
Gladstone, William 13
Glorious Revolution 27, 29, 32, 34, 47, 179, 241, 242, 244, 252, 253, 319
Goodwin, Timothy 56
Green, John 170
Grenville, Lord 278, 282-298, 300, 314, 317
Grindal, Edmund 1, 19
Gunpowder plot 82

Hackney Phalanx 227, 287
Hall, Joseph 207
Hall, Westley 159, 165, 197
Hallifax, Samuel 311
Harley, Robert 46
Harpsfield, Nicholas 14
Harris, Howell 6

Harsnet, Samuel 18, 25
Hastings, Sir Francis 24
Hatton, Sir Christopher 18
Haweis, Thomas 183, 193, 196, 204, 205
Haworth 177
Hay John 88, 91, 92
Hearne, Thomas 45, 67
Heber, Reginald 317-318
Heigham, Sir John 9, 24
Henry VIII, 17
Herbert, George 134
Hereford 47, 61
Hertfordshire 24
heterodoxy 27, 43-59, 61-80, 98, 194, 300-319
Hervey, James 187
Heylin, Peter 14, 206, 223, 227
Hickes, George 32, 65, 190, 227
high churchmanship 1, 30, 31, 38, 43-59, 183, 202, 220, 275, 286, 290, 294
Hildersham, Arthur 22, 24
Hill, Richard 176, 193, 197, 198, 204, 206, 210, 217, 225, 227
Hill, Rowland 187, 199
Hinchliffe, John 303
Hoadly, Benjamin 29, 31, 32, 38, 39, 40, 42, 47, 50, 52, 53, 57, 58, 59, 61-80, 190, 191, 205, 212
Holland, Thomas 22
Holles, Lord 24
Hollis, Thomas 184, 220
Hooker, Richard 64, 76, 190, 197, 203
Hooper, John 19
Hopton 23
Horne, George 33, 42, 162, 174, 183, 184, 192, 224, 225, 278, 287
Horsley, Samuel 181, 184, 187, 192, 205, 212, 217, 218, 219, 224, 225, 275, 278, 283, 285, 311
Howley, William 285
Hume, David 98, 103, 106, 132, 133, 232
Humphrey, Laurence 17, 22
Huntington, Countess of 171
Huntington, Earl of, 24

Hurd, Richard 103, 267, 268, 278
Hutcheson, Francis 232
Hutchinson, John 183, 287
Hutton, James 164, 165

Ingham, Benjamin 171
Ireland 29, 30, 120, 152, 191, 297
Italy 88, 187

Jackson, John 67, 74
Jacobinism 181, 191, 298
Jacobitism 27-43, 45, 53, 74, 81-95, 119-145, 160, 255
James I 24, 25, 81
James II 10, 20, 22, 33, 34, 38, 41, 81-95
Jane, William 44
Jebb, John 224
Jewell, John 19, 191, 197, 206, 221
Johnson, John 62, 65, 124
Johnson, Samuel 31, 121, 126, 141, 163
Jones, William 33, 42, 183, 188, 217, 287, 304

Ken, Thomas 134
Kennett, White 278
Kent, Duke of, 46
Kenyon, Lord 303-314
Kettlewell, John 44
King, Lord 150
Knolly, Sir Francis 24
Knox, James 169
Knox, Vicesimus, 271, 275

Lancaster, Joseph 211
Landor, Walter Savage 268
Latimer, Hugh 17
latitudinarianism 1, 27, 30, 31, 32, 38, 40, 42, 43, 51, 53, 137, 138, 161, 180, 182, 184, 185, 199, 210, 221, 222, 294, 300-319
Laud, William 12, 14, 15, 20, 21, 22, 23, 24, 52, 134, 174, 181, 182, 206, 212, 225
Lavington, George 173
Law, Edmund 303
Law, William 62, 190

Leeds 167
Leicester, Earl of, 24
Leicester, Lettice Countess of, 24
Leslie, Charles 27-43, 65, 190
Leslie, John 30
Lewis, John 65
Lincoln 278-291
Lindsey, Theophilus 154
Lisbon 111, 112, 116
Liverpool, Lord 285, 291, 317
Llandaff 301
Locke, John 29, 32, 107, 240, 241, 304
London 30, 52, 53, 79, 111, 112, 132, 133, 135, 140, 142, 172, 252, 259, 285, 305
'Long Reformation' 13, 145
Lowth, Robert 284
Ludlam, Thomas 199
Luther, Martin 165, 214, 221
Luxmoore, John 317

McQuhae, William 130
Maltby, Edward 298
Manchester 13
Mangey, Thomas 67
Mant, Richard 202, 294
Mar, Earl of/Duke of, 86, 87, 88, 91, 94
Markham, William 301
Marlborough, Duchess of, 69
Marsh, Herbert 209, 224
Mary I 17, 19, 205, 206, 293
Maynard, Sir John 24
Meade, Thomas 185
Mede, Joseph 217
Methodism 1, 2, 5, 131, 140, 147-178, 180, 183, 184, 188, 192, 195, 198, 202, 223, 282, 294, 295
Middleton, Conyers 62, 104, 105, 115
Middleton, John White 194
Mildmay, Sir Walter 24
Millar, Andrew 103
Millenary Petition, 21
Milton, John 38
miracles 106, 111, 115
Modena, Duke of 86

Index

Monmouth, Duke of, 35
Montagu, Richard 211
Mordaunt, Sir John 269, 274
More, Hannah 195, 196, 200, 201, 224, 226, 227, 228, 229
Morley, John 268, 269, 270, 274
Morrice, Roger 9-26
Morrice, Sir William 24
Moss, Charles 188
Murray, James 86, 87, 89, 90

national debt 244-245, 248, 249, 250
Neile, Richard 20
Nelson, Robert 44, 48
Netherlands 139, 140, 215
Newcastle on Tyne 151, 152
New England, 14
Newman, Cardinal J.H., 150
Newton, Isaac 99, 101, 102, 107, 108, 114, 116, 117, 207
Newton, John 217
Nicene Creed 265
Nithsdale, Lady 90-91
Nithsdale, Lord 90
Nonconformity, 5, 6, 17, 19, 20, 21, 75, 78, 186, 199
Nonjury 27-42, 43, 65, 142, 144, 182, 190, 206, 226
non-residence 3, 159, 283-298
Norton, Thomas 24
Norwich 169, 301
Nottingham, Earl of, 56

occasional conformity 41, 45, 46
Old Pretender ('James III') 30, 45, 81-95
Osgodby 23
Overall, John 18
Oxford 17, 22, 44, 45, 46, 48, 51, 55, 64, 136, 137, 157, 162, 176, 181, 185, 188, 221, 222, 228, 229, 257, 276, 285, 301, 306, 316

Paine, Thomas 225, 242, 252, 259
Paley, William 190, 191, 221, 298
Palmer, William 228
Parker, Matthew 18, 19
Parr, Samuel 267, 268, 270, 297

Pascal 107
Passover 66
Patrick, Simon 57, 76
Pelagianism 22, 124, 125, 141, 294
Pennant, Thomas 299, 313
Percival, Lord 46, 49, 53, 56
Percy, Thomas 68
Perronet, Charles 167
Perronet, Edward 167
Peter the Great 86
Petition of Right 25
Philaris debate 44
Phillip V 92
Pitt, William 171, 244, 270, 271, 277-291, 300, 302, 311
pluralism 3, 159, 302
Pocklington, John 211
Pope, Alexander 124
Popish plot 82
Porteus, Beilby 174, 191, 192, 224, 226, 278, 281
Potter, John 50, 173, 182, 184
Powell, William 57
Presbyterianism 18, 22, 51, 120, 127, 177
Pretyman-Tomline, Sir George 171, 186, 205, 206, 215, 224, 225, 226, 277-298
Price, Richard 231-254, 283
Prideaux, Humphrey 257
Priestley, Joseph 6, 225, 231, 237, 259
providence 101, 102, 106, 109, 113, 114, 115, 116, 218, 237, 264, 270
Prynne, William 15, 203
Puritanism 1, 9, 81, 129, 161, 164, 167, 168, 174, 175, 182, 184, 195, 196, 210, 212, 223, 289
Pym, John 12

Quakers 66, 160
Quebec 145, 248, 284

Racovian catechism 66, 69, 72
Randolph, John 281
rationalism 43, 53, 231-254
Reformation 76, 187, 190, 204, 205, 206, 207, 222

Regency crisis 287, 297
republicanism 41, 266
Restoration 13
Ridley, Nicholas 17, 18, 19
Ridolphi plot 82
Robertson, William 123, 125, 130
Romaine, William 176, 183
Rome 16, 17, 79, 90, 100, 103, 127, 190, 210, 211, 215, 216, 217, 221, 223, 263, 289
Rous, Francis 128
Rousseau 122, 123, 125, 126
Rye House Plot 35

St Asaph, 299-319
sabbatarianism 129, 130, 135
Sacheverell, Henry 30, 45, 47, 49, 50, 51, 53, 57, 59
Sackville, Thomas 25
Salisbury 61, 67, 74, 284, 299
Sancroft, William 30
Schism Act 45, 46
Scott, John 203
Scotland 29, 119-154, 148, 304
Secker, Thomas 173, 174, 182, 184, 192, 222, 278
Shaftesbury, Earl of 98, 232
Sharp, John 57
Shelburne, Lord 231, 244, 250, 303, 304, 305
Sherlock, Thomas 58, 59, 98, 104, 167, 182
Sherlock, William 57
Shipley, Jonathon 301, 303
Shipley, Bishop William 299, 302, 311
Shipley, William Davies 299-319
Sibthorp, Robert 25
Sidney, Algernon 38
slavery 240-251, 294, 295
Smalridge, George 43-59
Socinianism 22, 27, 31, 34, 36, 37, 39, 41, 54, 66, 67, 68, 69, 75, 77, 125, 141, 183, 199, 203, 212, 236, 289
Sobieski, Maria Clementine 86, 87, 88, 89, 90, 91, 92, 93
Somerset 185, 195
South Sea Bubble 83
Spain 89, 90, 93, 113, 219

Spanish Armada 17
SPCK 162, 294
Spectator 134
SPG 162
Staffordshire 20, 311
Stamp Act 248
Star Chamber 20
Stevens, William 186
Stillingfleet, Edward 57, 68, 150
St John, Oliver 24
Strickland, William 24
Sundon, Lady 68
Swift, Jonathon 31
Sykes, Arthur Ashley 50, 58, 59, 67

Talbot, William 57
Taylor, Jeremy 75, 76
Taylor, Thomas 165
Tenison, Thomas 44, 51
Test and Corporations Act 46, 77, 78, 79, 81, 84, 238, 253, 263, 296, 303
Thomas, John 68
Tillotson, John 30, 31, 35, 36, 37, 38, 39, 40, 41, 42, 75, 76, 124, 138
Tindal, Matthew 40
Toleration Act 10, 31
Toland, John 29, 67, 98
Toplady, Augustus 187, 204, 205
Tories 43, 265, 266, 268, 269, 275, 279-298
Tractarianism 1, 191, 208
Travers, Walter 17
Trelawney, Sir Harry 158
Trelawney, Sir Jonathon, 49, 55, 56
Trinitarianism 27, 28, 49, 53, 54, 66, 67-80, 117, 183, 203, 214

Uniformity, Act of 166
Unitarianism 28, 183, 238, 291, 295, 296
unity of Protestants 179-229
Ussher, James 21
Utilitarianism 233, 234

Van Mildert, William 227
Venn, Henry 176
Vestiarian Controversy 18

Index

Wales, 120, 152, 178, 299-319
Walker, Samuel 167, 168, 175, 176
Walpole, Horace 111
Walpole, Sir Robert 77, 78, 79, 275
Walsingham, Sir Francis 24
Wake, William 5, 46, 49, 50, 51, 55, 57, 65, 73, 278
Warburton, William 92-117, 172, 190, 191, 220, 221
Warwick, Frances, Countess of, 24
Warwickshire 255-276
Waterland, Daniel 48, 57, 62, 65, 72, 286
Watson Joshua 227
Watson, Richard 278
Wesley, Charles 147, 164, 165, 169, 170, 183
Wesley, John 5, 6, 147-178, 183, 184, 195, 204, 206
Wesley, Martha 160
Wesley, Samuel 158, 159
Wesley, Susannah 160
West Indies 148, 314-315
Westminster Abbey 134, 136, 159
Westminster Assembly 21, 126
Westminster Confession of Faith 122, 141

Westminster School 44, 301
Wharton, Duke of 93
Whig interpretation of History 25, 26
Whigs 27, 35, 41, 43, 65, 77, 221, 232, 241, 242, 258, 265, 267, 268, 294, 297, 299-319
Whiston, William 47, 48, 54, 55, 56, 57, 59, 62, 69
Whitby, Daniel 257
Whitefield, George, 5, 6, 183, 184
Whitgift, John 18, 25
Wilberforce, William 196, 197, 200, 201, 224, 229
William III 16, 32, 34, 35, 37, 40, 83
Williams, John Henry 255-276
Wilkes, John 132
Wilson, Thomas 14
Winchester 61, 67, 68, 74, 185, 213, 281, 285, 308
Wogan, Charles 87, 89, 90, 94
Wroth, Sir Henry 24
Wyvill, Christopher 246, 252, 304

Yelverton, Sir Henry 24
Yorkshire 4, 171
Yorke, Sir Joseph 139